Blue Monday

Blue Monday

Fats Domino and the
Lost Dawn of Rock 'n' Roll

Rick Coleman

Da Capo Press
A Member of the Perseus Books Group

Interior design by Lisa Kreinbrink

Cataloging-in-Publication data for this book is available from the Library of Congress
First Da Capo Press edition 2006
10-ISBN 0–306–81491–9
13-ISBN 978–0–306–81491–4
Published by Da Capo Press
A Member of the Perseus Books Group
http://www.dacapopress.com

Da Capo Press books are available at special discounts for bulk purchases in the U.S. by corporations, institutions, and other organizations. For more information, please contact the Special Markets Department at the Perseus Books Group, 11 Cambridge Center, Cambridge, MA 02142, or call (800) 255–1514 or (617) 252–5298, or e-mail *special.markets@perseusbooks.com.*

1 2 3 4 5 6 7 8 9–06 05 04 03 02

For my parents,
who loved music, history, and the written word.
Also for Vernon, Roy, and Stevenson.
Wish you all could be here.

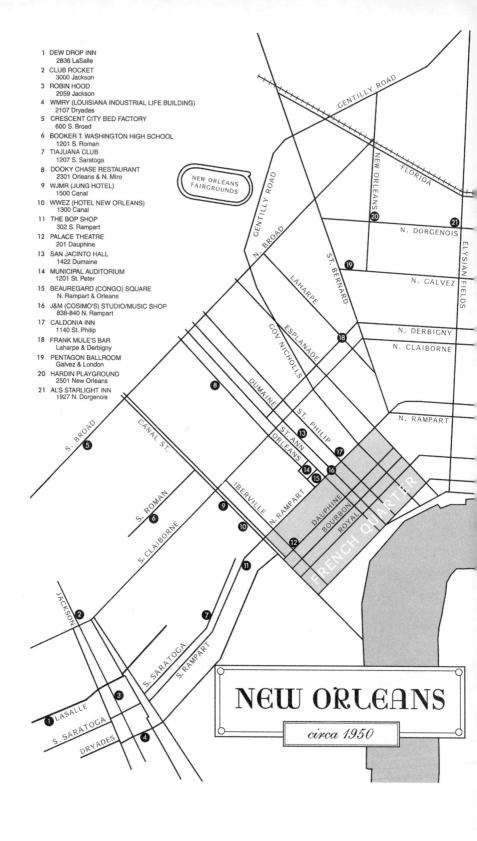

1. DEW DROP INN
   2836 LaSalle
2. CLUB ROCKET
   3000 Jackson
3. ROBIN HOOD
   2059 Jackson
4. WMRY (LOUISIANA INDUSTRIAL LIFE BUILDING)
   2107 Dryades
5. CRESCENT CITY BED FACTORY
   600 S. Broad
6. BOOKER T. WASHINGTON HIGH SCHOOL
   1201 S. Roman
7. TIAJUANA CLUB
   1207 S. Saratoga
8. DOOKY CHASE RESTAURANT
   2301 Orleans & N. Miro
9. WJMR (JUNG HOTEL)
   1500 Canal
10. WWEZ (HOTEL NEW ORLEANS)
    1300 Canal
11. THE BOP SHOP
    302 S. Rampart
12. PALACE THEATRE
    201 Dauphine
13. SAN JACINTO HALL
    1422 Dumaine
14. MUNICIPAL AUDITORIUM
    1201 St. Peter
15. BEAUREGARD (CONGO) SQUARE
    N. Rampart & Orleans
16. J&M (COSIMO'S) STUDIO/MUSIC SHOP
    838-840 N. Rampart
17. CALDONIA INN
    1140 St. Philip
18. FRANK MULE'S BAR
    Laharpe & Derbigny
19. PENTAGON BALLROOM
    Galvez & London
20. HARDIN PLAYGROUND
    2501 New Orleans
21. AL'S STARLIGHT INN
    1927 N. Dorgenois

NEW ORLEANS FAIRGROUNDS

FRENCH QUARTER

NEW ORLEANS
circa 1950

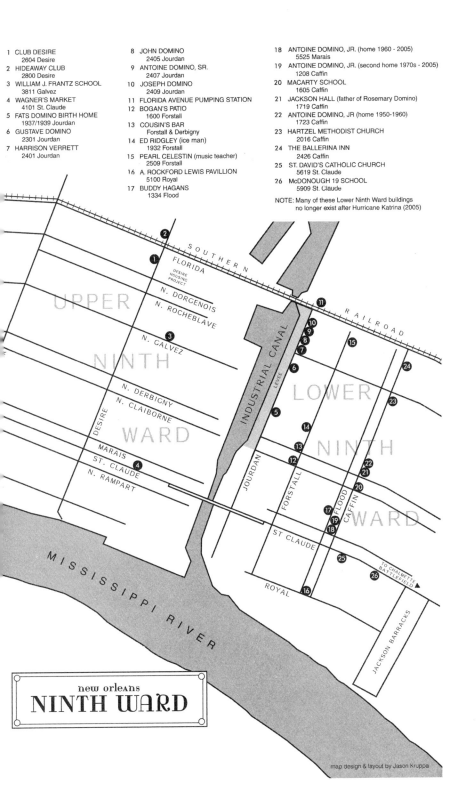

1 CLUB DESIRE
   2604 Desire
2 HIDEAWAY CLUB
   2800 Desire
3 WILLIAM J. FRANTZ SCHOOL
   3811 Galvez
4 WAGNER'S MARKET
   4101 St. Claude
5 FATS DOMINO BIRTH HOME
   1937/1939 Jourdan
6 GUSTAVE DOMINO
   2301 Jourdan
7 HARRISON VERRETT
   2401 Jourdan

8 JOHN DOMINO
   2405 Jourdan
9 ANTOINE DOMINO, SR.
   2407 Jourdan
10 JOSEPH DOMINO
   2409 Jourdan
11 FLORIDA AVENUE PUMPING STATION
12 BOGAN'S PATIO
   1600 Forstall
13 COUSIN'S BAR
   Forstall & Derbigny
14 ED RIDGLEY (ice man)
   1932 Forstall
15 PEARL CELESTIN (music teacher)
   2509 Forstall
16 A. ROCKFORD LEWIS PAVILLION
   5100 Royal
17 BUDDY HAGANS
   1334 Flood

18 ANTOINE DOMINO, JR. (home 1960 - 2005)
   5525 Marais
19 ANTOINE DOMINO, JR. (second home 1970s - 2005)
   1208 Caffin
20 MACARTY SCHOOL
   1605 Caffin
21 JACKSON HALL (father of Rosemary Domino)
   1719 Caffin
22 ANTOINE DOMINO, JR (home 1950-1960)
   1723 Caffin
23 HARTZEL METHODIST CHURCH
   2016 Caffin
24 THE BALLERINA INN
   2426 Caffin
25 ST. DAVID'S CATHOLIC CHURCH
   5619 St. Claude
26 McDONOUGH 19 SCHOOL
   5909 St. Claude

NOTE: Many of these Lower Ninth Ward buildings
no longer exist after Hurricane Katrina (2005)

new orleans
NINTH WARD

map design & layout by Jason Kruppa

Contents

Prologue

It was a very blue Monday when Hurricane Katrina devastated New Orleans. In the days following the nightmare, America and the world looked on in horror and disbelief at television images of a totally flooded and ravaged great *American* city and the tragic faces of so many people—most of them black—crying in fear, desperate in anger, sullen in despair. While many thought that the federal government's scandalously slow response to the apocalyptic emergency and the news media stereotypes of African Americans caught in the tragedy as "Third World" *refugees* and dangerous *looters* smacked of racism, in a CNN interview former Senator Carol Mosely Braun was slightly more philosophical when she said, "They don't see black people."

One of the myriad stories in the wake of the worst natural disaster in American history was the boat rescue of seventy-seven-year-old music legend Fats Domino and his family from his submerged Lower Ninth Ward home. His story indicated another perceptual disconnect. Though he had rarely sought publicity, the Katrina story was the most national attention that Fats had received in years, shocking even old fans who didn't even know that he was still *alive*. Though he had been the best-selling early rock 'n' roll star after Elvis Presley (whose continuous publicity beggared infinity), Domino had been all but forgotten.

I first met Fats almost exactly two decades before Katrina—after writing a newspaper article in which I outlined New Orleans' quintessential contributions to rock 'n' roll's genesis on the occasion of the music's purported thirtieth birthday (which the popular media then dated from "Rock Around the Clock," not Elvis). Before an outdoor concert on the north shore of Lake Ponchartrain I encountered Dave Bartholomew practicing his trumpet, blowing sweet notes into the pine trees. He took time out to introduce me to his musical partner, who was waiting in a recreational vehicle that served as his dressing room. Luckily for me, the concert was hit by an hour-long power outage, which allowed me time to get to know Domino. Dressed in a sleeveless T-shirt, the fifty-seven-year-old seemed small compared to his rotund legend, with a small Afro replacing his famous flat-top. He took an immediate liking to me, as I was obviously a fan. He even made a point of showing me his king's ransom in gaudy jewelry, including a golden piano ring and a diamond-studded starburst watch. When the power came back on, Domino proceeded to rock the multitude to happy exhaustion on that torrid August evening.

Two months later I interviewed the very private Mr. Domino at his home. The thick spicy aroma of Creole food was strong as I walked into his modest kitchen, where one of his neighborhood "podners" sat drinking beer and playing cards with him at a small Formica table. His grand pink-and-white split-level mansion had long been a landmark for tourists in the Lower Ninth Ward, the predominantly black neighborhood of New Orleans where he had lived since birth. But Domino no longer stayed in "the big house," the home of his wife Rosemary and some of his children. He now lived in the shotgun house next door—Fats loved his family, but he needed a little breathing space. He joked and laughed as he offered highly peppered samplings of red beans and rice. He even played some new songs on the electric piano in the house's tiny front room and took me to meet his wife, Rosemary, who was even more reclusive. Domino was incredibly shy for a rock star, but he gave me what may have been his most in-depth interview.

That day was the starting point for this book, a journey which for me would take far longer than I would have ever imagined. My friend Stevenson Palfi, an outstanding New Orleans filmmaker known for his brilliant tribute to Professor Longhair, *Piano Players Rarely Ever Play Together,* was, over the same twenty-year period, working on a documentary on another of the city's legendary pianists, Allen Toussaint. In fact, he filmed a couple of interviews for me and we joked about who would finish his own endlessly delayed project first. Our personal struggles emphasized the mind-numbing difficulty in documenting the New Orleans black music masters who should rightfully be revered by everyone. That travail was worsened by Katrina, which destroyed much of the city, dispersed its people, and killed many others—including, sadly, Stevenson, who, severely depressed three months after the flooding of his home and office, took his own life, his virtually complete Toussaint film still unreleased.

In February 2006 I revisited the Lower Ninth Ward, where Domino had lived all of his life. The devastation in the area could only be compared to the jagged, sad ruins after an intense bombing. Jourdan Avenue, the street adjoining the Industrial Canal where the Domino family had lived for eight decades, was ground zero—for miles below the canal levee homes were now torn in half, split into splinters, reduced to their foundations, mournfully stranded in the middle of the street, or even sitting on top of crushed cars. Everywhere the debris piles of a once vibrant neighborhood were heaped in jumbles. Forty years earlier, New

Orleans had shamefully bulldozed the house that Louis Armstrong had been born in, but in 2005 Mother Nature wiped Domino's birth house, 1927/1929 Jourdan, off the face of the planet—not even the foundation could be detected. A block or so closer to the North Claiborne Avenue bridge, a massive rusty barge from the canal was unhappily beached on the street.

Several blocks away, on Caffin Avenue, I entered Domino's famed house where I had visited with him on several honored occasions. Though it had been flooded to the ceiling, from the outside both it and the "big house" next door looked relatively undamaged. As I walked through the dark gutted building in eerie silence, phantoms called out to me—the musical legacies of Domino, the Ninth Ward, New Orleans. There in the gloom at the back of the house barely lighted by reflected sunlight was the only piece of furniture—the remains of Domino's couch built from the back of a Cadillac, the car that symbolized musical stardom in the 1950s. As I was leaving I noticed something else. Somehow I had missed it on the way in. In the front room Domino's electric piano, which he had more than once played for me, still stood proudly. On it sat a cassette tape. Wiping off the encrusted mud from the label, I gradually found a scrawled song title—the jazz funeral spiritual that had comforted so many over the last century, "Just a Closer Walk with Thee."

Domino's homes, his family's homes, his neighborhood, and a huge part of his beloved city had simply washed away. But even if New Orleans ceased to exist altogether, its soul lives on in the human spirit everywhere, since, as I have tried to document here, the city's music has—more than once—made the earth *move*.

■ ■ ■

In the fall of 1956 a black-and-white newsreel film sputtered onto movie screens showing a dark cherub of a man with a suit and a shiny flattop hairdo above his sweet plum face. He was sitting at an upright piano obliviously pounding away on its keys when a reporter interrupted him and asked the burning musical question of the day: "Fats, how did this rock 'n' roll all get started anyway?"

Antoine "Fats" Domino should have known. He was one of the fathers of rhythm & blues, which had paved the way for rock 'n' roll. But, like the name "rock 'n' roll" itself, he had only been nationally known to white audiences for a year. Rock 'n' roll was under fire everywhere for its "jungle rhythms" and its riots. In fact, Domino was the main perpetrator of both—he had triumphed rocking rhythms longer than anyone, and outbreaks of violence at his shows

had given him more national publicity than his music, leading to this very interview one week after a riot at a Newport servicemen's club. He replied softly
with a smile, "Well, what they call rock 'n' roll is rhythm & blues, and I've been
playing it for fifteen years in New Orleans."

It was an amazing statement coming from the normally very modest man,
and it remains so today, when only a relative few understand the towering im-
portance of Domino and the New Orleans r&b scene from which he sprang. In
fact, in the first weekend of July 2004, when a fire heavily damaged the building that had once housed Cosimo Matassa's legendary J&M Studio, where
Domino, Roy Brown, Little Richard, Ray Charles, Joe Turner, Lloyd Price, Professor Longhair, and many others recorded songs that ignited the fuse of rock
'n' roll, the story received little national press coverage besides a tiny Associated
Press story and a typed news crawl on CNN. Ironically, that same weekend
Memphis made worldwide headlines commemorating the fiftieth anniversary
of Elvis Presley's first recording at the Sun Records Studio as "the first rock 'n'
roll record." But Presley's "That's All Right" originally sold modestly and didn't
even possess the primary element that defined rock 'n' roll—a big beat. In fact,
Presley himself repeatedly denied his so-called invention, in one typical instance
in 1957 saying, "Rock 'n' roll was around a long time before me, it was really
rhythm & blues. I just got on the bandwagon with it."

Domino's own claim to rock 'n' roll creation certainly dates back to December 1949, when he recorded the thunderous rocker, "The Fat Man," but the
unlikely revolutionary made perhaps an even greater breakthrough years later.
In July 1955, at the same time as Bill Haley and the Comets' "Rock Around the
Clock" hit #1 and officially kicked off rock 'n' roll as a cultural phenomenon,
Domino's "Ain't That a Shame" cracked the pop top ten, an event that, more
than Haley's record, signaled a profound cultural change. At a time when the
few blacks on pop radio sang sweet ballads or novelties, "Ain't That a Shame"
landed with the sonic impact of a piano falling from the sky, as, decades before
today's gangsta rappers were born, Domino shouted out ghetto-accented staccato accusations about sad separations ringing like cannonades across a country
divided by segregation—*"You made* . . . BOOM! BOOM! . . . *me cry*
. . . BOOM! BOOM! . . . *when you said* . . . BOOM! BOOM! . . . *good-bye!"*

Those cataclysmic blasts were a nerve-shattering experience for adults accus-
tomed to wall-to-wall "Que Sera, Sera." They considered "Ain't That a Shame" a
cacophonous corruption of American culture, preferring Pat Boone's vanilla version, which simultaneously became a #1 pop hit. Boone, then an English major
at Columbia University, even tried to record it as *"Isn't* That a Shame." On *The*

Tonight Show, host Steve Allen ridiculed the song's teleg
like a Shakespearean sonnet. "I remember that he was very
song's co-writer and producer, legendary New Orleans
Bartholomew. "Ain't That a Shame" was in a sense a parody of
music of the era—a lyrically minimalist melodrama—though Do.   ssage
was not of romantic breakup, but rather one of liberating phy al release.
Teenagers soon phoned in radio requests and spent their jukebox nickels to
dance to Domino's starkly superior original. To many, Boone's insipid cover represented musical discrimination, a censored version of the loudest, most emphat-
ically rhythmic, and *blackest* pop hit yet. The song even symbolized a broader
revolt when, as Boone himself suggests, it helped put the most basic word of
working-class defiance—"ain't"—into the dictionary in the late 1950s.

Despite his Herculean role in the creation and rise of rock 'n' roll, Domino has
been disappearing for many years. Not only has he never been the subject of a
biography, recent 1,000-page reference works like *The Rough Guide to Rock, The
Great Rock Discography* (1st ed.), and *African American Lives* cite his r&b contemporaries like Bo Diddley and Chuck Berry but exclude Domino altogether. Even
the Rock and Roll Hall of Fame, which honored Domino as one of its first ten inductees, for years gave him a three-sentence website biography and couldn't get his
birth date right. Domino's music, like most early rock 'n' roll, was subversive in its
cultural impact, but, following the counterculture of the late 1960s, rock writers
demanded music of *overt* rebellion and began dismissing Domino as "harmless"
and "nonthreatening." Indeed, judged by the extremes of modern rock, Fats
wouldn't register on the outrage radar. He wasn't tortured, violent, or sexually
provocative. He didn't scream, take drugs, or trash hotels. But yesterday's rebellion
is today's status quo—even Little Richard and Jerry Lee Lewis, once seemingly
hell's heralds, are now found in easy-listening CD racks. This disregard reached a
nadir in James Miller's 1999 rock chronicle *Flowers in the Dustbin,* in which Miller
myopically equated Domino with Pat Boone and added a string of stereotypes:
"Domino was roly-poly, good-humored, and easily pegged as a happy-go-lucky,
wide-grinning, loud-laughing, shuffling sort of latter-day minstrel." In 2002, the
British music magazine *Q* likewise called him "a benign minstrel."

Such racial slurs once sullied another New Orleans icon. Louis Armstrong was
the leading genius of early jazz, yet by the 1950s modern jazz artists dismissed him
as an "Uncle Tom" after he became a worldwide musical ambassador. Certainly
overtly rebellious black artists suffered much worse. Paul Robeson's rousing calls
for civil rights for African Americans resulted in the revocation of his passport and
his personal ruin. Chuck Berry was more than once thrown in jail for crossing

...ies. Little Richard was effectively censored from TV in the 1950s due to his ...ild and provocative persona. Yet, in stark contrast to his later image, adults once also considered Domino a public menace. Unlike Elvis Presley's concerts, which were primarily attended by seas of white teenage girls, Domino's shows were ground zero for racial integration, and he was banned in several cities because those interracial shows were—more often than for any other Fifties rocker—the scenes of several rock 'n' roll riots. The 1956 movie *Shake, Rattle, and Rock!* accordingly showed him driving both teens and adults into tribal bedlam.

Domino's benign stereotype was really born on November 18, 1956, the night he first appeared on *The Ed Sullivan Show*. Just as Sullivan later famously showed Presley from the waist down, he hid Domino's powerful band behind a curtain to reduce the number of visible black men. Still bearing a wound on his hand from a recent riot ended by tear gas, Fats sang "Blueberry Hill" with a smile. At Sullivan's direction, he stood as he finished his song to better reveal his teddy bear stature. Sullivan made Domino *appear* harmless while propelling his new image and his version of the old pop hit to a massive cross-cultural popularity that glossed over the subversion of his rhythms. Subversion was the word. Armstrong and Domino, like Ray Charles, the Supremes, Stevie Wonder, and many other black artists, *smiled* their way into American homes. But, unlike the Mills Brothers, the Ink Spots, Nat "King" Cole, and other blacks who sang mostly pop songs, Armstrong, Domino, and others were a threat to the segregated American way of life because they popularized deeply rooted black music.

As Dave Bartholomew would later put it, Domino was the "cornerstone" of rock 'n' roll, strongly inspiring many later legends who began their careers as Domino fans: Little Richard, Elvis Presley, Chuck Berry, Buddy Holly, John Lennon, Paul McCartney, Van Morrison, John Fogerty, Bob Marley, and Bruce Springsteen. The fact that white-bread singers like Pat Boone, Teresa Brewer, and even a sixteen-year-old Ricky Nelson had huge hits with dead-fish imitations of Domino's hits only increased his cachet. For perhaps the first time, an African American made blackness not only hip but also wildly popular among whites. Dick Clark today suggests that teenagers were attracted to Domino partly *because* their parents loathed black rockers. "Fats was not a teen idol," says Clark, "but he was idolized—one of the founding fathers. Black people said, 'That's rhythm & blues, that's race music, that's ours.' White kids said, 'That's different.'"

Domino's statement—"Rock 'n' roll is rhythm & blues"—also helps explain why his star has dimmed since the 1950s. Although Alan Freed, the disc jockey who made the term "rock 'n' roll" famous, is now an icon, the almost exclusively African American artists he promoted when he first popularized the phrase are largely forgotten. Book and film histories of 1950s rock 'n' roll are likewise slanted toward the likes of Presley, Freed, Buddy Holly, and Jerry Lee Lewis. At least until Taylor Hackford's masterwork *Ray*, movies about the era tended to feature rebellious white teens inspired to rock by shadowy black musicians, who were heard but rarely seen. To paraphrase Nat "King" Cole's legendary racial pronouncement relating to 1950s television, in regards to the birth of rock 'n' roll America's mass media are *afraid of the dark;* the popular accounts of the music's creation have been so corrupted by commercial interests that they seem to reflect the segregation that the music once undermined. Indeed, since Freed used "rock 'n' roll" as a euphemism to integrate rhythm & blues into the white mainstream, placing r&b artists at the back of their own musical bus in history is a travesty of his intent. Just as journalists had crowned white bandleaders Paul Whiteman and Benny Goodman as the kings of jazz and swing, in the 1950s they enthroned Presley, Haley, and Freed as the kings of rock 'n' roll. Presley's unprecedented fame obscured black pioneers like a supernova obliterating neighboring stars, making him the unwilling figurehead of white denial, even as he insisted that rock 'n' roll began as rhythm & blues. After one such statement in 1957, Presley added, "Let's face it: I can't sing it like Fats Domino can. I know that."

If Presley wouldn't embrace his myth, a shot-from-the-lip remark by John Lennon—"Before Elvis there was nothing"—has often been used to justify it. That statement's popularity shows the ease with which black culture has been co-opted, a process that cultural theorist Joseph Roach eloquently calls "the staggering erasures required by the invention of whiteness." But, in fact, the first song that Lennon learned to play was "Ain't That a Shame," and shortly before his tragic death he put his famous remark about Presley into context with a searing indictment of the white myth of rock 'n' roll creation: "I know Fats Domino was makin' records in '48 [*sic*], and there was lots of stuff called rhythm & blues which you could've called rock 'n' roll, but it was hard to get in England. Rock 'n' roll only came into our consciousness when white people did it. I think it was a euphemism for fucking—the actual expression meaning being in bed and rocking and rolling. So this bit about, 'When did rock start?' really means, 'When did the honkies start noticing it?'"

Historians also love to romanticize the stark noncommercial purity of downtrodden delta bluesmen in a commendable attempt at black cultural appreciation that nonetheless seems to rationalize the ghettoizing of many of rock 'n' roll's more direct black fathers and mothers—the creators of rhythm & blues—into a historical no-man's land. Thus, there has been vast documentation of the blues, but so little research on *rhythm & blues* that even major figures have disappeared into shadow. It is not a good sign of the preservation of African American heritage when by far the most popular r&b artists of the 1940s and the 1950s, Louis Jordan and Domino, are today little known to most people. Likewise, it took nearly fifty years for doo wop vocal groups to reclaim a fragment of their seminal role in rock 'n' roll's birth, and then only through PBS public television pledge drive concerts. Historians also ignored many whites who bravely risked all to help black performers; in 2003 Terry Stewart, the president of the Rock and Roll Hall of Fame, told me that New Orleans studio engineer Cosimo Matassa, who recorded more music crucial to the birth of rock 'n' roll than *anyone,* would likely only be inducted after he was *dead.* Within these pages I mention many other shamefully neglected pioneers, both black and white, who helped turn rhythm & blues into rock 'n' roll, including "Big" Joe Turner, another colossus of twentieth-century music who has never been the subject of a biography; Roy Brown, the uber-influential gospel-blues shouter who inspired both the passion and the name of rock 'n' roll; Lew Chudd, the Imperial Records owner whose free-thinking chutzpah helped transform popular music; Hank Ballard, whose songs "Work with Me Annie" and "The Twist" sparked cultural shockwaves with their potent injections of black physicality into the white mainstream; Irvin Feld, rock 'n' roll's first super concert promoter, who smashed segregation barriers all over the country for more than a decade with his Biggest Show of Stars tours; and Bill Randle, the omnipotent Cleveland disc jockey who was perhaps as crucial to the rise of rock 'n' roll as Alan Freed.

Even with white performers playing their variations on rhythm & blues, rock 'n' roll was an African American cultural coup d'état. In fact, Chuck Berry, rock 'n' roll's poet laureate, declared the end of the European-rooted domination of popular music simply in 1956 when he shouted, *"Roll over Beethoven, dig these rhythm & blues!"* In an astounding coincidence, the music integrated into the fabric of society simultaneously with the rise of the civil rights movement. Rhythm & blues became rock 'n' roll and transformed America far more profoundly than jazz, since segregation was finally in question. Just as black children entered white schools for the first time, young whites absorbed the African American ethos significantly through both black *words* and music, as jazz had been primarily instrumental. Whites overflowed segregated boundaries to sit or dance next to blacks at Domino's shows and bought his records by the millions. As the first black rock 'n' roll superstar, Domino helped pave the way for integration, becoming the goodwill ambassador for a revolution. And, with their pocket change, teenagers changed the world. A year before his death, even

Martin Luther King, Jr., who had once condemned rock 'n' roll, said, "School integration is much easier now that they share a common music, a common language, and enjoy the same dances."

Still, even I had trouble accepting Domino's statement in 1956 that he had been playing rock 'n' roll for fifteen years in New Orleans. But, in fact, the city's piano-punishing musical warhorse, "The Junker's Blues," on which he based "The Fat Man," was first recorded in 1941 by Champion Jack Dupree, and the song dated back further still. Indeed, Domino's childhood obsession with rocking music would become the world's obsession. In New Orleans, the tradition of defiantly dancing your blues away, which was at the core of rock 'n' roll, went back for centuries.

"A Different Drummer"

Chapter 1

"The most important thing about my music is the beat."
—ANTOINE "FATS" DOMINO

X-ray America and you'll find the major artery, the magnificent Mississippi River coursing down the continent to New Orleans. Historian Jerah Johnson suggests that contrary to the British colonial policy of strict segregation from other cultures, the city represented the "apotheosis" of French colonial *assimilation*. With a true melting pot of French, African, Native American, German, Spanish, and Caribbean inhabitants, New Orleans became the heart that pumped a very different cultural message upstream against the overwhelming white-Anglo-Saxon-Protestant current in America.

Africans first arrived there in two slave ships in 1719, a year after the French founding of the city. In contrast to English Puritans, who viewed earthly pleasure as a sign of Satan, Africans considered physicality synonymous with the spiritual, symbolized by sacred drums used for dances and even communication. But after slaves beat out talking-drum messages of revolt in uprisings like the 1739 Stono Rebellion in South Carolina, slave drums were suppressed everywhere in America—except in New Orleans.

In an effort to help the struggling colony, New Orleans' French governors had passed the *Code Noir* in 1724, freeing the Africans to work for themselves on Sundays. On that day slaves were also free to dance to myriad rhythm instruments, notably in an earthen clearing outside the city's northern wall called *Place des Negres,* in a celebration that grew to a frenzied crescendo at sunset. Later known as Congo Square, the site would forever symbolize African heritage and freedom. Especially after Spain took control of New Orleans in 1769, slaves were even able to purchase their freedom. This relative air of tolerance in New Orleans was enhanced by the presence of free blacks, the *gens de couleur libre,* also known as the

Creoles of color, whose numbers increased as European men intermingled sexually with slave women, creating a unique mixed-race class of African Americans who were given privileges or, occasionally, freed altogether.

Still, the few freedoms that blacks enjoyed would be under assault for the next two centuries. In 1786, the New Orleans bishop denounced the "wicked custom of the Negroes, who, at the Vespers hour, assembled in a green expanse called Place Congo to dance the *bamboula* and perform the hideous gyrations." Cries for freedom were heard around the world in the late eighteenth century in populist revolutions in America, in France, and, most shocking of all, in the French sugar cane colony island of Santo Domingo, where the Haitian Revolution began in 1791. A former slave, Toussaint L'Ouverture, led the largest and only successful slave revolt in modern history, in which 500,000 slaves burned the plantations of the French, defeated Napoleon's army, and freed all blacks. The simple uprising of those abused sons of Africa reverberated with untold consequences for the western world. Due primarily to his loss of his most profitable colony, Napoleon became soured on the New World and accordingly sold the vast Louisiana Territory to the United States. Also, both French and black refugees fled in droves from the island nation, soon renamed Haiti, to New Orleans.

Protestant Americans also headed down to the city after the Louisiana Purchase in 1803. There they were shocked to witness French men and women, caramel-colored Creoles, Indians, and slaves carousing on the Sabbath. One New England visitor who witnessed the hip-shaking African dances in 1804 invoked witch-hunting Puritans, lamenting, "Oh, where are our select men of Salem?" In 1809, the new English-speaking citizens of New Orleans were mortified by yet another flood of Haitian refugees expelled from Cuba. In one year over 10,000 Frenchmen, free black Creoles, and slaves doubled the population of New Orleans and spread throughout Louisiana, bringing with them Afro-Cuban rhythms, voodoo religious practices, and seeds of revolt to add to the already potent cultural brew. Increasingly, Congo Square became the center of African American culture, and thus, foreshadowing condemnations of black music to come, a travel guide, *Paxton's Directory of 1822,* warned of the area's "great injury to the morals of the rising generation."

Over the next few decades Anglo-Americans gradually took over the reins of government in New Orleans, much to the dismay of slaves, who could no longer dance in public, purchase their freedom, or even keep their families intact under the harsher American laws. Still, in secret ceremonies and during the wild revelry of Mardi Gras, African Americans kept alive a music that symbolized a liberation of body and spirit antithetical to their oppression. Author and abolitionist Henry David Thoreau wrote about following "a different drummer," not imagining the role of the drummer in the black sense of freedom, which became literal when, in May 1864, blacks and Creoles gathered in the Square with Union troops, the new governor, and sympathetic whites to celebrate Louisiana's abolition of slavery.

But the mood was short-lived. In 1866, a massacre of at least forty-eight men—nearly all blacks—at a convention for African American voting rights at the New Orleans Mechanics Institute was the major factor in the congressional imposition of Radical Reconstruction in the South. The end of Reconstruction in 1877 was followed by the rise of the Ku Klux Klan, the suppression of black civil rights, and more than 350 lynchings in Louisiana over the next seventy-five years. In 1893 "For White Only" signs were placed in Congo Square, which was renamed Beauregard Square after the Louisiana Confederate general who fired the first shot at Fort Sumter (and who, ironically, afterwards strove for racial tolerance).

The mixed-race Creoles also lost the higher status they had enjoyed since colonial days, and they led the way in legal fights for black civil rights in court. In the most famous of these cases, New Orleans Creole Homer Plessy bravely boarded a whites-only train bound for Covington, Louisiana. He was arrested, leading to the 1896 *Plessy v. Ferguson* Supreme Court decision, which infamously justified segregation so long as it was "separate but equal."

Thrown together in a common cause against institutionalized racism, blacks and Creoles now mixed more freely together, merging their musical passions. Popular songs, military marches, ragtime, spirituals, and blues fused with African-rooted dancing rhythms and improvisation in the genesis of jazz. Following World War I, jazz hot-wired the American nervous system during a time of Prohibition, religious revivalism, and KKK terrorism. Moralists condemned early jazz and its 1930s offspring, swing, for their "jungle" rhythms, which, in the first hint of the musical, racial, and sexual revolution to come, allegedly corrupted the morals of young Americans.

During World War II radio networks largely purged hot jazz and reverted to pop music platitudes. The attrition of musicians who went off to fight, plus two musicians' union strikes and the rise of bebop, contributed to the decline of the big bands and dancing music in general. Meanwhile, the exorbitant royalty demands of the music publishing monopoly ASCAP led the radio networks to form BMI, which, in sheer desperation for songwriters, did not discriminate. After the war, the Federal Communications Commission opened up America's airwaves, increasing the number of radio stations from fewer than 1,000 in 1945 to more than 2,000 in 1949, and the influx of local stations playing regional favorites led to the rise of BMI, disc jockeys, independent record companies, and music previously only heard by minorities. Black music radio shows, primarily hosted by white disc jockeys, gradually debuted around the country.

African Americans advanced economically through war jobs and migration. But, as in the previous postwar period, the progress also led to a bitter backlash; there were at least six lynchings in America in 1946. After a South Carolina sheriff gouged out the eyes of a black GI heading home from the war, Louis Jordan, Nat "King" Cole, Count Basie, Billie Holiday, and others performed at a New York benefit for him. Ralph Ellison suggested that America was itself blind in a 1947 story that evolved into the firebell of twentieth-century novels, *Invisible Man*, about a black man's struggle for identity at a time when African Americans were ignored as though invisible. He emphasized Louis Armstrong's subversive use of that invisibility, as well as the transforming power of black music. Ellison later wrote that blues, spirituals, jazz, and dance were "what we had in place of freedom."

■ ■ ■

Just when dancing music had all but disappeared from radio, New Orleans delivered an incredibly prophetic new musical cry: *"I Heard the News, There's Good Rockin' Tonight!"* Blues shouter Roy Brown recorded the original version of his historically pivotal song in June 1947 at Cosimo Matassa's J&M Studio, across from Congo Square on Rampart Street. He declared an independence of body and soul that was shocking to churchgoing blacks as, long before Ray Charles, he mixed gospel-style shouting with jump blues music and sexual references—like "jazz," the word "rock" was black slang for sex. Brown was a musical Prometheus, stealing fiery spiritual wails for his earthy blues song, which became a local sensation. Vernon Winslow, an art instructor at Dillard University who fought discrimination to produce the first New Orleans black music radio program, the Poppa Stoppa show, in September 1947, even took phone requests from whites—"Play that nigger's record that talks about, 'I'm gonna take you out behind the barn and love you so much, don't mean you no harm.'" According to Winslow, Brown's song was an "earthquake" due to its controversial popularity, which led nightclubs to stock "20 or 30 extra cases of beer because they knew people were going to play it for hours."

First heard at the time of a devastating New Orleans hurricane, "Good Rockin' Tonight" slowly stormed northward. Strongly abetted by Wynonie Harris's bludgeoning-but-bloodless cover version, the song conquered black America in 1948. Elvis Presley first *roared* when he recorded Brown's original lyric (not the slightly altered Harris rendition) for Sun Records in 1954. After Presley's recording, Frankie Lymon, Hank Ballard, Buddy Holly, Jerry Lee Lewis, James Brown, the Beatles, Paul McCartney, and Bruce Springsteen would all shout out the song. Though the debate about the first rock 'n' roll record will never end, "Good Rockin' Tonight" was the first rock 'n' roll *anthem,* leading to the use of the word "rock" in scores of hard-partying rhythm & blues songs in the late 1940s and early 1950s and, eventually, its use in a musical context by Bill Haley, Alan Freed, and *everyone.*

"The name [rock 'n' roll] itself was generic," says legendary Cleveland disc jockey Bill Randle, who promoted r&b years before Freed and was a catalyst in the rise of Domino, Presley, and many other rock 'n' roll fathers. "The term was used as a sexual euphemism from the mid-1930s on. It was a party phrase. It went into the general culture because of 'Good Rockin' Tonight.'" The Rock and Roll Hall of Fame wants [fellow Cleveland radio icon] Alan Freed to be the creator of it because the Rock and Roll Hall of Fame is in Cleveland. They don't want somebody to say, "The Emperor has no clothes!"

In addition, as music scholars like Charlie Gillett, Sheldon Harris, and Robert Palmer suggest, Roy Brown's passionate wailing became the basic vocal template for much of r&b, rock 'n' roll, and soul. In fact, Gillett states that for his vocal style alone Brown's "influence was diffused throughout popular music."

New Orleans again shook music. In his essay "Hear That Long Snake Moan," Michael Ventura suggests that cultural radiation from the city's nuclear core of African quintessence was why early rockers arose "out of places within a half day's drive of New Orleans, and they would sing their music with holy fury and a bodily abandon that had simply never been seen before in Western performance." Even Langston Hughes, a jazz aficionado, admitted that rock 'n' roll combined the heartache of the blues, the hope of gospel, and the "steady beat of Congo Square—that going on beat—and the Marching Bands' loud and blatant yes!" Following Brown's liberating call, in 1949 the spirit of Congo Square, which permeated the adjacent Rampart Street, was channeled into rocking hits brimming with the city's revelry and rhythm, including four that actually mentioned that New Orleans avenue of black cultural life by name: Domino's "The Fat Man," Professor Longhair's "Mardi Gras in New Orleans," Stick McGhee's "Drinkin' Wine Spo-Dee-O-Dee," and Louis Jordan's "Saturday Night Fish Fry," which also incessantly repeated the word "rockin'."

In a November 1948 concert in New Orleans' Municipal Auditorium—on the site of Congo Square—Jordan had thrilled black fans when he publicly denounced their segregation in the balcony. Afterwards, Jordan told his fans to "mix a little politics with your love of entertainment." Jordan soon did just that, recording "Saturday Night Fish Fry," which, in another daring statement against discrimination, described a black New Orleans party brutally broken up by police. Amazingly, it even became a pop hit in late 1949 and gave a metaphorical glimpse of the city's next musical titan—just as Lew Chudd of Imperial Records discovered Fats Domino playing at the hole-in-the-wall Hideaway Club, Jordan's voice boomed from jukeboxes everywhere: *Over in the corner was a beat-up grand, being played by a big, fat piano man.*

In December 1949, Domino recorded his locomotive rocker "The Fat Man" at Matassa's studio. Johnny Otis, who then ruled the r&b charts, calls it "a revolutionary record." Echoing John Lennon's assessment that Domino was present at the birth of the revolution, musicologist Robert Doerschuk describes it as "punchy, to the point, and first-rate rock and roll." Likewise, Charlie Gillett suggests in his classic rock 'n' roll history *The Sound of the City* that Domino "achieved the spirit of rock 'n' roll from his early records, and he did not have to change much to meet his new audience."

If Roy Brown supplied the name, the revelry, and the vocal fire of rock 'n' roll, Domino and his producer Dave Bartholomew built its New Orleans rockhouse foundation with interlocking rhythms that would become the musical mainstream, which, like the Mississippi, everyone else would later ply. "We started what was called 'rock' music, with the big backbeat," says Bartholomew. "Fats and I started with the big, big beat. Little Richard helped; Professor Longhair, also. Earl Palmer helped create the sound. New Orleans music always had a beat." Several rhythms of *The New Orleans Sound* became pillars of rock 'n' roll. Domino's piano triplets spread like a rhythmic virus throughout popular music. Bartholomew's bass riffs were heard in scores of hits, including Bill Haley's "Shake, Rattle and Roll" and Elvis Presley's "Hound Dog." Drummer Earl Palmer fathered the pile-driving backbeat of rock 'n' roll on classics by Domino, Lloyd Price, Larry Williams, Eddie Cochran, Ritchie Valens, Sam Cooke, and Little Richard. Domino's offbeat rhythms even became the bedrock of Jamaican ska, the precursor of reggae. "New Orleans, as has often been noted, is a country unto its own. For a decade or two Mr. Domino brought the city's sense of joy, along with its rhythms and anarchic sensibility, to the rest of the country," Peter Watrous wrote in *The New York Times* in 1991 after catching a performance by Domino.

Rock 'n' roll, just like rhythm & blues, included gospel, jazz, boogie, country, pop, and blues influences, but its core was uniquely African American: raw emotional expression and relentless rhythm. "Be-bop didn't have any beat," remarked swing saxophonist and Dizzy Gillespie band member Howard E. Johnson, echoing a statement that Domino made many times, "There was very little dancing until Fats Domino brought back the beat again." Emphatic rhythms, which were unheard on pop radio in the early 1950s, hijacked the hit parade within a year after Domino unleashed the monolithic "Ain't That a Shame" in 1955. In fact, the phrase "the big beat" soon became synonymous with rock 'n' roll, titling Alan Freed radio, TV, and stage shows, a Domino hit, and even a movie. By the end of 1957, the standard criterion of a good record on *American Bandstand,* as judged by Dick Clark's teenage dancers, was, "It's got a good beat and you can dance to it."

Domino pioneered the very sound of rocking, the revolutionary music of our time, yet he sang few shocking lyrics, since he was merely amplifying his African-Creole-Catholic passion for living, which had never been shackled by rigid morality. In contrast, hell-fire rockers like Roy Brown, Elvis Presley, Little Richard, and Jerry Lee Lewis riotously broke away from Protestant upbringings to achieve much the same spirit. But, as British scholar Adam Fairclough writes in his Louisiana civil rights history *Race and Democracy,* "[I]n the context of the rural south, even the most innocuous act—reading the *Pittsburgh Courier,* driving a flashy car, failing to yield the sidewalk—represented a subversion of white authority and an assertion of equality." And Domino's sonic hammering was hardly innocuous, as he helped revive the African rhythmic tradition that had always threatened the white status quo. As Peter Shapiro suggests in *Turn the Beat Around,* from the late nineteenth century New Orleans marching jazz bands had even adopted the European martial beat, as they, in essence, launched a cultural war, culminating over half a century later with the "drill-sergeant precision" of Earl Palmer's drumming. The musicians turned even the rhythms of "killing machine" discipline into a drumbeat of social liberation and unfettered joy. Domino spearheaded the new musical insurgency for over a decade from near the dawn of rhythm & blues to the arrival of the Beatles, whose very name signified the triumph of rhythm.

■ ■ ■

For decades music historians largely ignored New Orleans' role in the birth of rock 'n' roll, a neglect that sadly can be attributed to the fact that the city's rockers were nearly all black, although there is a deeper explanation. Culture critics rarely exalt culture at its most common, which New Orleans exemplified with Mardi Gras, jazz parades, and, historically, the dances at Congo Square. The judgment that great art reflects self-serving ideals—in other words, that it must be "serious" or "respectable"—is rooted in the old European class system and is antithetical to egalitarian African-based culture. To put this point in perspective, few American academic institutions or encyclopedias made serious mention of popular music until the 1970s; European classical music was the unquestioned definition of "good" culture. I would suggest that a similar elitism still colors popular music writing, as the gatekeepers of art praise jazz and blues in which they perceive their egocentric ideals of dignity, virtuosity, introspection, and pathos, just as overt rebellion gives historians an egoistic handle on rock 'n' roll. Yet such cultural engineering distorts the intrinsic social nature of black music. Rock 'n' roll, like early jazz, was an anarchic musical antidote to such conceit, which was hardening into WASP dogma in 1950s America when rock 'n' roll exploded.

The great rivers of African American music all flowed from the source of call-and-response, a ritual dialogue of individual expression and communal reply heard in the shouts of gospel music, in the repetition of the blues, and in the interplay of jazz that was the wellspring of the Afrocentric aesthetic and a powerful form of democracy in action. Individuals taking center stage had vast leeway of free expression in "the call," leading to the improvisation and endless innovation of African-rooted music, but they (at least until the abstract introspection of modern jazz) also adhered to the social responsibility of "the response" reflecting the tribal demand for physical and emotional release. Thus, aspersions against common tastes like "commercial sellout" and "lowest common denominator" had little meaning, as even personally passionate art was *for the people.* To the Eurocentric aesthetic, classical music was the apex of sophistication, but African-rooted music was more complex rhythmically, improvisationally, and socially—that is, in the human terms of the everyday world.

For more than a millennium Western civilization had been dominated by "the mind-body split," a worldview that perceived the mind as superior and spiritual and the body as base or evil and which, in a social context, often rationalized hierarchy and ethnocentrism. That philosophy, which reached its sterile peaks with the Puritans and the Victorians, was the polar extreme from the socially fervid African way of life. Thus, white society historically condemned outward passion—uninhibited dancing, singing, sensuality, and other emotional expressions—as "common," "vulgar," "childish," or "sinful." From balladry to symphonies, Northern European–rooted music denied passion with strict form and abstraction; even dancing music—from the waltz to the square dance—was rigidly choreographed. In contrast, the shouts and rhythms of black music moved and joined people with visceral magnetism. As session guitar great Mickey Baker only half-jokingly put it, "[If it wasn't] for the blues, we'd all be sitting around sipping tea and listening to chamber music." One tradition was obsessed with abstract ideals; the other was a celebration of physical human reality. Texas singer-songwriter Butch Hancock calls that reality, reintroduced for many by Elvis Presley's hip-shaking 1956 television appearances, the dance "so strong it took an entire civilization to forget it. And ten seconds on *The Ed Sullivan Show* to remember." Indeed, both John Lennon and Mick Jagger described first hearing rock 'n' roll as the strongest reality they ever experienced. "It is the great strength of this music that it has been able both to reveal the disease and to further its healing," writes Michael Ventura. "And the disease, again and again, whether manifesting itself as racism or as an armaments race, is the Western divorce of consciousness from flesh."

But the music also made a direct hit on the driving force behind rigid and elitist social orders: the adult ego. Americans tried to deny self-interest by wrapping themselves in their flag, in their religion, or in their ethnically homogenous community. Thus, in a manner shocking to white sensibilities—and deliberately contrary to the discrimination that had long tried to destroy black self-esteem—uninhibited blacks sometimes flaunted egotism to the point of hyperbole for both attention and entertainment. Wild braggadocio—exemplified by the toasts, signifying, and dirty-dozens ancestors of rap heard in Bo Diddley's greatest hits—was a form of ego release in blues, r&b, and rock 'n' roll. Little Richard, rock 'n' roll's original wild man and, later, a lightning rod for ego jokes, appropriately unleashed the big bang of rock 'n' roll in his song "Tutti Frutti" at J&M Studio next to Congo Square—"*AWOPBOPALOOBOPAWOPBAMBOOM!*" The song, mocking not only white forms of communication, but even the singer himself, speaks volumes for the un-self-conscious free expression of the call-and-response. But Richard's shout, heard 'round the world, was also based on a rhythm by his New Orleans drummer Charles Connor, and was thus an African-rooted talking-drum battle cry in a literal sense.

Such subversive nonsense swept through rock 'n' roll and followed the mix of rhythm and humor revived by Louis Jordan in the African folkloric tradition of tricksters—including the old man Legba, the spider Anansi, and the signifying monkey—who punctured pretensions, a tradition that had served blacks well as they mocked white superiority. Nat "King" Cole's early Jordanesque hit "Straighten Up and Fly Right," along with songs by Jordan's disciple Chuck Berry (notably "Jo Jo Gunne" and "Brown Eyed Handsome Man"), were classic trickster tales. In Dave Bartholomew's "The Monkey Speaks His Mind" (which became a legendary record in Jamaica and so impressed Elvis Costello that he wrote a sequel to it, "Monkey to Man"), Bartholomew disputed evolution—not on creationist grounds, but with the notion that monkeys are in truth the superior species. The African-based folk wisdom judged that the exposure and deflation of ego—like the release of physical tension and emotions—was healthier than denial. From an individualistic adult perspective, early rock 'n' roll was dumb or nonsensical, but there was a method to its madness, as the music offered both physical and psychic catharsis, including temporary freedom from the real world's war of egos, in a remarkably tribal balm and bond. Rock 'n' roll's rebellion was thus rooted in fiery passions tempered by an un-self-conscious (or even self-mocking) ego release, which not only has largely disappeared, it has been ignored, since it is directly in the blind spot of cultural historians.

In New Orleans the call-and-response was so intrinsic that both the musicians and the audience received names. The marching jazz band was the "first line," while the everyday people parading after them became the "second line." In that same spirit, Domino always played titanic rhythms "for the people." His music demanded a visceral response and reflected a different ego release—from his unabashed theme song "The Fat Man" on, he scoured his ego down to raw everyman feelings. In fact, I would suggest a major reason why historians have so neglected Jordan, Domino, and doo wop groups is that their music is essentially *anti-ego*—self-effacing celebrations of common passions. African American scholar Jon Michael Spencer states that black "rhythmic insurgency" often embodies the duality of the trickster, "who reincarnates and re-christens rhythm in each new generation." Jordan, Domino, Berry, and Richard were just such tricksters, charming their way into white culture with harmless-sounding lyrics and seducing rhythms. Domino's thermonuclear 1950 rocker "Hey! La Bas Boogie" included only a handful of unintelligible Creole patois words—*"Hey! La Bas! Mooo-Nay Mooo-Shaww!"*—in a traditional New Orleans call-and-response perhaps unconsciously referencing Legba (known locally as "Papa La Bas"), the Dahomean trickster at the crossroads to the spiritual world. Domino himself was at the crossroads of the black and white worlds, as he led the way in the crucial fusion of popular music with the West African traditions of polyrhythms, which moved the body, and emotive storytelling, which moved the soul.

■ ■ ■

America began changing culturally in the 1950s partly because radio airwaves could not be segregated. Though teenagers had more free time and spending money than ever, in an era of paranoia and repression their minds and bodies were still shackled. Just by turning a radio dial, young Americans (like Elvis Presley) found a new world. Radios playing black music became modern Pandora's boxes, emitting sounds that adults labeled "evils," which were corrosive to segregation. Before children were integrated in schools, the music integrated their souls. "The musicians and their music elicited far more respect and admiration from us than did anyone in an adult leadership role," recalls civil rights historian John Egerton of his youth. "In truth, we marched to a different drummer."

In May 1954, the Supreme Court ruling in *Brown v. Board of Education of Topeka* overturned school segregation. Segregationists called the day of the ruling "Black Monday." A Mississippi circuit judge, Tom Pickens Brady, wrote *Black Monday: Segregation or Amalgamation . . . America Has Its Choice,* a manifesto that inspired white citizens' councils against integration, just when Dave Bartholomew's "Blue Monday," sung by Smiley Lewis, became a blues hit. Blue Mondays were a New Orleans tradition, with nightclubs offering free food or beer while musicians jammed. Monday was also washday, when red beans simmered all day as women (like Rosemary Domino) scrubbed clothes on washboards. Slaves had once found incredible joy at Congo Square on Sundays, but their Mondays were, in turn, unimaginably blue. Local blacks continued to stomp out their blues with rhythm, notably in the joyous parades of both jazz bands after funerals and the Mardi Gras Indians (blacks who kept African traditions of call-and-response and outrageous tribal display alive in the guise of honoring their Native American brethren). Domino brilliantly brought the barrelhouse blues and street rhythm traditions together, notably in the working-man's parade of life of "Blue Monday," singing about working *"like a slave,"* even as he pounded out a message of liberation.

If deliriously dancing your blues away created euphoria powerful enough to overcome the traumas of slavery, segregation, and even death, it gave the sensory deprivation of the WASP ideal—work ethic + a pious Sunday school life = pie-in-the-sky-when-you-die—the appeal of a prison sentence. Young rock 'n' roll fans exemplified the rite-of-passage state known as liminality, and the related social flux that anthropologist Victor Turner called "communitas . . . a liberation of human capacities of cognition, affect, volition, creativity, etc. from the normative constraints," which "contains the germ of future social developments, or societal change." The music removed physical and emotional bonds, along with prejudice and pretension. John Lennon once summed up Eldridge Cleaver's view of rock 'n' roll's visceral effect, saying that "blacks gave the middle-class whites back their bodies." Children conditioned to strict rules of behavior embraced the African American passions that soon inflamed the world in a wildfire of free expression. As music born of over two centuries of a larger human drama, it was a source of incredible release, a joyful noise that burst forth in a sound-and-fury signifying freedom.

For the Domino family that drama began not in New Orleans, but in dark green fields.

"Swanee River Boogie"

Chapter 2

(1824–1940s)

"Anywhere somebody had a piano, they had a friend. He slept music and he woke up music."

—Freddie Domino

For over a century before Antoine "Fats" Domino was born, his family worked the sugarcane fields in the small rural community of Vacherie along the Mississippi River above New Orleans. Miles of leafy emerald acres surrounded the majestic columned plantations of the mostly French-speaking white gentry and the cypress plank shacks of the dark-hued field hands. The cane grew from stubble to a forest tall as a man. Before the first hard freeze at the end of each year there was a frenzied climax to the harvest, when every available man, woman, and child chopped the pithy stalks with broad machete-like cane knives from "can't to can't"—can't see in the morning to can't see at night.

Native Americans had lived in the Vacherie area for hundreds of years, as evidenced by a huge shell midden (which was gradually leveled and sown with crops) seven miles from the current path of the Mississippi River. In the sixteenth and seventeenth centuries the expeditions of DeSoto and LaSalle respectively navigated the area. But the first documented inhabitants in St. James Parish were primarily black—African slaves who worked on a *vacherie*, a French cattle ranch, in 1763. The very next year the first Acadians in Louisiana— French Canadians who became known as "Cajuns"—settled there. After the successful granulation of sugar on a New Orleans plantation in 1795 and the exodus of thousands of sugarcane workers from Santo Domingo to Louisiana following the Haitian Revolution, sugar plantations sprouted up all over south Louisiana.

Whites feared the rebellious Santo Domingo slaves with good reason. In January 1811, former Haitians led the largest slave uprising in American history, which they fomented just below Vacherie between St. James Parish and St. John the Baptist Parish. Over 500 slaves brandishing fearsome cane knives and a few small guns marched downriver capturing plantations, intent on liberating blacks all the way down to New Orleans. Young drummers beating out a ferocious rhythm led them along the River Road. After they killed two whites, the rebels met a large and heavily armed force, which decimated them. The heads of the leaders were impaled on pikes along the River Road as a gruesome warning.

The uprising sent a shockwave throughout the slave-holding South and led to even harsher plantation conditions. Still, even the cruelest conditions of slavery didn't break the spirits of these children of Africa. St. James Parish Court records cite formal charges against slaves accused of assault, arson, speaking insolently, and even biting thumbs. Others escaped to swampy maroon camps and even free-dom. Stubborn retention of aspects of African language, religion, and especially music was itself a form of social defiance preserving their unique identity. As in New Orleans, lighter-skinned, mixed-race African Americans often enjoyed more privileges, becoming house servants rather than field hands. But all of the French-speaking blacks—light or dark-skinned—in the Louisiana countryside proudly labeled themselves "Creole" to separate themselves from broken-spirited and sub-servient English-speaking slaves who arrived from other parts of the South in the first half of the nineteenth century. The Creoles called them "Te Nig" (meaning "American Nigger") or, with equal disdain, just "American."

The tight-knit bonds and pride of the rural black Creoles help explain the very private and independent character of Fats Domino and his family. "The African Creole, he knew who he was," says Ronald Dumas, a Creole St. James Parish historian. "He don't mingle with anybody. Some blacks you could make quick Uncle Toms out of—they'd sell you like that—but a Creole stay by him-self. He don't care. He's bullheaded and he's gonna marry another Creole. They were the proud ones."

The name "Domino" itself suggests a possible connection to the defiant strain of slaves from Santo Domingo, though slaves were generally known only by their first names, with surnames not commonly used until after the Civil War. However, Fats Domino apparently has direct ties to Haiti in the ancestry of his mother, Donatile Gros. According to Dumas, her great-great-grandfather was Louis Jacco, who listed Santo Domingo as his birthplace in the 1880 St. James census, when he reached the incredible age of 108. Jacco was hard to kill, and so was his culture; even today Vacherie graveyards are filled with crosses displaying the "exploding heart" design common in Haiti.

The first known Domino in Vacherie was a mulatto slave born in 1824 known as Antoine Domino. The elder Domino had a large family, but he also sired another, smaller one, which resulted in the birth of Aristile Domino, Fats Domino's grandfather, in 1857. That same year, his grandmother Carmelite was born in Maryland. Her mother Emeline was literally sold down the river to Louisiana in 1860, when she was cruelly separated from her husband, Richard Brown.

Plantation owner W. S. Baker provided a modest education for Carmelite, who worked as his domestic during Reconstruction. After she married Aristile Domino, they lived on the Golden Star Plantation and raised four children, Mary, Gustave, John, and Antoine—Fats Domino's father—who was born on October 14, 1881. Carmelite was also a midwife, using herbal medicines and charms that could literally be traced to African roots. "A midwife was a priestess," says Dumas. "She had the knowledge of herbal remedies or she could 'fix' you and make you miserable. In this community the women was greater than men. The daddy was the provider, but the mama had the majority of the power. If you wanted to start an argument, all you had to [do] was talk about somebody's mama. That was taboo."

Shortly after the turn of the century, Antoine Domino, or "Calice," as he was known, married the teenage Donatile Gros, whose family included Creoles of light complexion, like her father and grandfather (both named Pierre Gros), who were teachers. Calice and Donatile settled in "the quarters," a group of twenty-seven cane worker houses on the Webre-Steib Plantation, an acreage a few miles from the Mississippi that had once been the back end of the famed Laura Plantation (where blacks told white men the African trickster tales of Compair Lapin, better known as "Bre'r Rabbit"). There the Dominos raised five sons and two daughters, who attended a one-room schoolhouse to learn English when they weren't playing in the fields.

Calice, a thin, dark-skinned man, wore a broad-brimmed hat to protect his head from the sun as he and his older sons plowed the cane rows walking behind a mule. At first he made less than a dollar a day for the back-breaking work, until he started getting paid by the tonnage of cane he harvested. The Dominos also fished, hunted, and gardened for food they could not afford at the Webre-Steib Plantation store's inflated prices. Donatile and her daughters sometimes worked in the fields, but they also cooked, sewed their own clothes, and made quilts for sale.

Though the Dominos worked hard, they played hard too. On Saturday nights they danced to blow off steam in a party called a *banco* or *la la*. They pushed their sparse furnishings against the walls of their plain frame home to make room for dancing and set up stumps for benches. The hosts sold food—like fried fish, pork stew, and coon gumbo—and homebrew for a nominal price to their guests. Sometimes a man would throw pennies for the children to chase after. On special occasions Donatile also made shortcake cookies and popcorn balls stuck together with cane syrup for the kids. The musicians included Calice Domino, who played both tenor banjo and fiddle.

In the African tradition, music wasn't just a part of life, *it was life*. "They had music in that [Domino] family," declares nonagenarian Ellis Bourgeois, who grew up among the plantation's white gentry. "Any piece of tool they had they made music with it, whether it was with the cane knife or the saw, they'd make a tune." John Woods, an elderly former cane worker still living in the last of the Webre-Steib worker shacks on the unpaved North Coteau Road, concurs. "All the time I used to see them," says Woods, "they used to look like they were playin' music with their hands." Like New Orleans blacks, the country Creoles also enjoyed music on Sunday. "Any worship you got to have music," says Ronald Dumas. "Sunday was a solemn time, but you leave the Catholic Church and you go party and dance. You couldn't do that if you were Protestant."

But things started getting worse. There was a devastating flood in 1912 in which the Mississippi River shifted in a crevasse in the Vacherie area. After World War I the new priest at the magnificent local brick Catholic church, *Notre Dame de la Paix,* was Father Delnom, a tall man with a terrible temper who would actually strike black parishioners in church if they did something he didn't like. Following the Mississippi flood of 1927, Calice was faced with having to go back to working for a dollar a day instead of the more profitable per tonnage pay. He decided to join his brothers in a move to New Orleans.

■ ■

In the mid-1920s, Calice's brother Gustave Domino took possession of land in a rural area of New Orleans at 2301 Jourdan Avenue. The muddy street adjoined the eastern levee of the newly constructed Industrial Canal that stretched from the Mississippi to Lake Ponchartrain in the Ninth Ward. The area had once been a swampland filled with cypress trees and alligators that few dared to enter, except for escaped slaves who found temporary refuge there. In 1899, a massive and lengthy drainage of the area began. By the time Gustave arrived, the land was dry, though settlement in the Lower Ninth Ward in the area east of the Canal was sparse. Services like paved roads, electricity, and indoor plumbing were unknown.

Loading their modest belongings onto a Model T Ford, Calice and his family at first moved to a duplex at 1939/1937 Jourdan Avenue. One half of the house (1939) was a small store that served the rural community. It was in 1937 Jourdan where Calice and Donatile's eighth and final child, a boy named Antoine, Jr., was born in New Orleans. Carmelite, who had been born into slavery, delivered her last grandchild into the world on February 26, 1928. The proud matriarch of the Domino family lived to see many wondrous things in the eighty-seven years before her death in 1944, including the boy's burgeoning musical talent, but even in her wildest dreams she could hardly have imagined his future.

Calice soon built a narrow shotgun house in the block next to Gustave's at 2407 Jourdan Avenue, and his oldest son, John, built a similar house next door, with a large porch where the families gathered. The Dominos slept near one another in the small rooms. They still spoke Creole French, but even when the family began to speak more English, they kept the rural Creole ideals of hard work, good times, and close family ties. For years the Dominos even traveled back to Vacherie at year's end to visit relatives and help with the sugarcane harvest. Calice at first worked odd jobs with Gustave, a jack-of-all-trades farmer, butcher, barber, salesman, trumpet player, and bandleader, but by the early 1930s he and his sons obtained jobs miles away at the Fairgrounds Racetrack. For decades they tended the grounds and the horses on the land where one day his youngest son would entertain vast crowds of adoring fans at the New Orleans Jazz and Heritage Festival.

Calice and Donatile rose every day at four in the morning, kindled a fire in the woodstove and sat and talked quietly over cups of strong coffee while the children slept. Then he tended to his small garden until six A.M., when he and his sons traveled to the fairgrounds. Before sundown, he went back to his beloved garden until his daughters called him to dinner.

In his few free hours of relaxation, Calice loved wine and music, as did his wife. Despite a gaudy nickname—"Zoot"—Donatile was a very reserved, short and thick Creole woman who wore her long straight hair in a single braid down her back ("I think Mama might have had a little Indian in her," says Fats) and sometimes played the accordion, though Fats himself doesn't remember her playing it. Her daughters, Philonese and Philomena, helped her with the housework and with their youngest brother's care. Antoine was a favored child, a baby in a family of adolescents and adults. And, like his parents, he was quiet; as a toddler he went missing for hours, only to be discovered in a barrel near the house steps when he finally cried out.

When Antoine reached school age, he attended the Macarty School on Caffin Avenue, six blocks away. After school his primary chore was chopping wood for the next day's cooking fire. He showed no sign of the girth that would later be integral to his fame, though even then he loved to eat. He remembers watching his mother cook—"If she happened to turn her back, I'd steal a couple of shrimp when she'd be soaking them for gumbo."

Antoine was a bit timid and solitary, but he was also resourceful and singleminded. He knew what he wanted—usually candy or other tasty treats—and he did what he had to do to get it. He made a habit of walking the muddy streets of the Lower Ninth Ward looking for small rewards. Sometimes the Florida Avenue pumping station lowered the level of the Industrial Canal, allowing the neighborhood children to catch fish, crawfish, and crabs stranded in the shallows. He and other kids collected scrap metal they found filling potholes in the street and coal from the railroad track just north of their homes to sell to a junk dealer who came by with his mule-drawn wagon and gave them a quarter. Antoine and his cousin Freddie (Gustave's son), who was three years older, even competed to help clean out a neighbor's cesspool. The other kids teased them about the filthy work, but the Domino boys earned the royal day's pay of a whole dollar.

Some nights Antoine walked the dirt path of Jourdan Avenue to St. Claude Street, lighted in those days only by oil lamps in the houses and the stars above. The only sounds Antoine heard in the dark were farm animals baying and foghorn blasts from the Canal. Philonese met him at the Desire streetcar line with big bags of leftover food—red beans and rice, stuffed peppers, and cornbread muffins—from her longtime job as a domestic for a white family, the Pillsburys. At Wagner's market, they bought large scrap meat packages, including hogshead cheese and hamhocks used for flavoring beans and soups, for twenty-six cents. At the Betsy Ross Bakery, they purchased day-old bread and cakes for a nickel each. Even during the Depression, when Antoine was happy to get a bag of marbles for Christmas, he didn't go hungry.

On languid Sunday evenings, the brothers played baseball out on the levee, though Antoine preferred boxing, which his brother, Joe, briefly pursued. They called Joe "Tenig," jokingly using the old Creole derogatory name. The other Domino brothers had nicknames too—John was "Ové," Aristile was "Jaco," Lawrence was "Bum," Morris was "King," and Antoine was "'Tit Frère," meaning "little brother" in French. In 1936, eight-year-old Antoine, Freddie, and other kids hung on the brass rails outside the Florida Avenue pumping station to listen to the thrilling radio broadcast of the fight between black boxer Joe Louis and the German Max Schmeling. The white man at the station taunted the boys when Schmeling won, though two years later Louis would become a hero for most Americans when he won the rematch, which, along with Jesse Owens's 1936 Olympics triumphs, became the first symbolic victories against Hitler.

From his earliest years, Antoine loved music. The family owned an old wind-up gramophone, and even when its winding string broke, he would twirl the 78s with his finger to keep the blues and jazz playing. When the family bought a radio, he listened to Glenn Miller and swing bands. Everyone was thrilled in 1938 when they heard a record by one of the few black performers then played on the radio. "I remember when Ella Fitzgerald first put that record out 'Ah-Tisket, Ah-Tasket,'" says Domino. "Everybody'd start running to hear that record and turn it up *loud.*"

The highlight of the week was still a Saturday night party. Calice delighted in plucking his violin strings, with his son John on trumpet, and Aristile on drums. Frank Hill, a neighbor, played guitar on some comical Creole songs, while everyone in the neighborhood danced and drank homebrew. Antoine and Freddie sometimes sneaked swigs of the potent drink and hid under the house until the alcohol wore off.

The turning point in Antoine's young life occurred at age ten, when the family obtained an old upright piano with keys so worn that rusted metal shone through the ivory. Though his brother Aristile played "A Salty Dog," Antoine's interest in the instrument only began to blossom after his brother-in-law Harrison Verrett sat down next to him. Verrett was both father figure and musical mentor. Born on February 27, 1907, in Napoleonville, Louisiana, he had moved to New Orleans as a small child and started his music career as a teenage banjo player in jazz bands, often playing in the Milneburg vacation camps on Lake Ponchartrain and later traveling with an eighteen-piece band in a medicine show. In the late 1920s he began playing on boats in Biloxi and at New Orleans' Fern Dance Hall. In 1932 he married Philonese and they moved into a house at 2401 Jourdan. Verrett taught Antoine piano chords and even wrote the notes on the keys so the boy could learn them.

Soon Antoine wanted to do little else besides play the piano. His parents, who had to listen to him practice for hours each day, put the instrument out in the garage, where their youngest son taught himself the songs he heard on the radio. Music was now his obsession, a word that once meant driven by an evil spirit, but the more he played piano, the more its music lifted him to a world beyond his muddy home, like the rays of the fiery sunsets breaking across the levee into his front door each evening. As he was a lonely child, it became his soul-filling companion.

His love of music and his shyness hurt his education at the Civil War–era Macarty School, where the black children of the Ninth Ward were educated in such poor conditions that their parents a decade later sued the New Orleans School Board over the unequal facilities. When Antoine was required to recite a poem, he played hooky simply to avoid having to get up in front of the class. The one time that he overcame his fear was when his teacher, Miss Lecage, left the classroom. As Oliver Morgan, a classmate who also became an r&b singer, recalls, Antoine sat down at the class piano and played a boogie that had his classmates rocking. The Lower Ninth Ward was loaded with future musical talent. Another friend was Lee Dorsey, who teased Antoine for going home after school and play-ing piano instead of playing with the other kids. Domino's fixation also hurt his Catholic catechism classes, and he failed to get his confirmation. Finally, in the fourth grade, eleven-year-old Antoine quit school and went to work.

■ ■ ■

"FRÈRE!" shouted Antoine's boss, a thin, blind black man named Ed Ridgley, his voice resonating down the street. He was calling for Domino, whose first real job was an iceman's helper. He awoke at 5:30 A.M. and worked delivering twenty-five to thirty blocks a day before the city's steamy heat set in. In the first half of the twentieth century, ice wagons were an essential part of city living for families that couldn't afford refrigerators or even electricity. The iceman's daily rounds were as familiar as those of the newsboy, the milkman, and the vegetable peddler. Ridgley pierced a frozen block three times with his ice pick, splitting it into four exact pieces. His small son, Ed, Jr., lifted a twenty-five-pound block of ice out of an insulated box in the back of their mule-drawn wagon. He walked up to a shotgun house, knocked, and announced: "ICEMAN!" He heard music nearby and found his co-worker Domino warming up the house where he had delivered ice—banging on the customer's upright piano.

Antoine also worked briefly as a stable boy at the New Orleans Fairgrounds Racetrack, where his father made $26 a week in the 1940s cutting grass and tending the horses, but he quit after he had to ride in the trailer with the horses on a harrowing trip to Kentucky. Next came jobs in a bakery, in a coffee factory, and at the home of the Pillsburys, the white family for whom Philonese worked. He cut the grass all day around their mansion for a dollar and a half. If he had any time at the end of the day, he had to clean the garage or wash windows. Philonese brought him his lunch in the garage, where he sat on a bench and ate in his dirty jeans—he was not even allowed in the kitchen, where his sister ate.

Domino was aware there were places he couldn't go because of segregation, but to him that was just the way things were. He was relatively happy in his small rural corner of New Orleans, and no one was really mean to him. In fact, he enjoyed washing the cars of white men—policeman Cliff Reuters, grocer Sam Clowery, and wealthy furrier Admiral Vaughan—who each gave him a dollar for a couple of hours of work. In the hierarchy of Antoine's pleasures, cars came right after music and food. He drove Harrison Verrett's Ford whenever he could and even went to work in the auto mechanic shop on Forstall Street of his cousin, Joseph Cousin (pronounced "Coo-ZAN").

Antoine sometimes even tended Cousin's bar next door to the shop. There he played the jukebox and learned songs like "Pine Top's Boogie Woogie." Recorded in the year of Domino's birth by Clarence "Pine Top" Smith, the song had fostered an entire musical style. The frenetic piano playing had developed from blues and ragtime in southern honkytonks and barrelhouse lumber camps, where a pianist was a one-man band who supplied dancing music for rousing weekend parties. Boogie piano became the early foundation of Antoine's music. He also played the "videophonic," a nickelodeon that played short films by black stars like Louis Jordan and Nat "King" Cole. Antoine often selected "Low Down Dog," in which chubby comedian Dudley Dickerson catches his wife flirting with the iceman in the kitchen and heavyweight boogie pianist Meade Lux Lewis in the living room. Dickerson shakes his finger at her and lip-synchs as Lewis plays and Big Joe Turner sings live off-camera, *Well, I ain't gonna be your low down dog no more!* It was a song that Domino would play for more than half a century.

On Saturdays in the early 1940s, Antoine went with his brothers to the Palace Theater at the edge of the French Quarter. For a quarter they saw a vaudeville show featuring a singer named Big Alma, a dancer, a comedian, five short films, and a full-length movie. "I used to see Gene Autry movies all the time," Domino recalls, "him, Roy Rogers, the Three Musketeers, and John Wayne—I used to like to hear him talk!"

Few African Americans had the money or transportation to go to night-clubs during World War II. So Philomena Domino and her husband, Robert Stevens, threw Sunday house parties in the backyard, with Antoine as the primary entertainment, performing before his first audience. His brothers-in-law usually accompanied him—Stevens on drums and Verrett on guitar. Philomena turned her garage into a little bar, where she sold beer for fifteen cents while her baby brother beat out boogies to the cheers of his family and friends.

But Verrett was grooming his protégé for his musical career in the world beyond the Domino homestead. He so closely bonded with the shy seventeen-year-old that in 1945 he was able to talk Antoine into overcoming his intense apprehension about leaving his home to take a month-long trip halfway across the country to Oxnard, California, where Harrison worked as a carpenter and Philomena cooked at the nearby naval base at Port Hueneme. After the war in 1946, Verrett took Domino to his gig with the Original Tuxedo Jazz Band, led by Oscar "Papa" Celestin, whose band had once included a young Louis Armstrong. In the courtyard patio of the French Quarter restaurant The Court of Two Sisters, Domino sat down and played his boogie woogie for white patrons, who deposited change and bills in the tip jar. "I picked up about eight or nine dollars within ten minutes," he recalls. "Oh, man! That was a lot of money." Verrett also took his young brother-in-law to a local piano teacher, Mrs. Pearl Celestin, two blocks away on Forstall Street, but Domino quit going after a month or so, as he was so adept at listening to records and then playing them by ear.

In fact, aside from Verrett's tutoring, Antoine received most of his musical education from jukeboxes booming out the blues and boogie of Amos Milburn, Charles Brown, Louis Jordan, Pete Johnson, and Meade Lux Lewis. Jordan, who scored one sly jump blues hit after another, dominated black music in the 1940s in the same way that Domino would in the next decade. Antoine especially loved the lubricious blues of Amos Milburn, whom he even came to resemble, hunching over the piano with a cherubic grin. "Amos Milburn was the only blues singer I tried to sing like," says Fats.

Domino's obsession with the piano was finally starting to pay some dividends beyond self-satisfaction. The positive feedback he received only intensified his desires. Now he knew that others could actually share his love of music, and he was thrilled to realize that he could even make money playing it. It was a discovery that opened his world to endless possibility.

■ ■ ■

Soon Domino found a close friend and ally. He was playing the piano in his patched mechanic overalls at Cousin's bar one night in 1946 when a short, portly soldier walked in. Soldiers were regulars there, as the bar was located not far from Jackson Barracks, but this one carried a saxophone with him. As Domino played a slow blues number in the dim glow of the bar's perennial Christmas lights, the soldier asked to sit in with him. Buddy Hagans stretched his stubby limbs before letting out an off-key bellow on his old C-melody sax. He warmed up and the two started playing. After several numbers, Hagans leaned in and said, "Why don't you come over to my house on Flood Street? Maybe we can start a little band."

Robert "Buddy" Hagans was born on December 18, 1922, in Bogalusa, Louisiana, renowned as both the birthplace of Roy "Professor Longhair" Byrd and as a longtime Ku Klux Klan stronghold. Hagans grew up in a musical family in New Orleans, but didn't start playing saxophone until 1944 at his army base in Fort Benning, Georgia. He was influenced by Louis Armstrong and saxmen like Gene Ammons, Chu Berry, and Coleman Hawkins, though his honking sound mostly reflected the influence of another Louisiana native, Illinois Jacquet of "Flying Home" fame.

Domino and Hagans spent many afternoons listening to records and trying to play songs. It was the beginning of a partnership that would last nearly a quarter of a century. They added a drummer, Victor Leonard, and a guitarist, Rupert Robertson. Harrison Verrett sometimes stopped by the rehearsals to help Antoine with his timing. The group began playing at Cousin's on Friday, Saturday, and Sunday evenings, and at the Ballerina on Caffin Avenue for Sunday matinees.

But the gigs were still modest to say the least. One weekend, Freddie Domino, who played trumpet in his own band, drove Antoine and two other musicians past the swampy Chalmette floodplain (where, over a century earlier, hundreds of British Redcoats had bled their last in the Battle of New Orleans) to a weathered fishing village, where a crippled peddler named Guy Minor owned a bar. Antoine looked in horror at the battered upright piano, with its warped, missing, and broken keys. Minor, a haggler by trade, spoke up: "Hey, he can't play that ol' piano; I'm only paying for three." But Freddie knew that Antoine could bang out *something* on the old box. He replied, "If you don't want him, you ain't got nobody," and started packing up his horn. Minor glanced at the bar full of people and reconsidered the two-dollar investment in a pianist. "W-e-l-l-l, okay," he croaked. "We'll take him." The Dominos proceeded to shake the shack's patrons with their crude blues beat.

But Domino needed something to make him stand out. That essential element of star quality first developed around a song he learned when working at the Douglas Lumber Yard in 1947. At lunchtime, he and his co-workers hung out in a café, where he played Albert Ammon's "Swanee River Boogie" on the jukebox. When he mastered Ammon's intricate fingerwork at a blistering pace, the song became a scintillating climax to his shows in the small bars of the Ninth Ward. "That's the one that kept me going before I had a record," says Fats. "People came in just to hear me play 'Swanee River Boogie.'" Ammon's boogie was based on Stephen Foster's "The Old Folks at Home," which nearly a century earlier was virtually the first song sung by people all over the world. Foster became the father of popular song largely by encapsulating the strong emotions, refrains, and rhythms of African American music in his compositions. The songs hit a universal chord, as Foster suggested by the alteration of the words "blacks" and "folks." Though his "Ethiopian" songs (as Foster called them) were associated with minstrelsy and stereotypes, black legends including W. C. Handy, Duke Ellington, Louis Armstrong, Ray Charles, and Domino all later recorded them. Though Antoine could later identify with Foster's homesick lyrics, at the time his rifling boogie instrumental stripped away any sentimentality with ass-shaking rhythm.

One day during the summer of 1947, a milling crowd of blacks gathered for a picnic on a Sunday afternoon. They arrived by cars and the busload at Hardin Park near the Gentilly section of New Orleans to see the city's new musical sensation, Paul Gayten. Schoolteachers sold hot dogs, sausages, pies, pig's feet, and soft drinks. Rip Roberts, the city's leading African American music promoter and a community leader, introduced Gayten at the piano. His band, including svelte singer Annie Laurie and towering sax player Lee Allen, started playing their suave ballads and blues novelties. In the crowd, Antoine Domino stood in his threadbare overalls. He had paid a nickel to sit at the back of the bus to get there and seventy-five cents admission to get his first look at the newly famed bandleader.

At one point, Gayten made a surprise announcement: "Ladies and gentlemen, Rip tells me we have a special guest in the audience, a young man who really plays the piano, Antoine Domino. Antoine, can you come up and play us a tune?"

Shocked, Domino nervously walked to the stage as the audience applauded him. He sat down at the piano and ripped into "Swanee River Boogie." Afterwards, the crowd cheered, giving him his first taste of fame. "Fats came on and stopped the show," recalled Gayten decades later, "and we were friends ever since."

Not long thereafter, Antoine walked on Orleans Avenue past Dooky Chase's, a popular black restaurant owned by a Creole who led a big band. Gayten, who was just arriving in his Cadillac, hailed Antoine and invited him to lunch. Still in his jeans, the nineteen-year-old Domino walked into the restaurant with the city's biggest black star. It was a moment he never would forget.

∎ ∎ ∎

That same summer Antoine had another life-changing encounter. He and his brother Joseph "Tenig" Domino paid a visit to a snowball stand on Caffin Avenue run by Tenig's friend Eva Breaux. The shaved ice cones, soaked with sweet syrup, were a fine way to beat the stifling Louisiana heat. Tenig introduced Antoine to Eva's family, the Halls, who lived next door. Jackson Hall was a hunter, who caught deer, muskrats, and raccoons in St. Bernard Parish as far down as Pointe A la Hachè. The Halls cooked the edible game and sold the hides. Rita LePage Hall, a prim-looking Creole lady, greeted the Dominos at the door. Antoine walked in and noticed the family's upright piano. He sat down and played a boogie. When he finished, Rita Hall burst into applause. Her support of him and uncritical enthusiasm for his music would be a source of inspiration for him for years to come. "She was crazy about me," says Fats, "and I was crazy about her."

He soon was also crazy about Mrs. Hall's daughter, Rosemary, who was the prettiest girl he had ever seen. She was even shyer than he, but her mother's adoration of the young man was infectious both ways; soon there was a corresponding attraction between Rosemary and Antoine. Antoine continued to stop at the Halls' house on Caffin Avenue to play piano and visit Rosemary, even though she was a serious churchgoing girl who would soon graduate from McDonough 35 High School with honors, and he was a poor grade school dropout. He couldn't afford a car, but with the money he was making from his music jobs he managed to buy a shiny secondhand tuxedo. He wore it proudly when Rosemary finally agreed to come see him play his first big show with Billy Diamond's band at the Rockford Pavilion later that summer of 1947.

Diamond, a small-time bandleader, would also become a major figure in Domino's musical life. Born in New Orleans on October 5, 1916, he was the son of a flamboyant local baseball pitcher nicknamed "Black Diamond." Louis Armstrong, a family friend, once gave him a trumpet, but Diamond followed the lead of his cousin, John Porter, a bass player, and took lessons from jazzman Narvin Kimball. "I wasn't a great musician," admits Diamond, "but I was good enough to get over." After World War II, he used his natural skills as a hustler to obtain steady work for his bands. He had recently seen Antoine play at a backyard party at the Dominos' and was impressed enough with the young man's boogie skills to ask him to play with his band. Once Harrison Verrett offered to accompany him, Antoine agreed. "Billy Diamond knew all the musicians and all the musicians knew him," says Fats. "He used to get a job when nobody else could."

Word of Domino's talent preceded the show at the A. Rockford Lewis Pavilion on Royal Street, the biggest ballroom in the Ninth Ward. Cornetist Melvin Lastie told future Domino sax player Clarence Ford, "There's a piano player named Domino, all he can play is boogie, but he can *play* the boogie!" From the Rockford stage the band beat out the slow-churning sounds of "The Honeydripper." Women, their hair swept up, and men, theirs slicked down, swayed in closely tangled dances. As Diamond introduced Domino to play his boogies, Antoine smiled at Rosemary, sitting at a table in her Sunday best, coughing on the cigarette smoke. She would never see him perform before an audience again.

On Wednesday, August 6, 1947, Rosemary Hall, then seventeen, married nineteen-year-old Antoine Domino. The Halls' minister, the Reverend Riley of the Hartzell African Methodist Episcopal Church, performed the ceremony at their home. The bride wore a floor-length white dress with puff sleeves and a ring she borrowed from her sister, Eva. The groom wore his tuxedo. Shortly afterwards, they set up housekeeping in one bedroom of the Halls' house. Though Domino would name several songs after Rosemary, he admits, "We never did talk too much about no music." Despite her daughter's academic achievements, Rita Hall had groomed her to become a dutiful wife and mother. That duty did not require an interest in her husband's career. "I looked at it as two separate lives," says Rosemary, "but I always wanted to see him successful."

Domino soon got a good job making forty dollars a week at the Crescent City Bed Factory on Broad Street. On the first floor Buddy Hagans bent the iron for the springs. On the second floor Domino fit the springs into the frames.

Thomas "Mac" Johnson, who would join Domino's band decades later, once saw him on a break at the factory, wearing a cap, overalls, and a bandana so he wouldn't inhale the mattress dust. The fourteen-year-old Johnson recognized the Ninth Ward pianist and told him, "I play trumpet." But Antoine didn't reply; he was too busy humming a tune.

One night after work Antoine went to see Dave Bartholomew's band performing at Al's Starlight Inn on North Dorgenois Street. Bartholomew was a powerful trumpeter who had recently capitalized on the jump blues trend to become the most popular black bandleader in New Orleans. When Bartholomew stepped down, drummer Earl Palmer took over to sing a couple of ballads while lightly brushing his drums. When Palmer took his break, the bar owner remarked, "Look, man, if y'all don't play, the people are gonna walk out." Bartholomew, who enforced a suit-and-tie dress code in his band, had encountered the poorly dressed Domino before and had not been impressed. But Palmer, seeing Antoine standing out like a sore thumb in his denim, wanted to encourage the young pianist. Domino agreed to play and disrupted cocktail conversations with a ripping boogie. After a couple of numbers, he stepped down and received some mild appreciation from the audience. Bartholomew, who had no idea that he would soon embark on a great collaboration with the young pianist, cornered Palmer and reminded him that he'd told him not to let Domino play. "Oh," said Palmer with a smile. "I forgot."

On May 15, 1948, twenty-year-old Antoine Domino and Buddy Hagans drove down to Local 496, the Musicians' Union at 1480 North Claiborne Avenue, and paid their $12 membership fees—it was a black union; the New Orleans American Federation of Musicians would not integrate until 1969. The pair had to get their union card to play their first "uptown" show with Billy Diamond at the Robin Hood, a nightclub at the corner of Jackson and Loyola where Paul Gayten and Annie Laurie held sway with their refined cocktail blues. Opening with a rhumba rocker, "Hey Little Girl" (which would later be recorded by Professor Longhair, Billy Wright, and Clifton Chenier), Gayten then sang softly as he caressed the piano keys; the sultry Laurie delivered both risqué blues numbers and stirring ballads, notably the original hit of the standard "Since I Fell for You." The thin Creole emcee, Sporty Johnson, praised the duo to the skies, and then reluctantly introduced Billy Diamond's combo.

Scattered applause greeted the five stubby musicians, but they quickly engaged the crowd with a Louis Jordan boogie. Hagans honked a noisy sax solo that amused Plas and Raymond Johnson of the Johnson Brothers band. After some instrumentals, Antoine, seated at the grand piano, committed the sin of singing Gayten's hits "True" and "Peter Blue and Jasper Too." Domino's style of playing was heavy-handed compared to Gayten's smooth, jazzy stylings. Sitting with a drink and a cigarette, Annie Laurie turned to her guitarist and said, "These guys can't play. That piano player can't sing *or* play."

The crowd thought differently, however, and rewarded the band with some warm applause. Diamond, holding a standup bass as tall as he, spoke into the microphone. "Thanks, folks. That's my boy, 'Fats' Domino. I call him 'Fats,' 'cause he's gonna be famous someday, just like Fats Pichon and Fats Waller. And if he keeps eating, he's gonna be just as big!" The crowd laughed. Antoine cringed a bit inwardly. The five-foot-five pianist had a fondness for his new family's cooking, especially hamhocks and pigs' feet, which gave him a sizeable gut, though he still only weighed 160 pounds.

"He got mad when I called him 'Fats Domino,'" says Diamond, "but he never gave the name up. I saw the dream because of Fats Waller. Don't be 'Antoine,' be 'Fats,' because 'Fats' is an outstanding name, you know what I mean? Like 'Minnesota Fats,' 'Fats Domino' was a classic."

Not long afterwards, Domino looked out on a swampy landscape of half-rotted trees, moss, and vines on either side of Airline Highway as he traveled with Diamond's band, including Harrison Verrett, to Shreveport in a Buick. In front of them Rip Roberts drove New Orleans' new blues sensation Roy Brown in the singer's Cadillac.

After dinner at Freeman's Chicken Shack in Shreveport's bleak ghetto, the musicians made their way to a local boarding house to rest. They were going to play after a baseball game at the club Palace Park, where Brown had once imitated Bing Crosby in a vaudeville act. Just before the show, Domino panicked—his shoes were missing. Roberts and Brown pitched in to buy some new shoes on the way to the club, though a couple hours later, something happened that made Brown regret his generosity. After Brown shook his six-foot frame as he sang like a hell-fire preacher heralding his planet-rocking news in "Good Rockin' Tonight," the band played an instrumental intermission. Then Billy told Fats to sing Paul Gayten's hits. The audience clapped along with Domino's rhythmically direct sound and warm, youthful voice. But Brown was furious at being upstaged. He told Domino, "I hired *you*, little Negro, to play, man. You're not supposed to be singin'. *I'm* the star!"

The club owner, Willie X, asked the group to stay another night. Rip Roberts agreed, though Brown also demanded Domino's silence. Roberts paid the musicians $8 each; Brown received $50. Late that night, Roberts heard a knock on his door. A young man who had never toured before handed him some items. "Mr. Rip, you wanna hold my eight dollars and my new shoes?" said Antoine Domino. "They tell me when you're on the road they steal your money."

A week later, Diamond's band sat on the curb of Rampart and Dumaine in front of Cosimo Matassa's J&M Music Shop. They were waiting for Roy Brown, who was supposed to meet them there for a trip to Memphis. Domino peered at the 78 rpm records and appliances inside, but he didn't even dream of recording in the little studio in the back where Gayten, Laurie, and Brown had waxed their hits. After they waited for hours, a man approached and said that Brown had already left, taking Edgar Blanchard's band instead. Domino was crestfallen; he felt he was to blame. Though he had achieved some neighborhood notoriety and had pleased crowds with his music, the local black stars, with the exception of Paul Gayten, seemed to belittle his abilities and his humble clothing. But the stinging rejections only made him more determined to succeed with his music, which possessed a visceral passion far deeper than outward appearances.

Billy Diamond cursed at Brown's rejection. Even a half century later he would still feel a twinge of regret over the missed opportunity. "That's how I lost the job with Roy Brown," says Diamond, "'cause I let Fats sing."

Chapter 3

"Hideaway Blues"

(1949)

"There is no, no, no, no place like New Orleans for music. The pioneers are here. We built the house. You can redecorate it, but we laid the foundation."

—DAVE BARTHOLOMEW

Charley Armstead, a strong-limbed Creole, dreamed of turning his little bar on Desire Street into a premier black nightspot. For decades, blacks in the neighborhood had ridden the Desire Streetcar made famous in 1947 by Tennessee Williams in which deceptively genteel signs FOR COLORED PATRONS ONLY provided them with convenient social filing tabs. Armstead's bar was in the Upper Ninth Ward, a working-class neighborhood between the Vieux Carré and the Industrial Canal. In the late 1940s, when he was hatching his plans, the neighborhood was supposedly improving, as the city began demolishing the area's tenements and building huge housing projects. But Desire Street (a corruption of the name of a nineteenth-century debutante named Desirée, whom the street originally honored) would accrue even more irony than Williams imagined.

Armstead cultured his big black pearl, doubling the size of the nightclub. Since the area had a bad reputation, he added signs commanding NO BOISTEROUS OR DISORDERLY CONDUCT WILL BE TOLERATED and two security guards; as a former boxer he sometimes grappled with troublemakers himself. Dave Bartholomew's big band presided over the club's glorious opening during Mardi Gras in 1948, and Armstead publicized his club with klieg lights blazing high into the sky and loudspeaker-equipped trucks blasting music as they drove around the neighborhood announcing that such luminaries as Count Basie and Billy Eckstine would be playing at Club Desire. Late that year, Billy Diamond grabbed a very juicy peach when his group became Armstead's house band.

On Saturday, January 22, 1949, Plymouths, Fords, and DeSotos deposited patrons at the club's front door, the men wearing stylishly baggy suits and the women in evening gowns. Some came all the way from Southern University, ninety miles away in Baton Rouge, to see the nightclub's ballyhooed floor show. Inside, their eyes filled with wonder seeing the colors dancing off the club's glass-brick walls, beautiful European landscape paintings, and a round-faced cabinet emitting miraculous blue light—a wrestling broadcast from the city's one TV station. Walking upstairs, the students took seats along a wrought-iron balcony and ordered boiled crabs, crawfish, and tenderloin trout. They looked down at the stage, where Lawrence "Big Four" Benton, a thin emcee in fishbowl glasses, told jokes, sang, and then proclaimed, "Now, it's showtime!"

An exotic dancer twirled with flaming torches while muscular acrobats bounded across the stage. Men in the crowd showered a belly dancer with silver dimes. All during the floor show, Diamond's band supplied a steady beat. Then they played for the patrons who wanted to dance. At one point, Billy let his chubby piano player, dressed in his one suit, take center stage and play a boogie and some blues. "Diamond's band is a much improved outfit and it's rumored that they will be recording soon for a large music firm," *The Louisiana Weekly* reported a week later, adding, in Domino's first press notice: "Featured in Diamond's outfit are Fat Man, the roly-poly pianist, and Seymour, the blind boy who blows a lot of fine trumpet."

Although Seymour's fate is unclear, the roly-poly pianist would continue to garner attention. Armstead's wife fawned over Fats, making the owner jealous. Jessie Lee Wells and Edwin Compass, the proprietors of the hole-in-the-wall Hideaway Club two blocks up on Desire Street, came to him with an offer to play at their club on Fridays, Saturdays, and Sundays. Domino was still working at the Crescent City Bed Factory and the few dollars he made with Diamond didn't go far, especially after his first child, Antoinette, was born, on January 2, 1949. Fats was flattered by the offer but also petrified with an insecurity that would mark each major transition in his career. He needed a venue where people didn't dress fancy, where a raw beat was welcome. Mostly, he needed a club to build his self-confidence, and the Hideaway seemed perfect for that.

But Fats knew next to nothing about running a band. Once again, Harrison Verrett and his cousin came to his aid. Freddie Domino hooked him up with a couple of sax players, Charles Burbank and Hiram Armstrong. Antoine's other brother-in-law, Robert Stevens, became the band's drummer. The fans at the Hideaway reminded Domino of the people at his sister's backyard parties, people who didn't make him feel shy or make fun of his working-class wardrobe. "It was a lot of fun!" says Domino. "I used to be *waitin'* for those three nights a week, just to go back there."

Unlike Club Desire, the Hideaway had nothing fancy. It was named for good reason; revelers had to walk past railroad tracks and an overgrown area to even get to the shack. Inside, the décor was haphazard; chairs didn't match, white tablecloths covered cheap wooden tables, tattered drink signs decorated the walls, and dusty crepe streamers hung from the ceiling. In the back the bandstand was merely an area with a small partition and an upright piano. But the cramped quarters belied the seismic shows that were taking place there.

Domino sat at the piano, both hands hitting the keyboard. His rumbling locomotive sound powered the band, as he had to develop an even more rhythmic style, since he was not supported by a bassist or guitarist. When the drummer upped the tempo, the two sax players circled the small dance floor like dervishes. Suddenly, they ran through the delirious crowd, leaping atop the bar and opposing each other like gunfighters as Scotty the bartender stood back, laughing as startled patrons grabbed for their drinks. The drummer rose to his feet, even beating his drums with gourds. Fats also stood, ripping the piano keys and sweating. The sax players jumped down, dodging club goers, and flew out the door, wailing "Flying Home" to the neighborhood. Then they ran back inside and fell down in front of the piano, blasting with their horns and legs in the air as Domino and Stevens crash-landed the song with an extended final note. The fans were out of their seats, screaming.

Domino played the jump blues and boogie hits of the day. His most popular song besides "Swanee River Boogie" was his raucous version of the bedrock New Orleans standard "The Junker's Blues," an eight-bar number sung with various lyrics over a barrelhouse beat. The city's first black disc jockey, Vernon "Dr. Daddy-O" Winslow, wrote in the *Louisiana Weekly* on August 27, 1949, "Don't forget, I'll be at the Hideaway next Saturday night . . . and I want Fats to play those Jungle [*sic*] Blues . . . !!!"—referring to Domino's crowd pleaser. New Orleans piano patriarch Champion Jack Dupree had recorded "The Junker's Blues" in 1941, but Domino learned the song from Harrison Verrett, who'd heard French Quarter pianists like Stormy Weather playing it. The song was sung by junkies in jailhouses from New Orleans to Angola prison. The punch line was a pun on ordinary junk dealers, who hawked odd bits of scrap loaded onto wagons, and the "junker" addict who was *loaded all the time.* Though the song had unknown folk origins, the man who first recorded the song calls it a cautionary tale. "'The Junker's Blues' comes from me bein' with junkers," recalled Champion Jack Dupree. "I seen the guys who used the needle and smoked and sniffed cocaine. I used all of my own blues to try and help the younger people." In Domino's chubby, piston-like hands, the lament of the ghetto's bane was no longer a blues but a holy houserocker.

Word of mouth about the wild pianist at the Hideaway shot across the city like lightning. Bass player Lawrence Guyton, who later joined Domino's band, remembers people asking "Where you goin' tonight?" According to Guyton, when someone replied "Over here across the tracks, they have FATS over there," it "sounded like the dude said Duke Ellington was there!" Dr. Daddy-O first noted the frenzy in the July 9, 1949, issue of *The Louisiana Weekly:* "Say, papa, have ya been out to the Hideaway lately?? . . . Fats Domio [*sic*] is out there making 'em shout and holler!!!" Winslow even planned to record Domino's band live at the Hideaway one night for his radio show and then present the disc to Apollo Records for an audition, but the recording engineer arrived too late.

Domino was learning more about music, as well as the dynamics of managing a band, as his musicians changed. Harrison Verrett sometimes jammed on guitar after his shows with Papa Celestin. A Ninth Ward neighbor, eighteen-year-old John "Little Sonny" Jones, wailed some blues songs. Freddie Domino and Buddy Hagans sat in on trumpet and saxophone, respectively. Domino loved the gutty sound of sax players. "Fats was a saxophone man," says Charles Burbank. "He'd have five saxophones up there before he'd get one trumpet player."

That summer Robert Stevens abandoned Philomena and took their two small children, never to be seen by her again. Verrett suggested a new drummer, Dave Oxley, who had played with Bessie Smith on her final tour and later with Papa Celestin and Dave Bartholomew. Oxley brought a showmanship and pop sound to the band that influenced Domino. From behind his drum kit, he sang jazz standards like "Coquette" (which Domino would later record) and novelties like "Down at the Zoo (They All Asked for You)." Fats still practiced constantly whenever he was at home. On days when he was not working at the bed factory, the band rehearsed during the day at the Halls' house, and then Fats worked a second job, selling snowballs to kids getting out of the nearby Macarty School; he sometimes made a hefty $25–$35 for a few hours' work.

After dinner he'd head over to the Hideaway, where club owners from as far away as Washington, D.C., and local musicians from around town were stopping in to check out Domino's wild shows. Members of Bartholomew's band performing at Club Desire walked down the street to the Hideaway to see Domino. They made fun of Domino's ill-fitting clothes, but Bartholomew's teenage pianist, Salvador Doucette, appreciated Domino's rough-hewn talent and showed him how to play his nightclub's theme song, "That's My Desire." Famed blues pianist Peter "Memphis Slim" Chatman also ventured from Club Desire to see Fats and was impressed both by Domino's blues singing and the size of the crowd. In late November 1949, Dave Bartholomew himself walked into the Hideaway. With him was a white businessman named Lew Chudd, who had come all the way from Hollywood looking for talent.

■ ■ ■

After World War II, American popular music went through a transformation. In retrospect, disc jockeys shooting off their mouths and independent record company owners hustling 78s to every storefront were the agents of change. They promoted the music of America's ethnic and cultural minorities—music that the major record companies and radio networks tried to ignore. Lew Chudd, who founded Imperial Records, remarkably had been present at some of the key scenes remaking popular music.

Chudd was the son of Russian-Jewish immigrants. His father, Abraham, fled Czarist conscription in the mid-1880s, making his way first to England and then to an ethnically diverse neighborhood in Harlem, where he married and raised a family. Lewis was the fourth and last child, born on July 11, 1911. His earliest recollections were of bitter New York winters and of the ghastly coughing spasms of his dying older brother John, who'd been exposed to poison gas during World War I. But while his parents worked long hours in the then Italian, Jewish, and Polish neighborhood, Lew, a small, wiry kid, enjoyed playing stickball on the streets and watching Babe Ruth swatting homeruns in Yankee Stadium.

Chudd was later known for his caustic tongue and acerbic personality. He also had a tendency toward embellishment, usually claiming that he went to college and even played minor league baseball, though once, in an apparently candid interview with *Fortune* magazine, he contradicted those statements by saying he "skipped college and after loafing for four years went to work at NBC in 1934." According to Chudd, he started at NBC radio as an advertising sales-man with the comedian Joe "Wanna buy a duck?" Penner and on the Ted Weems musical game show *Beat the Band* .

The ambitious Chudd helped sell radio time to the McCann-Erickson agency for a show that NBC premiered on December 1, 1934, *Let's Dance*. In the depth of the Depression, people stayed home on weekend nights for lack of cash, making the Saturday night party program, sponsored by Ritz Crackers and featuring the bands of Kel Murray, Xavier Cugat, and Benny Goodman, a hit. Crucially, it was Goodman's first big break, and he added arrangements by black bandleader Fletcher Henderson and the manic "jungle" drumming of Gene Krupa during the show's six-month run.

After the show, Goodman began a largely unsuccessful cross-country tour that ended in Los Angeles with a sensational stay at the Palomar Ballroom in August 1935. His L.A. success, which rang in the Swing Era, also foreshadowed the rise of disc jockeys. For radio's first two decades, nearly all music was performed live in the station's studio or in remote broadcasts from nightclubs. But the advance airplay of Goodman's records on KFWB—after publicist Charlie Emge paid disc jockey Al Jarvis $500 in payola—led to the Palomar success. At a time when the phrase "disc jockey" was a put-down, Jarvis was the first announcer to glamorize the playing of records by pretending on his *Make Believe Ballroom* show that the recordings were part of an all-star concert. A competitor, Martin Block, borrowed the show's format and the title and took it to WNEW in New York, where it became a huge success. Jarvis would later play a role in the rise of Chudd's Imperial Records, which eventually found a home in the same building as KFWB.

Though white bandleaders became the figureheads of swing, jazz historian Thomas J. Hennessey maintains that the music was really the volcanic resurfacing of the sound of hot black jazz bands, which "began developing the swing style as early as 1931." In New York, a few individuals were striving to break through racial barriers in music. Notably, record producer John Hammond discovered Count Basie, Joe Turner, Billie Holiday, and many others. He encouraged Goodman and other bandleaders to employ black musicians. Lew Chudd, who spent the late 1930s traveling around the country as a publicist and booking agent for big bands, once nearly got into trouble for trying to enter the segregated backdoor entrance of a Buffalo nightclub with Jimmy Lunceford's powerful black swing band. Chudd and many others reveled in the performances of jazz, blues, and boogie greats in the nightlife of 52nd Street in New York in a heady atmosphere that was briefly oblivious to racial distinctions.

With the outbreak of World War II Chudd enlisted and was mustered down south to the army boot camp at Fort Benning, Georgia. On a weekend pass one night he phoned for a taxi to take him to a black nightclub in Savannah, only to be called back by a local policeman, who told him to leave town. With his experience in radio, Chudd was eventually assigned to the army's Office of War Information in Washington, D.C., where he helped produce the *Five Minute Capsule* broadcasts, which countered the propaganda of Tokyo Rose.

At the end of the war Chudd came home to New York, where he caught the frenetic show of bandleader Louis Jordan. "I don't think I ever saw an artist I loved as much as Louis Jordan," says Chudd. "This guy had spirit in his face." Combining field hollers, a blasting saxophone, and a strong beat, Jordan's 1945 crossover hit "Caldonia" was a forerunner of rock 'n' roll, which inspired adolescents like Little Richard Penniman and James Brown to start performing.

Chudd started Crown Records that year at 521 Fifth Avenue. He signed a boogie pianist whom Jordan recommended, Maurice Rocco, who always stood up as he played. But Chudd soon sold out and headed west. In Mexico City, he heard mariachi musicians singing in a cantina and decided to record them with a more pronounced dancing beat. He recorded several Mexican artists before traveling to Los Angeles. There, in a storefront at 137–139 North Western Avenue in early 1946 with $2,500, he started the Imperial Record Company—which he named after an English beer. He soon bought out his original partner, Max Feirtag (who later started the Flip label and published "Louie, Louie"). Chudd, who often worked twelve-hour days, thought that Feirtag was lazy, though few people could get along with the Imperial owner; as the name of his company suggested, he was born to run his own empire.

Imperial was one of many new Los Angeles independent record companies. Significantly, most of the independent owners and entrepreneurs across the country who would promote ethnic music were, like Chudd, from minorities themselves and were acutely aware of discrimination. "The independents were more open-minded," he says. "To them, there were no color or language barriers." Many were Jewish, including Chudd, Art Rupe (Specialty Records), Syd Nathan (King Records), Leonard and Phil Chess (Chess Records), the four Bihari brothers (Modern Records), David and Jules Braun (DeLuxe Records), Billy Shaw (the Shaw Booking Agency), and Irvin Feld (the Biggest Show of Stars). Exclusive's Leon and Otis Rene, Swingtime's Jack Lauderdale, and Peacock's Don Robey were African American; Aladdin's Eddie and Leo Mesner were Lebanese; Atlantic's Ahmet Ertegun was Turkish; and J&M Studio owner Cosimo Matassa was Italian-American. The rise of black music during segregation would have been impossible without their color blindness.

At first, Chudd recorded nearly all Latino music. Manuel S. Acuna, originally from Sonora, Mexico, was the arranger for most of the Spanish-language records, which sold relatively well. The artists made little money from record sales, but they were able to play clubs all over the Southwest. Chudd also filled a void when he added the folk dance music of many other ethnic groups, as major record companies had turned away from dance music in favor of pop balladry. School boards bought the records for both cultural and physical education. By 1947, Imperial advertised a virtual United Nations of folk dances in the *Billboard Encyclopedia of Music*—Samba, Rumba, Spanish, Mexican, Gypsy, Italian, Scottish, Baltic, Philippine, Russian, and American—besides classical, boogie, and Latino records. Imperial's first "race" record was prophetically "8 O'Clock Stomp" by Dick Lewis and His Harlem Rhythm Boys in August 1947, a hard-driving piano and saxophone boogie instrumental.

Eduardo "Lalo" Guerrero, who sang boogie woogie songs in Spanish, was Imperial's first star. His "La Mula Bronca," a version of Frankie Laine's "Mule Train," became Imperial's biggest early hit in 1949, selling 200,000 copies. Instead of promoting the record only to Latino stations, Chudd took the unusual step of taking it to disc jockeys at pop stations, including KFWB, where Al Jarvis played it ten times in a four-hour period. Though he soon left Imperial, Guerrero enjoyed a long career in the Latino community. In 1981, his Imperial *pachuko* hits spiced up the soundtrack of the movie *Zoot Suit,* and fifteen years after that the seventy-nine-year-old singer received the National Medal of the Arts from President Bill Clinton at a ceremony that also honored Edward Albee, Lionel Hampton, Robert Redford, Maurice Sendak, Stephen Sondheim, and the Boys Choir of Harlem. He would not be the only Imperial Records artist who would receive America's highest cultural honor.

Like any good salesman, Chudd possessed a peripatetic streak, and in the late 1940s he traveled the Southwest with his car trunk full of records. In Mexico he sold them to peasants with torn clothes who bought music at the expense of their food. In Guatemala and Costa Rica, he even peddled his wares from a horse-drawn wagon. At a time when record stores were rare, he sold 78s to grocery stores and even automobile dealerships. "I put a lot of people in the record business," says a bemused Chudd. At the Acosta Furniture Company in San Antonio, the owner wanted records so badly that he stuffed more than $1,000 into the record man's pockets.

Chudd searched for new musical talent relentlessly and began recording several country and western artists in Texas. In Houston in the summer of 1947 at a black club called the Bronze Peacock, he caught Dave Bartholomew's band in a meeting that would have major consequences for the course of popular music.

■ ■ ■

Though New Orleans was the birthplace of jazz, it was not a recording Mecca in the early twentieth century. The city's stars, like Louis Armstrong, Jelly Roll Morton, and Louis Prima, migrated to cities with greater performing and recording opportunities. Largely because of segregation, the local music industry evolved slowly and didn't produce national hits until the late 1940s, when Cosimo Matassa boldly began recording black artists at J&M Studio, which legendary local disc jockey Vernon Winslow called "the center of so many things that were on the edge of something new."

The architect of "The New Orleans Sound" was Dave Bartholomew, a superb trumpeter and bandleader and a truly innovative arranger. Like the Dominos, the Bartholomew family hailed from the sugarcane country upriver from New Orleans, though soon after Dave was born on December 14, 1920, in the town of Edgard, his parents, Louis and Marie, moved to the city. After Louis, a barber who also played in the bands of Kid Clayton and Kid Harris, left the family, Marie, a housekeeper and seamstress, struggled to support her son and his three sisters in a modest house on Prieur Street. Still the boy visited his father in his South Galvez barbershop, where a flatbed truck with musicians playing jazz to advertise a dance often stopped for a rehearsal. Once when Kid Clayton, who could make his trumpet sound like it was talking, left the shop, he blew it saying "good-bye" to young Dave. From that moment on, Bartholomew wanted to be a musician.

One day, a thin man playing checkers in the barbershop noticed the young Bartholomew in a corner, pretending to play some imaginary instrument. "Louis," he said to the barber, who was snipping away at a customer, "I'm gonna take that boy." The man was Peter Davis, who had already made an immeasurable contribution to American music by teaching the young Louis Armstrong to play trumpet at the Municipal Boys' Home. Davis may have recognized the scars of poverty and paternal abandonment on Bartholomew, but as he liked to tell his young students, it didn't matter how down-and-out you were, "if you learn to play music, at least you'll know how to do something."

Davis became the first of many surrogate fathers for the boy, who began going to the older man's house for baritone saxophone and trumpet lessons, learning standards like "Sweet Sue." By age twelve Dave began sitting in with his father's bands. After stints in the bands of Joe Robichaux and Papa Celestin (who took Bartholomew out of the ninth grade to go on his first tour), coronet player Claiborne Williams, whose band played white society dances in oil-rich Morgan City, bought Bartholomew his first overcoat and taught him how to read music and to improvise. Groomed by some of New Orleans' best bandleaders, the teenager soon possessed a swaggering pride and a drive to succeed.

In the spring of 1936, bandleader Walter "Fats" Pichon invited the sixteen-year-old trumpeter to join a six-month cruise on the *Steamer Capitol* up the Mississippi River and Bartholomew accepted. Pichon, a pianist who resembled Fats Waller, liked to sing a Louis Armstrong song in which he asked for a "Big Butter and Egg Man." The young trumpeter answered the call with a solo. Though Bartholomew was following in the footsteps of Armstrong, he also loved swing music. One night in his ship bunk Dave was thrilled to hear the sound of Roy Eldridge's trumpet blaring from a shortwave radio.

As Aaron Bell, a bass player with Pichon who would join Duke Ellington, later recalled, "Bartholomew was a brilliant trumpet player—he had every-thing." When Pichon began playing solo in the French Quarter, he turned his band over to Bartholomew. The ten-piece band, renamed the Royal Playboys, played the San Jacinto, the Gypsy Tea Room, and the Rhythm Club, but couldn't expand their circuit. Bartholomew struggled in vain to keep the band together.

By age twenty, Dave was raising a family with his wife Pearl (King), a light-skinned beauty, and needed steady work. When in 1942 Jimmy Lunceford ap-peared at the Rhythm Club and offered him an audition to join his band—which Bartholomew considered "the greatest band in the world"—he jumped at the opportunity. Lunceford hired him for $105 a week, at a time when an average laborer in New Orleans was earning $25 a week.

But six weeks into the tour, Bartholomew received his draft notice. He would play in bands at various military bases for the next three years, backing a young Lena Horne at one show. On one crucial night, Abraham Malone, an older soldier who'd watched Bartholomew play, took him aside and told him he would teach him to write music. The trumpeter's musical knowledge took a great leap forward, just as his confidence was peaking. The high point of his army career occurred after the war, when he arrived in Europe with the 196 AGF Band on July 4, 1945. For Bartholomew, the tour was a "beautiful experi-ence" in which the band jammed all over the continent, playing swing for the soldiers, including prisoners of war, and for General Eisenhower himself. Although the band included outstanding players like sax player Art Pepper, Bartholomew's leather-lung solos stood out loud and clear. The AGF Band headed back home on Labor Day, ending the trumpeter's military stint, though not the lessons he'd learned in the service.

Back in New Orleans in the fall of 1945, Bartholomew joined the house band at the Dew Drop Inn on LaSalle Street. Built across the street from a new uptown housing project, the Dew Drop was the happening local club. Along with comedians, exotic "shake" dancers, and female impersonators, the club featured blues stars like Joe Turner and Wynonie Harris. Every weekend, musicians jammed until the sun rose. Big band music had faded away during the war as blacks became entranced with the comic blues style played by Louis Jordan's small "jump" combo. Billed as "America's Hottest Trumpet Player" (an appellation that earned him six dollars a night), Bartholomew headlined in guitarist Buddy Charles's band, including sax players Lee Allen and Joe Harris.

One night, Sam Cimino, the owner of Cimino's Cut-Rate Linoleum on Orleans Avenue, asked Bartholomew if he would form a band to play at a club he was opening in six weeks called the Graystone. With the help of Clarence Hall, a sax player from Papa Celestin's group, Bartholomew put together a band, buying them cheap striped suits. Cimino then shocked Bartholomew by agreeing to pay him what seemed a fortune: $20 a night for Bartholomew, $18 a night for the band. So on Friday, March 29, 1946, trumpet blasts rang out at the Graystone, at the corner of Eagle and Cohn streets. Bartholomew, now called "The Man Who Makes Rhythm," led his new band, including saxophonists Hall and Meyer Kennedy, pianist Fred Land, bassist Frank Fields, and drummer Dave Oxley. The next week, future r&b star Overton "Smiley Lewis" Lemons opened the show. Bartholomew's band played ballads, a few jump blues originals, Louis Jordan songs, and other hits like "Hey Bop A Re Bop." On June 22, Scoop Jones prophetically wrote in *The Louisiana Weekly,* "Putting it mildly, they make the house 'rock.'"

The band's musicianship improved greatly in 1947 when Bartholomew added alto saxophonist Joe Harris, guitarist Ernest McLean, and drummer Earl Palmer, who had seen the band at Tony's Tavern. On March 15, *The Louisiana Weekly* announced the arrival of "the new sensation on the tubs." As a boy Palmer had performed as a tap dancer in his mother's traveling vaudeville shows. As a man his dance rhythms became drumbeats behind exotic dancers. After Oxley went to work at the Municipal Boys' Home, Bartholomew hired

Palmer, who at first confused the band with his unorthodox beat. Meyer Kennedy complained, "That boy ain't gonna make it," but Dave had faith in his new drummer.

One night, as Bartholomew's band played at the Club Rocket on Jackson Avenue, a sharply dressed pale-faced black man in horn-rimmed glasses sat at a table smoking a cigar. "I gotta have that band," he said to his companions. He was Don Robey, and, as the kingpin of Houston's black nightlife, he was used to getting his way. In June 1947, Bartholomew's band headed to Robey's Bronze Peacock Club for a five-week engagement, where they were a smash hit, backing T-Bone Walker on some shows. While traveling through Texas, Lew Chudd witnessed one of the band's last nights at the club. Afterwards, he offered to buy Bartholomew a drink. Chudd told the trumpeter that he wanted him as both an artist and a talent scout for Imperial Records. Chudd said he would pay the princely sum of $125 a week. Bartholomew almost choked on his drink. He had received other offers in Houston, but this one was unbelievable. He gave Chudd his phone number, but then went back home and forgot about the offer. So too did Chudd. Or so it seemed.

■ ■ ■

An unnamed hurricane slammed into New Orleans on September 19, 1947, putting neighborhoods under six feet of water and killing ten people. At the same time, a musical hurricane was brewing in New Orleans that would eventually rock the planet. Roy Brown's "Good Rockin' Tonight," recorded at J&M for the Braun Brothers' DeLuxe Records, became an instant local sensation. The song took off on an afternoon radio show that debuted on WJMR three days after the storm.

The idea for the first black radio program in New Orleans began that summer when Vernon Winslow, an art instructor at the all-black Dillard University, had written local radio stations proposing a "colored" show. Winslow boldly walked in the front door of the segregated Jung Hotel and took the elevator up to the office of WJMR, the one station that had expressed interest in the program. WJMR certainly wanted black advertising dollars, but when Winslow auditioned the jive talk that he wanted to use on air, station manager Stanley Ray looked at the ivory-skinned gentleman and asked, "Are you a nigger?"

After Winslow said that he was a "Negro," Ray told him that he couldn't possibly announce the show—but he could coach a white announcer. Though greatly disappointed, Winslow agreed. He even created a jive name for the white disc jockey: "Poppa Stoppa." Winslow chose the records that Poppa Stoppa played, but he was surprised when the show diverged from the jazz that he had envisioned to what jukeboxes told him the music had to be, as he put it—"none other than Roy Brown tearing the place up!" The Poppa Stoppa show rode "Good Rockin' Tonight" like a racehorse. Brown's anthem to sex and partying shocked listeners who had never heard such fiery singing outside of church. "It divided neighborhoods," recalled Winslow, "and it just labeled rhythm & blues—we didn't call it rhythm & blues then."

There was now a growing commercial imperative to record in New Orleans, because for the first time black records could be heard on a popular radio show and not just on jukeboxes. Bartholomew also made his first recording that month for DeLuxe Records, whose owners, the Braun brothers from Linden, New Jersey, were cornering the local music scene with records by Roy Brown, Paul Gayten, Annie Laurie, Papa Celestin, Fats Pichon, and "Smiley" Lewis. Ironically, Bartholomew's band was now too big for the tiny J&M Studio. He had expanded to ten pieces to set his group apart from his main competitor, Gayten, whose small combo had become the toast of New Orleans with its romantic blues ballads hits during Bartholomew's extended stint in Houston. So Cosimo Matassa hauled his disc recorder to the Booker T. Washington High School auditorium stage and closed the curtains. Now Dave found himself between the two opposing trends—the cocktail blues of Gayten and the blues shouting of Roy Brown. Unsurprisingly, the unison chant and instrumental that he recorded didn't sell.

But Bartholomew began his own show on WJMR late that year. *"Hey, gang, you gonna meet me over by Al's?"* he'd shout into the microphone at J&M studio, from where his radio performances were broadcast. Through the winter of 1947–1948, Dave used his weekly WJMR shows to plug his evening gigs at Al's Starlight Inn, notably with a song called "Shrimp and Gumbo," with the type of Afro-Caribbean rhythms that had once been heard at the adjacent Congo Square. Earl Palmer ping-ponged a cowbell. Others clapped, snapped castanets, and beat beer bottles in a mad Latin rhythm as Bartholomew called out like a fish peddler: *"OK-RA GUM-BO! CRAAAB GUM-BO!"* The horns joined the happy fray for the climax. By the time they got to Al's each evening, the place would be packed. Throughout 1948 Dave was backing singers like Joe Turner, Gatemouth Brown, Chubbie Newsome, and even Annie Laurie. On holidays, he rented the San Jacinto, a large dance hall on Rampart Street, and drew as many as 3,000 people.

■ ■ ■

That summer, on July 26, 1948, President Harry Truman announced the beginning of the end of segregation in the armed forces; it was the first bombshell in the events leading to the 1954 *Brown v. Board of Education of Topeka* school integration ruling and the civil rights movement. On that very day, WJMR's Poppa Stoppa put on a record and left the studio for a moment. But when the record was over and the deejay still wasn't back, Vernon Winslow, the show's producer, had to stammer out a station I.D. An enraged Stanley Ray fired him on the spot—no *Negro* would announce on *his* radio station. Crushed by his abrupt dismissal, Winslow, the very dignified college professor turned radio visionary, had to take the usual black exit—down the freight elevator, past the blacks in the kitchen, and out through the service entrance of the Jung Hotel into the searing Louisiana heat.

Truman's stand on black civil rights was a major election issue in America that year, with Southern Democrats starting their own "Dixiecrat" Party with presidential candidate Strom Thurmond (who, unknown to the public at the time, had fathered a child with his black housemaid in 1925). Racists had almost totally purged African Americans in Louisiana from the state's voting rolls, but thanks to recent court decisions removing illegal voter obstructions, 1948 was the first year that blacks registered to vote in any numbers. They supported racial moderates like New Orleans Mayor de Lesseps "Chep" Morrison and Governor Earl K. Long, who actually encouraged black voter registration. Music promoter Rip Roberts led voting drives and held a benefit for the NAACP with singers Roy Brown, Larry Darnell, Cousin Joe, and even female impersonator Patsy Valadier. After Truman's hard-fought victory that November, Fats Domino's hero Albert Ammons graced an inaugural party with some rollicking boogie woogie piano playing.

Shortly after the election, Louis Jordan spoke out in New Orleans. On the Monday before Thanksgiving, blacks packed the balcony for his concert at Municipal Auditorium, which had a history of racial controversy since its construction in 1930 on the site of Congo Square. Only protests by African Americans in 1940 earned them even balcony seats to see black opera star Marian Anderson, who was famed for her concert at the Lincoln Memorial the previous year. During World War II, an "I Am an American Day" rally there excluded blacks. When the racially integrated Southern Conference for Human Welfare scheduled a convention in 1946, the auditorium adopted a formal policy of segregation.

Jordan became enraged when he found out that blacks could only sit in the balcony while a much smaller audience of whites sat in seats on the floor. At the end of the show he pointed to the balcony and announced, *"The next time I play here, I want to see ya'll down here—or I won't play here at all!"* It was a courageous act; if there had been trouble he would have been arrested. The balcony erupted in cheers. Backstage, Jordan was mobbed by excited admirers, who thanked him. "Well, you can thank me," replied Jordan, struggling to sign autographs, "but if you really want to do something, y'all need to mix a little politics with your love of entertainment."

Vernon Winslow, who was at the show, quickly followed Jordan's advice. On December 4, his guest column in *The Louisiana Weekly* appeared on the same page as a story headlined "Louis Jordan's Last Words Thrill Crowd." Winslow indicted the racism of New Orleans radio. "'Poppa Stoppa' is supposed to be a Negro character," he wrote, "not a black face minstrel." He invoked the city's musical heritage, which, he said, "today speaks the musical language of Paul Gayten, Annie Laurie, Dave Bartholomew, and Roy Brown."

Jordan issued an ultimatum in December that he would "play no Jim Crow dates." In February 1949, the arrest of sixty-five people for race-mixing at a French Quarter gathering was front-page *Louisiana Weekly* news over a story reporting that Nat "King" Cole and Dizzy Gillespie had joined Jordan's boycott. The next week, there was a similar raid at a nightclub in the Tremé neighborhood: "Sixty-eight persons were loaded into patrol wagons and hauled off." Jordan soon recorded "Saturday Night Fish Fry," one of the scores of songs in the wake of "Good Rockin' Tonight" that described a "rockin'" party. Jordan had journeyed from "Ain't Nobody Here But Us Chickens," which obliquely referred to a raid of a black house party, to a song that not only boldly exposed the racism of such a raid at a black New Orleans party but also reflected current headlines.

The black pride that Jordan had sparked in the city became a celebration when Mayor Morrison, who had never publicly honored an African American, presented Louis Armstrong with an oversized key to the city in March 1949 at City Hall on the Monday before Armstrong's Mardi Gras reign as King of the Zulus. The visit was national news, and Satchmo even appeared on the cover of *Time* magazine. Local blacks reveled deliriously in the streets the next day when their favorite son, wearing blackface makeup, traveled with the floats of the Zulus, who since 1909 had paraded with that same black grease paint, spears, and grass skirts. Named after an African tribe that had once annihilated British Redcoats, the Zulus were tricksters lampooning the Rex Mardi Gras parade that belonged to the city's white social elite. When Armstrong played at the Coliseum Arena on Mardi Gras night, he even jammed with his warm-up act, Dave Bartholomew's band.

That spring, Bartholomew rehearsed his musicians in the weekday stillness of the Robin Hood nightclub. Despite his years of experience, he still was searching for his own musical identity; like Domino, he would find it in rhythm. He told his horn section to play a rhumba pattern, a simple riff that would become his trademark copied on countless records: *"BOOOM BAAAA-DA, BOOOM BAAAA-DA—"* In April, the band recorded the song with the riff, "Country Boy," in their first real recording session at J&M Studio for DeLuxe. The pattern was part of the Latin tinge of New Orleans music in the "habanera" rhythm of pianists, first recorded by Jelly Roll Morton in his twelve-bar-blues from 1923, "New Orleans Joys." Bartholomew, who heard the bass line played by pianists like Professor Longhair and Tuts Washington, was the first to feature it as a dominating riff throughout his productions. Atlantic Records' arranger Jesse Stone later heard the riff when he traveled to New Orleans on Atlantic's second Southern scouting trip and ironically gained more acclaim than Bartholomew for employing variations of it, later noting that everybody "identified it with rock 'n' roll."

Nearly every month in 1949 brought another momentous event to the city's burgeoning music scene. On May 29, Vernon Winslow became the first black disc jockey in New Orleans. Winslow chose his new radio name, Dr. Daddy-O, from jive talk used by Louis Jordan during his stand at Municipal Auditorium. Despite threats of violence, the show on WWEZ, which was bravely sponsored by Jax Beer, went on the air without incident. Winslow's return to radio happily coincided with Roy Brown's sequel to "Good Rockin' Tonight," "Rockin' at Midnight." In recognition of all the rhythm hits, *Billboard* retitled the "Race" chart "Rhythm & Blues" in June (the same month that RCA introduced the 45-rpm record). Discovering that Winslow had to use the freight elevator in the New Orleans Hotel, Cosimo Matassa allowed him to use J&M for his shows. There, the disc jockey interviewed stars like Brown, Roy Milton, and Paul Gayten before neighborhood children. "It was an *event!*" recalled Winslow. "There was no such thing as civil rights. This was something moving through, that feeling of sound and opportunity, a strengthening of your own presence."

At the same time, the new Poppa Stoppa, charismatic white shouter Henry "Duke" Thiele, was tearing up the city. He had received a platinum record from

DeLuxe Records for breaking Brown's soulful blues "Long About Midnight," New Orleans' first #1 "Race" hit in late 1948. During Mardi Gras in 1949, Thiele revived a moribund 1947 record, "Drinkin' Wine Spo-Dee-O-Dee" by Stick McGhee and His Buddies, as a theme song for his sponsor, Monogram Wine. Ahmet Ertegun of Atlantic Records in New York heard about the song's local popularity. In order to sell several thousand copies to a New Orleans distributor, he had McGhee re-record it in a fast *rockin'* style and add lyrics about New Orleans. The subsequent national hit jump-started the struggling Atlantic Records company, with massive implications for the future of r&b. Even more astounding were the swelling ratings that Poppa Stoppa achieved with white audiences. Long before Alan Freed and Elvis Presley, Thiele established the music's early racial crossover, as demonstrated by the adoption of "Drinkin' Wine Spo-Dee-O-Dee" by a fourteen-year-old Jerry Lee Lewis, who shouted out the song at a Ford dealership in his hometown of Ferriday, Louisiana, that year.

Meanwhile, Bartholomew was riding high, garnering rave reviews opening for Nat "King" Cole and for Louis Jordan at the Booker T. Washington High School Auditorium (with both keeping their "No Jim Crow" pledges). After "Country Boy" was released in August, he traveled to Texas to promote the record, which became his biggest hit, selling 100,000 copies.

By November, New Orleans music was red hot. Professor Longhair's first record was released. Roy Brown's hardest rocker yet, "Boogie at Midnight," boomed out of jukeboxes. Even the suave Paul Gayten moved toward Brown's raging sound, producing a blues shout, "For You My Love," for Dew Drop Inn regular Larry Darnell, which became a #1 r&b hit. Bartholomew replaced his balladeer, Theard Johnson, with the versatile vocalist Tommy Ridgley, who could croon the standard "Stardust" *and* wail like Roy Brown. Louis Jordan ruled the airwaves with his song about New Orleans, "Saturday Night Fish Fry," which summed up the local scene: *"It was rockin'..."*

And then one morning Bartholomew heard a knock on the door.

Chapter 4

"The Fat Man"

(Late 1949–1950)

"Well, I wouldn't want to say that I started it [rock 'n' roll], but I don't remember anyone else before me playing that kind of stuff."
—ANTOINE "FATS" DOMINO

Dave Bartholomew stared in astonishment at a small white man in a suit standing on his steps at 1561 Lafreniere Street, not far from the new St. Bernard housing project. Two years after he'd met Bartholomew at the Bronze Peacock in Houston, Lew Chudd had finally arrived. Chudd had spent many nights on the neon-lit cobblestones of Bourbon Street listening to Dixieland jazz, but he wanted to record the *new* New Orleans music, rhythm & blues.

Bartholomew drove Chudd to the black business district where they met a sandy-haired, middle-aged man from New Jersey, Al Young, at his Bop Shop record store at 302 South Rampart. Young was a musical prospector, who, in defiance of convention, hung out in black nightclubs, listening to music and drinking heavily. For a time, his skills as a talent scout and salesman made him a kingpin of the local r&b scene. He could sell anything if he talked long enough. His phone calls to the Braun brothers of DeLuxe Records from his home state resulted in their New Orleans hits with Paul Gayten, Annie Laurie, and Roy Brown. Young, who also distributed Imperial Records, likewise drew Chudd to the city.

Both Young and Chudd were present on Tuesday, November 29, when Bartholomew conducted his first session at Cosimo's for Imperial, recording his new band vocalist Tommy Ridgley and also Jewel King, a lithe Creole beauty. From the start, Bartholomew produced his own New Orleans sound, notably on King's "3 x 7 = 21," which featured the kind of horn riffs and beat that became his trademarks.

In an effort to impress Chudd, Young acted like he ran the session. Bartholomew immediately resented both Young's brazen nerve and the growing bond between the two record salesmen. Chudd was impressed by Young's musical connections, notably with the very popular white r&b disc jockey, Duke "Poppa Stoppa" Thiele. Chudd, Young, and Thiele enjoyed lunch together at the home of WJMR, the Jung Hotel, where Bartholomew was excluded due to his skin color. As the record men ate, they talked about music, radio, and musicians.

Before Chudd left town, he decided to check out a boogie and blues pianist in the Ninth Ward whom Thiele enthused over. He called Bartholomew, and, together with Young, they traveled down bumpy roads past the Club Desire to a ramshackle club. Walking across railroad tracks, they heard boogie piano emanating from the Hideaway. Inside, they were shocked to see the bar packed with revelers. Antoine "The Fat Man" Domino was rocking the house.

Bartholomew knew Domino as the piano player who had sat in a few times at his shows playing boogies in mended denim, but he couldn't picture him in his adult nightclub world. Little Sonny Jones, who wailed a song while Domino played, represented the popular blues shouting style. Bartholomew asked Chudd how he liked him. But Lew, who had seen the legendary boogie woogie pianists up close in New York and had recorded several records in that style, loved Domino's train-rattling sound. He replied that he wanted to hear the piano player sing.

The patrons whispered among themselves at the presence of the three distinguished men in business suits, as Bartholomew whispered into Domino's ear. Fats filled the request to sing with his most popular song, lighting into the piano with a fevered frenzy. The fans erupted when it became clear he was playing "The Junker's Blues." After a pummeling piano prelude, he sang in his youthful Creole voice: *They call me a junker, 'cause I'm loaded all the time. . .*

Lew Chudd was thrilled. The pulsating, primitive beat and youthful wails were unlike anything he had heard before. Afterwards, Bartholomew told Domino that the man from Imperial Records wanted to meet him. The shy pianist, dressed in a jacket and pants that didn't match, slowly approached them. Chudd wasted no time, pulling out his standard contract and asking, "How would you like to make records?"

Antoine looked unsure. Al Young rallied the fans' support, asking, *Don't you think Fats should be on records?* Domino's friends and admirers yelled, *Yeah!* Antoine stepped aside to confer with his guitarist and advisor, Harrison Verrett, who told him, "You go for the royalty, don't sell none of your numbers," referring to the fact that many musicians sold their songs outright for quick cash. Finally, after he was reassured that he would receive royalties, Domino signed Chudd's contract.

After over a week in New Orleans, Lew Chudd flew home. Though he had also signed Bartholomew as an artist, he later discovered that the bandleader was still under contract to DeLuxe. Still, Dave was on his way to producing several Imperial hits. First off, he had to change the "The Junker's Blues," a song about a dope fiend, into popular music.

■ ■ ■

"THERE HE GOES! INTO THAT DRUGSTORE," announced a melodramatic voice emanating from radios and through screen doors and windows up and down Lafreniere Street. *"HE'S STEPPING ON THE SCALES. . . "* The voice was followed by the sound of a sliding counterweight. *"WEIGHT . . . 237 POUNDS . . . FORTUNE: DANGER!"* There was a flourish of horns. *"WHO IS HE? THE F-A-T M-A-A-A-N!"* Every Friday night at 7:30, the introduction to the popular radio program *The Fat Man* (based on Dashiell Hammett's companion to his other popular sleuth, *The Thin Man*) thrilled listeners. Dave Bartholomew heard the voice fade and rise in early December 1949 as he walked to his home, where his kids were sitting on the stoop, mesmerized by the latest murder mystery solved by the corpulent detective. As he listened, it hit him that Domino was also known as "The Fat Man."

A few days later, Buddy Hagans drove Fats to Bartholomew's house. When Domino sat down at the upright piano, Bartholomew told him that he was going to write new words to "The Junker's Blues," calling it "The Fat Man." They worked out lyrics describing a mythic version of Domino and his world.

On Saturday, December 10, 1949, Bartholomew's musicians arrived at J&M. In the tiny recording studio, Domino hammered the piano and shouted his theme song into a hanging microphone. "He did the *hell* out of it," recalls Bartholomew. Crammed next to the baby grand were drummer Earl Palmer, bassist Frank Fields, and guitarist Ernest McLean. The rhythm section strained to be heard over the shattering din of the piano. The horn players, Herbert Hardesty, Clarence Hall, Joe Harris, and Alvin "Red" Tyler, stood before a microphone blowing riffs into the hurricane of sound. In a tiny closet with a glass window, engineer Cosimo Matassa checked glowing level lights and Bartholomew gave orders. Tape recorders (invented in Germany during the war) were still not widely available. A lathe-like turntable plowed wax out of a giant shellac platter at 33 and 1/3 rpms, engraving the distorted sound for posterity.

Domino sang about standing on the corner of Rampart and Canal streets. The crossroads was a place of great significance in African-derived culture. Blues songs commemorated musical intersections in Robert Johnson's "Cross Roads Blues" (dusty Delta corners where "The Devil" supposedly gave midnight guitar lessons), Joe Turner's "Piney Brown Blues" (18th and Vine, near where the Kansas City music scene arose), and Professor Longhair's "Mardi Gras in New Orleans" (originally Rampart and Dumaine, where J&M was located).

Rampart and Canal were the major black and white thoroughfares in New Orleans, so Domino was metaphorically already suggesting the social intersection of black and white worlds through music, which would be his greatest achievement. In the early nineteenth century, Canal Street became the widest mercantile avenue in America and the rough dividing line between the original French-speaking inhabitants and the Americans who came later. Rampart Street was the northern border of the French Quarter, below the black Tremè district that once contained the Place des Negres, or Congo Square. The original eighteenth-century "rampart" had been a walled fortification against Indian attack.

In the song the Fat Man stood on the corner watching "Creole gals," who were the descendants of mixed-blood free blacks. Due largely to a lack of French female colonists, many of New Orleans' early male inhabitants had sexual relations with slaves. The offspring of these unions were often freed, adding to the *gens de couleur libre*. White men later took mulatto mistresses at "Octoroon Balls" and rented apartments for them on Rampart Street. Both white and black descendants of Louisiana's original French-speaking population claimed the name "Creole," but the word became most famously associated with the light tan offspring of both Europe and Africa. In New Orleans, the attraction of African American culture was highly visible: Café au lait–skinned Creole girls were renowned for their beauty.

At the midpoint of the century, the world was at a crossroads. News of the first Soviet atomic bomb and the Communist takeover in China had recently shaken everyone. In February 1950, Senator Joseph McCarthy would start his crusade against alleged "Reds." In June, North Koreans would invade South Korea, an act that would shape American foreign policy for the next generation. At the same time, a social revolution was taking shape. Jackie Robinson was baseball's first black Most Valuable Player. On December 2, 1949, President Truman banned discrimination in federal housing. Exactly one year before

Domino's session, Eleanor Roosevelt (who had long encouraged integration through music) achieved the passage of the U.N. Declaration of Human Rights, which seemed to indict America's segregation.

Music was also changing. The big bands were on life supports as sweet pop ballads and novelties dominated popular music and modern jazz became the domain of the cognoscenti. The more rhythmic elements of jazz melded with blues, gospel, and boogie woogie into rhythm & blues. The new Hank Williams hit was an old blues song, "My Bucket's Got a Hole in It." Five days before Domino's session, his piano idol Albert Ammons died in Chicago. The next day, Louisiana legend Huddie "Leadbelly" Ledbetter died just before his bittersweet lament "Goodnight Irene" became a massive hit by several artists, including Paul Gayten. Pop music soon adopted country, Latin, and r&b influences to spice up its whitebread palette. But there was little music that *moved* people. Domino would help change that.

The session at J&M for Domino's "The Fat Man" lasted close to six hours. Recording direct-to-disc, everything had to be perfect. If the musicians played for more than a few minutes, the transcribing stylus would grind to a halt. In the small studio with no baffles to separate the musicians, a good sound mix was difficult to attain. There was no editing or overdubs. The musicians recorded one bad take after another. But to Fats, who often practiced all day and performed all night, the long session didn't seem difficult. According to Matassa, Bartholomew was "a stern taskmaster," who made Domino focus; Dave's insistence upon making a record simple, direct, and commercial was Domino's "very salvation."

Domino drove "The Fat Man" with an almost maniacal frenzy. "Fats used to carry a heavy, heavy left hand," says bassist Frank Fields, who also played the backbeat, which was driven by Domino, not by drummer Earl Palmer. "I used to play most *all* of my piano," says Domino. "That's how I got that rock 'n' roll. Everybody used to use the 4/4 beat. Then we did that one-*two*-three—that added to the rhythm. The first song I recorded in 1949; that had the backbeat." Musicologist Robert Doerschuk, writing in *Keyboard* magazine, confirmed Domino's rhythmic innovations: "Unlike boogie-woogie patterns, in which rolled octaves move up and down the keyboard, Domino's variation repeated a low open fifth; when the chord changed, the pattern simply moved to the root of the new chord. This static beat froze the more fluid boogie-woogie feel into the kind of pounding rhythm eventually identified with rock. . . . Domino's piano beat is the driving element of the rhythm section."

"The Fat Man" jettisoned the despair of the original junker lyric. There was a touch of blues braggadocio, though bragging about being fat was hardly the stuff of ego. Fats disarmingly introduced himself and his world. But his thundering piano and his wordless cries—*"waah-waah-waah"*—said more about him. His piercing mouth harp turned another blues convention inside out, expressing feelings so boundless and new that—like Louis Armstrong with his scat and Jimmie Rodgers with his yodel—words weren't enough. Fats didn't care about artifice, he was crowing to wake the world. "The Fat Man" contained radically puzzling and pulsating sounds—the raucous musical cadence, emotion, and distortion that would echo through popular music for the rest of the century as "rock 'n' roll."

■ ■ ■

Lew Chudd didn't know what to make of the extraordinarily crude disc when it arrived at the Imperial office. He called Bartholomew to re-record the song, but events changed his mind. Al Young had taken acetate copies to the city's two r&b deejays, Duke "Poppa Stoppa" Thiele and Vernon "Dr. Daddy-O" Winslow. Both started playing Domino's record, creating an instant demand. Chudd started pressing thousands of copies to fill the orders.

It was a special Christmas for the Domino family. Over the holidays, New Orleans' black neighborhoods were filled with the sounds of "I Almost Lost My Mind" by Ivory Joe Hunter, "For You My Love" by Larry Darnell, "Silent Night" by Sister Rosetta Tharpe, "The Christmas Song" by Nat "King" Cole, and "The Fat Man." The proud pianist even walked around showing his neighbors his acetate copy. Fats didn't have a record player, but every day he went down to a grocery on St. Claude Street, passing a wino nicknamed Hadacol, who squalled the record's mouth harp scat. Fats smiled broadly as his friends played his songs on the jukebox.

Some assumed that the hit side was the more conventional-sounding "Detroit City Blues," which romantically described a distant place that, like Chicago and New York, was idealized by Southern blacks. The song also touched a chord with listeners, including Charles Neville of the Neville Brothers, who fondly remembers it from the time when he danced to it in school and thought that Fats was "so cool." "To this day," says Neville, "if I hear it I can taste Pepsi Cola." Fats himself thought that Bartholomew had visited the Motor City. In fact, Bartholomew wrote it for his sister-in-law, who had moved to

Detroit and sent back glowing letters about plentiful jobs and relative freedom from discrimination.

Some African Americans dreamed of racial equality even in New Orleans. In fact, as "The Fat Man" debuted, Creole attorney A. P. Tureaud held a hearing on the substandard quality of the Macarty School, Domino's "alma mater." It was the city's first lawsuit demanding improvements for black schools. In January, Mayor Morrison was reelected with a record vote by African Americans, who comprised a third of the population of New Orleans. Though he was a segregationist, Morrison gave blacks "backdoor" improvements, such as the paving of roads, which, according to one Ninth Ward resident, had been "so littered with trash, garbage, and dust that inside our homes, the dust would settle over the furniture and floors."

But Domino was still a struggling workingman, earning a hard living at the Crescent City Bed Factory. He and Rosemary were still living in a room in her parents' house, though they dreamed of owning their own home. With his first check from Imperial Records, Fats bought a small, 66-key Spinet piano from Valon's Music on St. Claude Street. But he and his wife did not anticipate any major changes in their lives.

Still, as the second half of the century dawned, Domino was becoming an unlikely local star. Al Young's NOLA Distributing Company placed an ad in *Billboard* on January 21 announcing, "10,000 IMPERIAL RECORDS #5058 SOLD IN NEW ORLEANS IN 10 DAYS." *Cash Box* raved that "The Fat Man" "should go wild in the boxes. Ditty is already kicking up a storm, and should spread like wildfire." Bartholomew brought Fats and Jewel King back into the studio to record more songs. Antoine also posed with a broad smile at Cosimo's grand piano for a rare promotional photo, one that Chudd cropped and used for years to come.

King's "3 x 7 = 21" was also hitting strongly. She and Domino were scheduled to begin a western tour with Bartholomew's band, but King demanded that her boyfriend, guitarist Jack Scott, join the entourage. When Bartholomew refused, she backed out. To replace King, Bartholomew would have Tommy Ridgley perform her hit.

Fats himself went into hiding for days to avoid the tour. He feared leaving New Orleans without Harrison Verrett. Eventually, the Musicians' Union sent a letter warning him to honor his contract, and Verrett persuaded him to join the tour. Domino was forced to go on the road that would become his second home for the balance of the century.

A caravan departed from the Dew Drop Inn on March 26, the day after Bartholomew's band played a dance at the San Jacinto. It was a new birth for New Orleans music, a fact that Domino felt personally with the birth of his first son, Antoine Domino III. In fact, he was arrested in St. Bernard Parish for speeding to the child's birth and, with the delay, missed the farewell show. Bartholomew's fans didn't miss Fats much; they knew that Bartholomew would return as New Orleans' new national star. After all, he had his own hit, "Country Boy," on the national charts and was now a producer/artist for a Hollywood record label; no one thought of the upstart Domino as the tour's headliner. Bartholomew's following was so strong that several cars escorted the two station wagons from their meeting place at the Dew Drop Inn out along Airline Highway as far as Moisant Airport.

The musicians crossed Texas and Oklahoma, imagining riches spilling from the oil wells, only to discover that the oil from many of the pumps could barely grease their hair. Most of the musicians had seen such places only in the movies; pianist Salvador Doucette had even left high school to join the tour. The band members teased Fats about his shiny shoes, and the joking got so far out of hand that sax player Herbert Hardesty actually tossed them out of the car window. Domino looked back, cursing as the shoes tumbled like prairie dogs in the barren fields.

The Dave Bartholomew Orchestra headlined at Joe's Skyline Club across the tracks on 4th and Easton in Oklahoma City at the end of March. Bartholomew sang the salty lyrics of his locally popular hit "Country Boy," as the crowd danced to the groove played by his musicians dressed in plaid coats and brown pants.

Stepping down for a break, Dave was surprised to see his army band buddy, Eugene Jones, collecting the dues for the black musicians' union. Bartholomew puffed like a peacock with pride over his band. He noted the piano player taking the stage. Bartholomew initially featured Domino playing the intermission by himself, as Fats had before in New Orleans. But, as Frank Fields recalls, over the course of the tour people asked to hear Domino play with the band. Bartholomew would soon resent the growing popularity of the piano player. In turn, Fats complained that Dave was making all the money—out of the $350 a night for the band, Domino received $50. Still, as Domino finished his short set, Bartholomew confided to Jones, "He's gonna be great someday."

From the beginning Domino was homesick and reclusive. He and seventeen-year-old Salvador Doucette often stayed behind when the band went out at night.

As a consequence, Fats didn't bond with the others, staying in his hotel room and sometimes even missing rehearsals. Bartholomew essentially took over the role of Harrison Verrett, talking to the homesick pianist in his room to keep up his morale. It was in those meetings that Dave began to learn how to deal with the shy pianist.

The band discovered the hard realities of the road. After singing his and Jewel King's songs, Tommy Ridgley counted people at the door. He came back at the end of the night shaking his head. They had only attracted a couple hundred people, not enough to earn bonus "percentage" money. That night they slept four men per room in a fleabag motel. Two slept in the bed, two on a mattress on the floor.

The caravan headed across the desert. Towns became sparse as Route 66 sliced through vast flatlands in Colorado and New Mexico between maroon mesas and steel blue mountains. Every forty or fifty miles they stopped to put water in Bartholomew's new Ford station wagon, which was running hot. One grease jockey after another failed to plug the incontinent behemoth. Eventually the car resembled a Bedouin camel, with huge water bags hanging from either side.

The musicians went hungry late at night when the few stores were closed— not that they had much money to spend on food. Part of his fear of going on the road derived from the fact that Domino had heard that restaurants didn't serve blacks on the road. Accordingly, he stocked a suitcase full of potted ham, tuna fish, sardines, crackers, cheese, sausages, pickled eggs, and pickled pigs' feet. Guitarist Ernest McLean discovered the stash and broke into it when the others went into the stores. To this day, McLean says with a laugh, "Fats ain't never caught me!"

In New Mexico, steam from the radiator of Bartholomew's 1950 Ford rose into the cobalt desert sky. To make matters worse, the band's show in Albuquerque was canceled. Bartholomew called Chudd to tell him of their plight. The musicians walked around the adobe city, amazed to witness a political rally for a black candidate for sheriff supported by Hispanics, Indians, and whites.

Finally, they reached Las Vegas, then a sleepy little desert town with only a few hotels along its nascent Strip. At the city auditorium, the band played a dance and met one of the Harlem Globetrotters. The promoters paid them in silver dollars in an attempt to induce them to put their money back into the slot machines. To African Americans, the city's reputation was not for vice, but for discrimination. The tourist-trapping Strip was as segregated as the French Quarter back home. Few blacks played there, besides the Will Mastin Trio (with Sammy Davis, Jr.) and Nat "King" Cole, and Domino heard a rumor that even Cole had to stay in a trailer. The Louisiana men bunked in Miss Harris' Rooming House across the tracks. The next day, they helped Fats spend his money at the local pool hall. Later they went into a bar. The bartender put their bottles of beer in a paper bag. He asked if they wanted a bottle opener. After an awkward moment, the black men realized that he was asking them to leave the all-white establishment.

So the guys left and drank their beer. They played a football game in a field. After returning to their room, Salvador Doucette and Earl Palmer, still wound up from the game, wrestled until Doucette crashed into the wall, smashing a hole in it. Now the money that Lew Chudd had wired Bartholomew went to pay for Miss Harris's wall.

Later that night, the musicians took one of the station wagons to see Nat "King" Cole, who was playing at the Thunderbird Hotel, but they were stopped at the door because of their race. The band had yet to find the kicks on Route 66 that Cole had promised in his song. Still, Bartholomew sent off cheerful postcards. Accordingly, Dr. Daddy-O reported a week later in his *Louisiana Weekly* column that in Las Vegas the musicians were "tearing the city apart."

The band headed across the Mojave Desert, with the wagons struggling up winding mountain roads before dropping into the San Fernando Valley, where they stared in wonder at the lights of Los Angeles.

"WELCOME: THE DAVE BARTHOLOMEW ORCHESTRA WITH FATS DOMINO" read banners across Central Avenue as the troupe arrived in Los Angeles. The musicians were thrilled by the reception, but their show was not in South Central L.A., but downtown at the Avedon Ballroom on Monday, April 10, and followed a standing-room-only Easter show with Harry James in the hall frequented by white big bands. Ernest McLean, who had invited his friends from a stint two years earlier with Joe Liggins, cringed as he played guitar in the nearly empty auditorium. Banners alone were not enough to bring blacks into an area where they were not welcome.

The next night Lew Chudd cheered up the musicians with a surprise. He took them to see Charlie Barnet's integrated big band. Barnet unexpectedly called Domino up to play and sing. Chudd had convinced the bandleader to arrange a big band version of "The Fat Man," which concluded with everyone hitting a booming final note.

The musicians then headed to the Bay Area, where they was shocked to see the name commanding the auditorium marquee: TONIGHT ONLY: "FATS"

DOMINO. "The Fat Man" was a big hit locally, and fans, including Louisiana émigrés, thronged the stage, asking for autographs. A lady even pulled up her dress and asked Fats to sign her leg cast. Police security helped the band get on and off the stage. After so much disappointment, the musicians thought they had stepped through the looking glass; Fats had never seen so many people. Earl Palmer teased him, telling him that girls wanted to meet him, but the young pianist was as yet too shy to take advantage of the fringe benefits of stardom.

The band celebrated with a raucous performance of their hometown standard "Hey! La Bas," a Creole song that Fats had learned from Harrison Verrett. During Mardi Gras, Creole men in drag performed the song with small guitars. Kid Ory recorded it as "Eh, La Bas" in 1946. Papa Celestin included Harrison Verrett on guitar in his "A-La-Bas" session in 1947. The song also became a Cajun standard. Fats omitted the French verses about the voracious appetites of the Creoles, though they certainly fit him. While many in the audience were familiar with the genteel, banjo-driven jazz versions of the song, Domino's version was an apocalyptic rocker much wilder than "The Fat Man."

The horns of Joe Harris, Clarence Hall, Herbert Hardesty, and Dave Bartholomew blasted to the stratosphere. The rhythm section of Ernest McLean, Frank Fields, and Earl Palmer played a pulsating beat. Hardesty blew a wild, extended solo. Domino lit into his piano with fiery arpeggios. Everyone in the auditorium shouted out the song's call-and-response patois: *"Hey! La Baww! Mooo-Nay Mooo-Shaww!"* Yet none of the homesick souls knew the origin of the words, let alone what they meant. The French translation was supposedly, "Hey, over there, my dear cousin," but Domino thought it meant, "Hey, over there, bring me my car," and Bartholomew interpreted it as "Hey, over there, how you doing over there?"

New Orleans jazz great Danny Barker agreed with that, but added:

It was used as *signifyin',* one housewife to another one. Maybe the fence is broke and they don't wanna mutually repair the fence or the kids is makin' too much noise while the husband is sleepin'. So it caused neighborly conflicts and they get to be sorta enemies, see. You know, "I don't like you and you don't like me." And so and so and so, versa versa, visa visa. So they signify: *"EHHHHH! LA BAS! OVER THERE YOU DIRTY FILTHY FILTHY SO AND SO AND SO!* I don't see no smoke comin' out the chimney! You might not be eatin' today, huh?! I don't see it. Seein' all your raggedy clothes on the line, why don't you get your husband to buy you some drawers?! Huh?!"

That's way ahead of my time, but them Mardi Gras people been singin' that all through the years. I was a little boy, and I'm eighty-two.

Both signifying and call-and-response were African cultural remnants, but something even more potent may have survived in the phrase "hey la bas." One of the primary deities of Dahomean and voodun culture was Legba, known in New Orleans as "Papa La Bas." Thus, the saying perhaps reflected an African cultural survival, as the esteemed African American scholar Henry Louis Gates, Jr., relates in *The Signifying Monkey:* "Called Papa Legba as his Haitian honorific and invoked through the phrase 'eh la-bas' in New Orleans jazz recordings. . . . Pa Pa La Bas is the Afro-American trickster figure from black sacred tradition. His surname, of course, is French for 'down' or 'over there,' and his presence unites 'over there' (Africa) with 'right here.'" It was perhaps a dim reference—like John the Conqueror Root, mojo, or hoodoo—to forgotten African religious practices. Slanderously identified with the Devil, Legba also bestowed musical powers at the crossroads (as documented by a 1920s interview with a New Orleans conjurer). West Africans invoked Legba any time that a service began, often accompanied by drums, his sacred instrument, and he alone communicated universally. He was also in the cultural canon of the tricksters, who, like music, had helped blacks psychically survive their terrible plight since slavery. In any event, the musicians blasted out an invocation to a brave new musical world with African-rooted traditions more powerful and enduring than anyone ever imagined.

But no one was thinking about the music's origins on the one triumphant night of the pitiful tour. After the show, Tommy Ridgley practically danced back from the door. The musicians were due to earn bonus percentage money from the overflow crowd, but Ridgley was so excited by the show's success that he forgot to count the people coming in the door. The musicians didn't let the lost money spoil their fun, though. They went out and partied—all except the underage Salvador Doucette and Domino, who was sorely missing his home. "When you first leave home, especially New Orleans," says Domino, "you always want to come home."

The truth was that they now all felt that way, and Bartholomew nixed a plan by promoter Harold Oxley that would have taken them to the farthest reaches of the erstwhile Louisiana Territory. In late April 1950, a month after they'd set out from New Orleans, they limped back home. Their travail was reminiscent of the 1935 Benny Goodman cross-country tour that ended with great success in L.A. and launched the Swing Era, but it was only after

Bartholomew returned home that he discovered the burgeoning impact of his "New Orleans Sound," with two more of his Imperial recordings, "Stack-A-Lee" by Archibald and "Tee Nah Nah" by Smiley Lewis, selling briskly, facilitated by the debut of New Orleans' first all-black radio station, WMRY, in May.

That month, Bartholomew's band enjoyed their newfound celebrity, backing up Big Joe Turner at a J&M session, with Domino ripping boogie licks on the songs. A triumphant show at the San Jacinto featured Bartholomew's big band, Smiley Lewis's bullhorn shouting, Professor Longhair's exultant rhythms, and Domino's barrelhouse rocking. "'Twas the grandest Mother's Day that ever was!" declared Dr. Daddy-O.

■ ■ ■

With his hard-rocking music, Domino was stepping beyond blues and jazz to the crossroads of a new, wider world that he would help create both musically and socially. His unfettered exuberance was the message that young people wanted to hear: *Things will get better*. Lew Chudd even managed to get airplay for "The Fat Man" on pop stations. "We had to fight for it," says Chudd. "Fats had a thump second to none." The song's influence was wide-ranging that year. Johnny Otis, whose risqué records dominated the r&b charts, was dining in a Los Angeles restaurant with guitarist Peter Lewis when he heard Domino's barreling piano. Otis was stunned by the thundering record, which he considered "revolutionary." In south Louisiana, a thirteen-year-old pleaded with his mother to buy "The Fat Man" after he heard it on the radio. "Fats Domino just stuck in my blood," recalled swamp rocker Huey "Cookie" Thierry. "And rock 'n' roll got into me, man." In Kenner, outside of New Orleans, sixteen-year-old Lloyd Price was struck by Domino's mouth harp cries. "That [*wah-wah-wah*] really was *penetrating*," says Price. "I think that's the first hook I ever heard that made any sense." L.A. blues pianist Willie Egans even based his best-selling record, "Wow Wow," on Domino's wails. In New Orleans, the record had an overwhelming influence on twelve-year-old Art Neville, who says, "Everything he did ever since then, I used to try to sound like Fats Domino."

With the rise of African American radio shows, young blacks who couldn't go into bars heard r&b heavily for the first time. They began making music in schools, in talent shows, and even on the street. Domino and Bartholomew spearheaded the youthful mainstreaming of rhythm & blues. "3 x 7 = 21" celebrated reaching legal adulthood. In "The Fat Man," the twenty-one-year-old

Domino turned a drug anthem into a pile-driving street corner ode to watching girls. Bartholomew also soon produced hits of teen angst by nineteen-year-old Lloyd Price and by two fifteen-year-olds, Shirley and Lee.

Domino's joyful cries divined a musical fountain of youth; his stomping blues blew the blues away. His ebullience contrasted with Roy Brown's holy-rolling mood swings between sin-laden, fatted-calf rockin' and cursed-by-God famine blues. "The Fat Man"'s pulsing beat and street-corner lothario trash-talk heavily influenced landmark hits like "Rocket 88" and "Lawdy Miss Clawdy." In fact, "Rocket 88" also had an extended piano intro and identical horn riffs, while "Lawdy" was also based on "The Junker's Blues" and would feature Domino prominently. As "The Fat Man" also predicted, it was the young people in the streets, not adults in bars, who would determine the fate of rhythm & blues.

Domino's Hideaway sax player, Hiram Armstrong, would soon have his own street-corner encounter with "The Fat Man." After he was drafted into the newly integrated U.S. Army for the Korean War, Armstrong walked down the streets of New York City in September and heard a familiar voice. He turned around. "All you could hear was Fats Domino all up and down Seventh and Eighth Avenue," recalls Armstrong. "You'd walk down the street and the radios would be loud with Fats Domino's tune—'*They call, they call me the Fat Man . . .* '"

■ ■ ■

The lights of New Orleans reflected off the curved silhouettes of cars aboard the ferry chugging across the Mississippi in the summer of 1950. When the boat hit the West Bank with a bump, Billy Diamond urged his ailing Ford up the levee ramp . . . until the motor died. He ordered everybody out and the musicians all helped push the car—all but Domino, who stood aside. Fats, who had quit his job at the Crescent City Bed Factory to go on tour, had gone right back to work as a musician, playing gigs at the Hideaway and elsewhere with Diamond's band. This particular show, at a club across the river, would prove important in his early career. Domino was still flush with the fact that he had outshone the great Bartholomew on their tour. He rightly felt that he now deserved his due. He was no longer a sideman. He was *a star.*

They headed for J. Hugh Riley's club in Sunrise, Louisiana. It was a bigger breed of chicken shack, holding 1,000 people for a dance, including hormon-ally driven young men who drank beer and started fights. Fats performed his new record "Little Bee," a song about a girl with a bumble-bee posterior, which included two suggestive words—the noun "bust" and the verb "ball." WMRY was playing it, but the fact that children were now regularly hearing risqué songs on the radio previously played only in bars stirred a controversy in the churchgoing African American community; even Vernon "Dr. Daddy-O" Winslow, who had kicked off the lusty "Good Rockin' Tonight," now refused to play the relatively tame "Little Bee" on WWEZ.

After the band took a break, Domino was talking with some fans when Billy Diamond told him that intermission was over. Domino kept chatting. A short time later, Diamond repeated the order. Emboldened by some drinks, Fats asked Billy if he had had any records out. The portly bandleader looked thunderstruck. Domino continued, "I have two records goin', so from now on I'm gonna be the bandleader. Do you wanna work in *my* group?"

From that point on, Domino became his own bandleader. He was also asserting his growing independence in other ways. After he received his first big royalty check for $20,000, Antoine and Rosemary moved out of her parents' home and bought the house next door at 1723 Caffin from his sister-in-law and her husband. More importantly, Fats was slowly establishing his own musical identity, separate from his mentors Verrett, Bartholomew, and Diamond.

Charley Armstead had presented Domino with his first car, a gray 1942 Buick, in order to persuade him to take up residence at Club Desire in June 1950. The club was still a bit of Hollywood in the poverty-stricken Ninth Ward, especially when the headliner was an actual movie star like Stepin Fetchit, who had taken his slack-jawed stereotype all the way to several banks. Continuing his independence, Domino formed a band including Lawrence Guyton on bass, Willie Barbarin on drums, Buddy Hagans on tenor sax, and Charles Burbank on alto sax. His support act throughout his residence at Club Desire was Alma Mondy, a brassy blues songstress who had become popular locally for a comedy sketch patterned after the song "Open the Door, Richard." Her partner, comedian Lollypop Jones, knocked on the door of a house facade. Alma popped out of a window exclaiming, *"I hear you knockin', but you can't come in!"* to a torrent of laughs and yells.

Domino's stardom at the Club Desire was enhanced by the release of his fifth Imperial single, "Every Night About This Time," in October. The song, a slow blues ballad that featured the hypnotic combination of a crying blues with pop hooks, became an instant jukebox favorite. Lew Chudd again promoted the infectious new record to pop radio stations. Domino, who wrote "Every Night" without help from Bartholomew, also came up with the crucial rhythmic hook—hammered 6/8 piano triplets throughout the song. "I first heard triplets on an Amos Milburn record," Fats recalls. "He and Little Willie Little-field, they both had the same style, but they just dropped off from it." Milburn's "Operation Blues" and Littlefield's "It's Midnight" featured the style, but only sparingly as a musical accent. Domino's trademark triplets would eventually become the rhythmic underpinning for rhythm & blues ballads everywhere.

By November, the success of "Every Night About This Time" led to another tour. Domino's departure from the Club Desire in the fall of 1950 signaled the end of Desire Street's brief musical glory. The Hideaway, which would remain dear to his heart, was demolished during the construction for the Desire Housing Projects, which became infamous as some of the most dangerous slums in the country, though they, too, would eventually disappear. Today, amidst trash and squalor, one sad relic of a bygone era with broken glass bricks still stands on the street named Desire, the once-magnificent Club Desire.

■ ■ ■

Domino started a second tour with Bartholomew's band in mid-November 1950. Again an Imperial artist backed out—French Quarter pianist Archibald of "Stack-A-Lee" fame, who developed ulcers. The irrepressible Professor Longhair, who then had his only national hit with "Bald Head" under his real name, Roy Byrd, replaced him, going along for the ride with Bartholomew's band, which also featured Tommy Ridgley and on this occasion the great saxophonist Lee Allen.

The musicians again headed west in two station wagons. Trying to avoid the automotive problems that had plagued the first tour, Bartholomew bought four new tires for each of his two station wagons. But as the band traveled to play shows in Texas, Arkansas, and Colorado, all of the new tires blew out. To kill time while they traveled, the musicians played cards. They didn't know that Longhair was a professional gambler, who took Domino's money playing "Coon-Can" by moonlight.

The band had an engagement at a nightclub in President Truman's hometown of Independence, Missouri, near Kansas City. Tommy Ridgley opened the show shouting the blues. Then Professor Longhair hollered out "Mardi Gras in New Orleans" and waylaid the piano, his skinny arms flying and his foot kicking the upright piano. Sometimes high on wine or marijuana, he even jumped up on the piano. Bartholomew followed with his big band arrangements and tautly rhythmic blues. Periodically the imposing figure of Lee Allen took center stage and unleashed cataclysmic solos that were an evolutionary step beyond the honkers of the 1940s. Finally, Domino appeared and discovered that Longhair had kicked a hole in the piano. He performed "Korea Blues," the popular b-side of "Every Night," just like he had on the record, with Bartholomew's bone-jarring bugle calls driving the song's military misery home. The show was New Orleans r&b at its finest, but the band's glory was soon shattered when the owner, a man named Johnson, admitted that he couldn't pay them.

Everyone in the band wanted to go home. It was too cold for their Louisiana blood anyway. Bartholomew told Johnson that if he didn't pay them he'd report him to the Musicians' Union and have his joint closed down. The owner stammered back that they could take all the admission fees and he'd just sell his liquor. They could sleep in the club and eat from his kitchen. After Bartholomew placed a call to their booking agent Harold Oxley, they agreed to stick it out.

The next night, people streamed in the door. Ridgley stood at the front and collected the band's money after he sang.

Then the blizzard hit. The musicians literally hibernated in the club. At least they enjoyed Thanksgiving dinner, raiding the kitchen and cooking steaks, eggs, and beans. Some, who had never seen such snow before, went out and frolicked in it like little children. Bartholomew, who hadn't equipped his two wagons with anti-freeze, had to thaw out their radiators.

Thanks to the snowstorm, instead of the $1,800 they were supposed to receive for the week, the musicians collected only about $200. After his fill of barbecue and gambling, Domino had to call his family to wire him money for a bus ticket. The others waited out the weekend. They decided to stay one more night to enjoy Kansas City's famed "Blue Monday" shows. They dressed up and walked from one club to another on Vine Street, listening to jazz and blues.

When the band finally headed home, Bartholomew, inspired by the Kansas City musicians, scribbled down a song he called "Blue Monday." "That came from me just knowing about the working man," he says. "But these guys were having a good time on Blue Monday. Lew Chudd said that's the best song I ever wrote, because it was actually life itself." The song bore a slight resemblance to T-Bone Walker's "Stormy Monday," which merged Texas blues with L.A. cool, but "Blue Monday" instead throbbed with the heart-pounding highs and lows of life.

After Bartholomew returned, he visited Al Young at his record store on Rampart Street. Young waved a year-end bonus check for $1,500 in Dave's face.

Lew Chudd had sent Young the check for his salesmanship but had thoughtlessly forgotten Bartholomew, who had not only produced Imperial's hit records but also went through hell in the two tours with Domino promoting them. The bandleader assumed a racial motive. He took his frustration back to his wife, Pearl. In a fit of anger, Bartholomew determined to quit Imperial, declaring, "I ain't doin' it no more!"

(1951–1952)

"Fats Domino is an outright institution. The man is one of the greatest artists who's ever lived. For twelve years this man was in the top ten. I think Fats is a genius."

— LLOYD PRICE, NEW ORLEANS R&B LEGEND

"If it hadn't a-been for that [New Orleans] rhythm section and Fats Domino doing a little ivory-tinkling, even behind some of the Lloyd Price stuff early—what-the-fuck! get real!—there wouldn't be much rock 'n' roll, dude! I mean, I was there."

— DALE HAWKINS, LOUISIANA
ROCKABILLY LEGEND

In January 1951, Chudd re-signed Domino for four more years. The Imperial owner sealed the deal with the presentation of a maroon Studebaker Champion. Fats drove the half-automobile, half-rocketship up to his new house on the still unpaved Caffin Avenue. His neighbors and in-laws were awed by the beautiful new car. Rosemary, however, standing in the yard with a baby in her arms, a toddler at her feet, and another on the way, was not impressed; unlike Antoine, she did not care about the material rewards of fame. That was fine with her husband, who had been deprived of nice things in his youth and now planned to spend plenty of money on himself. Having had to endure the laughing glances of others who scorned his sad clothing and tangled curls, Domino was also determined never to look poor again. He now wore fine suits and had his hair neatly stacked in a cube. He would remain mostly soft-spoken and modest in character, but expensive cars and jewelry would proclaim his musical royalty. In fact, a month later, when Fats was on tour in Nashville, he was mesmerized by a shiny diamond ring in a jewelry store. Not thinking of his pregnant wife or his children, he plunked down $3,600—a small fortune and virtually all the money to his name—for a bauble to adorn his hand.

At the same time Fats faced a major dilemma after Bartholomew quit Imperial over the bonus check incident. Both Vernon Winslow (in his Dr. Daddy-O column in *The Louisiana Weekly*) and Lew Chudd dismissed the first session Fats recorded by himself with his band in January as sorely missing Bartholomew's arranging skills. "It wasn't worth a damn," says Chudd. "With Dave he was a king."

Still, Domino was growing and improving as an artist. He appeared in his first-ever film, a commercial for black theaters in which he sang a song about Dr. Daddy-O's sponsor Jax Beer, and—following Winslow's instructions—he flashed the pearly smile that would become an integral part of his fame. In a February session, he recorded "Rockin' Chair," which had the makings of a hit. He also revised the piano intro from "The Fat Man" for an amusingly tough version of Tampa Red's '40s blues "Don't Lie to Me," which would later inspire Chuck Berry and, in turn, the Rolling Stones to record the song.

Domino still leaned on Harrison Verrett, who sometimes played guitar with Fats or simply accompanied him to his shows. Although Verrett continued to give good advice to his brother-in-law, Domino at other times made decisions that displayed his continuing naïveté, particularly in his choices of manager and attorney. Melvin Cade, a local nightclub owner and music promoter, became his manager. The slick Creole businessman with a smudge of mustache below his flat nose liked to pick up his young star in his Cadillac and drive him to shows. With Cade, Domino's income increased from $50 a night to the seemingly stratospheric sum of $103, although Cade himself often collected many times that amount for Domino's overflow shows. Cade also introduced Domino to his attorney, Charles Levy, Jr. The pasty-faced lawyer, who wore binocular glasses and spoke in a thick drawl, saw a major opportunity in controlling the talented, but uneducated, musician. He gave Domino a paper filled with legalese to sign, explaining that it would enable him to authorize contracts when Fats was on the road. Domino signed, giving Levy power of attorney. Soon, much of his money and properties were going through his lawyer. It was a power that Levy enjoyed—and some say abused—for nearly three decades.

By the time his daughter Andrea was born in April 1951, Domino constantly played dances around New Orleans and at ramshackle juke joints booked by Cade around the Gulf Coast "Gumbo Circuit," with the nucleus of the group that carried Fats through the decade. Together they defined the Domino sound on tour and on records.

Three of the musicians had already performed with Domino for years. Buddy Hagans, Domino's original band mate and close friend, blew raw sax solos in the manner of the honkers. The squat saxman even put on a show, walking the bar and bending forward with his sax between his legs. Offstage, though, Hagan's quiet maturity and sweet nature anchored the band.

Bass player Billy Diamond now accepted his subordinate role, and, according to Bartholomew, he was "the best road manager Fats ever had." He was a fast talker and a hustler, always trying to make little deals for extra money. He knew the ins and outs of the chittlin' circuit, and all of the farm roads in a five-state radius on the way to every town. The third member of this original trio was John "Little Sonny" Jones, Domino's warm-up singer, born April 15, 1931. At twenty, he was still a hotheaded young man who cried the blues, sometimes jumping on top of the piano when he got excited.

The other three band members were new and a bit suspect. They hung together socially in dark alleys and locked rooms. Fats accepted them at first out of pressing need, but they would become the musical nucleus of the band.

Cornelius "Tenoo" Coleman was a handsome left-handed drummer who claimed the job behind Domino that had already been held by Victor Leonard, Robert Stevens, Dave Oxley, Frank Parker, Willie Barbarin, John Cook, and Earl Palmer. Originally from the tough uptown neighborhood called "The Blade" on Rocheblave Street, Coleman, born July 5, 1928, began sitting in with Domino at the Mac Hansbury Lounge on Galvez Street. Everyone liked Tenoo, who possessed charm and a playful sense of humor. His rapid drum fills sometimes threw Domino off, but Fats soon appreciated him as a great drummer.

Wendell Duconge blew sweet alto sax solos and, like Tenoo, was a ladies' man. Fats was skeptical of the light-skinned hipster, whom Charles Burbank had recruited as his own replacement, but he grew to admire the aloof jazzman, who, according to Domino's brother-in-law Reggie Hall, "blowed the devil out of rhythm & blues." The mysterious saxophonist's name was, in fact, an alias he used to hide a secret past, including a stay in Leavenworth Prison alongside Sonny Stitt. He also used "E. Wendell" in an early news story and "Emmett W. Fortner" on session sheets. Though he claimed he was from Chicago, documents later proved that he was born Emmett Wendell Fortner in New Orleans on July 4, 1923.

The last member of the band was Walter "Papoose" Nelson, a skinny eighteen-year-old guitarist whose gold-toothed smile bobbed blissfully as he plunked hip-swiveling funk. Walter Charles Nelson, Jr., the son of the guitarist who had taught music to both Smiley Lewis and Professor Longhair, was born on July 26, 1932, and grew up in the poverty-stricken Tremè area, playing for dimes on the street. Fats heard Papoose when he was playing with Professor Longhair and persuaded him to join his band. Unfortunately, playing in shady clubs like Longhair's hangout, the Caldonia Inn, he had gathered some bad baggage, notably an addiction to heroin. Still, his driving-but-mellow style became, as Billy Diamond says, "the backbone of our band."

Despite their rough edges, Domino's musicians taught and inspired local kids. While Fats played at clubs like Bogan's Patio, Tenoo gave drum lessons to teenagers Charles "Hungry" Williams and Walter "Popee" Lastie, both of whom would later play drums with Domino. Buddy Hagans instructed Popee's older brother, David Lastie, who became a noted local saxophonist. Mac Rebennack (who became known as Dr. John) later saw Domino's band at the Cadillac Club downtown and idolized Papoose Nelson, who gave him formal guitar lessons. "Papoose wouldn't let me listen to just the blues," says Rebennack. "I had to key into other things, like pop and jazz. He was a real soulful player, probably the most soulful guitar teacher I had."

Likewise, to Domino his first road band was "the best band I ever had." "There wasn't but six of us," says Fats, "but we made as much music as a big band. We were so *together*."

But Domino's tranquil days spent near his home were numbered. On June 30, "Dr. Daddy-O" Winslow made a prediction in his *Louisiana Weekly* column: "Fats' popularity will skyrocket when 'Rockin' Chair' is released." That fall Winslow was proven correct: The ebullient song in which Fats sang that he wanted to *"rock away my blues"* was breaking out around the country and he began touring again. On October 20, 1951, the first real article on Domino, titled "'Fats' Domino, Blues King, Socko on Tour," appeared in *The Louisiana Weekly*. Its description of the pianist's performance would remain true over the next half century: "The clever finger work of the '88' specialist delighted the dancers as they roared with loud approval. It's no small wonder, because Fats is a tireless worker who strives for perfection."

By the end of 1951, both sides of Domino's new record blared from jukeboxes in black barrooms and greasy spoons. At Harrison Verrett's suggestion, Fats had recorded his first popular standard, "Careless Love," a year earlier with

Dave Bartholomew's band. But "Rockin' Chair" became Domino's first national hit without Bartholomew, whom Fats had rarely seen in the last year. He apparently didn't miss him much, as Domino's drawling but exuberant vocals over an easy-rocking beat created another influential style in his new hit. Lloyd Price would borrow the song's tune for his second hit, "Ooh Ooh Ooh," while both Professor Longhair and Little Richard would perform and, much later, record "Rockin' Chair."

Later that year, Dr. Daddy-O saw Domino riding through the streets of New Orleans in a black Cadillac. Fats had already sold the Studebaker (to Charley Armstead) and bought his new car in Dallas at Lone Star Cadillac, where the dealer would supply Domino with a new Caddy every year. Winslow made another prediction, "If things continue to move according to schedule, Fats should soon be a national idol!"

■ ■ ■

Rhythm & blues reached a turning point in 1952 as many white deejays and entrepreneurs publicly risked the social ostracism of segregation to bring rhythm & blues to a national stage. In January Duke "Poppa Stoppa" Thiele introduced Domino at New Orleans' Pentagon Ballroom. "HEY NOW!" shouted the coolly tailored, tall, and handsome disc jockey. "*HEY NOW!*" the black audience shouted back at him in the call-and-response he had made popular locally. Though Thiele had been making appearances for years, some in the black audience were still shocked to see the white announcer. Many listeners simply figured that *all* r&b deejays were black. Alan Freed, a white disc jockey who followed in the footsteps of Southern deejays like Poppa Stoppa and Gene Nobles (at WLAC in Nashville), made national news with the Moondog Coronation Ball in Cleveland on March 21, 1952, in which a riot occurred when thousands of black fans failed to get into a sold-out show featuring the Dominoes and Paul Williams. R&b shows were becoming larger and more unwieldy, as a younger generation took over black popular music.

Such disturbances seemed to mirror the streetwise and passionate turn of the music. Though New Orleans' great pioneer Roy Brown had faded in popularity, his crying gospel style influenced several 1952 hits, including "Weepin' and Cryin'" by the Griffin Brothers with vocalist Tommy Brown, "Have Mercy Baby" and "The Bells" by the Dominoes with singer Clyde McPhatter, and even "Cry" by Johnnie Ray, who became the first white singer to take the rhythm & blues sound to #1 in both the pop and r&b charts. But in the long run, the most important "crying" song was Lloyd Price's "Lawdy Miss Clawdy." Both Domino and Bartholomew, who built the musical foundation for Price's record, had ironically used the word "Lawdy" prominently in songs they'd recently recorded. The spiritual roots that the word suggested later became implicit in soul music, but the record was also in the direct line of a greater musical revolution. Historians would later label the Moondog Ball "the first rock 'n' roll concert," though Freed used the words "blues and rhythm" to describe the music he played throughout his stay in Cleveland. However, a more crucial event actually occurred a week earlier in New Orleans when Domino, Bartholomew and Co. forged the core sonic fusion of rock 'n' roll.

Art Rupe of Specialty Records in Hollywood had traveled to New Orleans because he loved Domino's sound. He was at Cosimo Matassa's J&M Studio at noon on Thursday, March 13, 1952, when a nervous teenager named Lloyd Price walked in. Matassa had introduced Rupe to Dave Bartholomew, who had heard Price in the New Orleans suburb of Kenner. At an earlier audition, Price had impressed Rupe when he literally cried to be heard.

Now, just three days after his nineteenth birthday, Price was there to sing for Rupe with Bartholomew's band: Herbert Hardesty (tenor sax), Joe Harris (alto), Salvador Doucette (piano), Ernest McLean (guitar), Frank Fields (bass), and Earl Palmer (drums). To the musicians, it was just another session. To Art Rupe of Specialty Records, New Orleans was the Southern Cibola, and he was a conquistador mining gold records. To Lloyd Price, the session was a dream coming true.

At first things did not go well. Bartholomew was not happy with his piano player, Salvador Doucette, who knew modern jazz better than the lowdown "Junker's Blues" piano style of the song.

Then a black Cadillac rolled up in front of J&M. It was Domino, who was just stopping by to say hello. Bartholomew broke the ice. "Hey, Antoine, how about sittin' in?"

"Man, you know I can't sit in!" fussed Fats, acting outraged. "I'm under contract." With his contract to Imperial Records, Domino was not supposed to record for anyone without Lew Chudd's permission. But after a couple of drinks, he laughed and moved toward the piano. "Well, I'm gonna have me some fun," he announced. "I'm gonna sit in anyway."

After hearing the song again, Fats played it through once, adding a majestic piano introduction and solo.

"Okay, that's it," said Bartholomew approvingly.

Cosimo switched on his tape recorder: "'Lawdy Miss Clawdy,' take one."

Domino started his piano rolling.

Price wailed.

Art Rupe thanked his lucky stars. He had just hired one of the top r&b stars for a pittance: a session musician's fee of $54.50. In fact, Fats helped sell the record even as an "anonymous" pianist. Domino's rolling trills at the start of the record in a cascading, horn-like procession was, as Bartholomew puts it, "one hell of an introduction," which he repeated in the solo. And the massive hit gave his piano triplets their widest exposure yet, with Price and others adopting them.

"Lawdy Miss Clawdy" became the forerunner of the primary rock 'n' roll sound, a powerful combination of Roy Brown–style fiery wails and New Orleans' rhythms anchored by the father of the backbeat, drummer Earl Palmer. Future #1 r&b hits, including Ruth Brown's "Mama, He Treats Your Daughter Mean," Joe Turner's "Shake, Rattle and Roll," Little Richard's "Tutti Frutti," and Elvis Presley's "Hound Dog," would all be heavily indebted to the Domino-Bartholomew-Brown sound. And, years later, Presley, Little Richard, and the Beatles all recorded "Lawdy Miss Clawdy."

Price's record grandly introduced *The New Orleans Sound* that became the signature of Domino and Bartholomew. As Mac "Dr. John" Rebennack notes, their interlocking rhythms were the forerunner of Phil Spector's "wall of sound" a decade later. "I don't know if Phil picked it up from Fats or from somebody who picked it up from Fats," says Rebennack, "but it started with Fats." There were at least three layers of rhythm in every Domino record, including piano triplets, some variation of Bartholomew's bass line played by various instruments, horns riffing in the background, and the drums usually delivering a pounding 2/4 backbeat, which made the rhythms virtually irresistible. Musicologist Robert Doerschuk describes the rhythmic fusillade of "The New Orleans Sound": "Each player essentially sticks to one part and plays it over and over against a solid snare hit on the second and fourth beats of each bar. Consider it a jigsaw method: The bass part fits snugly against the horn riff, the keyboard part settles into a cushion between the bass and drums." Another music scholar, Jonathan Kamin, noted its significance: "At the same time, the rhythmic impact of five players all providing different elements of rhythm, in several different patterns, was much greater than that of anything available in the pop market at the time, where the beat tended to be somewhat incidental. This complex, layered beat might also be compared to African polyrhythms." Doerschuk concludes that the New Orleans sound "is the foundation of pop music today, and it owes much to Domino's contributions as a rhythm player."

Still, Bartholomew and Domino were not yet back together as a team. That April, Fats traveled to Nashville for a long engagement at Grady's Supper Club. Grady's was a swank, two-story nightclub on Fourth Avenue, and Domino's pay there, subsidized by the club's illegal gambling, was an impressive take of $2,500 a week. After he thrilled the crowds, Fats high-rolled in the back room gambling parlor and drank whiskey from bottles with his name engraved on them till the early morning. Lew Chudd even traveled to Nashville to see Domino and supervise a recording session there on April 26. He met Ted Jarrett, a black talk show host at WSOK, who presented Chudd with two songs he'd written for Domino. At the session, Fats seemed to display his displeasure at recording someone else's songs and kept messing up. When Jarrett tried to make a suggestion, Domino snapped, "Do you want me to do the song or don't you?"

When Chudd later listened to the session tapes in Hollywood, he was not impressed. He asked Al Young to call Bartholomew, but the bandleader, who was still angry at Young, cursed him and slammed down the phone. Not long afterwards, Dave walked into A-1 Records on Camp Street in New Orleans with a 78 acetate of "Lawdy Miss Clawdy" to play for record distributor Joe Banashak, who took it upon himself to call Chudd, one of his clients, and play the song over the phone for him. With Banashak's help, Chudd persuaded Bartholomew to sign a contract with Imperial for $125 a week (which added to the $200 to $300 a week he made performing with his band). As Cosimo Matassa says, "Lew Chudd found out what side his bread was buttered on."

■ ■ ■

Prior to his reunion with Bartholomew, Domino enjoyed his biggest hit yet in the spring of 1952 with "Goin' Home." Lew Chudd had watched the previous October as Al Young's so-called arrangement of the "Goin' Home" session resulted in a terrible sound mix and an off-key saxophone solo by Buddy Hagans. Young even managed to cajole a co-writing credit on the song out of the naïve Domino, who was used to giving half credit to his producer. Still, the song's powerful feeling was locked in the grooves, as Fats shouted a story that everyone could relate to their own lives. "Goin' Home" swamped the Southland and then moved north. The song, which again displayed Domino's amazing ability to tell a moving story with just a few words, was inspired by his musicians always saying that they wanted to go home to New Orleans during his tours. Domino's piano prelude on "Goin' Home" rang like chimes before a storm. "When Fats plays that, it's *magic,*" says New Orleans pianist Allen Toussaint. "It's beyond just a general grace note in musical terms. It's a little bigger than life, just the way Fats is." The shouts and churning horn riffs hit with a visceral, heart-rending impact. The message of longing for a familiar safe haven resonated with black émigrés, including those serving in the Korean War and those who had moved away from the South.

The record's influence was obvious in the horn riffs of the subsequent #1 r&b hits "Shake a Hand" by Faye Adams and "The Things That I Used to Do" by Guitar Slim—a record that featured piano triplets by none other than its arranger, Ray Charles, who spent several crucial months in New Orleans in 1952–1953, notably in the company of Guitar Slim, which would heavily influence his turn to passionate and rhythmic gospel r&b. Both Domino and Bartholomew also recognized "Goin' Home"'s influence on Leiber and Stoller's contemporary song "K.C. Lovin'" by Little Willie Littlefield, which later became famous as "Kansas City." R&b legends including Professor Longhair, Clifton Chenier, Little Richard (with Jimi Hendrix), Roscoe Gordon, James Brown, Percy Sledge, and Dr. John would all record "Goin' Home."

Fats had a good reason to go home, as on May 10, 1952, his second son, Andre, was born. But exactly a week later he was shocked by a welcome-home concert that was literally riotous. At the show 700 Domino fans jammed the Pentagon Ballroom after a Saturday football game at Hardin playground between uptown blacks and downtown Creoles. The uptowners flirted with the fair downtown girls. At 10:30, promoter Rip Roberts ejected a troublemaker. Two policemen took others in tow. Then a rowdy group upstairs started throwing beer bottles into the crowd below as Domino sang his own version of "Lawdy Miss Clawdy." Bottles popped like firecrackers, scattering glass across the floor. Fats and the band stopped. Rip Roberts ran over and shouted, "Keep playin'! Maybe they'll stop!" As Domino struck three notes and sang, *"GOIN' HOME TOMORROW!"* a bottle crashed near the stage. *The Louisiana Weekly* later reported, "The house was rockin'!" as "a staccato chorus of whizzing bottles" began falling all around the musicians, who stopped in mid-riff. People scattered and screamed, fighting for the stairway and the exits. Some even jumped out of the second-story windows. Domino ducked under the piano with

Billy Diamond, who clutched his bass as a shield. Diamond's eyebrows rose when he saw Al Young's wife looking for handsome saxophonist Wendell Duconge, not Al, in the bedlam. The fights flowed out of the club and into the street. Six police cars squealed to the scene. Fourteen people, mostly teenagers, went to Charity Hospital with stab wounds, cuts, and bruises.

With the success of "Goin' Home," promoters deluged Domino with concert requests. At a club called the Longhorn Ranch in Dallas, he made a crucial connection with promoter Howard Lewis, a hulking black man who controlled much of the Southwestern r&b circuit from his Empire Room in north Dallas. Lewis, in turn, contacted the Shaw Booking Agency in New York, which represented the biggest names in black music. The owner, Billy Shaw, flew to Dallas to check out Domino and sign him to a booking contract. Shaw had made a name for himself by defiantly launching such black musical acts as Billy Eckstine, Sarah Vaughan, and Dizzy Gillespie at the William Morris Agency in the mid-1940s. He started his own booking firm in 1949 with clients like the Orioles and Charlie Parker. At the same time as Domino joined the agency, Shaw prophetically expressed his vision to one of his agents: "Black music is on the threshold of something big."

By the third week of June, "Goin' Home" became Domino's first #1 r&b hit. Much more shocking, though, was the song's crossover to pop radio—it had reached #30 on the pop charts the week before. Because of the racial divide in America, for years rhythm & blues only trickled into the white mainstream, though in culturally diverse New Orleans, disc jockey Duke "Poppa Stoppa" Thiele had attracted a huge white audience since 1948. In Mallory's record store on Canal Street, whites nervously requested r&b records "for the maid" or "for the handy man." Sadly, the deejays who kicked off New Orleans r&b did not enjoy its ultimate crossover—Vernon Winslow soon began playing only gospel on WMRY, while Thiele quit WJMR in April 1952 and not long afterwards contracted a mysterious illness.

In other parts of the South, segregation and the tight squeeze of the Bible Belt limited the exposure of rhythm & blues. One deejay who had moved from Cleveland to Texas discovered that white teens liked r&b, which they euphemized as "cat music." But, he complained, "There are only two or three dances a year because of the Baptists here." Likewise, John Richbourg and Gene Nobles on WLAC in Nashville attracted white listeners to their late-night programs, who, due to the heavy stigma of segregation, usually only bought r&b by mail-ordering 78s from the station's sponsors. Even in Cleveland, Alan

Freed's fans were still overwhelmingly black. The music, as yet, was no threat to pop music.

In the early 1950s, r&b records broke into the white hit parade only when key pop disc jockeys dared to play them. Lew Chudd, who always sought pop airplay, found the perfect ally in another Cleveland deejay, Bill Randle. In fact, Chudd says, "Bill Randle broke almost all of Domino's records." Randle, who was then far more popular than Freed, used his extremely influential pop program on WERE to break r&b and other ethnic music nationally. "I played every record Fats Domino ever made from the beginning," states Randle. "Oh, God, yes, I played 'Goin' Home'! God, yes! Those are records you play and get a visceral response. I just got goosebumps on that. Fats Domino was an *icon* in Cleveland."

The seeds of Randle's revolt were sewn in the working-class politics of his father, a Detroit union organizer during the Depression. In 1944, after race riots in Detroit over war jobs killed more than thirty blacks, the twenty-one-year-old Randle hosted *The Interracial Goodwill Hour* jazz radio show. "I did anything I could to subvert the system," says Randle, who hung out in the black community and ran a jazz nightclub. "I was playing black music to say to the white establishment, 'Fuck you!'" After Randle moved to Cleveland in 1949, the WERE station manager fired him for playing Sister Rosetta Tharpe's "Silent Night." However, when the controversial airing drew new listeners, the owner rehired him. Randle's subversive airplay aided the pop success of r&b songs about racist police brutality ("Saturday Night Fish Fry" by Louis Jordan in 1949), unabashed sexuality ("Sixty Minute Man" by the Dominoes in 1951), and drug addiction ("Junco Partner," in a faithful cover of James Wayne's original by pop singer Richard Hayes in 1952). After Randle broke Johnnie Ray's massive hit "Cry," *Down Beat* called the deejay "the single most important and powerful record-spinner in the country." He would play a major role in the crossover of several r&b acts, notably both Domino and Elvis Presley.

Ironically, the record that Domino revamped with his rumbling piano, Lloyd Price's "Lawdy Miss Clawdy," knocked "Goin' Home" from #1 in the r&b charts in July and racked up over a million sales to a mixed audience, though it failed to make the pop charts. Lew Chudd enjoyed another kind of crossover in August, when "Indian Love Call," a country record by Slim Whitman, became the first Imperial record to make the pop top ten.

■ ■ ■

Domino was, as usual, running late for a show on Friday September 5, 1952. His manager Melvin Cade insisted on driving him, speeding his Cadillac down Highway 90, through Morgan City toward Rayne, Louisiana. Billy Diamond had left earlier, driving the band through Baton Rouge in his '49 Ford station wagon. Four miles outside of Franklin, Louisiana, Cade hit a sharp curve and lost control of the Cadillac. The car slammed into an embankment and hurtled ten feet in the air. It rolled over three times, throwing Cade onto the ground. Domino, who had been sleeping in the backseat, was uninjured. He and the other two in the car, Cade's chauffeur, Bernard Dunn, and his assistant, Elzia Duckett, found Cade, his life ebbing away. An ambulance sped him to New Orleans' Charity Hospital, where he died the next morning at age thirty-two. Thousands soon paid their last respects to the popular music promoter at the Majestic Funeral Home. For Domino, however, the tragedy freed him from a contract that paid him only $150 a night, when Cade might pocket several hundred dollars. A decade later, Harrison Verrett put it bluntly: "If Cade hadn't got killed, Fats would have been screwed up today."

Still, the wreck cast a pall over Domino's session the next Wednesday. He wrote a melancholy instrumental called "Dreaming" featuring Wendell Duconge on alto sax, which was, in effect, an elegy for Cade. But, as in jazz funerals, the musicians also celebrated life. Fats kicked off a version of Professor Longhair's "Mardi Gras in New Orleans," fingering a right-hand flourish that cut through the gloom like a clarinet leading a second line parade. Though it was Domino's first session with Bartholomew in two years and included musicians from both of their bands, they kicked right into the groove. Longhair and Domino influenced each other. "He used to sing one of my numbers, 'Goin' Home Tomorrow,'" says Fats. "I did 'Mardi Gras' and 'Hey Now Baby,' but I called it 'Hey Little Schoolgirl.'" Domino's "Mardi Gras in New Orleans" was not a simple imitation, but a rocking version, with Fats re-installing the crucial piano prelude. As jazz critic Gary Giddins notes, "The instrumental chorus is gone and the rhythmic support tidier." It set the pattern for Longhair's 1958 version, which would become the primary anthem for Mardi Gras thereafter.

On Tuesday, September 16, Fats appeared in Durham, North Carolina, at the start of an East Coast tour. Domino was red hot, making up to $500 a night, but he and his musicians faced the hardships of touring in the South. They could buy gas at service stations but couldn't use the restrooms. They had trouble finding places to eat and sleep, occasionally parking on the side of the road or even driving home between shows to sleep. Domino's showstopper

"Goin' Home" accordingly hit home in yet another way. To some blacks, the "evil ways" Fats sang about described the discrimination they faced every day.

But social changes were brewing even at Domino's southern shows, which attracted adventurous "white spectators," who, as advertised in black newspapers, could pay $1 to sit in a segregated section or balcony, while blacks enjoyed the dance floor for $1.50. At the same time as the incipient musical crossover, African Americans were striving for integration in other areas besides sports. Fittingly, Ralph Ellison's 1952 novel *Invisible Man,* a soul-shocking indictment of racism, would win the National Book Award. On the day of Cade's fatal accident, attorney A. P. Tureaud filed the *Bush v. Orleans Parish School Board* lawsuit, which challenged segregation on behalf of the students of the Macarty School, which Domino had once attended, though the lawyer soon put his case in abeyance so that the Supreme Court would review similar cases in South Carolina, Delaware, Virginia, and, most famously, Kansas, in *Brown v. Board of Education.*

A month later, there was a campaign rally in "Beauregard Square" for war hero and presidential candidate Dwight Eisenhower. Jazz trumpeter Al Hirt led a parade of brass bands through a crowd of 60,000 people stretching from Canal Street to the former Congo Square. Livid with his own Democratic Party's civil rights moves, Louisiana Governor Robert Kennon crossed party lines to introduce Ike, a Republican who delivered a speech defending "States' Rights"—code words for the segregation status quo. But outgoing Governor Earl K. Long had succeeded spectacularly in registering black voters, increasing their number from fewer than 10,000 in 1948 to nearly 110,000 in 1952. For the first time since Reconstruction, black voters made a difference in Louisiana, giving Eisenhower's opponent, Adlai Stevenson, a narrow victory in the state.

In late October, the other half of the New Orleans one-two r&b punch, Lloyd Price, played frenzied shows at the Apollo in Harlem that included his version of Domino's "Goin' Home." Fans ripped his clothes when he jumped into the crowd for an encore of "Lawdy Miss Clawdy." After the show, fans asked Price when they would see Domino, who still had not made it to New York City.

Fats headed for Pittsburgh, where he opened for the famed vocal group the Orioles in mid-November. He traveled through the Midwest during the holidays. Accompanied by sobbing horns and stinging guitar licks, Domino cried an ancient blues refrain in his new hit, "How Long," that winter—*"How long? How long must I wait for you?"*

"Going to the River"

Chapter 6

(1953–1954)

*"TEENAGERS DEMAND MUSIC WITH A BEAT, SPUR
RHYTHM & BLUES"*
—*Billboard,* APRIL 24, 1954

"SUPREME COURT OUTLAWS SEGREGATION"
—*Louisiana Weekly* BANNER HEADLINE, MAY 24, 1954

On New Year's Day, 1953, Bernard Dunn was driving Domino south from
Chicago back to Nashville as the lonesome voice of Hank Williams emanated from the car radio. A disc jockey came on after the song and announced
that Williams had died on the way to a show. The news upset Fats, who loved
both Hank's bluesy heartsick cries and the joie de vivre in his Cajun anthem
"Jambalaya," which had recently even made the New Orleans r&b charts. He
felt the loss of a kindred soul. "That country music tells a story," says Domino,
"that's just like rhythm & blues. Look at Hank Williams—he was twenty-nine
when he died, and the songs he wrote, man!" Fats would later record several
country songs, including three by Williams.

In mid-January Domino's musicians gathered before a big national tour at
Frank Mulé's bar at Laharpe and Derbigny in New Orleans. They drank beer
and bought foot-long fried oyster and sausage "po-boy" sandwiches wrapped in
butcher paper for the trip. Sonny Jones, Domino's warm-up singer, walked
in the door and boasted, "Things ain't what they used to be, man! I got me a
record!" Holding a 78 that he had recorded with Bartholomew's band, Jones
could taste the "overnight" stardom that both Domino and Lloyd Price
achieved with Bartholomew, and accordingly quit Domino's band. With a few

African Americans finding national success in sports and music, young blacks now dreamed the American Dream, but for 99.9 percent of them, including Jones, it was still only a dream.

Billy Diamond asked Roy Brown to replace Jones. The wheel of fortune had turned so that the once-mighty Brown was now slated to be an opening act for the man who'd once played during his intermissions. But Fats, in a pique of revenge for the day when Brown left them stranded at Cosimo's nearly five years earlier, told Diamond not to pick him up. In Mobile, Domino instead hired Jimmy Gilchrist, a six-foot blues wailer with a thick conk who looked and sounded like Roy Brown.

Domino played piano behind both Gilchrist and the Clovers, the red-hot vocal group from Washington, D.C., that headlined the tour. The Clovers, who had forsaken Tin Pan Alley songs for down-in-the-alley rhythm & blues, bonded with Domino's musicians. "Fats' band was tighter than wallpaper is to paint or shirttail is to rectum!" declares Harold Winley, the Clovers' bass singer. "We drank, bullshitted, and raised hell together. Tenoo, Papoose, Wendell, and Buddy, with his little half-a-pint hidin' in his pocket; we loved to play with 'em!"

The first show was at the Star City Auditorium in Roanoke, Virginia, on January 15. The two-week tour was booked by Ralph and Eli Weinberg, whose home base was a furniture store in Bluefield, West Virginia. The father-and-son team promoted dances along the Eastern Seaboard and in a 1,000-mile swath along the Mason-Dixon Line to the Mississippi. After Ralph's death in April 1953, Eli continued "The Weinberg Tour," which, together with the Howard Lewis Southwestern circuit, dominated the rhythm & blues heartland. Musicians who made both tours often achieved national stardom.

In Virginia and the Carolinas, tobacco barns became makeshift dance halls and truck flatbeds served as stages. Like the "jitterbugs" of the swing era, dancers took turns showing off acrobatic moves, including twists, dips, splits, and flips. With their baggy clothes flying, they whirled like tops as the audience formed a circle echoing African ring dances around them. The musicians also competed in "battle of the bands" shows in which singers, guitarists, and saxophonists attempted to blow each other off the stage in cutthroat "cutting contests." Such improvisational musical warfare was a major reason why black music was the wellspring of innovation in America.

Rhythm & blues sowed the seeds of integration even in virulently racist areas. There was a curious turnabout, as whites now felt the bondage of both the ropes that segregated them away from the dance floor and their own repressive moral dictums, as they enviously watched the blacks dance. As early as August 1950, the Ku Klux Klan raided an African American bar, Charlie's Place, in Myrtle Beach, South Carolina, to stop the "race-mixing" dancing there. The Klansmen even shot up the offending jukebox. They kidnapped and savagely beat the black club owner, Charlie Fitzgerald, though he, like the music, survived. On the Eastern Seaboard, r&b, including Domino's music, was later euphemized as "beach music." It accomplished what laws couldn't, becoming the great bridge between the races on the southeastern coast, where whites and blacks continued to dance "the shag" to beach music, which in 2001 became South Carolina's official state music.

■ ■ ■

At a Dallas nightclub in February, Fats sang "Going to the River," a swampy swansong that he had recently recorded. Chuck Willis, a talented young r&b singer from Atlanta, opened for Domino. Backstage after the show, he asked Fats to play the song again. An enraptured Willis said that he would love to record it.

Ironically, Dave Bartholomew had belittled "Going to the River" as "a nothing song" when Fats first played it for him. Bartholomew and Domino soon had their collaboration down. They each wrote songs, but Bartholomew arranged them all in the studio, usually humming patterns to the musicians in impromptu instrumental charts called "head arrangements." There were never many chord changes in a song because, as bass player Frank Fields says, "Fats' musical vocabulary didn't carry you that far." The two were proving a dynamic musical pairing, though to this day, Bartholomew, who admits that Domino came up with the basic ideas for many of the Domino-Bartholomew hits by himself, still insists that "Fats didn't do any of the music. All of the music—the arranging and everything—was done by Dave Bartholomew."

To be sure, Bartholomew gave the songs their arrangements and musical notation—Fats, like many great songwriters, did not read or write music, but he nonetheless came up with strong tunes and direct, emotion-packed lyrics. He conceived songs like "Ain't That a Shame" and "I'm Walkin'" with simple but emotion-laden lyrics, which his co-writer denigrated as "nursery rhymes." In contrast, the songs that Bartholomew originated often possessed a relatively elaborate narrative, as in "Blue Monday" and "I Hear You Knocking." He envied Domino's stardom, while Fats resented his partner's imperious attitude.

Somehow, the two immense talents managed to harness their egos and work together for years, becoming the first great rock 'n' roll songwriting team, predating Leiber and Stoller. "Dave mostly did the arrangement to the music," says Fats, "but I wrote most of the things. I give Dave a lot of credit, because he knew just what I wanted. He knew how to place the music. It looked like we were just two people workin' together and understanding each other."

On his way to the West Coast, Fats heard "Going to the River" on the radio, but it was not his version. Chuck Willis had rushed into the studio to record the song too. For the first time, he had a chart race on his hands. Domino felt that Willis had knifed him in the back, and he would never again trust anyone with his song ideas.

When he reached Los Angeles, Domino climbed the stairs to the 5-4 Ballroom, the top black club in the city. Movie stars like Clark Gable, Mae West, and Humphrey Bogart had once sipped martinis as jazz combos played at the 5-4 (named after its address at 54th and Broadway). With heavy African American migration to L.A. during and after World War II, the 5-4 catered primarily to blacks after 1947.

Fats made himself at home in L.A. There were so many Louisiana émigrés there that the 5-4 served New Orleans–brewed Jax and Dixie beer. The city became Domino's playground away from home, where he drank heavily and met women. He also wanted to look fashionable; after shopping for clothes in South Central, Fats turned up at the Imperial office in an oversized chartreuse zoot suit, much to the amusement of the secretaries.

But though he was enjoying some of the prerogatives of stardom, a star attitude and image would always be at odds with Domino's reticent personality. He still felt a closeness with Rosemary and his family that his success had not diminished. He even brought gifts back from L.A. for everyone, including brightly colored clothes for his eighteen-year-old brother-in-law, Reggie Hall, an aspiring musician. Fats then missed a week of gigs in Louisiana, Alabama, and Georgia due to an illness, which was really homesickness. While he was in Hollywood Domino had recorded his next hit, a rocker called "Please Don't Leave Me" and "Rose Mary," a slow blues about missing his wife: *"If you see Rose Mary, tell her I'm coming home to stay . . . "*

In a June session at Cosimo's, Domino rerecorded "Rose Mary" with a faster dancing rhythm, though Hollywood recording engineer Abraham "Bunny" Robyn obtained a similar effect on most of Domino's recordings simply by mastering the tapes using a capstan that sped up the music and lifted the key a halftone. The process, which Lew Chudd considered a secret to Domino's success, emphasized the beat and made Fats sound younger. It also created odd musical keys that confounded his imitators. "They couldn't find the damn notes on the piano!" says Cosimo Matassa with a laugh.

That same month, "Going to the River" muscled past Chuck Willis's version and stayed at #2 in the *Billboard* r&b charts for weeks. The phrase "going to the river" represented many things to African Americans, and to Domino himself, as the Mississippi River was less than a mile from his home. Rivers symbolized bloodlines, life, death, rebirth, and, if all else failed, a tempting suicidal solution, which another Louisiana-bred bluesman, Percy Mayfield, had recently described in the haunting "The River's Invitation." Blacks gathered by the river for baptisms, celebrated in spirituals like "Down by the Riverside" and "Wade in the Water." In both the Bible and American slavery, crossing over a river meant an escape from bondage. Incredibly, Domino's dark blues itself crossed over, reaching #24 on the pop charts and spawning many imitators. Chuck Willis wrote a sequel titled "Changed My Mind," in which he reneged on drowning himself. Tommy Ridgley recorded a rewrite with Ray Charles himself playing the piano triplets at J&M, as did Little Milton at Sun Studios in Memphis. Professor Longhair, Snooks Eaglin, Wilbert Harrison, Taj Mahal, Prince Buster, Ronnie Hawkins, and Johnny Rivers would all record the song.

Domino was increasingly attracting young white listeners. Twelve-year-old John Fred Gourrier pedaled his bicycle from Sacred Heart School in Baton Rouge to a drive-in, where he heard a mysterious wailing emanating from a jukebox. The only clue to the sound's origin was the song listed below it— "Mardi Gras in New Orleans." At a party, John Fred heard Domino and Joe Turner 78s that sounded totally unlike his Frankie Laine and Les Paul and Mary Ford records. He rode his bike the next day to the Moss Street record shop that sold the mystery music. "'Going to the River' was like a *haunting* song to me," says John Fred (who would gain fame for the 1968 #1 hit by John Fred and the Playboys, "Judy in Disguise"). "The way he did that *'wah-wah-wah-wah,'* it just captured me, man."

Farther south in Louisiana, a fifteen-year-old in Abbeville took advantage of his parents' inattention while bickering in French to turn the radio from the Cajun music station to one playing Hank Williams and then to an even stranger sound on the dial. "I heard Fats Domino and that changed my life forever," says Bobby Charles, who would later write Bill Haley's "See You Later Alligator" and Domino's "Walking to New Orleans."

In west Texas, high school musicians Jerry Allison and Buddy Holly listened to r&b on Shreveport's KWKH late at night on a car radio. "The first 45 rpm record I ever bought was 'Going to the River' by Fats Domino," says Allison. "That was one of the first rock 'n' roll records I heard."

In Memphis, a deejay at the famed black radio station WDIA was a young B. B. King, then a popular bluesman who was also a huge Domino fan. Across town at Humes High School, a senior with distinctive sideburns named Elvis Presley bought nearly every 78 by Domino, one of his favorite artists.

■ ■ ■

In July, Domino appeared at the Showboat on Lombard Street in Philadelphia. He played a blistering piano intro and wailed like a train whistle in his new hit, "Please Don't Leave Me," causing the fans to shriek like they were at a church revival. In the African American tradition, Fats originally sang the nonsense syllables in the song at home just to fill out the rhythm, but Rosemary asked him, "Why don't you do a record where you go 'woo-woo-woo' in it?" Unlike Domino's mild later image, the raucous piano work and yells of "Please Don't Leave Me" would define wild abandon in r&b until Little Richard recorded in New Orleans. Jump bandleader Tiny Grimes recorded it as "Ho Ho Ho." The Spaniels performed it as an uptempo closer. In 1956, the Johnny Burnette Trio, Johnny Otis, the Four Lovers (the incipient Four Seasons), and the Fontane Sisters all revived the song, while Clarence "Frogman" Henry rearranged the *woo woo woo* part for his "Ain't Got No Home." Zydeco creator Clifton Chenier pumped his accordion like bellows, stoking the fire to his version, titled "Woo Woo Woo."

Bartholomew flew up to Philadelphia to join Fats for the weeklong nightclub gig, and he was amazed by the *woo woo woo* fever that Domino had spread throughout the city. Raymond Allen, an old friend from the Ninth Ward who now lived in Philly, was so thrilled by the performances that by week's end, he agreed to quit his job to become Domino's valet. He and chauffeur Bernard Dunn would serve Domino like his two arms for over two decades.

Fats and his band played bigger and more exciting shows. They opened for Louis Jordan at the Oakland Auditorium in California. At a Cincinnati theater, Domino's musicians made good on a promise to "cut heads and kick ass" on the headliner, Buddy Morrow's white big band, who had a hit cover version of "Night Train." That summer Fats toured with the Orioles—then riding their historic crossover hit "Crying in the Chapel"—on the Howard Lewis circuit, arrowing deep into the heart of Texas. On August 29, Domino appeared at a historic Alan Freed show in the cavernous Cleveland Arena that included Joe Turner and the Harptones, with both Clyde McPhatter and the Drifters and the Moonglows making their debuts.

As Domino's fame grew, both his audience and his music were diversifying. Taking a break at the 5-4 Ballroom on September 18, Fats had a drink with a large Native American whom he had seen dancing in the crowd. "There were white bars, Mexican bars, black bars, and actually three or four Indian bars in Los Angeles," remarks Dennis Alley, an Otoe-Missouria tribesman from Oklahoma who became Domino's longtime friend. "That's all we played was Fats Domino on the jukebox."

While in L.A., a photographer captured Domino, accompanied by Chudd and Bartholomew, for the cover of *Cash Box* magazine. Fats held two gold 78s representing more than two million total records sold, a massive figure for r&b. In October 1953, as "Rose Mary" became Domino's third major hit in a row, *Billboard* announced that Imperial had signed an amazing nine-year contract with the singer.

Fats now felt he could perform almost anywhere, though he was at first intimidated by the huge black theaters, including the Apollo in Harlem, where, he had heard, audiences threw eggs at performers they didn't like. When he appeared at the Royal Theater in Baltimore with comedienne Moms Mabley, he coached his musicians backstage: "Just play like the record, that's what they want to hear." The band met each larger challenge, including its first New York appearance at the Audubon Ballroom on October 11, 1953. A week later, Domino joined an all-star show at the Laurel Gardens in Newark, New Jersey, with Amos Milburn, Margie Day, Ruth Brown, and the Paul Williams Orchestra.

In November, Ruth Brown and the Artists Society of America held a press conference in Washington, D.C., decrying the "low quality of service and exorbitant fees in hotels and restaurants." "The vicious discrimination practiced against show folk on the road," said Brown, reading from a prepared statement, "is, in many cases, a two-edged dagger. They are given the choice of humiliation because of race or exploitation because of occupation. These deplorable conditions are not confined to prejudice in the South. They are often implicit in criminal economic injustice in other parts of the country. Unscrupulous Negroes in business have as unclean hands in this matter as prejudiced whites."

Indeed, even in the North, Domino and his musicians often had to stay in a rooming house or in private homes, and nightclub managers set up tables in the kitchen for the musicians. Fats often cooked Creole dishes on a hot plate in the band's hotel to avoid such problems, but he and his band continued to suffer from segregation.

■ ■ ■

Two white station wagons zoomed past rows of Louisiana fields on their way to Texas in late December 1953. FATS DOMINO and THE CLOVERS were painted in bold black letters on the sides of the two cars. Behind the wagons, Domino and two of the Clovers played cards and drank scotch in his Cadillac.

The Clovers wore "do-rags" tied around their heads—scarves to keep their process hairdos in place. Papoose also sported a process. Billy Shaw had actually shamed Billy Diamond into cutting his off. With soft hair inherited from his mother's family, Fats didn't need to undergo the grueling process of straightening the hair with caustic lime and heat. He kept his hair stacked flat with Murray's Pomade grease and a little water.

Promoter Howard Lewis booked the bands from Dallas to California. In Richmond, near San Francisco, Fats again tore up the crowd. "Man! Just to see the frenzy!" says the Clovers' Harold Winley. "Fats did that 'Woo-woo-woo!' Papoose was answering on guitar. Tenoo was back there. That shit was *gone*, man!" On one of their few nights off, some of Domino's musicians went out to hear live jazz. Harold Lucas of the Clovers talked the reluctant Domino into going out and seeing blues acts like B. B. King, T-Bone Walker, and Lowell Fulson.

In January 1954, *Cash Box* reported that r&b listeners were gradually catching on to the more melodic sound of Domino's new record, "Something's Wrong." His increasing mixture of pop, country, and r&b (evidenced in his occasional performance of Patti Page's classic "Tennessee Waltz," which was a #1 r&b hit in New Orleans and many other cities) reflected the fact that young music fans were beginning to mix racially, even in nightclubs in a major social development that the popular press never reported; the musical integration only became news when tensions overflowed at the jam-packed dances, including a Domino-Clovers show in Indianapolis in which a riot occurred. Afterwards, the club owner counted broken bottles and chairs, while the Clovers' manager, Lou Krefetz, counted greenbacks on the dressing room floor.

That same month Domino again played the Showboat in Philadelphia. Outside of the Douglas Hotel late one night, Buddy Hagans walked warm-up singer Jimmy Gilchrist around in fourteen inches of snow, trying to keep the much taller man steady and conscious. Gilchrist had high-grade heroin running through his veins, and Hagans knew from his experiences in the army that he had to keep him awake.

Marijuana and heroin were black musicians' drugs of choice. The use of the needle was a measure of cool in the night world of musicians, a defining defiance. Though "The Junker's Blues" had kicked off his career, Fats stuck to alcohol. He was only vaguely aware of his musicians' drug use, though at the end of 1954 his band members would run into trouble again in Philly when police arrested Wendell Duconge, Walter Nelson, and Cornelius Coleman for drugs in a raid on their hotel room. The City of Brotherly Love's police liked to shake down black musicians (including Ray Charles and Billie Holiday) like mahogany money trees; once they got a pound of cash, they often dropped the charges. The cops found hypodermic needles and thirty empty cellophane bags with heroin residue, and Domino ended up paying $1,000, which Lew Chudd wired to him to spring Duconge, the only one who received formal charges. Two years after that Tenoo would be busted there again, though the police, fishing for any harassment, replaced the "suspicion of narcotics violation" charge with a firearms violation.

Walter "Papoose" Nelson was the worst offender. Though he was cheerful, friendly, and enormously talented, he was also a junkie. Billy Diamond once gave him his own form of drug intervention when he slapped a heroin syringe out of Papoose's hand in Muncie, Indiana. The young guitarist also had a habit of spending all his money on drugs and gambling and then pawning his guitar, knowing that Domino would redeem it so that his guitarist could go on tour. "Most of the time I'd get it out," recalls Fats. "Even when I told him I wasn't gonna do it, he'd go do it again." Later, Domino even paid the back payments on child support that Papoose owed in order to get him out of jail.

Jimmy Gilchrist did not survive the night. Billy Diamond, as usual, had to do the dirty work, including calling Gilchrist's family in Mobile with the terrible news. "Jimmy died in his sleep," recalls Diamond. "I went down and identified the body. Of course, they say 'a heart attack'—it wasn't that. He took that *her-oin* all the time."

Fats hired r&b pianist Jalacy Hawkins to replace Gilchrist. After a few gigs in New Jersey, however, Fats fired him for his vulgarity and because he had a disquieting way of screaming his songs; he would soon become known as "Screamin' Jay." Later, Hawkins claimed that Fats fired him because he was jealous of his dynamic singing and his leopard-skin suit.

■ ■ ■

Back in New Orleans on February 21, Rosemary Domino gave birth to Anatole, her fifth child in just over five years. "I had them right in a row there," she says. "It was very difficult. My mother lived next door to me. She influenced him to go out on his own. Then the trips became longer. We lived two separate lives. That was his life. So I was mother and father both. I accepted that he wasn't going to be happy doing anything else." Though she had found unwanted fame in the hit Fats named for her, Rosemary was simply a housewife whose husband was rarely home, as Domino's many travel-themed songs attested. Her desire for a simple life was extreme. She rarely went out in public and disdained show business. The expensive cars and jewelry that her spouse cherished didn't impress her. In turn, Fats appreciated the fact that Rosemary never asked for much from him. And while he was hardly an ideal husband, he called her every day and wired her money regularly. Reflecting his Catholic background of sin followed by confession, Domino was always conflicted. Tempting as the women on the road could be, from time to time he would claim illness, cancel a few shows, and hurry back to New Orleans.

At the news of Anatole's birth, Domino's homesickness recurred. At Lew Chudd's request, Harrison Verrett quit Papa Celestin's band and drove up from New Orleans to Baltimore, where Fats was again playing the Royal Theater, to replace the band's broken-down Chevrolet station wagon with a new Chrysler and to provide moral support for Fats. Little Sonny Jones accompanied Verrett; he had recently recorded some drinking songs, so-called rhythm & booze records, with Bartholomew for Imperial, but he needed steady money to support his family. He pleaded for his job, and Fats took him back.

On March 6, 1954, Domino was named the top-selling r&b artist in the *Billboard* Jukebox Operators Poll, overtaking the Clovers, just as his "You Done Me Wrong" made the r&b top ten. The next month Lew Chudd visited his major r&b competitors Ahmet Ertegun and Jerry Wexler at Atlantic Records in New York. Though their acts dominated the r&b charts, the Atlantic men coveted Chudd's star; they would ask several artists, including Screamin' Jay Hawkins, Bobby Darin, and even Ray Charles, to try to sound like Domino. In July 1953, Wexler had even written a *Down Beat* editorial supporting r&b in which he asked, "Can't you envision a collector in 1993 discovering a Fats Domino record in a Salvation Army Depot and rushing home to put it on the turntable? We can. It's good blues, it's good jazz, and it's the kind of good that never wears out."

Ertegun liked to tease the irascible Chudd. He once called him saying he had phoned an Atlanta deejay and said, "I'm Lew Chudd and if you don't play my fucking records, I'm coming down there to break both of your legs!" Another time he pretended to be Domino's uncle, "Chester Domino," and demanded royalties. Chudd later nearly got revenge when he talked to Nesuhi Ertegun about starting an Imperial jazz line, but Ahmet made his brother a partner, beginning the Atlantic jazz series.

The Atlantic Records founder once saw Domino at a huge nightclub near Birmingham, Alabama. His feet crunched on shards of broken beer bottles as he walked through the crowd. "Fats had a great band, man," says Ertegun. "There was so much beautiful blues in the playing and the singing, even when they were playing a pop song. . . ." Afterwards he saw a handsome trunk in Domino's dressing room. Fats opened it to reveal a portable bar with every kind of alcohol imaginable.

"Can't you get liquor wherever you go?!" asked an incredulous Ertegun.

"Man," smiled Domino, "you never know when you might hit a dry spot."

∎ ∎ ∎

On April 24, 1954, a stark headline appeared in *Billboard:* "TEENAGERS DEMAND MUSIC WITH A BEAT, SPUR RHYTHM & BLUES" in the latest evidence of musical integration. Cracks were suddenly appearing everywhere in America's walls of segregation—two weeks later, on May 7, black schoolchildren fittingly led the first civil rights protest in New Orleans, a boycott of the discriminatory annual parade of children to honor John McDonogh, a nineteenth-century school benefactor, in which blacks always marched last. Ten days later, the Supreme Court declared school segregation unconstitutional in the case of *Brown v. Board of Education.* The ruling of basic human rights reverberated around the world like a new Declaration of Independence, though there was a heavy backlash. During the paranoid atmosphere of the Red Scare, many southern whites considered integration tantamount to communism. Echoing the secession of the Civil War, Georgia, South Carolina, and Louisiana threatened to abolish their public school systems. The Louisiana legislature created the Joint Committee to Maintain Segregation and passed a raft of bills to prevent integration.

Rhythm & blues supporters were, of course, thrilled by the ruling. To Lew Chudd, the ruling "opened up the whole world." With his typical entrepreneurial verve, he envisioned the pop market opening up for his black artists.

Dave Bartholomew, who insulated himself from segregation by both prosperity and pride, was "amazed and elated," but later skeptical. Those who denounced integration also decried rhythm & blues, just as teenagers in the South began to demand the music. "Politically there was prejudice [in the South], but not musically," says Art Rupe of Specialty Records. Jerry Wexler and Ahmet Ertegun likewise observed in a *Cash Box* article on July 3 that the first white listeners of rhythm & blues were in the South. They noted that northern pop disc jockeys at high school record hops were soon besieged by kids demanding danceable hits by acts like the Clovers and Fats Domino that had gained popularity below the Mason-Dixon line.

In such an atmosphere, embracing rhythm & blues became dangerous. On WGST in Atlanta, Zenas "Daddy" Sears, a white r&b deejay who advocated integration, was kicked off the air with a stream of racist epithets. "He was threatened a number of times by the KKK," says fellow disc jockey Bill Lowery. "He worked on me to play black artists like Fats Domino, but I was afraid my listeners wouldn't like that kind of music. It was mostly young kids who were diggin' it then." Rhythm & blues was still alien to most white radio stations.

Domino himself did not envision great changes in the racial status quo. "I know my children went to school," says Fats, "but my mind was on my music. It used to be great every night to play different towns. All I wanted to do was *go*." Domino was an unlikely civil rights hero, as he didn't seem rebellious or even politically conscious, but his single-minded drive to *rock* everyone who heard him would have a significant effect on race relations. His big beat diplomacy—the drive, energy, and strong emotions his music conveyed—was infectious in a way overripe pop music was not, and his unaffected charm made him the perfect ambassador for the coming rhythm & blues revolution.

At the time of the Supreme Court ruling, a song topped the r&b charts that caused a major backlash against r&b records and made Domino's music seem mild by comparison. The Hayes Code censoring movies had reached a puritanical peak, but the Kinsey Reports on sex, the new *Playboy* magazine, sex symbols like Marilyn Monroe, and rhythm & blues all ignited suppressed passions. The Midnighters' "Work with Me Annie" kicked off a trend for sexy r&b songs that made the Detroit group Public Obscenity #1 by the end of the year. "Man, I had a couple of lines in the song," recalled Midnighters singer Hank Ballard, "that said, *'Annie please don't cheat, give me all my meat,'* and that busted me!"

There were many reasons why rhythm & blues appealed to teenagers. Besides its physical and emotional release, the music represented forbidden fruit.

America preached WASP values of patriotism, puritanism, and consumerism, but kids related mostly to the latter. With the booming economy and the mass exodus to the suburbs, they had more spending money and free time. Cruising, watching movies and TV, and listening to radio made them conscious of the outside world. At the same time, young psyches also bore the brunt of nightmarish fears. The Apocalypse—via the Bomb, World War III, Communists, flying saucers, Jesus, or Negroes—seemed imminent. In the whitebread cultural landscape, kids were confused, scared, aimless, and bored. They sought their own identity in entertainment perverse to the dull WASP credo, with sick humor and cheap thrills—in magazines like *Mad* and in movies about juvenile delinquents, atomic horrors, and aliens from outer space. Just as the book *Seduction of the Innocent* created an uproar over "evil" comic books in congressional juvenile delinquency hearings, a controversy arose over r&b "leer-ics" (as *Variety* dubbed the songs' words). Even TV's *Jukebox Jury* host, Peter Potter, uttered the racially sweeping dictum, "All rhythm & blues records are dirty and as bad for kids as dope." Many teenagers, however, reveled in the condemnation.

■ ■ ■

"Keep alive and listen in to Huggy Boy! All night long from Dolphin's of Hollywood with the king of rhythm & blues, Fats Domino!" After playing at the Madison Rink in Chicago with Joe Turner and Muddy Waters in July, Domino appeared in the picture window of the Dolphin's of Hollywood record store on Central Avenue in Los Angeles. Fats waved to the teens on the sidewalk as white deejay Dick "Huggy Boy" Hugg played his records on the late-night KRKD radio show.

L.A. deejays, including Huggy Boy, had recently kicked off the historic r&b hit, "Sh-Boom" by the Chords. Cleveland deejay Bill Randle then persuaded a Canadian group, the Crew Cuts, to cover the song in a version that went to #1, dragging the Chords into the pop top five. The song's infectious nonsense radiated a subversive alternative to the banned sex songs, though, ironically, the word "boom" was hydrogen bomb–inspired New York ghetto slang for sex. Foreshadowing a similar cry by Little Richard, the black teens blissfully celebrated a new, nihilistic American Dream—simultaneous orgasm and annihilation—in one crazy, euphoric refrain—*"Life could be a dream, doo, doo, doo, SH-BOOM!"*

For r&b to fly below the radar of the moralists, sexual overtones had to be hidden. As Alan Freed noted, "the rhythm [is] what they want, and with rock 'n' roll rhythm the lyric could be sung in Sanskrit and they'd still get what they're looking for." "Sh-Boom" crystallized the use of voices as "talking drums." When the beat was the message, the words didn't have to make sense. Unable to relate to the wrenching passions of gospel or blues, the labyrinthine mysteries of bop, or the vacuous homilies of pop, young blacks parodied Tin Pan Alley lyrics with nonsensical cries that communicated in the African tradition. "It is common knowledge that African drumming was originally a form of sign language," Gunther Schuller wrote in *Early Jazz*. "But beyond this, drum patterns, which in African music are thought of not as mere rhythms but as 'tunes,' are identified by so-called nonsense syllables." The groups sublimated the revolt of r&b into subversive nonsense that, with unimaginable synchronicity, thrilled alienated white teens.

There was a spiritual link between the anarchic sensibility of New Orleans and the wild new r&b, which entranced listeners like the egalitarian cacophony of a jazz parade. Doo wop echoed both the scat that Louis Armstrong started in his own teenage street group and Domino's wordless cries in "The Fat Man" and in several of his 1953–1954 hits. Uninhibited celebrations of free expression became common in rock 'n' roll, which reveled in novelty; "Lawdy Miss Clawdy," for instance, kicked off several New Orleans–connected hits with rhyming names. The Spaniels, the Four Lovers/Four Seasons, the Del-Vikings, and Dion and the Belmonts would all perform Domino songs. Most doo wop groups also used his triplets, which gave ballads a slow dancing rhythm and a bedrock foundation for vocal flights of fancy.

The joke was on adults. Bandleader Les Brown complained that "rock 'n' roll is not only unintellectual but practically anti-intellectual, making a virtue of non-communication." The nonsense was inconceivable to adults who based their lives on respectable outward appearance, whereas the young had little to lose. Physical and emotional abandon stripped away pretenses, inhibitions, and individual egos. The whimsical wailing turned passion into nonsense, nonsense into the all-important beat, and the beat into passion in a cooling-and-heating process that powered the engine of rock 'n' roll. The driving mechanism was the call-and-response, which unleashed egalitarian musical expression previously unknown in Western culture. The music was individually liberating and socially conscious simply because it was *unself-conscious*—a blast of joyous chaos into an uptight world.

A month after the Supreme Court integration ruling, WDIA in Memphis became the nation's most powerful black radio station, with 50,000 watts of power. In his first radio interview in July 1954, Elvis Presley told Memphis dee-jay Dewey Phillips on the white station WHBQ that he was from Humes High, thereby reassuring listeners that he was a "good ol' boy" from a segregated high school. But as was obvious by his record, Elvis had also graduated from the r&b school of broadcasting.

The music also broke down racial barriers in the North. When Domino was in Cleveland to play a black theater on 105th Street in Cleveland, he spent the day with Bill Randle, visiting both black and white high schools. After a film on hygiene, the evils of smoking, or civil defense, Randle played Domino's records while the singer sang and banged along at a piano for the cheering teens. "I did maybe fifty shows with Fats like that in Cleveland," says Randle. "It was all revolutionary. I'm sure I did help Fats cross over, but to me, a black audience was as important as white audiences. I wanted to have it *all*. You're talking about a very greedy son of a bitch, which is what one guy called me. That was Alan Freed. He was very satisfied to have the black audience in Cleve-land. He didn't get the white audience until he went to New York."

Freed started his nightly rhythm & blues crusade on WINS radio in New York City in September 1954, exactly seven years after the debut of Vernon Winslow's Poppa Stoppa radio show and Roy Brown's "Good Rockin' Tonight" rocked New Orleans. While parents watched Uncle Miltie and Lucy on televi-sion, their children listened to the radio. Freed soon attracted a fanatically de-voted audience of teenagers, both black and white.

Ironically, Elvis Presley's version of "Good Rockin' Tonight" also appeared that September. Presley followed Brown's urgent wails (*"meet me in* a hurry *be-hind the barn"*), instead of the flat, urbanized version of Wynonie Harris (*"meet me in* the alley *behind the barn"*). Elvis created a powerful "rockabilly" hybrid, but it didn't sell; he was still missing the key r&b ingredient, drums, which were taboo voodoo in Tennessee, where the tight-necked Nashville hierarchy banned any "jungle" influence. Buddy Holly's drummer, Jerry Allison, asked Elvis when he visited Texas early the next year why he didn't have a drummer. "Aw, man," replied Presley, "if I had a drummer I'd sound just like Bill Haley."

Haley's "Shake, Rattle and Roll" created a devastating racket on the pop charts in the fall of 1954. His version whitewashed the words of Joe Turner's ver-sion, but arguably had more rhythmic drive than the original (which didn't pos-sess the pulsating propulsion of Turner's New Orleans–recorded progenitor, "Honey Hush"). Haley, who admitted a New Orleans influence, had his saxo-phones booming out the Bartholomew bass riff. In fact, Presley and white rockers who achieved major success soon followed Haley's lead in moving from rockabilly toward heavy-bottomed rhythm & blues. Hard drums and thumping riffs eclipsed the slapped bass; shouting, crying, and swooping nonsense displaced echoed hiccupping and twangs. Rhythm & blues—not rockabilly—would become the mainstream of rock 'n' roll.

On September 13, Domino developed severe tonsillitis in Baton Rouge and checked into a New Orleans hospital. For six weeks, promoters tried to get him back on the road, but Domino, whose health concerns bordered on hypochondria, took his time getting a tonsillectomy. As he feared, the operation *did* have a lasting effect on his voice. With his vocal cords weakened, he could no longer wail the blaring mouth harp sounds on "The Fat Man," which were thereafter delivered by a muted trumpet. On November 1, Domino finally hit the road with his former hero, Amos Milburn, circling the East Coast and the South.

A major trend was established that year when several pop/jazz package tours lost money, whereas the most successful tour was the Gale Agency's "Rhythm & Blues Show," featuring Faye Adams, the Drifters, the Spaniels, and Roy Hamilton. Winds of musical change were blowing. At Moriarty's, a Manhattan bar on 51st Street, Alan Freed drowned his sorrows on Wednesday, November 24, after losing his "Moondog" moniker and a $5,700 judgment in court to Louis "Moondog" Hardin, a blind street musician who dressed in a robe and Viking headgear. Freed had used Hardin's weird, howling record as a theme song for his nightly *Moondog Party* r&b show on WINS, which had been a smashing success since his arrival in the Big Apple. Freed sank a drink and declared his intentions to rename his program *Rock 'n' Roll Party* after words popularized in rhythm & blues long before he adopted them as a catchphrase.

"Ain't That a Shame"

Chapter 7

(1955)

"Ain't That a Shame' will never die. It'll be here when the world comes to an end."

—DAVE BARTHOLOMEW

"HELLO ROCK 'N' ROLLERS!"

Seventy-five hundred teens screamed for their hero, a disc jockey dressed in plaid named Alan Freed. Kids who had waited for hours in the cold jammed into St. Nicholas Arena in New York, a boxing venue fit for 6,000. Police held back hundreds and hauled out the toughs and fainters. Freed's "Rock 'n' Roll Jubilee Ball" on January 14 and 15, 1955, featured an all-black line-up—Buddy Johnson, Joe Turner, the Clovers, Fats Domino, Clyde McPhatter and the Drifters, the Moonglows, the Harptones, Red Prysock, and others. But unlike Freed's previous shows, nearly half the crowd was white. Though their parents had heard r&b pulsing through bedroom walls, most would have been appalled to see their children amidst black faces. On banners behind the stage between the words ALAN FREED and his radio address WINS 1010 was the new title of his radio show: ROCK 'N' ROLL PARTY. Due to the sweaty humidity caused by the overcrowding, it was raining *inside* the arena, but the teens were oblivious to the water dripping on them. "The enthusiasm of the audience was transferred to the performers," reported *Cash Box*. "The latter loved the kids and reacted to the frenzy with tremendous performances."

The beat united everyone. *Variety* noted that the musicians "based their arrangements on a bedrock repetitive rhythm that seemed to hypnotize kids into one swaying, screaming mass." For an encore at two A.M., the performers crowded back onto the stage in a wild half-hour finale in which everybody danced and sang as Domino played piano and Joe Turner shouted, just as they had played together years earlier. Freed joked that his next show would be at Madison Square Garden. The shows were ground zero for endless cross-cultural tribal rhythm rituals to come, spreading to encompass the planet in a musical global village. "Once limited to the Negro market, the r&b influence has now crossed all color lines into the general pop market," reported *Variety*, estimating the two-night take at $30,000—"bigger than any jazz concert" ever in New York.

The revolution that Freed now claimed had evolved from a decade of black innovation. Ever since Roy Brown and Wynonie Harris rocked roughshod across the airwaves, the black slang words "rock" and "rock and roll" had been pervasive in r&b. Freed had used the latter phrase in his "blues and rhythm" WJW show *Moondog House* in Cleveland, but not, as often reported, in the title of his show. Even Freed's biographer, John Jackson, debunks the myth that Freed renamed r&b in the early 1950s, noting that the words "rock 'n' roll" became synonymous with music only after the Rock 'n' Roll Jubilee Ball. In fact, music journalists reviewing the ball were confounded by the new name, writing that it was "a straight rhythm & blues concert" (*Variety*) with "only rhythm & blues talent" (*Billboard*).

Shouting into his microphone and beating on a phone book like a church pulpit, Freed followed Roy Brown in another sense—as a preacher shouting the rockin' news. The Jubilee was labeled a "revival" by *Cash Box*. *Variety* called Freed a "rhythm & blues evangelist." Even rival deejay, black bandleader Lucky Millinder, said Freed announced with "the fire and excitement of a Reverend Billy Graham." Freed's congregation was now an audience of both blacks and whites. Incredibly, Freed later said that the Jubilee Ball was *the first time he realized that whites listened to rhythm & blues*. Since r&b had acquired a heavy stigma as obscene "jungle music," the phrase "rock 'n' roll" now became his euphemism for selling r&b to whites. New York journalists ran with the phrase, legitimizing both the name and audience shift in a *Variety* headline over a story about Freed's first show directed at whites a month later: "ROCK & ROLL TO GET OFAY THEATER SHOWCASING."

"Ofay" was black slang for whites, derived possibly from the Yoruba (Nigerian) word *ofé* for a "charm" to protect oneself; or it may have just been pig latin for "foe." Likewise, the phrase "ofay and oxford gray" meant whites and blacks together. A decade earlier, after cracking the pop top ten with his primordial rocker "Caldonia," Louis Jordan had performed "Ofay and Oxford Gray," which optimistically envisioned integration: *"Discrimination has gone its way. There's no line between Ofay and Oxford Gray."* Because of segregation, the song was never released. Now Freed, with the Supreme Court integration ruling in his rear-view mirror, boldly took the ball that the fathers of r&b handed him and ran with it.

He became an instigator. Whereas Bill Randle had been subversive, Freed was confrontational. When he pounded on phone books during his shows, he was pounding on everybody in them—i.e., adults. He used apostrophes in "rock 'n' roll" in a mocking jab at stereotypes of black speech, à la *Amos 'n' Andy*—the controversial radio and TV show that the NAACP had castigated as demeaning. His euphemism cleaning up the image of obscene r&b was itself the old blues slang word for sex; if Randle was secretly saying "Fuck you" to the white establishment, Freed was saying it almost literally. His three little words symbolized a gathering insurgence among white youths, who listened to the music in defiance of their parents' prejudices. Freed would lay down the gauntlet in the April 20, 1955, issue of *Down Beat:* "This campaign against 'Rock 'n' Roll' smells of discrimination of the worst kind against the great and accomplished Negro songwriters, musicians, and singers who are responsible for this outstanding contribution to American music."

Still, Freed lacked the crucial direct connection to the pop market. Lew Chudd, who once got a headache from spending three hours as a guest on Freed's show, says that the deejay "had his hand out" for payola, but he "never sold records" like the coolly professorial Randle, who now commuted to New York for a Saturday CBS network show. In light of the massive pop hits like "Sh-Boom" that Randle had broken, in February 1955, *Time* called him "the top U.S. deejay." He even played Elvis Presley's "Good Rockin' Tonight" when few northern deejays thought much of "The Hillbilly Cat."

Rhythm & blues, increasingly known as "rock 'n' roll," was the buzz of the music industry. L.A. deejay Al Jarvis, who had helped kick off swing, enthused, "I believe that youngsters have taken to rhythm & blues in much the same manner that youngsters of a generation ago took to swing, the Lindy hop, and swooning to Frank Sinatra." *Cash Box* prophetically eyed the social ramifications of r&b's crossover in a February 5, 1955, editorial titled "Breaking Down the Barriers!"

> The whole movement has broken down barriers, which in the ordinary course of events might have taken untold amounts of time to do. How better to understand what is known to you than by appreciation of the emotional experience of other people? And how better are the emotions portrayed than by music?

All factions in our country have a vital contribution to make to our culture and understanding. The music and record industries could never accomplish anything greater than to contribute to that achievement.

In the early 1950s, BMI music publishers persuaded pop singers to record ethnic and country songs (which ASCAP publishers ridiculed) to liven up blandly romantic pop. The songs started fads for folk, Latin, hillbilly, and mambo music. Now BMI's latest fad was rhythm & blues. Even Frank Sinatra recorded the Charms' "Two Hearts, Two Kisses," which became Pat Boone's first hit. Pop singers considered r&b songs silly novelties. They had no clue that they were tampering with a firewall of segregation that had held back flaming passions for centuries.

■ ■ ■

At Imperial, the big news in February was Chudd's hiring of Eddie Ray, a black salesman at L.A.'s Central Record Sales, to head promotions. *Cash Box* called the hiring the "biggest news to hit the music field in several months." African Americans in management positions at white companies were almost nonexistent. Now, along with Dave Bartholomew, Chudd had *two* in his tiny record company. He caught hell from others over the hiring, but he didn't give a damn. *Cash Box* wished Ray "good luck in his new venture," likely implying the nearly impossible task of getting along with the caustic Chudd. Though record men bet that he would last at Imperial at most sixty days, the soft-spoken Ray developed a working relationship with Chudd that lasted as long as the company. Due to Chudd's lack of personal charm, Ray and Bartholomew would prove to be crucial liaisons for Imperial. In fact, Ray would soon go where no black man had gone before. He walked into white school board offices to promote Imperial's folk dances, into country radio stations to plug the hillbilly line, and into pop radio stations to promote all of Imperial's records. Lew wanted Eddie to always have first-class flights and accommodations. However, Ray (who was originally from Virginia) insisted on traveling to the South, despite segregation.

Though his records had not made the r&b charts in nearly a year, Domino was still Imperial's best-selling artist. In late February, as Fats began a western tour in Texas, a handsome saxophonist walked the bar of a nightclub while blowing a rousing solo. Herbert Hardesty, who had played on Domino's records since "The Fat Man," had finally joined his band.

Born March 3, 1925, in New Orleans, Hardesty began playing music at age eleven when he blew "The Music Goes 'Round and 'Round" on a trumpet as he watched a Mardi Gras parade. During World War II, he first picked up a saxophone when he was a radio technician for the Black Army Air Corps. Returning home, he played with Roy Brown, Professor Longhair, and Smiley Lewis. He also led bands, ranging from a Nat "King" Cole–style trio (in which he played stand-up bass) to an r&b combo that backed up Ray Charles in 1953. Hardesty joined Bartholomew's band in 1949 and became his top soloist. When the session work slowed, Hardesty accepted a standing offer from Domino to join his band.

With his personal and musical sophistication alone, Hardesty stood out from Domino's other musicians. But he also performed with wild showmanship, running and sliding across the stage, playing on his back, and even riding down banisters. His solos playfully fused polished melody with rhythm. Musicologist Charlie Gillett compares his tone to that of New Orleans clarinetists Sidney Bechet and George Lewis, "with a sort of blurred edge that gave a buzz effect to every note."

In Texas, white sheriffs harassed Billy Diamond when Fats played past the one A.M. curfew. Domino often ignored Diamond's pleas to stop playing, but when Hardesty spoke up, Fats listened. He had to respect his impressive new foil, who would raise the level of Domino's music for over half a century.

By the first weekend in March, Domino and the band were in Los Angeles, playing an engagement at the 5-4 Ballroom. The band was still staying at the dingy Dunbar Hotel at 4215 Central, but Fats had upgraded to the ritzy Hotel Watkins at 2022 West Adams, which catered to well-to-do blacks, including stars like Duke Ellington, Ella Fitzgerald, and Sidney Poitier. To Dave Bartholomew, who flew in to supervise a session, the hotel was the hippest African American gathering place on the continent. "Nat 'King' Cole used to be in the bar at the Watkins Hotel every day," remembers Bartholomew. "We all would be in one place, because we were supposed to be segregated. All I mean, it was a white man's world. You want to hear something? I'm sorry [segregation is] gone, because we had more fun." Domino could often be found in the hotel's Rubyiat Lounge; when Eddie Ray came by the Watkins to pick him up, Fats would insist on having several drinks there, thereby purposefully missing radio interviews that Ray had scheduled for him.

One night, Bartholomew went out with Chudd and Ray to hear black pianist Earl Grant at a club on Figueroa Street. They were amazed to see an integrated audience. Blacks and whites loved Grant's cool renditions of songs by artists as diverse as Nat "King" Cole and B. B. King. "That's what we need," said Chudd, motioning his glass at Grant. He elaborated on the drive home: "We need a crossover thing away from rhythm & blues. We need something that's going to sell pop."

Bartholomew was at a loss. He and Domino had never deliberately aimed their music at the pop hit parade. As it happened, pop music came to them.

■ ■ ■

On March 15, 1955, Domino recorded "Ain't That a Shame" at Master Recorders in Hollywood. Bartholomew complained that the song was too simple and didn't tell a whole story, but Fats wouldn't change it. So the bandleader had Domino's band echo the telegram lyrics with a similarly simple beat, with a musical break like his father had played in the jazz standard "Tin Roof Blues." Papoose Nelson drove the song with a killer guitar riff. Herbert Hardesty added a mellow solo.

On the same day, Domino recorded another future #1 r&b hit, the jaunty "All by Myself," which, like "The Fat Man," was based on an earlier blues, a hokum song of the same title recorded by Big Bill Broonzy in 1941 with pianist Memphis Slim. "All by Myself" introduced another Domino trademark, his double-fisted "two-beat" piano style, which propelled a string of up-tempo hits. The rhythm placed him firmly in the New Orleans tradition. "Fats got more New Orleans music across than anybody else from having so many hit records in his time," says Mac "Dr. John" Rebennack. "For a band to play a good ol' second line feel with that pattern is so natural."

In New Orleans jazz funerals, a brass band slowly sashayed to a cemetery playing religious dirges. Then the band would perk up mourners with up-tempo two-beat songs like "When the Saints Go Marching In." A parade of "second-liners" followed the band, waving handkerchiefs and dancing to celebrate living. *Variety* would later call Domino's "driving, grinding" version of "The Saints" "about as far from the basic intent of the old spiritual as could be imagined." But the rhythms were spiritual in the African sense. Robert Palmer wrote that rock 'n' roll rhythms "can ultimately be traced back to African music of a primarily spiritual or ritual nature." Michael Ventura adds that African Americans "built their cathedrals and wrote their scripture within their bodies, by means of a system that could be passed from one generation to the next. That system was rhythm." But to Western religions, rhythms that inflamed passion were sinful, as former rocker Reverend Jimmie Rodgers Snow reaffirmed when he preached against *THE BEAT! THE BEAT! THE BEAT!"* of rock 'n' roll from a church pulpit in a famed newsreel. Domino was a Catholic who carried a Bible and ended shows with "The Saints," but, in the African tradition, his rhythms sparked spine-tingling musical electricity surging through the bodies and souls of both performers and listeners in a spirit circuit. "Of course his music is spiritual," says r&b queen Ruth Brown, who played many shows with Domino. "That's what he's about and always was. It made you want to *move.* There was nothing you could do; you *had* to move."

■ ■ ■

"Look, don't we have to be in Phoenix by eight?" asked a nervous Eddie Ray, adding, "Isn't it about five hundred miles from here?" He was drinking with Fats and his chauffeur Bernard Dunn in the Watkins Hotel. Domino laughed. Dunn raced them across the desert, arriving at the dance hall just as the band was finishing the warm-up. Ray wondered, "How do they do it and not get in an accident?" After the third day of touring, the Imperial salesman got on a plane and went home. "I'd go see them," says Ray, "but no more on the road with them!"

Ray promoted Domino's new hit "Don't You Know" and his grandly titled first extended-play record, *America's Outstanding Piano Stylist,* at a time when rhythm & blues albums were exceedingly rare. Domino's EP was a cheap sampler for teens, like Johnny Ramistella in Baton Rouge, who would find fame as "Johnny Rivers." "I used to get those little EPs," says Rivers. "They had four songs on 'em, two on each side. That was still considered r&b, it wasn't even rock 'n' roll yet."

In late March, at the same time that *Variety* asserted that rock 'n' roll would be "just a passing fancy by June," Fats recorded another crucial session at Abraham "Bunny" Robyn's Master Recorders Studio. Robyn, a classically trained musician, was an unusual engineer for rock 'n' roll. He found Domino agreeable and quiet, but he especially appreciated Bartholomew, an articulate arranger who knew his material, the musicians, and what he wanted. Lew Chudd depended upon Bartholomew to arrange the music and on Robyn to master the results for records. But for this session Chudd suggested that Domino rerecord an old Bartholomew song, "Blue Monday." "It's the description of a week of what a workingman does," says Chudd. "He works all week and he has a beer on Saturday night if he's lucky." It would become the favorite Domino recording of the Imperial triumvirate—Domino, Bartholomew, and Chudd.

Fats had met sax player Sam Lee, Harrison Verrett's cousin, at the Watkins Hotel and invited him to play on the session. Lee, nicknamed "Hold That Note" for his ability to play extended notes, was supposed to play the baritone solo on "Blue Monday," but the versatile Herbert Hardesty had to step in to play another classic solo. "'Blue Monday' is as close to perfection as one can imagine," music writer Hank Davis would later observe. "The eight-bar sax break is a gem of almost frightening economy. It is one of the most memorable, bluesy, and yet simple runs in all of r&b." Ironically, Hardesty had never played baritone saxophone before and didn't even like the instrument. The song was the third future #1 r&b hit that Domino recorded that month.

In the spring of 1955, the movie *Blackboard Jungle* became the nexus of the raging controversies over juvenile delinquency, school integration, and rhythm & blues. Clare Boothe Luce, the U.S. ambassador to Italy, managed to have it banned from the Venice Film Festival. Offended also by the sympathetic role played by Sidney Poitier, Memphis censor Lloyd T. Binford (who in 1947 had banned the jazz film *New Orleans* because of Louis Armstrong's role) called *Blackboard Jungle* "the vilest picture I've seen in 26 years as censor." The inclusion of Bill Haley's "Rock Around the Clock" in the film added to the controversy. Ironically, the first major media story on rock 'n' roll appeared in the April 18 edition of *Life* owned by Luce's husband, Henry Luce. One photo showed Herbert Hardesty lying on the floor of the 5-4 Ballroom in white shirtsleeves, blasting a solo in front of enraptured black fans at one of Domino's three recent sold-out weekends at the venue.

On May 1, Domino headlined a show over Ray Charles (then riding "I Got a Woman") at New Orleans' Labor Union Hall. The fans went wild as Domino segued from the wails of "Please Don't Leave Me" to "You Done Me Wrong." Tenoo rolled across his drums and stuck his tongue out at girls in the front row. The show stopped when a girl jumped on the stage and grabbed him. Women chased Fats and his musicians all over the country, a couple of them even following them from Fort Worth to Cleveland in a '55 Cadillac. They had local girlfriends, too; Domino's chauffeur and close friend Bernard Dunn even dated New Orleans' Sweetheart of the Blues, Shirley Goodman of Shirley and Lee. While at home, Domino began bar-hopping early in the morning, driving from one bar to the next, drinking with his card partners and flirting with women.

Then he would go home, rest awhile, change his clothes and his car, and head back out. When he finally got tired, he'd drive home. Frank Mulé's bar on Derbigny Street was his favorite of dozens of haunts, where Fats would drink, eat po-boy sandwiches, and play pinball. He trusted Mulé so much that he sometimes gave him checks for $5,000 or more to cash. Everyone greeted Domino, but few actually penetrated his aura of privacy to become close to him.

"Ain't That a Shame" (which Imperial incorrectly labeled "Ain't *It* a Shame") began an eleven-week stay at #1 on the *Billboard* r&b charts, just as the magazine reported that Fats was the first rock 'n' roller to be banned. An article titled "Fear of Rock-Roll Nixes Conn," reported that Bridgeport, Connecticut, police canceled Domino's May 22 dance at the Ritz ballroom after a near-riot at the New Haven Arena.

But Domino soon made even bigger news. Prior to the release of "Ain't That a Shame," Lew Chudd had sent an advance copy to Bill Randle. "He liked it because it was ignorant," says Chudd, "because he was an English professor at [Case] Western Reserve University." The deejay was again the catalyst for Domino's crossover through a connection with Randy Wood of Dot Records. "I got Pat Boone to cover that," says Randle. "I sent the acetate that I had of that to Randy through [distributor] Art Freeman. Again, it was a case of one day, *BAM! BAM! BAM!,* and the competition was on the street. I played both versions—both versions were #1 in Cleveland." At a time when pop stations would not play r&b, Randle was the driving force behind cover hits by Boone, the Crew Cuts, and the Diamonds, knowing that their success helped the black originators.

Boone was the scrub-faced self-admitted "ultimate WASP." He had at first tried a grammatical version of Domino's song in a Chicago recording studio. "I tried to change it to 'Isn't That a Shame!'" says a laughing Boone. "I was just transferred to Columbia University in New York and I was majoring in English." Better sense prevailed, and soon Boone recorded the song, officially titling it "Ain't That a Shame."

That summer, Domino heard Boone's record constantly. "When I first heard it I didn't like it," says Fats. "It took two months to write and he put it out almost the same time I did. It kind of hurt. The publishing companies don't care if a thousand people make it." Likewise, Bartholomew detested white cover versions, despite the substantial royalties he received from them. "Pat Boone was a lucky white boy," says Bartholomew. "He wasn't singing shit. Randy Wood was doing un-Constitutional type stuff. He was successful with it, but that don't make it right." But Boone's infamously bland covers of Domino and Little Richard were the beginning of the end of long-held music industry practices. Not only did glossy pop versions of r&b songs sound false to white teenagers, they reeked of discrimination, especially since black performers were so powerfully idiosyncratic that they simply couldn't be imitated. In fact, by mid-June, Lew Chudd called Domino saying, "Your record's going pop." Fats tried to comprehend. Despite Chudd's ongoing machinations to crack the pop market, Domino had never really considered selling records to whites. "He didn't know what a pop record was," says Chudd.

Chudd promoted "Ain't That a Shame" heavily, putting on the hard sell. He chartered an airplane for a cross-country promotional tour, hitting mostly pop radio stations in thirteen cities in nineteen days. "You have no idea what I went through changing 'race' records to 'pop' records," says Chudd. "Oh, boy, I fought like *hell*!" Upon hearing Domino's Creolese, deejays sometimes commented to Chudd, "He doesn't talk English." "It's New Orleans English!" argued Chudd. "What the hell! Haven't we taken the country down there yet?"

Meanwhile, Eddie Ray put on the soft sell, sometimes going on the air live in the studio with pop disc jockeys and smoothly spieling, "I got a new artist out of New Orleans who's gonna be another Louis Armstrong." The deejays were shocked to see an articulate black man promoting r&b and country records. Their expectations took another jolt when, instead of hearing a tasteful Satchmo-like recording or a Pat Boone–style big ballad, Domino's disk emitted booms that nearly shook their Mitch Miller and Perez Prado records off the racks. But the jocks soon had to play it themselves; young listeners weaned on pop pabulum called in droves to say that they liked the "new" version better than Pat Boone's.

At a restaurant one night, Domino and Bartholomew sat watching *The Tonight Show* with Steve Allen. Allen adjusted his glasses to read a "poem" like a freshman in interpretive speech. Allen looked earnestly at the camera and gushed his melodramatic reading of the remedial lyrics of "Ain't That a Shame." His studio audience laughed. The "poets" looked at each other sheepishly. "Steve Allen made us feel like shit," says Bartholomew. "He was making fun of us." But the New Orleans men would have the last laugh.

On July 9, Fats became only the second r&b artist (after Johnny Ace with "Pledging My Love") to capture the *Billboard* Triple Crown Award, topping the r&b sales, jukebox, and disc jockey charts. The next week, Domino again found himself at another historic crossroads, when his record followed Boone up the pop charts, eventually reaching #10. Imperial Records was red hot. Slim Whitman's "Rose Marie" became the best-selling record in England for 1955. Smiley Lewis scored his biggest r&b hit with "I Hear You Knocking," which Bartholomew had originally written for Domino in the backseat of his Cadillac near San Francisco.

Just as Domino had declined the song, he also turned down another hit when he played Robinson's Recreation Center in Abbeville, Louisiana. The audience was all black, except for a young Cajun with slicked-down hair and rolled-up jeans named Bobby Charles Guidry. After the show, seventeen-year-old Guidry offered Fats his song, "See You Later Alligator." But Fats just laughed at the lyric about the swampland carnivore. Guidry was disappointed, though he would soon record the song himself as "Bobby Charles."

Whites were now common at Domino's shows. After a northern tour including several white clubs, Fats played the Pentagon Ballroom in New Orleans on Saturday, September 17. After the show, he hung out at the Dew Drop Inn, where he would play a piano instrumental, eat fried chicken, play pinball, or even flash a roll of thousand-dollar bills to impress the owner, Frank Painia. That night he met Specialty Records producer Bumps Blackwell, who himself had just made music history; three days earlier, he had recorded Little Richard's world-wrecking "Tutti Frutti" with the New Orleans musicians at Cosimo Matassa's studio. "The Fats Domino concert was jammed," Blackwell wrote in a letter to Art Rupe of Specialty Records. "It was the first all-white rock 'n' roll concert—so 'blues' has definitely gone 'white' here also. All of the white spots have now changed to 'colored' bands." Dallas promoter Howard Lewis, whose top artist was Domino, likewise reported to *Variety* that whites now outnumbered blacks at his r&b shows at a rate of three-to-one. "For those who say that the music with a beat is doing terrible things to the nation's youth," wrote Ruth Cage in *Down Beat,* "it might be pointed out that this music is doing a job in the Deep South that even the U.S. Supreme Court hasn't been able to accomplish."

On September 23, Domino recorded another #1 r&b hit, "Poor Me." Three weeks after that, he recorded yet another.

■ ■ ■

"Take one." A short, balding Italian American spoke from behind the glass window of a closet-sized control room. Cosimo Matassa, who had already recorded historic records by Roy Brown, Professor Longhair, Lloyd Price, Shirley and Lee, Ray Charles, Guitar Slim, Jerry Lee Lewis, Joe Turner, and Little Richard at his J&M Studio, now engineered one of the most important sessions for his biggest client, Domino. Though his equipment was never state-of-the-art, Matassa was a great engineer. As Dave Bartholomew says, "Cosimo *had* to be a great architect."

Domino sang what almost sounded like a Cajun two-step, the bouncy "Bo Weevil." At one microphone stood saxmen Lee Allen, Herbert Hardesty, and Clarence Ford. In the corner were guitarist Ernest McLean, bass player Frank Fields, and drummer Earl Palmer. The final mike was on Domino. Behind the glass next to Matassa, Bartholomew instructed McLean to play a real hillbilly guitar lick.

Domino next recorded the two-beat rocker "I Can't Go On (Rosalie)," which *Cash Box* would call "of the 'Maybellene' school." Chuck Berry's recent crossover hit was so country that he was tagged "the black Hank Snow." Similarly, Domino's barnyard novelties "Bo Weevil" and "The Rooster Song" (both inspired by old black folk songs) reflected the rural setting of his childhood. Fats is almost country & western," says Bartholomew. "That's one reason Fats is so successful, because that country music never dies in him."

Domino had a song called "I'm in Love Again" that needed lyrics. During a break, the musicians listened to records in Cosimo's music shop. Frank Fields picked up a screwdriver and resumed his part-time job repairing televisions. When they returned to the studio, Lee Allen played a rock-solid tenor solo on "I'm in Love Again." Then Fats impishly threw in a line inspired by one of the records he had just heard: *"Baby, don't you let your dog bite me!"* Once again Bartholomew was not impressed with a future #1 r&b hit. "I said the song would be shit," he says, "and I was wrong."

Fats was soon riding west in a white convertible El Dorado Cadillac that displayed the word "FATS" and crossed dominos on the trunk. The car was a gift from promoter Howard Lewis for all the money Domino had made him. Ray Charles opened for him again, this time in Texas and Oklahoma. In Arizona, Fats even performed at the Navajo reservation, where he ran into his friend Dennis "Big Chief" Alley at a huge tribal dome. The fans erupted when he sang "Along the Navaho Trail."

In late October and November, Fats played the 5-4 Ballroom and r&b deejay Hunter Hancock's Los Angeles TV show *Rhythm & Bluesville*. Hancock presented Fats with his second *Billboard* top r&b artist award in as many years, with "Ain't That a Shame" named the top record. Articles in the awards issue of *Billboard* noted a greater integration in popular music than in America as a whole. But the news didn't help Domino's #1 r&b hit "All by Myself," which failed to make the pop charts, despite cover versions by Eddie Fisher, Vaughn Monroe, and Roy Hall. Nor did it help Smiley Lewis, whose "I Hear You Knocking" made #2 on the r&b charts, while Gale Storm's version made #2 on the pop charts. Segregation was still the rule in pop music. Reflecting the song's lyric, black artists were knocking, but, for the most part, they couldn't come in.

While staying at the Watkins Hotel, Domino met one of his biggest fans. "Fats, let me play you my record!" exclaimed Little Richard in the Rubyiat Lounge, banging out "Tutti Frutti" on the piano. "He [Domino] was *everything* to me," says Richard. "I felt honored just to shake his hand. I *still* feel that way about Fats Domino." Fats didn't know the flamboyant singer from Adam (or Eve), but he was impressed by "Tutti Frutti," especially when he learned it was recorded in New Orleans with Lee Allen blowing the sax and Earl Palmer pounding the drums. "Don't worry, Richard," Fats assured him after hearing the song, "your record's gonna be a hit."

Lew Chudd labeled Fats "The King!" in a November *Cash Box* ad for "Poor Me," Domino's third straight #1 r&b hit. Nationally, Domino's only serious rocking competition was Bill Haley and the Comets. A midwestern tour booked by Colonel Tom Parker in October featured Haley (billed as "The Nation's No. 1 RHYTHM & BLUES ARTIST"), Hank Snow, and "Elvis Presley with Scotty & Bill" third on the bill. Alan Freed declared himself "The King of Rock 'n' Roll," though his kingdom was confined to New York. He was still not as influential nationally as Bill Randle, who filmed Haley, Pat Boone, and Presley for his legendary unreleased short film, *The Pied Piper of Cleveland,* and was a key player in Presley's signing by RCA-Victor in November and the booking of his crucial *Stage Show* TV appearances. "Rock Around the Clock" and movies kept Haley popular, but he reached the top ten for the last time in early 1956 with a song that Domino had turned down, "See You Later Alligator."

■ ■ ■

On December 1, 1955, Rosa Parks refused to move to the back of a Montgomery, Alabama, bus. She followed the legacy of Homer Plessy, the New Orleans Creole whose attempt to integrate Louisiana's trains more than sixty years earlier had led to the "separate but equal" ruling that Parks now sought to overturn. On that same day, another Creole, attorney A. P. Tureaud, argued the *Bush v. Orleans Parish School Board* lawsuit in federal court, seeking full integration of the Macarty School, which Domino had once attended. Within a few days, the then little-known Reverend Martin Luther King, Jr., consulted with the National Baptist Convention Secretary, Reverend Theodore Jemison, who over two years earlier had led the first mass civil rights protest in the South, the Baton Rouge bus boycott. King was preparing for a similar boycott in Montgomery.

In that landmark week for civil rights, the pop top ten included "Sixteen Tons," "Love Is a Many-Splendored Thing," "Love and Marriage," and "The Yellow Rose of Texas." Only two songs on the top ten had a rhythm & blues connection—"Only You" by the Platters and "I Hear You Knocking" by Gale Storm. Both songs borrowed Domino's triplets and Bartholomew's bass line. Incredibly, New Orleans with its one small recording studio *ruled* the *Billboard* r&b charts that week. The top fifteen r&b charts, exemplifying Alan Freed's rock 'n' roll, included *seven* New Orleans records: "Feel So Good" by Shirley and Lee, "I Hear You Knocking" by Smiley Lewis, "Poor Me"/"I Can't Go On" and "All By Myself" by Domino, "Witchcraft" by the Spiders, "Those Lonely, Lonely Nights" by Earl King, and "Tutti Frutti" by Little Richard. It was a prophetic moment, as for the next two years the city's rhythmic and vocal influences would *power* the sound of rock 'n' roll.

Henry David Thoreau, whose essay *Civil Disobedience* inspired the passive resistance of both Gandhi and Martin Luther King, Jr., wrote, "If a man does not keep pace with his companions perhaps it is because he hears a different drummer." The influences of Congo Square suggested in Domino's earliest recordings were again unleashed. With supernaturally synchronous timing with the civil rights movement, a cultural revolution brewing for centuries was channeled into music. The fusillades were rhythms. The war cries were led by Little Richard's talking drum howl, *"AWOPBOPALOOBOPAWOPBAMBOOM!"*

Lew Chudd was now obsessed with making another crossover hit. He went to lunch with publishers who encouraged him to record their hoary standards. He passed their suggestions on to Bartholomew, who showed the sheet music for the songs to Domino. Fats, who often listened to pop radio stations, didn't need much convincing. His musical mentor, Harrison Verrett, carried a black book of songs that he had played with Papa Celestin. "Harrison used to tell me always to play some of those standard old songs because they never die," says Domino. The day before Christmas Eve, 1955, he recorded "My Blue Heaven," an enormous 1927 pop hit by Gene Austin that had even been in the repertoire of blues icon Robert Johnson. Eschewing Austin's violin prelude, Domino pounded one power chord and tore into a solidly hewn two-beat rhythm. The colorful lyrics added warm imagery to his persona, as he sang in his thick Creole accent. The song was an end-run on the guardians of popular music. New Orleans musicians had once scandalized America by adding anarchic jazz horns and rhythms to pop standards. Now Domino's wall of rhythms would *rock* pop songs. "We had the young people," says Bartholomew, "and we were out to get the older people in." The old ASCAP music publishers would reap huge royalties from Domino's versions of their standards, but the all-white musical ethos that they represented would soon lose the larger war.

Chapter 8

"My Blue Heaven"

(Early 1956)

"The obscenity and vulgarity of the rock 'n' roll music is obviously a means by which the white man can be driven to the level of the nigger."
> —ASA "ACE" CARTER OF THE ALABAMA WHITE CITIZENS' COUNCIL, MARCH 1956

"Eeny, meeny, and miney moe, told me you didn't want me around no more."
> —FATS DOMINO, "I'M IN LOVE AGAIN," MARCH 1956

The symbols of segregation were everywhere in the South. Restaurants, theaters, buses, restrooms, and water fountains all had signs enforcing the racial divide. In the cities, ramshackle ghettoes and run-down schools were heart-sickening symbols of inequality. In the country, shacks near fields of crops were continuing reminders of the former evils of slavery. Domino performed in a Mississippi town with the prime symbol of racial terrorism staring him in the face: *the rope.*

A century earlier, the rope had been used for binding cotton or those who picked it. After Reconstruction, it became the weapon of choice for brutal lynchings initiated on the slightest whim. Mississippi was the home of the blues for good reason; it was the scene of more than 500 such lynchings. Recently, though, the former redneck mob bloodsport had turned to cowardly murders. In March 1955, and again a year later, NAACP leaders were furtively shot dead there. In August 1955, Emmett Till, a fourteen-year-old black boy from Chicago, was brutally beaten to death for saying "Bye, baby" to a white woman.

The weapons of oppression were now primarily symbolic intimidation. Now the rope merely divided. At Domino's show, the rope ran down the middle of the nightclub. Whites danced on one side, blacks danced on the other.

Fats Domino's dance-defying rhythms laughed at the blues. Everyone swayed to his euphoric music and the dancers started knocking down the rope. Alarmed, the sheriff tried to put it back up, but the mayor stopped him, saying it was all right because, "Everybody here knows each other." The dancers kept dancing, now mixing freely. Domino's valet, Raymond Allen, was astonished. "I had never seen this before!" recalls Allen. "It was so shocking. And it was beautiful. It was beautiful!"

Even in black neighborhoods, white teenagers now appeared regularly at Domino's shows. "Fats *made* integration," says Billy Diamond. "Fats was the Martin Luther King of music. He brought whites and blacks together, Indians, everything."

"Everywhere Fats went he tore up the place," adds Eddie Ray. "He'd go to Klamath Falls [Oregon], and it'd be packed with Indians. He'd go to Colorado and Arizona, and it'd be packed with Mexicans. He was an absolute superstar." As Herbert Hardesty concludes, "When people get started dancing and having a good time, they don't care what color you are."

In his State of the Union address on January 5, President Eisenhower announced for the first time that he favored a Civil Rights bill. But despite integration rumblings, the white status quo seemed invulnerable. Though Dave Bartholomew had made a major breakthrough for a black songwriter with two of the top ten pop songs for 1955, he still viewed white cover versions as a form of discrimination. *Down Beat*'s Ruth Cage suggested that the music's new name was itself becoming a segregation symbol: "Rock 'n' roll is what you get when somebody lifts a piece of material from a 'rhythm & blues' performer."

Neither of Domino's last two #1 r&b hits, "All by Myself" and "Poor Me," scratched the pop charts, but strange things were happening. Teens gagging on Pat Boone's ultra-vanilla version of "Tutti Frutti" opened the pop inner sanctum to Little Richard's banshee wails, which joined the African American physical and spiritual worlds at the crossroads in a time of crisis and catharsis. Just as Roy Brown's cries had transformed black music, Richard's even wilder yells, when coupled with a bludgeoning New Orleans beat, revolutionized pop. "Tutti Frutti" was launched from Cosimo Matassa's J&M studio past all the banging, clanking prototypes, redefining rock 'n' roll as shouting music with a driving backbeat. Even Fats noticed the change. "We played a slow number, they called it 'rhythm & blues,'" he says. "We played a fast number, they called it 'rock 'n' roll.'"

The crossover of the earth-shaking rhythms was the *Gotterdammerung* for European-rooted popular music. "It just would not have occurred to [whites] to pound a piano the way Little Richard or Fats Domino does," wrote music scholar Jonathan Kamin, noting that such r&b instrumentation reflected the African tradition "to use non-percussion instruments percussively." The pounding kept repairmen busy. In Kansas City, New Orleanian O. J. Dodds told a convention of aghast piano tuners horror stories about replacing bass strings broken by the hammering of rock 'n' roll.

Domino concluded his nightly revolution with a smile, which, rock historian Dave Marsh writes, had always made black performers more welcome, adding, "Fats' singing style amounted to one long, gregarious grin." But the unearthly look and persona of Little Richard was, in contrast, as subtle as a Martian landing on the White House lawn for tea with Ike and Mamie, a fact that would pave the way for his imitators, who were not so outrageous, or so *black*.

■ ■ ■

The more success that Domino achieved, the worse certain of his habits became. When he was drinking or seeing women, he was not only late for shows, he sometimes missed them altogether. His impatient fans would scream, stomp, or even riot. Billy Diamond begged Fats to be on time, but he was fighting a losing battle with his headstrong bandleader.

In January 1956, the problem reached a breaking point. As the band waited in the station wagon to hit the road for its next gig, Fats procrastinated for three hours in a Kansas City hotel room. With 300 miles to cover in snowy conditions to get to that night's show, Diamond got fed up with Fats and quit the band. "He didn't want to listen to me," says Diamond. "You're behind the gun all the time, and he's never ready." Billy had filled many shoes. Herbert Hardesty became the band's driver, and Bernard Dunn became road manager, but they were short a bass player.

While Fats toured the Midwest, Elvis Presley, the first white to truly sound and *move* like a black rocker, made his television debut on the Dorsey Brothers' *Stage Show*, introduced by Bill Randle. Elvis shocked America with his pelvic motions and heavy-rhythmed r&b covers. He soon recorded "Lawdy Miss Clawdy," "Shake, Rattle and Roll," "Tutti Frutti," and three other Little

Richard songs. Presley's TV appearances paralleled the bizarre 1954 CBS television production of Mark Twain's *The Adventures of Huckleberry Finn,* which, in startling evidence of Ralph Ellison's *Invisible Man* thesis, totally omitted the black slave Jim; the producers portrayed Huck riding a raft down the Mississippi by himself, thus eviscerating the revolutionary soul of the book—Huck and Jim seeking freedom together. Racists, who threatened television sponsors, pressured networks to exclude blacks. Though Ed Sullivan later censored Elvis from the waist down, some black rockers, most notably Little Richard, were censored altogether from network TV in the 1950s.

On radio, though, the integration continued. In fact, a revolutionary crossover was going *both ways.* Many blacks thought that "Blue Suede Shoes" by Carl Perkins and "Heartbreak Hotel" by Elvis Presley were by black men. Both songs, with stop-time, call-and-response structures remarkably similar to "Ain't That a Shame," climbed the r&b charts. As winter turned into spring, some listeners thought Frankie Lymon, the singer on the Teenagers' "Why Do Fools Fall in Love," was a white girl. The Platters became the first r&b act to score a pop #1, the triplet-driven tear-jerker "The Great Pretender." "People in the South did not know we were black until we got on *The Ed Sullivan Show,*" says Paul Robi of the Platters, "and by that time it was too late."

A *Cash Box* editorial, "Rock and Roll May Be the Great UNIFYING FORCE," praised the musical mixing: "We in the music business can be very proud of this development, for it is rock 'n' roll which is instigating it all. It is the music business which is so vitally affecting the entire entertainment world and, by extension of that, the lives of everyone in our country."

Most adults, however, did not view integration so favorably. Even in the North and other predominantly white sections of the country, the influx of black culture was an unwelcome jolt to the status quo. The Red Scare was joined by *The Black Scare.* Tension was heavy in the South as a mass boycott of the Montgomery, Alabama, bus system began, led by Martin Luther King, Jr. Riots erupted as Autherine Lucy, a black student, attempted to enroll at the University of Alabama.

Not even a delirious New Orleans street party like Mardi Gras was immune from controversy. The Krewe of Zulu, under heavy pressure for degrading Negroes in a time of racial tension, expressed shock at the rap—and paraded as usual in grass skirts and blackface makeup, while throwing the prized painted Zulu coconuts from their parade floats.

The next day, February 15, 1956, New Orleanians awoke on a rainy Ash Wednesday to news of Judge J. Skelly Wright's ruling on the *Bush v. Orleans Parish School Board* lawsuit. Wright, who was ridiculed as "J. Skelly Wrong" or "Judas Scalawag" for his courageous rulings, became the first district judge in the Deep South to order the integration of local schools "with all deliberate speed." Four days later, at the first Sunday mass in the Lenten season, priests read a letter from New Orleans Archbishop Joseph Rummel that shocked the half million Catholics in his archdiocese with the words, "Racial segregation as such is morally wrong and sinful." That night on the archbishop's lawn, a cross was burning.

Enraged by both the bus boycott and r&b crossovers, the White Citizens' Council in Birmingham, Alabama, held a rally in March, charging that rock 'n' roll was a plot by the NAACP to introduce "nigger bop" to white teens. Its leader, Asa "Ace" Carter, called and threatened New Orleans radio stations. Carter was interviewed live on WNOE, where the white disc jockeys defended the music. One of them, Dave Banks, later interviewed Dave Bartholomew, who called the conspiracy theory "laughable," pointing out that the record companies that sold r&b were owned by whites, not the NAACP. "New Orleanians, white and Negro, feel they've cut their teeth on rhythm & blues," wrote Banks in *Down Beat,* "and are quick to resent any attempt to drag a legitimate musical expression into the realm of hate politics. We'll keep right on rockin' and rollin'. . . "

In response to the integration developments, the newly formed Citizens' Council of Greater New Orleans held a rally on March 20 in Municipal Auditorium that drew 8,000 Confederate flag–waving whites singing "Dixie" on the former site of Congo Square. The Council, led by powerful Plaquemines Parish boss Leander Perez, issued a flyer:

NOTICE!
STOP
Help Save The Youth of America
DON'T BUY NEGRO RECORDS
(If you don't want to serve Negroes in your place of business,
then do not have Negro records on your jukebox or listen
to Negro records on the radio.)
The screaming, idiotic words, and savage music of these records are
undermining the morals of our white youth in America.

Call the advertisers of the radio stations that play this type of music
and complain to them!
Don't Let Your Children Buy, or Listen
To These Negro Records

Though the anti–rock 'n' roll campaigns of the Citizens' Councils appeared ludicrous, their other actions were no laughing matter. The New Orleans Citizens' Council became the largest anti-integration group in the South, though segregationists had suffered a setback with the reelection of eccentric Governor Earl K. Long, who was single-handedly responsible for registering the vast majority of the state's 160,000 black voters. State Senator Willie Rainach and the Citizens' Councils waged a successful war against the threat to "our historical Southern Social Institutions." They soon suppressed Louisiana's NAACP, disqualified thousands of black voters, and intimidated all opposition.

Domino fought his own small integration battle. As he toured the country, he heard his song "Bo Weevil" on the radio. Lew Chudd had heavily promoted the record to L.A. pop disc jockeys like Al Jarvis of KFWB and Jim Ameche of KLAC (who posed with Fats for a *Cash Box* cover photo). But it was a chirpy white cover version by perky songstress Teresa Brewer that Fats heard most often. Like the Krewe of Zulu, the song spoofed stereotypes. In black folklore the boll weevil was a trickster, a subversive little bugger making a home in the white man's money crop, cotton. As Mahalia Jackson wrote in her autobiography, "God sent the boll weevil to jumble" the plantation owners, who went bankrupt. Domino was still taking a backseat—Brewer's version reached #5, while his original barely dented the top 40. But, like its namesake burrowing into a plump white cotton boll, "Bo Weevil" was a crucial entrée for Domino back into the pop charts.

■ ■ ■

Lawrence Guyton, who had previously played with Domino at Club Desire, replaced Billy Diamond on bass, taking a train to meet the band in Knoxville, Tennessee. Guyton, who had struggled to play modern jazz, thought he was joining "The Big Time." But, after a couple of weeks of Domino's hard road life, he was soon asking, "When are we gonna go home?"

Guyton walked up to a window marked "COLORED" and picked up a sandwich and a drink. He took his meal and walked to the band's table in the kitchen of the nightclub where they would be "stars" later that night. His salary of $21 a night would have been great money at home, but he had to pay for his suit, food, room, and laundry before sending money home. He ate sardines and crackers and slept crossways on beds to save money.

"Man, I don't know how much longer I can take this!" complained Guyton. "Look at Elvis and Pat Boone, they ain't gotta go through this! And their groups ain't got to go through what we go through!"

The Domino veterans were silent. They were used to such treatment.

Travel anywhere in the South was difficult for blacks. The musicians stocked up on nonperishable food items to avoid worrying about the next place that might serve blacks. Fats filled a cooler with bologna, ham, beer, and other drinks. The musicians asked any black they saw about sleeping accommodations. "Sometimes we had to go 100 miles out of the way to get a place to stay," recalls Fats. Though Domino himself was ostensibly treated well, he too was hurt by the cold knife edge of segregation that cut them away from white society.

Domino ran into a different sort of trouble in Hartford, Connecticut. Starting on March 23, 1956, Fats headlined a three-day Alan Freed show at the State Theater that included the Cadillacs, the Harptones, the Turbans, and the Teenagers, who were making their debut. Wearing white sweaters bearing the scarlet letter "T," the Teenagers firmly established the adolescent role in rock 'n' roll. Thirteen-year-old Frankie Lymon slid across the stage, knocking out a stage light with his foot. At the climax, Fats drove the crowd into a frenzy. Eleven fans were arrested that weekend, mostly for dancing uncontrollably to the rousing reveille of rock 'n' roll. One twenty-one-year-old fan stood up in his seat and began howling, leading to a fight. Alarmed Hartford officials held a hearing to revoke the theater's license. Psychiatrist Dr. Francis Braceland testified that rock 'n' roll was "a communicable disease with music appealing to adolescent insecurity and driving teenagers to do outlandish things. It is cannibalistic and tribalistic."

■ ■ ■

A bus proclaiming the RHYTHM & BLUES SHOW OF 1956 drove into the former capital of the Confederacy, Richmond, Virginia. On the conjunction of Easter Sunday and April Fool's Day, a show there began a tour promoted by Lou Krefetz and Eli Weinberg with the Shaw Booking Agency. Placards on telephone poles shouted the line-up: FATS DOMINO, RUTH BROWN, THE

CLOVERS, THE CADILLACS, THE TURBANS, LITTLE RICHARD, and LITTLE WILLIE JOHN.

Backstage that night, Domino met Washington, D.C., record store owner Irvin Feld, whose continent-sweeping Biggest Show of Stars tours made him the top rock 'n' roll promoter in the land. Feld reminded him to play "I'm in Love Again." Fats was surprised—the flipside "My Blue Heaven" was the big hit in the North.

White boys in crew cuts and plaid shirts and white girls in starched dresses looked down from the balcony at the blacks on the floor. The r&b stars put on two shows, with each act performing a few songs, culminating with a booming half-hour set by Domino. The promoters took in $12,180 after taxes in Richmond—an impressive haul. The next show in Charlotte, North Carolina, drew $19,064, with a total attendance of 11,649—1,000 more teens than a Bill Haley show with the Platters, LaVern Baker, Shirley and Lee, the Drifters, Joe Turner, and Bo Diddley had attracted there in January. The promoters knew that even with only a couple of pop hits, Fats brought out whites in droves. The tour played theaters, armories, VFW halls, municipal buildings, and new auditoriums built as the country boomed along new highways. As dances became too big, rock 'n' roll shows became "concerts," in a vain attempt to confine teens to their seats and prevent race mixing.

The barnstorming tours with a busload of black stars gave new meaning to the phrase "grueling one-nighters." The Italian-American bus driver would stop at white restaurants that didn't allow blacks and order takeout for everybody. Or Ruth Brown played den mother, making sandwiches from groceries bought at a roadside store. "We used to have a ball on the bus!" recalls Herbert Hardesty. "They would gamble and shoot dice all night. Nobody got any sleep." Domino still rode in his Cadillac. He spent his time in his car drinking, eating, sleeping, playing cards, and listening to the radio, his crucial link to popular music. Once, a girl came up to Domino after a show. She held his car antenna in her hand, explaining that she had to have a souvenir. Fats politely declined her offer to pay for it, but inwardly he thought of the next 300 miles without a radio.

Domino soon had worse car trouble. As Bernard Dunn and Herbert Hardesty drove his El Dorado to Washington, D.C., the rear wheels caught on fire. They spotted a D.C. fire station down the street. The white firemen looked at the black men driving the luxury car they themselves couldn't afford. They told them that the car was across the line in Virginia and out of their jurisdiction. Domino's Cadillac burned to a shell while they waited for a fire truck from Richmond.

Still, the band members went sight-seeing in the capital before their show at the Howard Theater. At the Dunbar, the city's best black hotel, Fats cooked on his hot plate. Walking around the White House, Congress, and the Lincoln Memorial, the black men experienced something they rarely felt—pride in being American. Returning to the hotel, the musicians smelled a spicy aroma wafting down the hall. They lined up for Domino's red beans and rice, thick with ham hocks and sausage.

Domino's first album, a collection of hits titled *Rock and Rollin' with Fats Domino* with a woodcut drawing of Fats on the cover, appeared in April. The words "A Robyn Recording" on the back suggested that Hollywood engineer Bunny Robyn produced the record. There was no mention of Bartholomew, though he was more concerned "about what went on the inside."

As Bill Simon noted in *Billboard,* many credited Domino "with starting the whole business of triplets." The triplet beat became the primary rhythmic underpinning for ballads that kept dancers swaying for years to come. "Fats made it popular," says Bartholomew, "then it was on every record." Stan Freberg's parody of "The Great Pretender" featured a jazzbo pianist (voiced by Freberg) who detested "that *cling-cling-cling* jazz." After playing the physically demanding triplets at length, he cried, "My hand is falling off, man!" Freberg's actual session pianist, Ella Fitzgerald sideman Paul Smith, soaked his hands in ice water between takes and couldn't play for three days afterward. "The rhythm & blues guys were really being looked down upon by the jazz musicians," says saxophonist Gene "Daddy G" Barge (the soloist with Gary U.S. Bonds). "They talked about Fats Domino like a *dog;* they really did—playing those triplets on the piano. . . . They said, 'Who is this idiot? . . . That's not music!' The same things that guys are saying about rap, they were saying about rhythm & blues." Jazz musicians ridiculed piano triplets as numbingly repetitive, but, as musicologist John Storm Roberts writes, "Those who use the word 'monotonous' in criticism of black music are on the wrong cultural wavelength." Contrary to the overemphasis on improvisation by jazz critics, the *dominant* African-based musical tradition was always in strong, persistent rhythms. There was a ritual effect to the repetition in the call-and-response that emphasized social bonding, which was crucial in the Civil Rights era, especially as that bonding crossed racial and cultural lines more than any music before. But Domino's music also incorporated a variety of influences from blues, boogie, country, pop, big band, jump, jazz, and Latin music. As Simon concluded, Fats experimented with "all varieties of beats and rhythms, always looking for something different."

With his new record, Domino had a two-sided pop and r&b smash hit. "My Blue Heaven" became the paradigm for the rocking of pop standards. As Chudd and Bartholomew hoped, it gained him adult fans. With a feisty vocal, a howling Lee Allen tenor solo, and a throbbing beat, "I'm in Love Again" steam-rolled a lame cover by the Fontane Sisters and bulled up the pop charts in late April in a twenty-three-week run peaking at #3. It would later be recorded by Pat Boone, Bill Haley, Ricky Nelson, Little Richard, Carl Perkins, Johnny Rivers, Randy Newman, and Paul McCartney. Fats Domino had crossed over to pop for good.

The song's seemingly nonsensical words hid deeper implications. Like Little Richard's suggestive lyrics, Domino's complaint that he needed love like a mad dog surprisingly passed censorship. Fats also twisted an old racist children's rhyme: *"Eeny, meeny, miney moe, catch a nigger by the toe . . ."* just as Asa Carter of the Alabama White Citizens' Council made headlines suggesting that rock 'n' roll was reducing teenagers "to the level of the nigger." Fats sang, *"Eeny, meeny, and miney moe, told me you didn't want me around no more,"* as if he were commenting on segregation and the backlash against rock 'n' roll.

The Rhythm & Blues Show traveled for five weeks, winding from the East Coast into Toronto on April 10. The tour rambled from the Midwest into Texas and down to New Orleans, where people were "dancing in the aisles [and] jumping up in the seats." Everyone enjoyed the show except for the terminally starchy black writer Elgin Hychew of *The Louisiana Weekly*, who decried black fans "acting like savages and non-human beings" at the April 22 concert at Loyola University Field House.

In Memphis, the shows were totally segregated; the first performance for whites, the second for blacks. By showtime, Domino had not arrived. Musicians were playing cards and smoking backstage. The white teenagers were restless. They clapped, stomped, and hollered: "W-E W-A-N-T F-A-T-S-!-!"

Little Richard, whose second New Orleans–recorded hit, "Long Tall Sally," sat at #1 on the r&b charts and was overtaking Pat Boone on the pop charts, tried to save the night. "Little Richard took it upon himself to go out there and sing Domino's songbook damn near!" laughs Harold Winley of the Clovers. "When he got through they said, 'WHERE'S FATS?!' You know, it's like sayin', 'Yeah, but!'" Throughout the tour, Little Richard assailed the keyboard and screamed. "He would jump on top of the piano!" laughs Fats. "He was a real great entertainer." Richard would soon head back to New Orleans to record the all-time classics "Rip It Up," "Ready Teddy," and "Lucille." He was a nuclear

force, but Domino was the crucial mortar that held all of the audiences together—rhythm & blues, rock 'n' roll, black, white, young, and, soon, even old.

A full-scale riot occurred at the American Legion Auditorium in Roanoke,
Virginia, on May 4. Over 2,000 white teens tried to squeeze into the balcony to
see the all-black show headlined by Domino. Half of the whites went downstairs where blacks were seated. Some even started dancing among the blacks.
As Domino concluded the three-hour show at 1:15 A.M., somebody in the balcony threw a bottle down at the mixed crowd. With whiskey bottles soon "flying through the air as thick as hailstones," Fats ducked behind the piano. Fights
spilled into the streets near the Dumas Hotel, where the performers stayed. The
rioters broke seats, light fixtures, and windows. Three dozen policemen arrested
four whites and two blacks.

After the show, the American Legion banned integrated shows. The
Roanoke City Council likewise discussed a ban in light of the "racial sentiment
over the [Supreme] court decision." *The New York Times* dismissed the riot as a
"Negro affair." Adults tried to ignore the cutting-edge changes that the music
was causing.

The tour ended soberly the next day in Birmingham. On April 10, members of the White Citizens' Council had assaulted Nat "King" Cole during a
concert there. In the wake of all the violence, Domino's Rhythm & Blues Show
was canceled. A month later, at a Bill Haley–led show in Birmingham, white
teens bravely counter-protested segregationists, one of whom carried a sign that
read "ROCK 'N' ROLL BREEDS INTEGRATION."

■ ■ ■

Domino was relieved to go home. After sleeping heavily he played with his six
kids and enjoyed Rosemary's cooking. He helped his six-year-old son, Antoine,
III., who was learning to play piano and drums.

On May 25, Fats Domino rocked the Guy Lombardo standard "When My
Dreamboat Comes Home" nearly beyond recognition in a session at Cosimo
Matassa's new Governor Nicholls Avenue studio, on the eastern edge of the
French Quarter. "Cosimo's" was roomier than J&M, though still primitive—the
recordings were still single-track mono. Lacking an air-conditioner, the studio
was cooled by fans blowing over huge blocks of ice in the torrid Louisiana heat.

During May, the Louisiana Legislature passed a raft of anti-integration bills
banning integration in all social activities, including television's "Communist

technique of brain-washing for racial integration." Meanwhile, New York news-papers blasted Elvis Presley's TV appearances. However, the powers-that-be continued to underestimate the subversive power of radio.

Shortly before Rosemary gave birth to another girl, Anola, on June 10, Fats "integrated" a huge all-white high school prom held in a hangar at Ryan Air-port in Baton Rouge, ground zero for all the racial legislation. Future rock 'n' roll stars Jimmy Clanton, John Fred, and Johnny Rivers heard Domino per-form like a living jukebox. Papoose impressed the young guitarists with his Gibson Les Paul and his shiny gold tooth.

On June 23, Billy Shaw of the Shaw Booking Agency died of a heart attack. He was memorialized as a "good friend to the Negro." His son, Milton, who had delved so deep in the world of black musicians that he spoke jive talk and shot heroin, took over the company and put out a "Not for Sale" sign in *Billboard*.

Traveling to California in late June, Domino met Alex Gordon, a movie producer for the low-budget movie studio American International Pictures at a show in the L.A. suburb of Ontario. AIP's competitor, Sam Katzman at Colum-bia, would premiere the first real rock 'n' roll film, *Rock Around the Clock,* in July. When Gordon explained that Fats would get $1,500 for performing three songs, Domino said he had an open day in a couple of weeks.

When Fats played his old haunt the 5-4 Ballroom with Ray Charles open-ing, Lew Chudd reserved him a suite in the Garden of Allah at 8152 Sunset Boulevard. The Hollywood landmark, consisting of an apartment building and several Spanish-style bungalows, had been the haunt of every movie star imagi-nable, but Domino was uneasy in the white hotel. On the first day he called Chudd three times saying, "I can't go outside!" The Imperial owner took him to two other white venues: an upscale restaurant, Romanoff's, and a music pub-lishing convention. "I was making a stand for him, so he wouldn't be afraid," says Chudd. "You might laugh at it now, but it was very, very serious. You have to go through it to appreciate it. I was aware he wasn't welcome everywhere."

On the afternoon of Wednesday, June 27, Fats tried to play the old stan-dard "Blueberry Hill" at Master Recorders in Hollywood. First recorded by Gene Autry in 1940 for the film *The Singing Hill,* the song was a #1 hit for Glenn Miller that year. Louis Armstrong recorded it with the Gordon Jenkins Orchestra in New York in 1949. Fats had heard Louis Armstrong's version and was determined to one day record the song. But he couldn't remember all of the words, so Harrison Verrett played it through on the piano, once again teaching him chord changes. Domino devised a beautiful piano introduction ending

Antoine, about the same age, wearing his first suit (courtesy of Antoine "Fats" Domino).

The young Antoine Domino, Jr., about age nine, circa 1937. He was about to encounter something that would become a major part of the rest of his life—a piano (courtesy of Antoine "Fats" Domino; restoration by Jason Kruppa).

The Industrial Canal levee that served as the extended front yard for five Domino families—it was Antoine Domino's playground until he moved to Caffin Avenue after his marriage in 1947. Though the Domino families enjoyed their proximity to the levee and the canal, that nearness also led to disaster for them in Hurricane Betsy in 1965 and in Hurricane Katrina forty years later (photograph by author).

Antoine Domino and (left) Harrison Verrett, the brother-in-law who taught him to play piano, on their trip to California in 1945, when Antoine was seventeen and playing boogie woogie on every piano he could find. The sign "Hollywood Air Lines" is above the head of Domino, who would later earn one of the first stars in the Hollywood Walk of Fame in 1960 (courtesy of Antoine "Fats" Domino).

A skinny Antoine Domino and Robert "Buddy" Hagans, his first band member, soon after they started playing music together, circa 1946. Note that Domino (left) is dressed in patched mechanic's overalls and Hagans is still wearing his army uniform (courtesy of Antoine "Fats" Domino).

Rosemary Hall, the seventeen-year-old beauty who would enter Domino's life and become his wife on August 6, 1947. They would still be married nearly sixty years later (courtesy of Antoine "Fats" Domino).

The Hideaway Club in New Orleans, where Antoine Domino rocked the house every Friday, Saturday, and Sunday from the spring of 1949 to early 1950. This was essentially the same scene that Dave Bartholomew, Lew Chudd, and local music promoter Al Young saw as they walked into the club in late 1949 and discovered Domino, except that another singer, John "Sonny" Jones, and guitarist Harrison Verrett were also there that night. Left to right at back: Domino (at the piano), Charles Burbank (alto sax), Hiram Armstrong (tenor sax), Dave Oxley (drums) (courtesy of Frank Oxley; restoration by Jason Kruppa).

North Rampart Street in New Orleans, with Cosimo Matassa's J&M Music Shop (and recording studio) in the center, circa 1950. Between 1947 and 1956 Matassa recorded scores of records crucial to the birth of rhythm & blues and rock 'n' roll at J&M. (Photograph Collection New Orleans Public Library).

Cosimo Matassa, about age nineteen, when he first began recording musicians at J&M, originally an appliance store that sold records, in 1945. Matassa's color blindness in recording African-American musicians that others shunned would have earth-shaking musical consequences (courtesy of Cosimo Matassa).

Roy Brown shouting the news. The Prometheus of rock 'n' roll, Brown started everyone rocking when he combined gospel-fire singing and earthy jump blues, declaring, *I heard the news, there's good rocking tonight!* at Cosimo's J&M Studio in 1947. He and Matassa are the most egregious exclusions from the early fathers in the Rock and Roll Hall of Fame (author collection).

ROY BROWN
And His Mighty, Mighty Men

UNIVERSAL ATTRACTIONS
347 Madison Ave New York, 17, N.Y.

Dave Bartholomew receiving a libation at The Graystone nightclub at Eagle and Cohn Streets in 1946. Bartholomew, then the leading black bandleader in New Orleans, would join with Domino in one of the most important collaborations in twentieth-century music (courtesy of Jeff Hannusch; restoration by Jason Kruppa).

The Dave Bartholomew band in 1948, including musicians that would form the core of the New Orleans studio group, turning out hit after hit from the late 1940s to the early 1960s. Clockwise from bottom left: Ernest McLean (guitar), Clarence Hall (tenor sax), Joe Harris (alto sax), Salvador Doucette (piano), Frank Fields (bass), Earl Palmer (drums), Alvin "Red" Tyler (baritone and tenor sax), Theard Johnson (vocals); center: Dave Bartholomew (author collection; restoration by Jason Kruppa).

Movers and shakers of New Orleans r&b at Cab Calloway's concert at Booker T. Washington Auditorium on September 9, 1951. Left to right: WBOK DJ James "Okey Dokey" Smith (whose catchphrase "Lawdy Miss Clawdy!" inspired a classic hit), WJMR DJ Duke "Poppa Stoppa" Thiele, promoter Rip Roberts, WMRY DJ Ernest "Ernie the Whip" Bringier, Cab Calloway, Dew Drop Inn owner Frank Painia, Domino's agent Melvin Cade, (unknown), and WWEZ DJ Vernon "Dr. Daddy-O" Winslow (courtesy of Martha Thiele).

Antoine "Fats" Domino, at Cosimo Matassa's J&M Studio circa January 1950, posing for his first promotional photograph, shortly after recording "The Fat Man." Note that Harold F. Oxley, the former big band agent who booked Dave Bartholomew's two 1950 tours with Domino, is listed; also, Domino's name is misspelled (courtesy of Michael Ochs Archives).

FATS DIMONO   IMPERIAL RECORDS   *Harold F. Oxley*

Fats Domino and fans, circa 1953 (courtesy of Hogan Jazz Archive, Tulane University; restoration by Jason Kruppa).

Lew Chudd of Imperial Records presenting Domino with two gold records for sales of two million records, on the cover of *The Cash Box*, November 21, 1953. Left to right: Jim Warren (Central Record Sales distributors in Los Angeles), Eddie Ray (Central Record Sales and, later, head of Imperial Records' promotions), Chudd, Domino, Bartholomew, Cliff Aaronson (Shaw Artists), Billy Berg (5-4 Ballroom), and Carl Taft (*Cash Box*) (courtesy of Edna Albert).

Jimmy Gilchrist, Domino's new warm-up singer, wailing the blues Roy Brown–style as Fats plays piano, circa 1953. Left to right: Domino, Billy Diamond, Gilchrist, Wendell Duconge, Buddy Hagans. In early 1954 Gilchrist would become the first Domino musician to die of a heroin overdose (courtesy of Doris and Gregory Hagans).

On the road drinking Cokes at a gas station, circa 1955. Left to right: Domino, Bartholomew, Bernard Dunn (chauffeur), Sonny Jones (Domino's warm-up singer, who returned after Gilchrist's death), and Billy Diamond. Bartholomew rarely toured with Domino in the 1950s (courtesy of Herbert Hardesty).

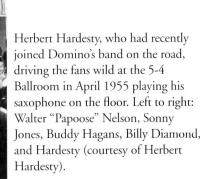

Herbert Hardesty, who had recently joined Domino's band on the road, driving the fans wild at the 5-4 Ballroom in April 1955 playing his saxophone on the floor. Left to right: Walter "Papoose" Nelson, Sonny Jones, Buddy Hagans, Billy Diamond, and Hardesty (courtesy of Herbert Hardesty).

As rhythm & blues became "rock 'n' roll" and gained a heavy white audience, the parallels with racial integration were clear. White singers like Pat Boone covered r&b artists for pop hits. The "Ain't That a Shame" sheet music with Domino on the cover is extremely rare, as some ninety percent of the copies printed had Pat Boone's face on the cover (author collection).

AIN'T THAT A SHAME !
By ANTOINE DOMINO and DAVE BARTHOLOMEW

Recorded by
Pat Boone - - - Dot Re...
Fats Domino - Imperial Record...
Ronnie Gaylord - Wing Records

Price 50c
in U.S.A.

COMMODORE MUSIC CORP.
6425 Hollywood Boulevard
Hollywood 28, California

Fats singing to an integrated audience in Albany, New York, in 1956. (courtesy of Antoine "Fats" Domino).

NOTICE!
STOP

Help Save The Youth of America
DON'T BUY NEGRO RECORDS

(If you don't want to serve negroes in your place of business, then do not have negro records on your juke box or listen to negro records on the radio.)

The screaming, idiotic words, and savage music of these records are undermining the morals of our white youth in America.

Call the advertisers of the radio stations that play this type of music and complain to them!

Don't Let Your Children Buy, or Listen To These Negro Records

For additional copies of this circular, write
CITIZENS' COUNCIL OF GREATER NEW ORLEANS, INC.
509 Delta Building   New Orleans, Louisiana 70112

Permission is granted to re-print this circular

In early 1956, at the time of the Montgomery, Alabama, bus boycott led by Martin Luther King, Jr., citizens' councils against integration in the South began condemning rock 'n' roll as "nigger music." Accordingly, the Citizens' Council of New Orleans produced this infamous flyer. Domino, the first black rock 'n' roll superstar, attracted more and larger integrated audiences than anyone and accordingly became the goodwill ambassador for a revolution, both musically and socially (courtesy of collection of Adam Woodward).

Domino's musicians posing before leaving for their next show, circa mid-1956. Left to right: Cornelius "Tenoo" Coleman, Walter "Papoose" Nelson, (unknown), Wendell Duconge, Buddy Hagans, (new member) Eddie Silvers, and (unknown) (courtesy of Antoine "Fats" Domino).

The aftermath of a riot in Fayetteville, North Carolina, at a Domino show in which racially integrated dancing led to fights that, in turn, led to the police throwing tear gas bombs. Domino suffered more riots than any other rocker during that period (courtesy of Antoine "Fats" Domino).

On the 20th Century Fox movie studio lot during the filming of *The Girl Can't Help It* in October 1956, Domino posed with Robert Wagner (dressed for his title role in the Fox movie *The True Story of Jesse James*), Jayne Mansfield, and Lew Chudd. In December, as *The Girl Can't Help It* premiered and Domino's song in the movie, "Blue Monday," was released, the photo would make the cover of *Cash Box* (courtesy of Andrew A. Chudd and Reeve E. Chudd).

IRVING FELD'S BIGGEST SHOW OF STARS. Washington, D.C. super-promoter Irving Feld promoted many of the biggest rock 'n' roll tours in America for over a decade. His two most successful tours were headlined by Domino in 1957. (author collection).

Ricky Nelson sang his weak version of Domino's "I'm Walkin'" on his parents' long-running television show—*The Adventures of Ozzie and Harriet*—in April 1957. The handsome sixteen-year-old sold nearly a million records, mostly to white teenage girls, and soon the television-driven teen idol trend swung into high gear on *American Bandstand* and other programs. Lew Chudd of Imperial Records noted the teenage reaction and soon signed Nelson (author collection).

Domino and Bartholomew listening to the playback of a recording in the control booth at Cosimo Matassa's new studio on Governor Nicholls Street in New Orleans, circa July 1957. Photograph by Charles Franck (courtesy of Michael Ochs Archives).

Antoine Domino helping his wife, Rosemary, cook red beans in their kitchen, circa July 1957. Fats, who had learned to cook from his sister Philonese, would become a great New Orleans chef, specializing in very spicy Creole soul cuisine. Photograph by Charles Franck (courtesy of Michael Ochs Archives).

The Domino family posing in front of their modest home at 1723 Caffin for photographer Charles Franck, who was taking publicity photos for Imperial Records. Left to right: Rosemary, Anola, Andrea, Antoinette, Antoine III (top), Andre (bottom), Antoine, Jr., and Anatole (courtesy of the Historic New Orleans Collection).

The great saxophonists Herbert Hardesty and Lee Allen (who briefly joined Domino's band in 1957) flirt with Eartha Kitt between shows in Wildwood-by-the-Sea, New Jersey, August 1957 (courtesy of Herbert Hardesty).

Domino appearing on *American Bandstand* with his band, circa August 1957, to perform a medley of hits. The show made the transition from a local Philadelphia television dance show to debut on the ABC network on August 5, and Domino—much to Dick Clark's joy—appeared twice in one week during a club stay in Philadelphia. Left to right: Dick Clark, WFIL-TV cameraman, Domino, Herbert Hardesty, Tenoo Coleman, Clarence Ford, Jimmy Davis, Bill Jones, Lee Allen, and Buddy Hagans (courtesy of Dick Clark Productions).

Lew Chudd and Fats Domino celebrating selling twenty-five million Fats Domino records, in a photo that would appear on the October 5, 1957 cover of *Cash Box* (courtesy of Andrew A. Chudd and Reeve E. Chudd).

The second 1957 Biggest Show of Stars, from September 6 to November 24, was the greatest rock 'n' roll package tour of all time, with artists who, at the time, had amassed twenty-two #1 hit records. Most of them would later enter the Rock and Roll Hall of Fame. Dick Clark still marvels at Feld's tours. "If you look at the lineup of the old posters, every big star in the world was on those tours," says Clark. "It was unbelievable" (author collection).

A Day in the Life. On Thursday, November 21, 1957, Irvin Feld's Biggest Show of Stars played the Brooklyn Paramount in New York City. The next four pages tell the story of that show from the headliner's perspective, thanks to the magnificent photos of Charlotte Brooks, who captured Domino's day in photos for a *Look* magazine article that was not published. This is the first publication of these photos.

Fans arriving early that cold November morning to see the Biggest Show of Stars. Note the movies playing—*Reform School Girls* and *The Tommy Steele Story* (Charlotte Brooks, Photographer, *Look* Magazine Collection, Library of Congress, Prints and Photographs Division).

Antoine Domino, Jr. presumably calling home to his wife, Rosemary, from his hotel room (Charlotte Brooks, Photographer, *Look* Magazine Collection, Library of Congress, Prints and Photographs Division).

Fats Domino fanning himself with $1,000 bills backstage. Photographer Charlotte Brooks appears in the mirror, left (Charlotte Brooks, Photographer, *Look* Magazine Collection, Library of Congress, Prints and Photographs Division).

A tailor measures Domino's famous girth backstage (Charlotte Brooks, Photographer, *Look* Magazine Collection, Library of Congress, Prints and Photographs Division).

Domino kicks back the piano stool to rock at the Brooklyn Paramount (Charlotte Brooks, Photographer, *Look* Magazine Collection, Library of Congress, Prints and Photographs Division).

Fats tears into his piano as Jimmy Davis watches (Charlotte Brooks, Photographer, *Look* Magazine Collection, Library of Congress, Prints and Photographs Division).

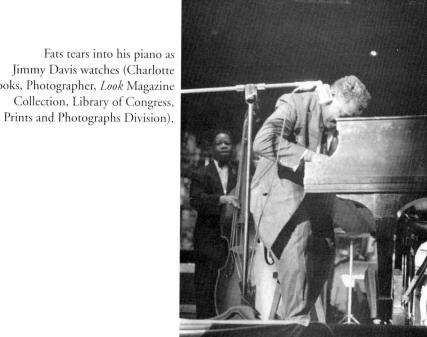

The classic Fats Domino (Charlotte Brooks, Photographer, *Look* Magazine Collection, Library of Congress, Prints and Photographs Division).

After the show Domino is wearing his leather coat, as he is heading out into the cold night to play a show in Norfolk, Virginia—after playing number seventy-six of the tour's seventy-nine dates (with only two off-days) (Charlotte Brooks, Photographer, *Look* Magazine Collection, Library of Congress, Prints and Photographs Division).

with a trill and sang with a honey-toned drawl. Walter "Papoose" Nelson added a mellow guitar riff that dominated the rhythm section, including Lawrence Guyton on bass and Cornelius Coleman on drums. "Papoose had a big influence on me," says Bartholomew. "In the studio, I could *feel* him, man. He added so much more to it—a lot of feeling." Bartholomew instructed the sax players—Buddy Hagans, Wendell Duconge, and Eddie Silvers (a new band member from East St. Louis)—to gently roll the song along in unison. But after the session, he listened to the tapes and shook his head. He didn't get a full take of "Blueberry Hill"; they had only completed the hard-riffing "Honey Chile." He put the tape on Chudd's desk and went out to dinner. At the restaurant, Bartholomew told his boss, "Lew, I don't think I have nothin'."

■ ■ ■

Domino took a break at his hotel on Sunday, July 1, to watch a singer on *The Steve Allen Show*. For a joke, Allen had Elvis Presley constricted in a tuxedo as he leaned over to sing a vampish version of "Hound Dog" to a basset hound. While "I'm in Love Again" enjoyed a nine-week stay at #1 on the *Billboard* r&b charts, Presley was #1 on the pop and country charts with "Heartbreak Hotel." Domino even heard deejays comparing his and Presley's records, asking listeners which one they liked better. "Me and him was runnin' pretty close together in popularity when he first started," says Fats.

Presley's version of Leiber and Stoller's "Hound Dog" sounded familiar to the New Orleans musicians. The frenzied shouting recalled Roy Brown and Little Richard. Rhythmically, it was radically different from Big Mama Thornton's original (recorded with Johnny Otis's band) or Presley's Sun recordings. It featured Bartholomew's three-beat Latin riff, which had been heard in Bill Haley's "Shake, Rattle and Roll." Haley's disciples, Freddie Bell and the Bell Boys, used the riff in their version of "Hound Dog," which Presley copied. The riff was also heard in scores of New Orleans records, the Platters' "Only You," Jim Lowe's "The Green Door," Gene and Eunice's "Ko Ko Mo," the Five Keys' "Ling, Ting, Tong," Eddie Cochran's "Twenty Flight Rock," the Cadets' "Stranded in the Jungle," Bobby Darin's "Splish Splash," and even the Beatles' "Rock and Roll Music." Robert Palmer called Bartholomew's riff "the most overused rhythmic pattern in 1950s rock 'n' roll," though triplets and the backbeat were even more pervasive. D. J. Fontana played the type of hard-driving backbeat that Earl Palmer institutionalized on Little Richard's records.

Fontana's rapid drum runs even echoed Richard's apocalyptic shriek in "Tutti Frutti," returning *"Awopbopaloobop"* to the tribal drumming message of revolt from which it had sprung. The new lyrics also reflected r&b's new youthfully perverse bent, distorting a ghetto alley blues into nonsense.

"Hound Dog" was the culmination of a decade of r&b and reflected the real revolution—the integration of black culture into white. Leiber and Stoller, Otis, Haley, Bell, and Presley were in the white vanguard following a different drummer. Presley was a brilliant synthesist, the electrifying amplifier for shouts and rhythms not yet heard in Main Street America, where blacks were virtually unseen and unheard. Now everyone heard "Hound Dog," which screamed like an air raid siren of the changes to come. In keeping with the blindness of segregation, there was a vast cultural disconnect. The white media and most Americans myopically viewed Presley's music as *white music*. But the modest Presley told the *Charlotte Observer* on June 26, "The colored folks been singing it and playing it just like I'm doin' now for more years than I know. . . . I got it from them." Blacks, in turn, admired Presley's talent. "I know one thing, that son of a gun could sing!" says Domino. "He had to [play black music], 'cause that was the only thing happening."

Presley expressed his admiration for Domino to Lew Chudd when they met at the Hermitage Hotel in Nashville and at a Hollywood barbershop. "He's quite an artist," enthused Elvis. "Nobody can bang a piano like he does." "Along came Presley and joined the parade," says Chudd. "That was the biggest help Fats ever got. He made rock 'n' roll a national institution. He was so hot he dragged us along."

Aside from the uproar over Presley, there were news stories about the presidential campaign, the British transfer of the Suez Canal to Egypt, the first widespread use of Jonas Salk's polio vaccine, and the sinking of the *Andrea Doria*.

In Santa Cruz, California, the police chief broke up a rock 'n' roll ball at the Civic Auditorium where teenagers were dancing in "an obscene and highly suggestive manner." In a move that proved prophetic, the city banned Domino's scheduled show, as he attracted "a certain type of crowd." Shortly afterwards, Fats made a headline of his own in another California city.

2,500 WHITE TEEN-AGERS IN ROCK AND ROLL RIOT—
FATS DOMINO ESCAPES INJURY

"Blue Monday"

Chapter 9

(Late 1956)

"The Fats Domino brand of rock 'n' roll wasn't the kind that inspired teenage riots."

—NEWSMAN ED BRADLEY AT THE GRAMMY
LIFETIME ACHIEVEMENT AWARDS, 1987

Sonny Jones was crying the blues, warming up the largest crowd ever to see a rock 'n' roll show in San Jose, California. White, Latino, and black teenagers entered the Palomar Ballroom soon after dark on Saturday, July 7. Fights had jostled the crowd since the band took the stage at nine o'clock. Now the thick crowd hindered Domino, who was already late, from reaching the stage. Jones ducked an oncoming beer bottle. By the time Fats started his first song, more bottles were flying. Suddenly there was a sound like machine gun fire. Someone had thrown a lighted string of leftover Fourth of July firecrackers into the mob. Fans ran for the doors and the windows. Domino and his band dove for the dressing room. The five policemen providing security were overwhelmed. Thirty officers who had been celebrating nearby at San Jose's annual policeman's ball headed for the Palomar to stop the riot in progress. *The San Jose Mercury* later reported that upon their arrival they were hailed by beer bottles "popping around them like confetti." In fact, the fans were still fighting even after the musicians packed their instruments and escaped. It took fifty policemen nearly an hour to control the mob. A dozen young people required medical treatment. Another dozen were arrested. Tables and chairs were splintered across the scene, along with 1,000 broken beer bottles.

San Jose police chief Ray Blackmore blamed "the fifth-to-the-bottle rather than the eight-to-the-bar"—that is, the alcohol rather than the music—but newspapers nationally, in Domino's first major mainstream publicity, reported that "the pulsating rhythms of Fats Domino" drove the teens wild. The news reports led *San Francisco Chronicle* writer Ralph J. Gleason to interview Domino. As Fats carved his steak and eggs in an Oakland ghetto hotel diner, Gleason asked him what he called his music.

"The only thing is the rhythm," replied Domino between chews. "You gotta keep a good beat. The rhythm we play is from Dixieland, from New Orleans. I don't know what to call it. I really don't."

While Domino's July 21 show in Stockton was canceled, a substitute appearance was quickly booked in Tracy, where 1,500 attended. On July 29, Fats was rescheduled in San Jose by the same promoter who had booked him there in the first place; he was determined to refute the theory that rock 'n' roll caused riots. Fats played San Jose again before a crowd of 1,400 people. In twenty-eight West Coast dates, Fats grossed an impressive $80,000, with thousands of under-aged teens turned away.

Domino's new record, "When My Dreamboat Comes Home," quickly made the pop charts. The flipside, "So Long," which featured smoldering piano breaks recalling "Lawdy Miss Clawdy" and a dreamy alto solo by Wendell Duconge, was a classic New Orleans blues ballad. Both Fats and some disc jockeys would use it to conclude their shows.

In late July, movie producer Alex Gordon, attempting to pick up Fats to film his part for the American International Pictures movie *Shake, Rattle and Rock!* asked for Antoine Domino at the front desk of the Roosevelt Hotel in L.A. He soon discovered he was at the wrong place—there was also a hotel of the same name in a black neighborhood.

Domino almost didn't appear in the movie at all. Since Gordon's meeting with him a month earlier, Twentieth Century Fox had offered the singer an appearance in a major rock 'n' roll film—tentatively titled *Do Re Mi*—for $7,500, five times the money of *Shake, Rattle and Rock!* (which was budgeted at a meager $79,000). Lew Chudd told Samuel Z. Arkoff of AIP the deal was off. But Chudd relented when Arkoff threatened a restraining order to prevent Domino from appearing in the Fox film, soon to be retitled *The Girl Can't Help It*. Even so, Gordon had to wrangle his way past Domino's bodyguards to get the pianist to the studio.

In the film, Mike (Touch) Connors (later of *Mannix* TV fame), playing a TV dance host pre-dating Dick Clark, slips in a reference to the San Jose riot. When he is told that Fats was coming to rehearse before his teenagers, he exclaims, "You know what he does to 'em! They'd tear up the place!" But Domino was the movie's star, performing "Ain't That a Shame," "I'm in Love Again," and introducing his next single: "I just wrote a new number called 'Honey Chile'; would ya'll like to hear it?"

Things were looking up. In an issue of *Down Beat* that generally condemned rock 'n' roll, Ralph Gleason's positive article on Domino noted that he "draws a mixed audience wherever he goes." "I'm in Love Again" became Domino's first chart hit in England. His performance fee had increased from $450 to $750, plus everything else beyond the next $1,500, the promoter's take. He sometimes grossed $2,000 or more a night, from which would be deducted taxes, the band's payment, ten percent for Shaw Artists, and five percent for his lawyer, Charles Levy. *Jet* dubiously claimed that Domino "is currently a hotter rhythm-and-blues personality than even Elvis (The Pelvis) Presley." The magazine listed his luxuries: "a fire-engine red El Dorado trimmed in gold, a shocking pink Fleetwood Cadillac, a Chrysler station wagon, 50 suits, and 200 pairs of shoes." But some upstanding African Americans did not approve of Domino's lowdown rocking or his success with white teens. "'Fats' Domino is riding a wave of popularity as he has never ridden before, whether you like him or not," sniped columnist Elgin Hychew in *The Louisiana Weekly*. "He is now tops all over the nation, except in his own New Orleans."

Domino's second album, *Rock and Rollin'*, included the old standard "Careless Love" from 1950 and eight unreleased songs from 1953. In contrast to most rock 'n' roll album covers, which avoided showing black singers, it featured a three-times-life-size dot-matrix blow-up of Domino's face, as if Lew Chudd wanted to emphasize his star's black facial features. In contrast to his first album, the liner notes also noted his New Orleans heritage and "arranger Dave Bartholomew." At the time white adults accounted for nearly all album sales. *Billboard* noted that even *releasing* an album was a major step: "The recent 'Fats Domino' lp released by Imperial Records is one of the few r&b albums that uses a single vocalist thruout. . . . Manufacturers voiced the attitude that only vocalists of the stature of Domino, Presley, Haley, or the Platters would have the 'personality pull' to make a really successful lp seller." When *Rock and Rollin'* sold an impressive 20,000 copies in the first week of release, Lew Chudd rang cash registers in his mind as he calculated the string of albums he could release simply by dipping into Domino's pre-1956 catalog.

Traveling back home through Texas, Domino narrowly averted another riot. At a segregated show at the Houston Auditorium on Sunday, August 12, only blacks were allowed to dance on the main floor, while whites watched from the balcony. The fear was that the races would mix in a dancing frenzy. But as the rocking commenced, whites also hit the dance floor. A black policeman tried to stop the mixing by directing *all* of the dancers to sit down. This incensed a white cop, who announced that only whites could dance. Fats refused to continue. "I won't play if Negroes can't dance," an angered Domino told the police. Though the teens said they didn't mind mixing, the officers stopped the show. Fifteen hundred fans began a run on the box office for refunds. A dozen were arrested for cursing and threatening policemen. The kids defiantly serenaded the cops with Shirley and Lee's current hit "Let the Good Times Roll" as they left.

Soon afterwards, the Houston chief of police reported that "members of both races have been allowed on dance floors in other Texas cities without trouble." But, in the wake of the San Jose riot, dances were banned as far away as New Jersey. The American Civil Liberties Union (ACLU) took up rock 'n' roll's case, as it was "largely the product of Negro bands." Manager Buck Ram, touring with the Platters, Joe Houston, and others, thought that "rock 'n' roll," a euphemism for rhythm & blues, was now itself tainted by racial, sexual, and riotous implications. He suggested it should be re-titled "Happy Music," with the slogan "The Happy Beat for Happy Feet."

Though Elvis Presley was still widely condemned, he was hardly America's worst nightmare. Aside from his shouting and shaking, he was son-in-law material: shy, modest, well-mannered, God-fearing, a mama's boy, rich, and *white*. The powers-that-be soon began erecting pedestals for him when they realized his commercial value—and *the alternatives*. By mid-1956, Domino, Little Richard, Chuck Berry, the Platters, Frankie Lymon, and other artists unacceptable because of their skin color were overtaking the other white midwives of rock 'n' roll. White adults were horrified by the black hordes invading the radio airwaves with their raucous music, which no amount of musical laundering seemed to stop.

Attacks against rock 'n' roll acquired increasingly racial overtones. The *Encyclopaedia Britannica* stated that rock 'n' roll was "deliberately competing with the artistic ideals of the jungle itself." Likewise, Sir Malcolm Sargent, conductor of the BBC Symphony, said, "Rock 'n' roll has been played in the jungle for centuries." The attacks followed the pattern of the condemnations of jazz in the 1920s and even outcries against Congo Square a century before that. One of the most vehement condemnations appeared in *Music Journal:*

> The illiterate gangsters of our younger generation are definitely influenced in their
> lawlessness by this throwback to jungle rhythms. Either it actually stirs them to

orgies of sex and violence (as its model did for the savages themselves), or they use it as an excuse for the removal of all inhibitions and the complete disregard of the conventions of decency. Aside from the illiteracy of this vicious "music," it has proved itself definitely a menace to youthful morals and an incitement to juvenile delinquency.

Suddenly America's children were revealing physical and emotional impulses that were alien to their repressed parents. *Look* magazine reviewed rock 'n' roll as if it were conducting an anthropological study for *National Geographic:*

> Going to a rock 'n' roll show is like attending the rites of some obscure tribe whose means of communication are incomprehensible. An adult can actually become frightened. Two notes are played on-stage and, like one vast organism, the assembled teen-agers shriek on exactly the same pitch. Or, just as suddenly, they become deathly quiet except for the rhythmic clapping of their hands on the second and fourth beat of every measure. Another number is played, and like one voice, they sing, *"Why-iey do foo-ools fall in lu-uve?"*—their youthful enunciation and melody somehow sweet and haunting. Sometimes, a few of them dance—in the aisles if there is no other place. More rarely, they engage in more strenuous exhibitionism.

When riots broke out at screenings in England of the movie *Rock Around the Clock, The Manchester Guardian* likewise commented, "Perhaps it is a case for the anthropologists to study, an echo in staider surroundings of tribal dances to the drum, or the slogans to which dervishes revolve."

The loss of inhibitions or "self-respect" in public was cathartic in a way that was inconceivable to white adults. Jazz, having largely lost its original essence of physical release, had become respectable music for "highbrow" adults. But young people were now again dancing in the streets, in gym sock hops, and at rock 'n' roll shows to the new reveille of rhythm. Parents now imagined their children gripped in a virtual voodoo spell. Unlike previous assaults on dirty lyrics, adults grabbed at phantoms in this musical anarchy that didn't play by *their* rules. Rockers seemed to mock them at every move. Psychiatrist Francis Braceland's description of rock 'n' roll as "tribalistic and cannibalistic" was echoed by the archbishop of Dubuque, who called it "a Communistic endeavor, a pretext for cannibalistic rhythmic orgies." Sure enough, the Cadets' "Stranded in the Jungle" had tribal chants, Amos 'n' Andy–style voices, and *cannibals.* Like the blackfaced, grass-skirted Zulus at Mardi Gras, r&b singers, including

Domino and Little Richard, were throwing black stereotypes back at whites with a laugh. To white Americans already paranoid about communism, civil rights protests and rock 'n' roll were like ominous *Heart of Darkness* drumbeats boomlay-boomlay-booming in their own backyard, signaling an uprising on the Great American Plantation. America, which in prior centuries had figuratively cannibalized Africa, was now suddenly shocked to discover *it was what it ate.* Parents endured a nightmare similar to that of the Cadets' singer, who found himself in a cannibal boiling pot and hollered, *"Great Googa Mooga! Lemme outta here!"*

▌▐ ▌

On Wednesday, August 29, Alan Freed, a small, unremarkable man in a bow tie, welcomed his teenage army of insurrection to his second anniversary show. Teens lined up around the block of the Brooklyn Paramount for the nine-day show featuring Domino, Frankie Lymon and the Teenagers, Big Joe Turner, the Cleftones, the Harptones, the Penguins, the Moonglows, and hitless white opening acts. The big news, though, was Domino's first appearances before mostly white fans in the Big Apple.

Backstage, a huge singer draped in a tent-like suit, Joe Turner, showed off a royalty check to his old friend, Dave Bartholomew, who had flown up to lead Domino's band. But Dave was incensed that the check was for $2,500 instead of $25,000. He didn't miss Domino's appearances with Freed, who to him was "one of the greatest disc jockeys that ever lived." Playing six or seven shows a day from noon until two A.M. was hard on all of the musicians. Fats tried to nap, but he could rest only briefly before he had to perform again. The musicians stood around smoking, rolling dice, or watching the show.

The discomforts of fans and musicians disappeared in the musical frenzy. An old-school *Variety* reviewer who was unimpressed with the vocal groups credited Domino and Turner with "some fine blues shouting in the old jazz tradition." Kids danced in their seats as police and ushers tried to keep order. A boy pushed past the gauntlet and ran down to the stage before he was seized. The show was teenage heaven, the marquee event in rock 'n' roll, but also the last major Freed package show with all-black headliners. He would trumpet its statistics—a gross of $220,000 from 140,000 tickets—for months to come.

In the midst of the shows, Freed's Cleveland counterpart Bill Randle also featured Domino on his CBS network radio show. In the WCBS studio,

Domino, wearing a tailored suit, rings, and a slick hairstack, chewed broken words in his thick *patois*. He thanked the deejay as he left, shaking his hand with a roll of $20 bills and telling him to buy his daughter something. Randle thanked him, but then handed the roll to his engineer, telling Fats, "He'll play more of your records that way." Allegations of Freed's payola were already rampant among music insiders. Word of the incident with Domino solidified Randle's straight-arrow reputation. "That story *made* me in New York," declares Randle. "I wasn't in *anybody's* pocket."

On Sunday, September 2, 1956, Fats also made his scintillating network television debut on *The Steve Allen Show*. The plum-faced, flat-topped singer appeared head first across America, mouthing words from a lexicon that was all his own: *"Wimh mah dreamboat c-o-u-m-s home . . . "* The camera panned back to reveal a battery of five horn players, including Bartholomew, blasting like pistons in a rhythm factory. Herbert Hardesty released two thrilling solos, while a split screen revealed Tenoo's rapid-fire drumming. After Allen presented Domino with a *Cash Box* award for Best R&B Male Vocalist, Fats stomped into "I'm in Love Again," with Eddie Silvers playing Lee Allen's solo. Steve Allen, who had introduced the talk show format and several other television innovations, was again on the cutting edge in even allowing the controversial black rockers on his show, easily making up for his earlier humorous swipe at "Ain't That a Shame." Allen, who had stirred controversy two months earlier with Elvis Presley's "Hound Dog" appearance, now spoofed Gene Vincent's "Be-Bop-A-Lula" by reading it like an Elizabethan rhyme. He referred to Vincent, Presley, and Domino with the grim anticipation of the end of civilization: "Let's face it, rhythm & blues—uhhh—is *here*."

Domino's new record would play a part in ensuring that the music was here *to stay,* achieving a massive crossover to white adult and even country audiences. Imperial promotion man Eddie Ray pitched "Honey Chile" in Philadelphia and other cities. However, some deejays were playing the flipside. Despite a warning from Bartholomew that "Blueberry Hill"—edited together from half-finished takes by engineer Bunny Robyn—would "ruin" Domino, Lew Chudd had placed it on the b-side. "We never got a full good take," says Robyn. "I took his first chorus and repeated it because it was so damned good." One of the first to push the song was New Orleans disc jockey Clarence Hamann, who had claimed the "Poppa Stoppa" moniker on WJMR after Duke Thiele left the station. He was sitting at Delicate Jerry's restaurant when a man put new 78s in the jukebox. Soon a majestic piano roll and a warm voice entranced the diners. They demanded to hear the record again and again. Hamann played it on his show the next day. But the days when Poppa Stoppa ruled the rockin' universe were long gone. New Orleans rhythms were now heard constantly all over the country.

An article in *Billboard* called Fats "New Orleans' high priest of r&b" and noted that he was now making big bucks for ASCAP publishers with his hit versions of old standards. Another story stated that Domino, "one of the great entertainers of our day," was booked in nightclubs never previously played by a rhythm & blues act. But few white nightclubs had ever witnessed the full intensity of rock 'n' roll. When Fats rocked the Rhode Island Naval Station enlisted men's club in Newport that month, some joker turned out the lights. One thousand sailors and marines and their dates found themselves in a bottle-throwing, chair-swinging war zone, with fights spilling into the street. "With the Navy and the Marines *everybody's* fightin'," says Herbert Hardesty. Lawrence Guyton, who saw people stepping on a pregnant woman, called it "the worse stuff I ever seen." Ambulances and police cars screamed to the scene. Ten sailors were hospitalized. Nine others went to jail. Still, Rear Admiral Ralph D. Earle, Jr., blamed the mêlée not on alcohol, race-mixing, or intra-military friction, but rather on the "excitement accompanying the fever pitched 'rock 'n' roll'" and banned the music for a month.

In late September, a Hearst-Metrotone newsreel reporter asked Domino about the riot. After making his "rock 'n' roll is rhythm & blues" pronouncement, Fats downplayed the violence and commented on the negative publicity surrounding rock 'n' roll: "Well, maybe the people that are criticizing it are the older people who can't dance by the beat." He also hinted at the music's *positive* subversion. At a time when the State Department was arranging cultural exchanges with the Soviet Union, Louisiana Senator Allen J. Ellender (infamous for leading a twenty-seven-hour filibuster against an anti-lynching bill in 1938) remarked, "Americans are barbarians, if the best we can offer as a symbol of our culture is be-bop and rock and roll music." Prompted by the reporter, Domino joked that rock 'n' roll might thaw Cold War relations.

"I'd like to go into Russia and show 'em the rock 'n' roll beat," said Fats.

"You think the Russians could dig your kind of music?" asked the reporter.

"They'll dig it," Domino assured him.

■ ■ ■

The cultural war raged. In England Queen Elizabeth requested a private screening of Bill Haley's movie *Rock Around the Clock* to try to comprehend the riots it ignited. In Pittsburgh, promoters banned Haley from his own—otherwise all-black—rock 'n' roll tour in order to segregate the performers. In view of the protests and the music's new name, Haley changed the name of his next movie from *Rhythm and Blues* to *Don't Knock the Rock*. Meanwhile, ASCAP president Paul Cunningham returned from Europe declaring, "From this point on we can expect a revival of good music in the style of the Gershwins, the Kerns, and the Rombergs."

In October 1956, Little Richard staged more assaults on Domino's kingdom. In his final New Orleans sessions, he recorded several future hits, including "Good Golly Miss Molly," "Jenny, Jenny," and "The Girl Can't Help It," the new title song for the 20th Century Fox film also featuring Domino, the Platters, Gene Vincent, and Eddie Cochran. Art Rupe of Specialty Records achieved a coup after he presented Fox with a color film of Richard cavorting at his piano. According to Rupe, Domino was supposed to sing "The Girl Can't Help It" until Rupe convinced director Frank Tashlin, a former cartoonist, that Richard would be more "animated."

Domino flew to California on October 24 with Bartholomew to film his scene for *The Girl Can't Help It*. The movie starred Tom Ewell (fresh from his success blowing up Marilyn Monroe's dress in *The Seven-Year Itch*) and the new blond bombshell, Jayne Mansfield. Though Fats received the top rock 'n' roll billing, his part was indeed reduced to give Richard more time. He was originally supposed to sing "My Blue Heaven," but Chudd didn't own the publishing on the standard and suggested that Fats perform his year-and-a-half-old recording, "Blue Monday."

While in L.A., Domino went to the Chudd home for dinner. At the family piano, he played a new song, "I'm Walkin'," even before he auditioned it for Bartholomew. Chudd's seven-year-old son, Andy, lost a tooth that night. With six children of his own, Fats knew just what to do. He gave him a quarter.

In between Elvis Presley records that fall, "Blueberry Hill" became an instant classic, topping the r&b charts for eleven weeks. Jukeboxes everywhere wore out multiple copies. Domino's piano intro pealed like a flourish of horns announcing a king, his bass line then intertwining with Papoose's sensuously bobbing guitar riff, and the saxes blowing cool and breezy. His warm Creole drawl evoked a misty tryst of romantic mystery as the record became a primary soundtrack for slow dancing and making out; the sexual implications of the lyrics riveted teens hopped up on suppressed hormones. Domino's delivery impressed even poet, songwriter, and singer Leonard Cohen, who names it as his all-time favorite song. "You want to hear a guy's story," says Cohen, "and if the guy's really seen a few things, the story is quite interesting. . . . When you hear Fats Domino singing, *'I found my thrill on Blueberry Hill,'* whatever that's about, I mean, it's deep." The success of the record would cause a noticeable shift in Domino's music. Like Louis Armstrong, he now co-opted pop music with both rhythm and personality. The song was now inexorably Domino's, though an amazing number of artists later recorded the song, including Elvis Presley, Ray Charles, Little Richard, Johnny Cash, Loretta Lynn, Jerry Lee Lewis, the Beach Boys, and even Led Zeppelin (on the band's best-known bootleg, *Live on Blueberry Hill*). Bartholomew was finally sold on "Blueberry Hill," taking pride in his horn arrangement. "When I'm dead and gone a million times," says the bandleader, "they'll still be playing *'da-da-da-da-dee dah.'*"

■ ■ ■

In early November the presidential election headed for a climax, Soviet troops poured into Hungary, three nations bombed Egypt over the disputed Suez Canal, and Fats Domino made yet another riot headline.

Twenty-five hundred people, many of whom were soldiers, jam-packed Breece's Landing Hall in the Fayetteville, North Carolina, red-light district, which catered to the nearby Fort Bragg army base. Minor fights broke out early during the racially mixed dance. White r&b manager Ben DeCosta attended the show and saw nothing wrong with whites and blacks dancing together. "What the hell!" declares DeCosta. "They was dancin', not fornicatin'! But the military police were hittin' 'em over the head and draggin' 'em out and just really inciting a riot."

Shortly before midnight, a full-scale brawl erupted. Fists, bottles, and knives went flying. A bottle hit police sergeant W. A. Davis in the back. His response was to pull the pin from a tear gas grenade and fling it into the crowd. Police then threw more gas grenades into the building's ventilator ducts. Blinded by the hellish gas, the frenzied crowd broke through bars covering a window at the back of the hall, not knowing that the building was built on posts over a creek ravine. Lawrence Guyton, Domino's bass player, lifted a chair to smash the glass, but the mob surged and pushed him through the window. He plummeted through trees and brush to the ground below. It took a human chain of men to rescue him.

More than fifty fans, including two soldiers who were stabbed, received medical treatment. Broken chairs and bottles were strewn across the floor. At the local hospital a doctor slapped crushed ice into Guyton's hemorrhaging hand, telling the "black so-and-so" that the musicians started it. Guyton finally got his ticket home. He would never play with Domino again, and, with his permanently damaged hand, he would thereafter only play the bass with two fingers sticking out.

As Domino tended his own hand wound in a local hotel, a package arrived. He was heartened by a pounding sound, as Bernard Dunn put an advance 78-rpm pressing of his next release, "Blue Monday," on the turntable. Many blue-collar rockers would record the workingman's anthem; the piano intro would be echoed by Buddy Holly's guitar at the start of "That'll Be the Day," and the same booming beat would be heard in two other #1 hits, "Stagger Lee" by Lloyd Price and "The Wanderer" by Dion. But unlike those macho songs, Fats celebrated the Everyman—like Billy Lyons in the Stagger Lee saga. The song hit a profound chord of both blues and joy in the mundane, a precious universality in its lack of ego. Indeed, Domino went right back to work, playing the Petite Ballroom in Portsmouth, Virginia, on the Monday after the Fayetteville debacle. He fingered the keyboard with stitches in his hand and started a rousing ode to his dreamboat coming home.

1956 was Domino's Blue Monday. At year's end he found himself on a hard-won beachhead. Elvis Presley's highly hyped popularity was the most visible sign of a musical revolution, but the controversy over "The Pelvis" was a red herring. Postwar America was controlled by those who claimed to be more American and righteous than anyone else; President Eisenhower, who represented that status quo, won a landslide election that month, becoming the first Republican presidential candidate to capture Louisiana's votes since Reconstruction. Outside of the pariah South, racial fears were euphemized with hot-button words like "integration," "jungle music," "juvenile delinquency," "white flight," and "rock 'n' roll riot." As evidenced by the actual violence at Domino's 1956 shows, he was leading the musical revolt in the trenches. Rock 'n' roll was venting pent-up passions the same way New Orleans jazz had in the 1920s, but now segregation walls were cracking. The integration of Domino's shows was a major factor in the riots, but there was a crucial point that the newspapers ignored: In the vast majority of his shows everyone mixed—and even danced—together peacefully.

In *Invisible Man*, Ralph Ellison singled out Louis Armstrong's "What Did I Do to Be So Black and Blue," calling Armstrong's music poetry "because he's unaware that he *is* invisible." Likewise, sometimes the greatest agents of change are unaware of the revolution. In some ways, Domino's relative invisibility helped him—similar riots involving Elvis Presley would have been shocking front-page headlines everywhere. If Fats was not making poetry, his simple rhythms and emotions certainly went straight to body and soul. Rock 'n' roll was the clarion call of young Americans learning to express themselves freely for the first time. And in the maelstrom of controversy, hatred, violence, and overwhelming joy that surrounded him, Domino was the eye of the storm.

■ ■ ■

It was a cold Sunday on November 18 when Domino appeared on *The Ed Sullivan Show*. Sullivan featured rockers on his show, though not without censorship. He had tried to ban Bo Diddley's "jungle"-rhythmed signature song, "Bo Diddley," the previous year. In 1957 he would solve the Elvis problem by showing the gyrating singer from the waist up. Sullivan scheduled Domino at the show's end in case he had to cancel a guest—a year later he would do just that to Sam Cooke, actually cutting him off in the middle of "You Send Me." Given the controversies over both rock 'n' roll and blacks appearing on television, Lew Chudd strongly emphasized to Sullivan Domino's similarities to Louis Armstrong, who even to most whites was an American icon. After all, Satchmo's 1949 version had inspired Fats to sing "Blueberry Hill" and—re-released—it followed Domino's hit up the charts.

Backstage, Fats was all nerves after many rehearsals. Sullivan announced the singer from "New Or-lee-uns" with his granite jaw clenched so tightly that his tongue tripped over the word "million-seller." Aware that many white adults considered Domino a threat, Sullivan hid his band behind the curtain, reducing the number of black faces. He presented Fats alone at his piano singing the Tin Pan Alley ballad, as if he were a young Nat "King" Cole or Fats Waller.

Domino and Little Richard were often stereotyped on the rare occasions they received white publicity—Fats as a harmless, chubby "colored" man and Richard as a screaming wild man. Sullivan emphasized the stereotype when he had Fats stand up during the last verse of the song to reveal his pudgy figure. To this day those racial rubber stamps have made it easy to disregard Domino's and Richard's incalculable influence on popular music and American culture.

Still, there was a youthful dignity about the singer. Though others could manipulate his appearance, he and Bartholomew controlled the music, and Domino's New Orleans soul now radiated into living rooms everywhere. With the blessing of the high lama of show biz, Fats Domino became a household name. "I figured the night I went on there," says Fats, "the next day we sold over a million records on 'Blueberry Hill.'"

Now, Domino's influence was spreading everywhere.

At a party in Baton Rouge, a teenage singer bent over coughing in the middle of a Little Richard song. "I can't sing," he croaked. A gangly teen, John Fred Gourrier, who had sung every Domino record in his bedroom since "Going to the River," volunteered. Soon he would lead his own band, the Playboys, learning both sides of every Domino and Little Richard record as soon as they came out.

In New Orleans, nineteen-year-old Clarence "Frogman" Henry, who also learned Domino's hits immediately, met his idol shortly before a tour for his Domino-influenced hit "Ain't Got No Home." Aladdin Records sent Domino's inspirations Charles Brown and Amos Milburn to Cosimo's to try to capture some of his sound. Modern Records likewise sent Richard Berry and Jimmy Beasley to New Orleans. "Fats was superhot," declares Art Neville. "Fats could burn a piano, and Fats had a vocal sound that everybody loved. I ate, drank, and slept Fats Domino."

In south Louisiana, Domino's triplet sound blended with Cajun and country influences to create "swamp pop," pioneered by Bobby Charles. "A lot of people don't realize how big of an influence Fats Domino was," says Charles. "I don't *like* Fats Domino, I *love* Fats Domino."

In Lubbock, Texas, Buddy Holly and his band played r&b at venues like the Lubbock Roller Rink and made homemade tapes of songs by Domino and Little Richard. Holly even played Domino's songs on his family piano.

In San Antonio, fifteen-year-old Doug Sahm performed at the Tiffany Lounge. "I was playin' all them great Fats Domino tunes at night," recalled Sahm, "and I decided that's what I wanted to do . . . that's what really started changing my life."

In Hawthorne, California, Brian Wilson, his kid brothers Dennis and Carl, and their cousin Mike Love listened in the bedroom at night to rhythm & blues on the radio. "Fats Domino's music got to my soul," says Brian Wilson. "I loved all of his records. He's got to be one of the greatest singers of all time."

Also in California, a piano player actually born in New Orleans felt a genetic link. "I loved Fats Domino. Like nobody else," says Randy Newman, who would later record "I'm in Love Again," "Poor Me," and "Blue Monday."

In the Bay Area, Doug Clifford heard "authentic Fats Domino piano" coming out of his junior high music room and soon formed a band with the pianist

John Fogerty that would become Creedence Clearwater Revival. "I always considered Fats the equal of Chuck Berry, or Elvis, or Little Richard," says Fogerty.

In the Spring Wood area of Liverpool, England, a pretty, auburn-haired lady named Julia showed banjo chords to her son, John. "The first song I learned was 'Ain't That a Shame,' an old rock hit by Fats Domino," John Lennon later stated. "It has a lot of memories for me."

Domino likewise gave George Harrison a memory he would recall vividly over thirty years later. While walking past Picton Clock Tower and the Abbey Cinema in the Wavertree district of the same city, the thirteen-year-old heard a record playing nearby that "touched somewhere deep" inside him—Domino's "I'm in Love Again." "That was the first . . . rock 'n' roll record I ever heard," recalled Harrison.

Mick Jagger famously remarked in a *Rolling Stone* interview that when he was very young he read an interview in which Domino said something that really influenced him: "You should never sing the lyrics out very clearly," though, in fact, Domino *tried* to sing clearly, but his heavy Creole accent was unshakeable.

The great Louisiana-Texas pianist Marcia Ball sums up Domino's influence for a generation. "I don't think anybody," says Ball, "who plays music today wasn't moved in that direction by Fats Domino."

The rhythms and release of rock 'n' roll imbued young whites with a visceral rush bordering on a new reality, as Jagger noted: "I was crazy over Chuck Berry, Bo Diddley, Muddy Waters and Fats Domino, not knowing what it meant, just that it was beautiful. My father used to call it jungle music and I used to say, 'Yeah, that's right, jungle music, that's a very good description.' Every time I heard it, I just wanted to hear more. It seemed like the most real thing I'd ever known."

In a statement remarkably similar to Jagger's, John Lennon expressed why he thought rock 'n' roll meant so much to people in a *Rolling Stone* interview:

Because it is primitive enough and has no bullshit, really, the best stuff, and it gets through to you [through] its beat. Go to the jungle and they have the rhythm and it goes throughout the world and it's as simple as that. You get the rhythm going, everybody gets into it. I read that Eldridge Cleaver said that blacks gave the middle-class whites back their bodies, you know, put their minds and bodies together through the music. It's something like that, it gets through, to me it got through, it was the only thing to get through to me after all the things that were happening when I was 15. Rock and roll was real, everything else was unreal.

In the South especially, the music was radical both musically and *socially*.

"At the outset we couldn't listen to that music," says Buddy Holly's guitarist Sonny Curtis, "'cause it was considered 'race music.' We had to go out in the car late at night, listening to rhythm & blues from Shreveport. Along came Little Richard, Fats Domino, Ray Charles, and, of course, Chuck Berry." Holly soon identified with the black artists. While touring on a mostly black show with Domino in 1957, he told his mother, "Oh, we're Negroes, too! We get to feeling like that's what we are."

"We didn't consider ourselves white back then!" recalled John Fred. "I'm not kiddin' you! Parents didn't like the music we were playin'; it was called 'nigger music,' 'jungle bunny music.' But the kids loved the music. We didn't do much Elvis, because in our opinion Elvis was just copying black music."

■ ■ ■

"The big man of the year was Fats Domino, whose sensational set of hit recordings made him nationally known almost overnight," stated *Down Beat* when Domino beat out Joe Turner and Elvis Presley for "Personality of the Year" in the magazine's first rhythm & blues poll in December, which Fats added to his *Cash Box* and *Billboard* top r&b awards for the year.

Meanwhile, Shaw Artists finally realized that Domino was even more popular with white audiences. "I got him $10,000 a week," recalled booking agent Larry Myers. "He was worth even more, because he was packing the places."

While Domino appeared at the Blue Note jazz club in Chicago, the movie *Shake, Rattle and Rock!* premiered nearby at the B&K Roosevelt Theater. The film related rock 'n' roll's relation to early jazz and even Africa with more humor and less preaching than Alan Freed's movies. "It was an important time for young people," recalled the movie's producer, Samuel Z. Arkoff. "The oddity is that the old people were afraid of rock 'n' roll. And the girl might be dancing here and the boy way over there! I don't know why, but adults all thought that rock 'n' roll was immoral."

In Hollywood, *The Girl Can't Help It* premiered with a smiling, swaying Jayne Mansfield. Attracting a large adult audience, the movie gave the much-maligned rock 'n' roll some respectability, though *Films in Review* called it "a showcase for the leading purveyors of the jungle caterwauling known as rock 'n' roll, and . . . thereby a cultural debilitator our descendants won't forgive us for (let us hope)."

On Tuesday, December 4, there was an impromptu session at Sam Phillips's Sun Studios in Memphis with Elvis Presley, Carl Perkins, Johnny Cash, and Jerry Lee Lewis, whose first record, "Crazy Arms," struck a *Billboard* reviewer as possessing "a Domino-type piano backing which brings a distinct New Orleans feeling to the rendition." The group gathered around Elvis practicing "Blueberry Hill," a song he would play to the very end of his career. A photographer from a Memphis newspaper popped a flashbulb. It was about the only song actually performed by the full group—Johnny Cash left soon after the picture was taken. "Elvis headed for the piano and started to Fats Domino it on 'Blueberry Hill,'" reported Robert Johnson in *The Memphis Press-Scimitar*. "If Sam Philips had been on his toes, he'd have turned the recorder on when that very unrehearsed but talented bunch got to cutting up on 'Blueberry Hill' and a lot of other songs. That quartet could sell a million."

That month the *New York Mirror* suggested that rock 'n' roll was not only selling millions of records, it was sweeping the world like a cultural tsunami:

> Rampaging youths of both sexes, aroused to an uncontrollable state of frenzy, have rioted in nearly every city in the British Isles. Precisely the same thing has happened in Paris; in Norway; Australia; and even in Jakarta, Indonesia. And in each instance, the cause of these youth riots has been the same—exposure to the insistent beat of rock 'n' roll, the rhythm its practitioners and addicts call a compelling new form of music which fulfills a need, and which its detractors either call a bore or denounce as a pernicious influence and an inducement to delinquency without even being music. The European viewers-with-alarm, who always look askance towards these shores, say that rock 'n' roll is probably the greatest evil that the United States has ever exported. . . .

"One time we used to set the pace for the world."
—DAVE BARTHOLOMEW

Over the holidays there were lines at movie box offices across America, where marquees proclaimed Hollywood spectaculars: *Oklahoma, The Ten Commandments, Around the World in 80 Days, Lust for Life, Anastasia . . .* Three controversial films, *The Girl Can't Help It, Shake, Rattle and Rock!* and *Baby Doll,* incredibly featured singers—Fats Domino, Little Richard, Joe Turner, and Smiley Lewis—who were veterans of Cosimo's studio and hole-in-the-wall New Orleans nightclubs.

After *The Ed Sullivan Show* and his appearance in two movies, Domino was becoming a superstar. On January 19, "Blueberry Hill" reached its pop peak at #2 for two weeks on the *Billboard* Juke Box chart behind "Singing the Blues" by pop singer Guy Mitchell. After the record's eleventh week at #1 in the r&b charts, "Blue Monday" replaced it at the top. Lew Chudd bought an impressive four pages in *Billboard* to advertise Domino's twelve gold records and attendance records broken in twenty-one cities. Imperial sold two million records in January, a million and a half in February—the vast majority of them 45 and 78 rpm singles by Domino. Though white adults rarely bought albums by black singers, except artists like Nat "King" Cole or Harry Belafonte who were essentially singing pop, Domino's second album, *Rock and Rollin',* invaded the snow-white pop album charts, reaching #18. It was followed by *This Is Fats Domino,* which hit #19.

In New York, BMI held the first "Rhythm & Blues Awards" luncheon on January 23 to celebrate blowing away ASCAP. Domino and Bartholomew won six "citations of achievement" for their hits, the most of any songwriters. Fats also did great business for ASCAP with his revivals of old standards.

Fats was wide-eyed with pride as he flipped through his five-page "King of Rock 'n' Roll" layout in *Ebony*. The article rolled up the figures of his success: 340 days a year on the road, up to $2,500 a night to perform, over $500,000 gross income in 1956, fifty suits, 100 pairs of shoes, a $1,500 diamond horseshoe stick pin, and a $200 monthly phone bill from calling Rosemary daily. Pictures also told his story: crowds jostling to beat the fire marshal's audience limit, whites mixing with blacks, and the broken bottles and splintered chairs of the Newport and Fayetteville riots.

But there were a couple of sour notes in the midst of the coronation. George Oliver, owner of a Ninth Ward bar, the Jail Drop, talked Fats into going to the all-black Gallo Theater to see *The Girl Can't Help It,* which had premiered downtown at the segregated Saenger Theater. There was no red-carpet treatment for Domino. "I don't guess nobody knew I was there," says Fats. At the same time, he canceled a stay locally at the all-white Safari Room on Gentilly Highway when he found out that the management expected him to dress in a trailer behind the club instead of giving him a dressing room.

On January 3 Domino recorded a session in Cosimo's studio that included "I'm Walkin'," a song that added fuel to his fire. Bartholomew challenged Earl Palmer to come up with a different beat. Following Domino's unique two-beat piano, the drummer added his own parade rhythms. "Fats was a hell of a lot better musician than people give him credit for," says Palmer. "He had a lot of original thoughts and they were all creative." Palmer pumped a bass drum introduction that harked back a generation to the parade beat of Little Jim Mukes with the Eureka Brass Band. Then he started a steaming snare two-beat. Papoose Nelson played a scintillating guitar riff, with a tuba bass pattern accelerating to double-time. He also added a crucial sixth note. Frank Fields blended his bass between the guitar and Domino's rumbling left hand.

Bartholomew wasn't satisfied. He told Matassa he needed more bottom.

"I can't give it to you, I'm overloaded now," replied the engineer.

"Well, take it from the top and give it to the bass," Bartholomew demanded. "Just give me something to stand on!"

The musicians soon kicked off on an exhilarating second line parade rhythm with an extended solo by Herb Hardesty.

After the session, Bartholomew called a couple of kids from out on the street into the studio. He then rewound the tape and played "I'm Walkin'" for them. As if shot with a jolt of electricity, the kids immediately started dancing. "The only record I ever really felt that we had a big hit on was 'I'm Walkin','" says Bartholomew. "You put the clarinet in 'I'm Walkin'"—*'Doomp-doomp-doomp deedly-deedly-dee'*—and you got traditional jazz. You got Dixieland."

"I'm Walkin'" was also one of Domino's most "country" recordings, with a swinging beat like "Hey Good Lookin'." Country fans also loved Domino's records. His version of Gene Autry's "Blueberry Hill" made #23 on the *Billboard* Country & Western top 50 Best Sellers for 1956, even though—likely to avoid incensing racists—it never appeared on any other country chart, making Fats the only black artist to make the c&w charts during the early civil rights era and foreshadowing the country crossover of Ray Charles by six years. As Gerald Early writes in *One Nation Under a Groove:* "What made Motown possible was not that Elvis Presley covered r&b but that Fats Domino, in the end a more significant artist, not only crossed over with r&b hits in 1955 but with a Country and Western tune, 'Blueberry Hill.'"

■ ■ ■

In late January, blues guitarist Earl King and teenage pianist James Booker performed for a few barflies at the Dew Drop Inn. Rock 'n' roll had hurt black nightclubs, as under-aged teenagers now ruled r&b. A pale, chunky man, tenor sax player Clarence Ford, sat at the bar. A veteran of the bands of Bartholomew and Guitar Slim, Ford (born December 19, 1929) had played many nights at the Dew Drop for ten dollars. Even a musician with a large family like Ford could survive off a few such gigs. At midnight, the owner Frank Painia announced he was canceling the show. Turning to Ford, whom he had nicknamed "V-8," after the powerful car engine, Painia said, "Here's a dollar, get a cab and come back tomorrow."

Ford swallowed hard, accepting the bill. He walked into a biting rain, turning up the collar on his overcoat as he walked to Claiborne Avenue to await a bus. As he soaked, Ford decided that he needed to change his location.

The next day, Herbert Hardesty knocked on Ford's door with an invitation to join Domino's band. Ford quickly accepted. He borrowed a baritone sax from Buddy Hagans to play the solo in "Blue Monday." "I played it up until the time I left the band," says Ford, "which was thirteen years and two months later."

Fats also needed a bass player. "Abdul," a replacement bass player from Philadelphia, hadn't worked out as he was a Black Muslim who labeled whites "The Great Satan." Bartholomew's guitarist, Ernest McLean, was recruited as a fill-in.

Domino also enlisted the services of Lew Freedman, a white middle-aged bartender from Pep's Bar in Philadelphia, as his new road manager. While serving Fats drinks, Freedman had regaled him with his supposed knowledge of the music business. "Lew just wanted to see the world," says Bartholomew. "I thought Lew was okay, but he never had the ability like Billy Diamond."

After a show in Washington, D.C., Domino headed to New York for his February 2 appearance on *The Perry Como Show.* The musicians arrived at the NBC studio at eleven A.M. to rehearse. Como even joked with them, saying, "I sure wish I had a little band like this, I would take it out on the road myself." But following Ed Sullivan's theory that most black musicians should be heard and not seen, Como would also show only Domino at the piano, as racial tensions were still high. In New Orleans, Martin Luther King, Jr., organized the Southern Christian Leadership Conference (SCLC) that month, while black Mardi Gras organizations raising money for civil rights causes pledged not to dance while those boycotting buses had to walk.

Como was even blander than Pat Boone, though he had jokingly covered his namesake r&b hit, "Ko Ko Mo." His other singing guests mirrored his pop style: Jaye P. Morgan, the Four Lads, and Tab Hunter, who performed his #1 hit, "Young Love." But milksop pop embalming the status quo had passed its expiration date, a fact suggested by the slippage of *Your Hit Parade,* a long-running radio and TV show featuring Caucasion crooners chirping innocuous tunes. Ray Charles, the white music director for both *Your Hit Parade* and Como's choristers, the Ray Charles Singers, realized that the emphasis had shifted from the song to *the performance,* as black artists firebranded their music with passion. "They didn't want anybody except Fats Domino doing 'Blueberry Hill,'" says Charles, whose *very name* would soon be usurped by the fame of a singer who epitomized the innovation of black music. Similarly, Domino burned like a nuclear reactor in the white-on-white tableau, as he banged out a medley, ending with "Blue Monday." It was probably the first time a black man uttered the word "slave" on *Perry Como.*

After the high of the Como show, Fats was brought down to earth five days later when he returned to Fayetteville, the scene of his last debacle. This time a fifth of whiskey came crashing into a cymbal stand. The rowdy Fort Bragg dancers and Native Americans from the local Lumbee tribe were drinking heavily. A fight again engulfed the audience, though Domino exited through a back door.

"This your Daddio of Raddio, your Porkulatin' Poppa . . ." In Masontown, Pennsylvania, fifty-five miles south of Pittsburgh, a sixteen-year-old named Richard Nader listened to deejay Porky Chedwick every day after school on a red plastic radio, the wire antenna wrapped around his bedsprings to attract every juicy drop of rock 'n' roll ether. Nader was thrilled to hear about The Biggest Show of Stars, which Chedwick promoted. It would be first rock 'n' roll show he ever attended.

On February 15, Nader and his friends traveled to the Big Show in his brother's green '55 Mercury with all the "cool" automotive accoutrements: knockers, mud flaps, lowering blocks, fuzzy dice, and roaring glass pak mufflers. Nader sped through the Liberty Tunnel, incurring a hefty $15 speeding ticket, though he forgot the fine's sting as he took his seat in the fourth row of the Syria Mosque. "Rock 'n' roll was still under a great deal of adverse publicity," says Nader. "Up came Fats Domino and everybody that was anybody. It was an *incredible* experience."

A dozen years later, Richard Nader would realize Alan Freed's dream of putting rock 'n' roll in Madison Square Garden when he began his Rock 'n' Roll Revival concerts, which also paid tribute to rock 'n' roll extravaganzas even greater than Freed's New York–only shows—Irvin Feld's The Biggest Show of Stars.

Backstage at the Syria Mosque, Feld, a small, blond man with owlish horn-rimmed glasses, a loud jacket, and a cigar, greeted the performers. With his Biggest Show of Stars tours sweeping the continent, Feld was the first super concert promoter of rock 'n' roll. "Irvin Feld had more guts than any man I knew," says Lew Chudd. "From record-seller to taking on the circus, man, that guy had guts!"

In the 1930s, a teenage Feld and his brother Israel started hawking "snake oil" at carnivals near their home of Hagerstown, Maryland. By 1939, with $500 saved up, they opened the Super Drug Store in Washington, D.C. From the beginning, the Felds were in tune with the local black community; in front of their store an old black man with a pet gila monster sold Nature Tonic and played blues records. In 1942, the Felds began sponsoring a "race" music radio show on WWDC. They soon started Super Disc Records, including Arthur ("Guitar Boogie") Smith, Erroll Garner, Bullmoose Jackson, and Sister Rosetta Tharpe. By the 1950s, the Felds owned a chain of Super Music stores and booked spiritual and jazz acts, operas, ballets, and even stars like Bob Hope, Jerry Lewis, Ella Fitzgerald, and Harry Belafonte every summer in D.C. The Felds also became the top promoters for Ringling Brothers' Circus by 1957.

The Big Shows started as jazz caravans in the early 1950s. By 1956 the tours took rock 'n' roll all across North America. "Irvin had an incredible amount of vision," says his assistant Allen Bloom. "From '56 we really controlled, by and large, the live music business. The two shows in '57 were probably the biggest ones we had. Definitely Fats was a huge factor in it."

Feld was passionate about rock 'n' roll. He sometimes spoke to his young stars, declaring, "You guys don't know! This is the thing of the future! You're at the beginning of something here, so take this seriously. This is the new music." Like Bill Randle, Feld risked his "legitimate" business reputation by promoting rock 'n' roll. "Irvin Feld had his thumb on the public's pulse," says Herb Cox of the Cleftones, who toured with the Big Show in 1956. "I think he had *more* impact than Alan Freed, because he brought those shows all over the country. They played a major social impact on integration obviously, but also in broadening out the expression of voices of young people."

Feld also promoted black performers to an even greater degree than Alan Freed. After several tours in 1956 headlined by Bill Haley or Carl Perkins over black stars, the first 1957 Big Show was all-black. "In the spring of '57 when we went out there," says Allen Bloom, "there weren't any white acts that meant anything. We booked Fats Domino because he was the biggest thing out there. Fats was hot." With the quick disappearance of Haley, Perkins, and Gene Vincent from the hit parade, the rock 'n' roll milieu beyond Elvis was then dominated by black artists, led by Domino, whose hits from the spring of 1956 stayed at #1 on the r&b charts—still representing rock 'n' roll far more than the pop charts—for an incredible seven months out of the next year. Not until mid-1957 did white acts like Eddie Cochran, Ricky Nelson, the Everly Brothers, Jerry Lee Lewis, and Buddy Holly & the Crickets emerge in the second wave of white rockers.

The Biggest Show of Stars for early 1957 crossed North America in a tour of Odyssean proportions. Only Feld's experience with years of music and circus tours prepared him for the logistical nightmare of a grueling, eighty-day bus and plane trek. No one else had the *balls* for such a tour—an all-black show for mostly white audiences in the midst of civil rights protests. White teens had heard rock 'n' roll records, but they had rarely *seen* the acts. The Feld tours were in fact the first mass, face-to-face convergence of black culture with white teenagers.

Domino, Bill Doggett, LaVern Baker, and Clyde McPhatter were the "Big Four" of the tour, and their pictures appeared largest on posters. Doggett, a former pianist and arranger with Lionel Hampton and Louis Jordan, was actually co-billed with Fats (though he was paid $4,800 a week, compared to Domino's $10,000 salary) because of his massive hit instrumental "Honky Tonk," which guitarist Steve Cropper calls "the record that changed my life." Known for nu. brassy Latin-tinged novelty hits, LaVern Baker was then red-hot with "Jim Dandy." Feld had pried the former Dominoes and Drifters lead vocalist Clyde McPhatter out of the army and became his manager for a solo career including the #1 r&b ballads "Treasure of Love" and "Without Love." Fifth-billed, Chuck Berry was still best known for "Maybellene," though his classic "Roll over Beethoven" had edged into the pop top 30.

Also on the show were vocal group veterans the Five Keys and the Moonglows, along with the Five Satins, Ann Cole, Eddie Cooley and the Dimples, and the pre-teen Schoolboys. At the bottom of the bill were two r&b stars from the late 1940s—blues pianist Charles Brown and Paul Williams, whose orchestra supported the acts. With road managers, roadies, valets, publicists, and several wives and girlfriends, there were more than one hundred people on the two Big Show buses.

▌ ▌ ▌

"WELCOME TO THE BIGGEST SHOW OF STARS FOR 1957!" The Big Show's diminutive announcer, Harold Cromer (once half of the famed song-and-dance team Stump and Stumpy), tap-danced from behind the curtains each night, cracked a couple of jokes, and then announced the Paul Williams Orchestra.

Chuck Berry kicked the show into high gear with electrifying guitar licks and his scissoring duckwalk. The Five Satins romanced the crowd with "In the Still of the Night." The Moonglows, the Five Keys, and Clyde McPhatter completed the seduction. Finally, the teenagers screamed with a rush of hormones when Domino stomped out his massive rhythm hits.

"Domino's Fat $22,700 in SRO Pitt Pair" read the headline in *Variety*, which noted, "There hasn't been anything like this lineup at the box office locally in years." Scalpers hawked tickets to the sold-out shows. Three nights later, Buffalo r&b disc jockey George "Hound Dog" Lorenz, a former associate of Alan Freed who had a popular show on WKBW, m.c.'d the concert at the Maple Leaf Gardens in Toronto.

After the shows, Domino took off in his Cadillac. The others loaded onto the buses and hit the highway winding into the night. The driver knew every black motel in every town. Most shared rooms to save money, if they managed to get off the bus at all. Sometimes after an all-night bus ride, the performers simply showered at the auditorium and waited until showtime.

A headline in the black St. Louis *Argus* newspaper reported, "3,500 Shriek for Fats Domino and Other R&R Stars," after the Kiel Auditorium show on February 23. Due to Domino's reputation for riots, there was a strong police presence. The *Argus* writer emphasized the fact that "no one was injured."

Though the Big Show was big news to teenagers, mainstream newspapers ignored it. There were few blacks in white schools—in places like Toronto many had never even *seen* blacks before—but teens still idolized them as the bearers of *their* music. The main reason for the impressive crowds was clear. "Fats had crossed the line," states Herbert Hardesty. "He was drawing the white audience."

■ ■ ■

"This is a smash, man!" exclaimed singer John Fred upon hearing "I'm Walkin'" on a Baton Rouge radio station in late February. He considered it "an explosion" for its scintillating combination of Dixieland, r&b, pop, and country. The song would be recorded by an amazing variety of artists—including Hank Williams, Jr., Jerry Lee Lewis, Count Basie, Peggy Lee, Ella Fitzgerald, Blues Traveler, and Harry Connick, Jr. Paul McCartney, who imitated Domino's vocals in "I'm Walkin'" as a teenager, would later record an unreleased version of the song.

That winter, sixteen-year-old Ricky Nelson, the younger son on TV's *The Adventures of Ozzie and Harriet,* was driving his date home. To stop her from gushing over Elvis, Ricky declared, "Well, *I'm* gonna make a record." Ricky went home and listened to Domino's "I'm Walkin'." "It was about the only song I knew at the time," Nelson recalled later. "It had about three chords, so I could play it on guitar, and that's why I did the song. I really liked his version of it."

Echoes of "I'm Walkin'"'s two-beat would be heard over a broad spectrum—in the r&b of the Coasters' "Yakety Yak," in the rockabilly of Rick Nelson's "Hello, Mary Lou," in Phil Spector's production pop of Curtis Lee's "Pretty Little Angel Eyes," in Motown hits like the Supremes' "You Can't Hurry Love," and even in the booming bass drum of disco. Max Weinberg admits the song's influence on his drumming in Bruce Springsteen's "Workin' on the Highway."

While everyone heard Earl Palmer's massive beats in "I'm Walkin'" and in Little Richard's hits, New Orleans rhythms were assimilated directly by the Big Show's musicians through Cornelius "Tenoo" Coleman. "Everybody used to ask

'Where's your drummer?'" recalls Fats. "They were lookin' for Tenoo everywhere we go. He was so fast. He threw so much stuff in there, but he'd be on time."

Coleman's fiery rhythms were strongly rooted in the hip-shaking African tradition, in contrast to the cool jazz style of another noted New Orleans drummer, Ed Blackwell, whom Tenoo once bested in a local "Battle of the Drummers." "Tenoo was one *hell* of a drummer," says Bartholomew, "one of the best drummers in the world, but nobody could touch Earl Palmer." The Big Show musicians stood in the wings to watch Coleman play. "Everybody paid attention to Tenoo," adds Bill Doggett. "He had that funny kind of rhythm that later became the style, that double stuff on the bass drum. The way he played his snare was, in what we call the vernacular now, a real *funky* beat."

The word "funky" dates back to at least the beginnings of jazz in New Orleans, circa 1900, when the first jazz legend, cornetist Buddy Bolden, played at a club called "The Funky Butt." Music historian Robert Farris Thompson traces the word back to the African Ki-Kongo "lu-fuki," meaning "positive sweat." In either context, the word reeks of people having a rollicking good time. A funky beat meant a drummer who improvised extra beats, not just for show, but to force people to dance even harder, creating more positive sweat. New Orleans was the home of funky rhythms, dating back to Congo Square and Second Line parades, but notably played by drummers like Tenoo, his pupil Charles "Hungry" Williams, Joseph "Smokey" Johnson, and Joseph "Zigaboo" Modeliste of the Meters. In fact, James Brown admitted his debt to "the New Orleans beat"—as did Brown's drummers Clayton Fillyau and John "Jabo" Starks, who states that he "learned some of that funk by listening to Tenoo."

■ ■ ■

Backstage during the Big Show musicians crouched in a circle throwing dice on the floor. Harold Cromer held "the pot" of bills in his derby. Charles Brown, an inveterate gambler, always seemed to lose. Clyde McPhatter and Domino were the "Big Fish" that the gamblers aimed to hook.

In his dressing room, Fats was nervous. He worried that the people might not like him, despite overwhelming evidence to the contrary every night. Allen Bloom thought that Domino "was scared to death of being on stage." He watched Fats drink heavily, perform his show without speaking, play cards, and then go to sleep. "It's amazing he's still alive," says Bloom. "Fats had a lot of problems with his ears, an enlarged heart, an enlarged liver, but kept on drinking. He said his daddy drank two fifths a day, why couldn't he do the same?"

Despite the grueling schedule, at least some of Domino's band members found time to have their fun. After a show in Toledo, two of them were arrested and fined $50 for having girls in their room for immoral purposes. Ironically, a *Jet* article named the white girls, ages seventeen and nineteen, but not the musicians.

At the end of February, Irvin Feld chartered two Convair planes, nicknamed *Honky Tonk I* and *Honky Tonk II*. The Big Show musicians flew for ten days crossing the Northwest, landing first in Denver on February 26. Allen Bloom had to assuage Domino's nerves to get him on the plane.

In Los Angeles, the performers stayed at the Hotel Watkins or the Dunbar Hotel. Domino's new hangout was the white hotel where he had once been afraid the stay, the Garden of Allah. Ernest McLean walked the deteriorating Central Avenue strip where he had seen stars like Roy Rogers, Harry James, and Betty Grable in the audience when he had played with Joe Liggins a decade earlier. Earl Palmer, who had just moved to L.A., visited Fats backstage at the Shrine Auditorium. After the show, the musicians went out to party. McLean and others went to see Roy Milton at Club Alabam. Then they headed to the Last Word, across the street from the Dunbar. Sitting in the audience was a wisp of a woman, Billie Holiday, who was encouraged to sing a song. The frail goddess of jazz crept up and delivered a song made even more chilling by her shaky delivery.

■ ■ ■

"Oh, you're having trouble sellin' the Spiders' records, huh?" As part of his daily routine at the Imperial office, Lew Chudd harangued East Coast distributors and disc jockeys beginning at seven A.M. Pacific Time. He told the distributor he could send the stiffing records back if he also shipped his red-hot Domino hits back. Chudd smiled wickedly as the phone emitted a frantic squawking sound; the distributor agreed to try harder to sell the Spiders' records.

While in L.A., Fats overdubbed vocals over tracks that Bartholomew had recorded in New Orleans with his musicians, including Lee Allen on sax—"Valley of Tears," "It's You I Love," and "Wait and See." Pianist Edward Frank played softly with no microphone on the session to guide the band. "Fats would sing and put his piano on top of it," recalled Frank. On some records, like "It's You I Love," the piano was inaudible, reflecting the original sound of the background track.

Domino's popularity was at a peak. On March 9, he achieved an amazing feat for any artist, with four hits simultaneously in the *Billboard* Top 100— "Blue Monday" at #10, "I'm Walkin'" at #35, "Blueberry Hill" at #43, and "What's the Reason (I'm Not Pleasing You)" at #83. A week later, Chudd presented Fats with more gold records, announced the release of both the *Here Stands Fats Domino* and *This Is Fats* albums, and even moved toward adult album sales by signing Liberace's brother, George Liberace, who arranged a bizarre violin-led album of Domino-Bartholomew songs titled *George Liberace Goes Teen-Age*. Domino's heavy airplay also revived his first album, which climbed to #17 on the *Billboard* charts. On March 23, "I'm Walkin'" took over the #1 spot on the *Billboard* r&b charts, which New Orleans was again dominating, with "Blue Monday," "Lucille" by Little Richard, and "Just Because" by Lloyd Price also in the top five. Further down the top 15 list was an irony a decade in the making—Domino-styled comeback hits by his former detractors, Annie Laurie and Roy Brown. Domino's dizzying dominance went to the head of Lew Chudd, who announced, "When an artist sells 1,000,000 or more records, he's a pop artist." He more than doubled the first pressing of "Blue Monday" by ordering three-quarters of a million copies of Domino's next record, "Valley of Tears." Such massive orders had only been exceeded by the million-record advances for Elvis Presley hits.

Chudd likely envisioned "Valley of Tears" as a new "Blueberry Hill"–type ballad, but he decided to go one step further to try to increase its pop crossover potential. When Domino received his copy of the new single in the midst of the Big Show tour he was surprised to hear female white singers cooing behind him. Chudd had Imperial pop arranger Jimmie Haskell overdub the singers. Women also sang curious *"bum-bum"* sounds to the beat on the B-side, "It's You I Love." It was an ominous turn for Domino's recordings.

■ ■ ■

"WE WANT FATS!! WE WANT FATS!!" On Sunday, March 17, a daytime crowd in Tucson yelled and stomped when Domino was late for the performance. Bothered by chronic ear and throat problems, Fats was sick. Finally, Harold Cromer stepped out and introduced Domino, who whispered to the fans that he had laryngitis and couldn't sing. As the crowd filed out, road manager Lew Freedman went with Domino and Bernard Dunn to the local hospital, where to appease the promoters they obtained a doctor's statement ordering Fats to rest.

With Domino absent at the next date in Houston, Chuck Berry opened the show with a thrilling performance and then went up to the segregated balcony filled with only white fans. He was risking the racial divide for forbidden fruit, hoping to charm a white man's virginal daughter out of her panties for some *one-on-one integration*. A policeman asked him to leave. He was about to seize the guitarist when Allen Bloom showed up. He apologized to the cop and dragged Berry out of the balcony.

"I saved Chuck from near death many, many times," says Bloom. "In those days, it wasn't exactly 'Southern hospitality.' Chuck had a perverted sense of whatever. The closest call was in the Carolinas. He was caught in the backseat of his car with a young white girl. I was able to talk the police out of putting him in jail forever or lynching him and got him out of town." "Chuck was a little wild," adds Bill Doggett. "All we would do was sign autographs. Sign and don't even talk. *Don't get caught mumbling!* Man, those cops were *terrible* down there. They were just waiting for an opportunity."

The next day, March 27, Fats, still sick, flew home, promising to return the next night. In Little Rock, the scene of integration riots later that year, Chuck Berry tempted fate again. After the show, Paul Williams spotted Berry making out with a white girl as he left the auditorium. A chill ran through the veteran bandleader. Instead of waiting for the bus, he hightailed it to the hotel in a cab.

With as much trouble as Berry was creating, Domino would cause even more. The next night at the Ellis Auditorium in Memphis, Howard Lewis, the big black promoter who booked the Big Show concerts through the Southwest, hung up the phone minutes before showtime. A pissed-off Lewis announced, "Fats says he's sick and can't make it." The news shocked everyone, including Lew Freedman.

The shows in Memphis were again totally segregated. That afternoon, Harold Cromer announced at the first show—for whites only—that Domino was sick. Still, 5,134 fans ignored the offer of a ticket refund and stayed. LaVern Baker, wearing a sequined red dress, stole the show singing "Jim Dandy," with Harold Cromer as the eponymous hero, dancing out to her rescue. With Domino's absence posted in advance for the second show, only 2,500 African American fans paid the $1-$3 ticket prices, even in a benefit for a construction of a Negro YMCA swimming pool.

It was perhaps no coincidence that Domino missed Memphis shows twice in a year. He often played two shows in one day, but he didn't like such blatant segregation. *Tan* magazine even suggested that Fats had won "his own Civil

Rights demand" by boycotting the show. But Allen Bloom saw his absences differently. "Fats was one of a kind," says Bloom. "He was the sweetest, nicest person you ever want to meet, and about as responsible as a four-year-old. But you can't hate him. If he got within 300 miles of New Orleans, he'd disappear. It didn't make any difference how closely you tried to guard him."

■ ■ ■

"AHHHHHHHH-HA-HA-HA-HA-HA!" Tommy "Weepin' and Cryin'" Brown's histrionic cries interrupted his signature song at the Loyola Field House in New Orleans. The wails of the Atlanta singer were patterned after Roy Brown, but his performance was somewhere between the collapsing-and-reviving act that James Brown would make famous, and Tarzan. According to Bartholomew, who joined Domino's band that night and later recorded Brown, "Tommy was one of the greatest entertainers in the world in person." The singer hammed it up with a hanky across the stage, leaping into the orchestra pit and walking up the stairs. He soon stood on the lip of the balcony, contemplating his fate below. Tommy gave into his "sorrow" and jumped, crumpling on the stage, then he got up to screams from the fans. He performed the stunt twice a night and never broke a bone.

Each night on the Big Show, Clyde McPhatter, wearing an immaculate suit and a waved process, cried "Without Love," a spiritual of secular heartbreak, in the lonely glare of a single spotlight. White girls swooned in the front rows. Domino loved McPhatter's voice and sometimes watched him from the wings.

Another of Domino's favorites was the blues balladeer at the bottom of the bill. Charles Brown was now reduced to singing his cover version of Sonny Knight's hit, "Confidential." But Fats hadn't forgotten the great pianist who had influenced him. He often asked Brown to play privately for him. "He treasured me over everybody else," recalled Brown.

After the vocal groups, rockers, and torch singers, Bill Doggett created an uproar with his massive hit, "Honky Tonk." The fans went berserk when saxman Clifford Scott acted out the bump-and-grind of his sexy solo. Blacks danced all over the auditorium. The police signaled Doggett to stop, but he continued into "Honky Tonk, Part 2." Kids from the white sections joined blacks in the aisles. Everybody was having a good time, except the police, who pulled Doggett's plug, causing a premature intermission. "The cops down there didn't want that mixture," says Doggett with a laugh. "They weren't ready for *prime time!*"

Backstage after the show, Fats displayed a pained expression to Allen Bloom, saying, "I feel really sick. I don't think I'll make it tomorrow night." Bloom replied that he'd better talk to Howard Lewis.

They went to see the promoter, who had gotten to know Domino well since he had hooked him up with the Shaw Agency five years earlier. Lewis, who always carried thousands of dollars and a pistol, was sitting at a table counting money when Fats walked in. He acted like he didn't hear Domino's complaint and asked him to repeat himself, while casually placing his .38 revolver on the table.

Fats looked at the gun. "I didn't say nothin'," he replied and walked out.

Despite this attempt to put a scare into him, Domino was again a no-show in Mobile. Allen Bloom chartered a plane back to New Orleans. He rented a car and sat in front of Domino's house on Caffin Avenue until Fats came home at seven A.M. after cruising the bars all night. Bloom shoved the singer into the shower, and they left at 8:30 to catch an eleven o'clock flight. But Fats insisted on stopping on the way to the airport at Frank Mulé's bar, just to say good-bye to his buddies. After a few drinks, they missed their plane, though they caught the next flight to Atlanta.

Though Domino claimed he wanted to spend time with his family, he was very susceptible to the temptations of wine and women. He also liked hanging out with his hometown friends. At heart he was still a private person and the pressures of stardom were hard for him to endure on a continuous basis. He always longed for the safe haven of home, as many of his songs attested. "I was the star of the show," says Fats, "but I'd drink my little whiskey, eat, and forget about it. The man still paid me, whether I was there or not. I didn't realize how important it was—the people waitin' for you. I guess I didn't take nothin' too serious."

■ ■ ■

A huge crowd of Elvis fans, eighty percent of whom were white teenage girls, squealed in unison at the Ottawa Auditorium on April 9. Onstage, Presley, wearing a gold boudoir jacket, gave a plug to Domino's Big Show appearance nine days later there when he sashayed to the piano, fingered out four notes, and sang "Blueberry Hill."

The next night on one of the longest running early TV situation comedies, *The Adventures of Ozzie and Harriet,* Ozzie Nelson asked an actor playing a bandleader in the episode, "How about Ricky singing a rhythm & blues tune?"

Ricky Nelson, a skinny sixteen-year-old in a tuxedo deadpanned a nervous monotone version of "I'm Walkin'." Shocked parents stared at the good clean kid corrupted by the "jungle" music. Shocked teenage girls screamed when he performed an inept Elvis wiggle. No blacks were seen on *Ozzie and Harriet,* but longtime bandleader Ozzie Nelson needed them to simulate rock 'n' roll—he hired two New Orleans expatriates, drummer Earl Palmer and saxophonist Plas Johnson. But Ricky's first producer, jazz guitarist Barney Kessel, failed to duplicate Papoose Nelson's scintillating riff. Under instructions, Palmer likewise played a bland, wooden beat. As fond as he is of Nelson, rock 'n' roll revivalist Marshall Crenshaw admits the stilted record sounds "quite a bit like what Pat Boone was doing to Little Richard's material at around the same time." "Rhythm & blues turned into [white] 'rock 'n' roll,'" says Palmer, who would play a crucial rhythmic role in much better L.A. sessions. "It wasn't as bluesy and soulful as the blacks had been doin' it. It had that white influence, which relates to country or a stricter feeling in regards to rhythm. As with everything else, once something becomes theirs, they took the whole music over."

Nelson's "I'm Walkin," coupled with the triplet ballad "A Teenager's Romance," reached #2. Though its sales failed to top Domino's million-plus seller, it was much more insidious than Pat Boone's r&b travesties, which had the indirect positive effect of sending retching teens to the originals. Nelson's hit signified that the music could be sold *visually* to teenage girls. The formula was clear: Good-looking white kid (no special experience or talent necessary) + "clean" rock 'n' roll + television exposure = $$$. Since television was virtually all white, the writing was on the wall for black rockers. Nelson soon made fine rock 'n' roll records, but he had paved the way for the television teen idol trend, which had tacit adult approval. "It was a time when many a mother ripped pictures of Fats Domino off her daughter's bedroom wall," says Russ Sanjek of BMI.

The Big Show buses traveled East. Musicians tried to sleep with arms cocked beneath their heads, their bones aching. In the back, dice bones were rolling and tempers were flaring. There were arguments over talking, lights, smoking, and living space. Sleep deprivation, drug and alcohol abuse, arthritic joints, colds, and the flu were just some of the problems. One consolation for traveling all night was saving money on hotels. Some slept hardly at all. Some dreamed about *sleeping.*

Every night, Ann Cole, a petite black songstress, shouted her new rocker, "Got My Mojo Working," which Muddy Waters would soon co-opt for one of his signature hits. The mojo was about to hit the tour again upon its return to

Pittsburgh on April 10, which *Variety* noted with the headline "Domino Unit Fat 18g in Return to Pitt." After the show, Allen Bloom instructed LaVern Baker, who had the flu, to stay in bed until she felt well enough to rejoin the troupe.

The next night, Baker surprised Bloom when she showed up at the Big Show in Erie, Pennsylvania. She explained that she heard that Fats wasn't going to show up, so she figured she'd better. He'd left after a girl he was fooling with stole his diamond stickpin. In a panic, Bloom called Domino's favorite joints from the East Coast on down to New Orleans, but the headliner missed shows in Syracuse, Rochester, Providence, and Boston. Each night, the tuxedoed Harold Cromer walked to center stage, took off his derby and bowed. He suggested that the fans pray that Fats Domino might get well soon.

Bostonians watched the Celtics in a thrilling championship. Professional basketball was ninety-nine percent white, but the Celtics were led by a black rookie, Bill Russell, a Louisiana native who the state's white universities had not bothered to recruit. In the same year that Hank Aaron became the National League's Most Valuable Player and Jim Brown was the National Football League's Rookie of the Year, Russell started a racial revolution in basketball, leading the team to eleven championships. Walter Brown, the owner of the Boston Garden and the Celtics, was so happy over winning that when Allen Bloom told him Fats was a no-show, he couldn't care less, though the Better Business Bureau later condemned Domino's billing.

On the fifth day of Domino's absence, Bloom had an inspiration in the dead of night. He remembered the Garden of Allah in L.A., which Domino now loved. He placed a person-to-person call, telling the operator: "Let me speak to Fats!"

From across the continent came a sleepy voice. "Liberace," said Fats, using his nickname for the pompadoured tour manager, "are you the CIA and the FBI?"

"Fats, get your ass back here and get it back tonight!"

In New Haven, Fats finally showed up and rocked the house—the concert would later be called the third greatest rock 'n' roll show in Connecticut's history (after Rolling Stones and Bruce Springsteen concerts).

At the Big Show's Ottawa appearance on April 18, Bloom was surprised to see a baby-faced teenager backstage. Irvin Feld would later claim that "Fats Domino's own mother couldn't have gotten past the police guards." The fifteen-year-old Canadian, who was getting autographs on his new white jacket, ducked into a dressing room and announced, "Mr. Domino, I've got a song for you." Upon hearing the song, Fats told him he ought to record i/ kid also visited Chuck Berry, who was more interested in an eigh with an autograph book who would inspire his "Sweet Little Sixteen." New showtime, Allen Bloom again saw the teen and grabbed him by the collar to eject him. The kid handed Irvin Feld a piece of paper and exclaimed, "My name is Paul Anka and one day I'm gonna be the star of your show!"

At the end of the month, Chuck Berry's "School Day" finally dethroned Domino, who had held the top spot in the *Billboard* r&b chart for an incredible twenty-two straight weeks with "Blueberry Hill," "Blue Monday," and "I'm Walkin'." At the same time, Bill Buchanan, radio-TV editor of the *Boston Daily Record,* wrote a letter to the preeminent black newspaper, *The Pittsburgh Courier,* condemning "Little Richard, Fats Domino, and others like them [who] have done much to hurt the Negro race."

On Sunday, May 5, 1957, the highly successful spring edition of The Biggest Show of Stars of '57 finally wound up its punishing schedule with a party. Clyde McPhatter bought champagne for everyone. Swimming in money, Irvin Feld gave out gifts. Despite Domino's absences—Bill Doggett claimed to have closed the show thirteen times in his place—Fats had still played nearly seventy shows on the backbreaking tour. Incredibly, he soon would headline even bigger shows.

Back home Fats enjoyed a "working" rest. He succeeded in his demand for a dressing room in the Safari Room, where he played a one-week engagement. He also played a benefit at the local Rosenwald Gymnasium on May 18 for the construction of the Ninth Ward's St. David Catholic School, which his children would later attend. Forty policemen were on hand to keep order at the show, at which alcohol was banned. "The big beat and whiskey don't mix," said Domino. "Anywhere liquor is served anything can happen. I don't know why music should make anybody fight. It makes me happy even when I'm feeling bad."

(Late 1957)

"[Domino's] reputation rivals that of Elvis Presley with rock 'n' roll fans."

— *Time* MAGAZINE, JUNE 10, 1957

Soothing strings were heard on Saturday, May 25, as a voice announced, *"The Perry Como Show*!" Como opened his television show singing "Toot Toot Tootsie, Good-bye," an Al Jolson minstrelsy, amid swirling Southern belles and prancing riverboat gamblers. After pop songstress Jo Stafford crooned a number, he introduced his next guest, "a very happy, little rotund fellow named Fats Domino."

Domino and his band, including Bartholomew, swayed through the ballad "Valley of Tears." During "It's You I Love," Tenoo beat out a steaming parade rhythm. Afterwards, Como asked Domino to play "some of that rock 'n' roll stuff." In a joke on his reputation for causing riots, Fats refused, saying he "might wake up everybody and the whole house'll be rockin'!" But Como persisted. His dancers surrounded Domino, whirling in spasmodic teenage fashion, and Tenoo kicked into the heart-jacking beat of "I'm Walkin'." The dancers performed a stylized riot, complete with Fats and his band beating a hasty exit through the audience. Back on the stage, Como appeared shaken.

The carefully choreographed appearance was another attempt to smooth over Domino's image. A similar "sweetening" process was taking place with Elvis Presley and others. Would Domino become, as some viewed Nat "King" Cole, a black Perry Como? Or, like earlier blacks, a "happy, little rotund" minstrel?

Not likely. For the first time since *The Steve Allen Show*, Domino's band was seen on TV. And Fats, a perfectionist who always wanted to perform his hits *exactly* like his records to please his fans, notably didn't use Como's female chorus to duplicate the background singers that Lew Chudd had added to his current record. The appearance was the most prime time exposure that any black rockers received in the 1950s, and much more significantly, it was the first time that television—a virtually all-white medium at the time—actually mocked stodgy whites like Perry Como for their lack of hipness, spontaneity, and rhythm—in essence, their *lack of blackness.*

"Valley of Tears" peaked at a relatively disappointing #6 on the pop charts. It even failed to top the r&b charts. "Frankly, I got all kinds of negative reactions to the girl singers," says Imperial's Eddie Ray. "Fats wasn't meant to be a Nat 'King' Cole."

A few days later, 6,000 teenagers screamed as Domino's diamond-studded digits plastered the piano at the Dallas Sportatorium. Six extra loudspeakers amplified the pounding. Twenty-six policemen herded fans back to their seats. But even the cops couldn't control Domino's crowds; when he returned to Dallas just six weeks later fights would break out among the racially mixed fans exiting the show, with six fans, including a girl, stabbed or beaten.

There were more personnel changes in Domino's band. Squat bassman James Davis (born March 12, 1912), who had played banjo and guitar in New Orleans bands since age eleven, would solidify the rhythm section for more than a decade to come. Saxophonist Eddie Silvers briefly rejoined the group. After Papoose Nelson got into trouble again, this time for failure to pay his child support, another local guitarist, Bill Jones, temporarily replaced him.

Backstage, Fats talked to a *Time* reporter, revealing that it was his ninety-seventh one-night stand so far in the year and that he expected to gross between $600,000 and $700,000 that year. Fats scoffed when the reporter replied that some fans called him the "undisputed king of rock 'n' roll." Still, the article on Domino in the lily-white news magazine was another indication of his arrival. As the *Time* reporter noted, Fats then dominated rock 'n' roll outside of Elvis. He would soon take the music to even larger audiences across the continent, at the same time as news events signaled cultural changes that would shape the world to come.

■ ■ ■

Back in New Orleans, Dave Bartholomew began work on a new song. The producers of Domino's forthcoming movie *The Big Beat* wanted an eponymous title track. Traveling to Jackson, Mississippi, to play a show with his band, Bartholomew sang a simple rhyme into his tape recorder. The bandleader recorded the instrumental track at Cosimo's on June 5 with his studio band. But the recording featured an annoying high-pitched piano riff by session pianist Edward Frank. The lightweight sound, belying the song's title, was typical of Domino's later 1957 recordings, which Bartholomew's band recorded, with Fats overdubbing his vocals later. With the decrease of Domino's participation in the creative process, Chudd's insistence on a pop sound, and a lack of solid material, Domino's records began slipping on the charts.

As Fats trekked westward he had more trouble in Salt Lake City, where he refused to appear at a segregated show until finally his black fans were admitted. He began a week-long show at Zardi's in Hollywood on June 9. Lew Chudd, hoping to place Domino even more solidly into the entertainment mainstream, invited gossip columnist Louella Parsons to the shows. His plan backfired when Domino drank heavily, skipped shows, and left a day early.

A week earlier, Chudd had tried to take advantage of Domino's drinking. He invited Fats to join him in the sacrosanct private bar in his office for a drink before renewing a contract. But Fats replied cannily, "Not until we discuss the contract." Domino knew that Chudd was a tough businessman, but he earned so much money that he didn't worry about the additional fortune that was likely slipping through his fingers. Chudd tried to set up a corporation, "Fats Domino Orchestra, Inc.," but Domino's lawyer Charles Levy didn't want anyone else touching his golden goose's money. Domino also turned down Chudd's suggestion to invest in the new company IBM. If he put $100,000 in computers, Chudd said, in twenty years everybody would kiss his ass. "He was right," admits Fats. "I didn't know what a computer was."

Also in June, ASCAP publishers successfully lobbied for a Senate hearing on BMI's alleged "monopolistic practices." In a *Variety* story Sid Bernstein, then a Shaw Artists agent, argued that rock 'n' roll was still strong, noting that Domino was earning up to $12,500 weekly, while Shaw's next biggest star, Ray Charles, made $5,000 a week.

In fact, Domino grossed $104,000 for his West Coast tour, netting $46,405 for himself. He earned another $5,000 upon filming his appearance for *The Big Beat*. No doubt impressed by Little Richard's shimmying performance in *The Girl Can't Help It*, the movie's director asked Fats to dance during the title song, and the big piano man shocked everyone with some nifty steps. As the movie featured mostly pop and jazz acts past their prime, *Billboard* reported on July 15 that Fats "may lend an aura of rock 'n' roll" to the movie, "which may be carrying a misnomer as *The Big Beat*." A week later, Vanguard Productions, makers of

Alan Freed's *Rock, Rock, Rock,* began work on another low-budget movie titled *The Hit Record,* with scheduled stars Fats Domino, Little Richard, Count Basie, Carl Perkins, and Slim Whitman. While his band drove home, Fats lip-synched a song with a band composed of black extras, who didn't seem to know their instruments, for the movie, soon to be retitled *Jamboree.*

In July children ducked under school desks in a national atomic drill. Fire and brimstone rained on Yankee stadium, where Billy Graham preached to 100,000. Backsliding preacher Jerry Lee Lewis performed his apocalyptic "Whole Lotta Shakin' Goin' On" on *The Steve Allen Show,* while Lennon and McCartney met at a church picnic and practiced songs from *The Girl Can't Help It.* The same Sid Bernstein who declared in *Variety* that rock 'n' roll's "full earning potential has not yet been tapped" would later book the Beatles' shows at Carnegie Hall and Shea Stadium.

Fats flew to New York with Lew Chudd to appear on Alan Freed's ABC summer show *The Big Beat* on Friday, July 26. The show's stars included Patsy Cline, Clyde McPhatter, and Louisiana natives Domino, Jimmy Newman, and Dale Hawkins. Despite the obvious talent, Freed's show, which was soon hurt by a racist backlash after Frankie Lymon danced with a white girl, was not renewed. Three days after Freed's final broadcast, *American Bandstand* debuted on ABC on August 5, featuring the white female barbershop quartet the Chordettes. Whereas Freed preached rock 'n' roll, Clark captured America's young like an ice cream man, feeding them mostly soft-serve vanilla with sprinkles of rock 'n' roll.

During a stay in Philadelphia, Domino appeared twice on *American Bandstand.* Clark's fledgling show did not yet have a piano, so Fats lip-synched his chirping new single "When I See You" standing alone. Later that week, Domino again appeared on Clark's show, this time sitting at a piano and blasting through a live medley with his band. "He was one of the few artists to appear on *Bandstand* that played live," says Clark; "everybody else had to lip-synch."

Also in August, Congress finally approved a civil rights voting bill. Ford introduced the Edsel, a failure that would cost the company $400 million. In a *Jet* article, Elvis Presley said he could never equal the musical achievements of Domino or the Ink Spots' Bill Kenny. Police escorted the first black family in the model suburb of Levittown, New York, to their home through rock-throwing mobs.

In *Variety* on August 28 Imperial announced record grosses of $3,162,000 for the first six months of 1957, almost all due to Domino, whose five albums had sold 250,000 copies, an unheard-of amount for an r&b artist. But Lew Chudd had also seen the visual impact that Elvis Presley had on young girls and realized the potential of TV star Ricky Nelson after his cover version of "I'm Walkin'." The same issue reported in a tiny article, "Imperial Records has inked Ricky Nelson to an exclusive contract."

"His father had a television show, that's why I signed Ricky Nelson," says Chudd. "He couldn't sing. I walked by the studio. The kid was playing guitar and he sounded pretty good. I had known Ozzie from New York when he was a bandleader. We made a deal in five minutes. I was a wide awake little boy!"

■ ■ ■

"OOH-POPPA-DOO, HOW-DO-YOU-DO? This is your Spaceman, Joc-ko, back on the scene at the A-poll-o with Fats Dom-i-no!" The crowd at the Apollo Theater screamed as black WOV disc jockey Jocko Henderson ("The Ace from Outer Space") delivered his patented jive rap for Domino's Labor Day week show at the Harlem landmark. Domino and Bartholomew roomed at the Park Sheraton downtown at 56th and Seventh, while the band members stayed at the Hotel Theresa in Harlem, where they jammed with other musicians to the wee hours of the morning.

During the show the lilting tones of Philly's Lee Andrews and the Hearts challenged Harlem's own Harptones. Blues belter Big Maybelle, with her 200-pound curves stuffed into red satin tights like giant jalapenos, slew the crowd with her fiery wails. Bo Diddley beat out a voodoo beat with the eerie "Who Do You Love."

Bartholomew worried that Fats was now too pop for the tough Apollo crowd. But Domino opened with the steamrolling "I'm Walkin'," and the fans jumped up and started clapping. The promoters added more daily shows to satisfy the overflow "pepper-and-salt" audiences—many whites ventured to Harlem to see Domino. Sunday, September 1, was the theater's biggest single-day gross, a remarkable fact considering a star-packed Alan Freed show featuring Little Richard and Buddy Holly and the Crickets was playing simultaneously across town at the Brooklyn Paramount.

Domino's international appeal was also impressive. *Billboard* reported astounding tour offers from Australia and England. Clarence "Frogman" Henry confirmed Domino's popularity in Jamaica when he toured there that month. "'Blueberry Hill' was the biggest thing over there," says Henry, "and I sang it."

■ ■ ■

On Friday, September 6, class was back in session for Irvin Feld's 1957 Biggest Show of Stars at Pittsburgh's Syria Mosque. Returning former Big Show stars included (in order of billing) Domino, LaVern Baker, Frankie Lymon, Chuck Berry, and Clyde McPhatter, along with an integrated cast of mostly freshmen: (Buddy Holly and) the Crickets, the Everly Brothers, the Spaniels, the Drifters, Paul Anka, Johnnie and Joe, and the Bobbettes. Musical backing was provided by the Paul Williams Orchestra, featuring Tommy Brown. "If you look at the lineup of the old posters, every big star in the *world* was on those tours," remarks Dick Clark. "You got in for like a buck and a half or two dollars. It was unbelievable."

There was bad news before the tour even began, as *Jet* reported: "Fats Domino Banned in Nation's Capital." *The Washington Post* placed the story on its front page on August 30, next to the news of Strom Thurmond's record one-man twenty-four-hour filibuster of the civil rights bill. Washington, D.C., commissioners banned the tour from Feld's hometown, declaring that with Domino's riotous reputation they would need "just about every policeman in town to maintain order"—presumably jeopardizing the president and national security. The September 8 show was rescheduled for Annapolis, Maryland.

The caravan grossed more than $21,000 for the Pittsburgh shows, though it was the third time the headliners had played there that year. The troupe would tour twenty-eight different states and five Canadian provinces in eighty days. Jack Kerouac's 1957 novel *On the Road* had nothing, travel-wise, on the Big Shows led by Domino that year, though even the bebop-loving beats listened to the big beat as they zoomed across America's highways. Allen Ginsberg wrote in *First Blues* that he, Kerouac, and Neal Cassady listened "to car radio Rhythm & Blues of Louis Jordan & Fats Domino, moans of Slim Gaillard & shrieks of Little Richard, so I had some kind of American Blues in my heart without knowing it."

The Big Show buses often traveled all night on 400–600-mile jaunts. Upon arriving in the next city at seven o'clock in the morning, the musicians did their laundry, got a bite to eat, and tried to sleep before the show. For matinees, they had to be at the theater before noon. "It was a horrible life," recalled Niki Sullivan of the Crickets. "You're at the mercy of your booking agent, your managers, the record company, the radio jockeys, and especially the fans."

On the bus, the young black stars were literally having the time of their lives. After the Big Show, everything would be an anticlimax, if not a freefall. Though he was a year younger than Paul Anka, fifteen-year-old Frankie Lymon lived in the fast lane. He had already toured England, appeared on TV and in movies, slept with countless females, and ingested a stream of intoxicants, but his solo pop hit of Ella Fitzgerald's "Goody Goody" would be his last big hurrah. The even younger Bobbettes enjoyed knocking Clyde McPhatter's "Long Lonely Nights" out of #1 on the r&b disc jockey chart with "Mr. Lee," but most of the r&b singers would fail to have a second hit. White entrepreneurs exploited young blacks and spat them out. Lymon would o.d. on heroin at age twenty-five. Even the great McPhatter would struggle with alcoholism and fade into obscurity before an early death.

Late at night, the Drifters sang haunting spirituals like "Burying Ground" or "How Deep Is the Ocean" in an ethereal *a capella,* with their four voices filling the cigarette-lit bus. The group included original Drifter Bill Pinkney, famed for his baritone lead vocals on the classic "White Christmas." "Once we'd get started on the bus," says Pinkney, "we'd have it rockin'!"

▌▌▌

The fans at the Maple Leaf Gardens in Toronto on September 14 groaned when Harold Cromer announced that Chuck Berry had the Asiatic flu, but when he added that another star would play a double set—*"PLEASE WELCOME THE SELLER OF OVER SIXTEEN MILLION-SELLING RECORDS, 'FATS' DOMINO!"*—screams erupted as the curtains parted and Fats shouted "I'm in Love Again." At the end of each show, the artists all gathered for a grand finale. Six-foot-four saxophone great Lee Allen, who had joined Domino's band, blew a towering solo.

The next night, the show broke records at the Forum in Montreal, taking in an incredible $51,890 and 30,000 fans for two shows, with thousands turned away. The teenage girls wanted to see sixteen-year-old Canadian Paul Anka. Hearing Anka's record "Diana" in his D.C. record store, Irvin Feld had booked the kid he had kicked out of the Ottawa Big Show in April. "Diana" received airplay on *American Bandstand* after ABC-Paramount gave the b-side's publishing rights to Dick Clark. Anka bragged about his record hitting #1. He also claimed that he had felt racism in Canada due to his Lebanese ancestry. The other musicians were not impressed by Anka's claim, but the fact that young whites suddenly wanted to relate to blacks was news indeed.

Two buses with "THE BIGGEST SHOW OF STARS FOR 1957" painted across the side rolled along highways like an inoculation shot against racism in the bloodstream of America. Despite the Supreme Court integration ruling, one of the few places that white and black teens mixed together was at rock 'n' roll concerts like the Big Show. Inside, the bus was a microcosm of racial integration in reverse. Riding their first hit, Buddy Holly and the Crickets were, as drummer Jerry Allison puts it, "in hog heaven" to be touring with a pantheon of great rockers.

"It's so great to be out here," Holly confided to Bill Pinkney of the Drifters. "Just six months ago, I was pushin' a wheelbarrow carrying cement up and down a ramp, doin' construction work. I've been lovin' my guitar, pickin' and singin'. I just didn't give up. Now I'm not pushin' a wheelbarrow anymore!"

"I can understand that," nodded Pinkney, "because I came from a cotton field in South Carolina, and I don't plan to go *there* no more—not to pick cotton!"

Three weeks after the Big Show began, the Crickets' "That'll Be the Day" hit #1. Dick Clark played the song after it broke out in Cleveland, where disc jockey Bill Randle plugged it heavily. Randle had a major hand in the pop breakthroughs of the Big Show acts Domino, Buddy Holly, and the Everly Brothers, and he soon kicked off Sam Cooke's career by breaking "You Send Me." "A lot of the records got broken in Cleveland because of Bill," says Clark. "He was a very studious, intelligent man who had his finger on the pulse of the kid market like [Alan] Freed did."

In stark contrast to the growing social ties on the Big Show, the major news story in America was about a racial firestorm taking place in Arkansas. Two days before the tour began, Governor Orval Faubus had the state militia bar nine black students from Central High School in Little Rock.

On September 9, the first civil rights legislation since Reconstruction became law. That day, segregationists beat a Birmingham minister who was leading black children to a white school. The next day, a bomb ripped through a Nashville school that admitted Negroes. On September 24, President Eisenhower federalized Arkansas National Guard troops who led nine black students to class through an angry mob of 1,500 white protesters. NBC and CBS provided live news updates on the tense situation. The riots helped *American Bandstand*, which was the only "riot-free" TV for ninety minutes, five days a week. Meanwhile, Nat "King" Cole, the only black network TV star, lambasted companies for lacking the courage to sponsor his program. "Madison Avenue," said Cole, "is afraid of the dark."

Likewise, before the intervention in Little Rock, another normally apolitical black icon, Louis Armstrong, had declared that the president had "no guts" and withdrew from a proposed tour to Russia. Domino, of course, had jokingly offered to go to Russia the previous year to help thaw the Cold War. But, in fact, the Big Show buses were having a great positive effect on integration of America's youth, crisscrossing the country like freedom riders.

In Greenville, South Carolina, a group of white teens, who had attended Domino's concerts locally, watched the racial disturbances on television. As disc jockey Harry Turner recounts in *This Magic Moment,* his memoir of growing up with rock 'n' roll, one of the boys blurted out, "They ought to shoot those niggers!" Shocked by the uncharacteristically racist statement, Turner asked his friend what he would do if Fats Domino stood in front of those black kids. His friend reconsidered and replied, "They'd have to shoot me first!"

Given the racial climate in the country, the Big Show musicians regularly ran into prejudice. At one Southern roadside café, a man told the Big Show musicians as they entered, "We don't serve niggers."

"That's all right," Chuck Berry replied with a wicked smile, *"I don't eat 'em."*

"If you can't feed these fellas," said Buddy Holly, "we're not gonna eat here either!" as he exited with the others.

Curtains divided blacks and whites in the Carolina concert halls. "A lot of times [the blacks] couldn't get into the hotels or restaurants," recalls Anka, "and we'd all sleep and eat in the bus." In turn, the white artists were annoyed when they couldn't stay in black hotels. In a preplanned move, beginning September 23, Irvin Feld removed the white acts from five southern cities—Columbus, Chattanooga, Birmingham, New Orleans, and Memphis—which didn't allow integrated performances.

The Crickets flew from Atlanta to Lubbock. "We were tickled to go home," says Jerry Allison, "but we didn't like the reason we weren't playing." They then flew to Oklahoma City, where their producer, Norman Petty, set up a session. They revved up the formerly hillbilly song "Maybe Baby" with a riff derived from the locomotive pattern played by the New Orleans studio band in Little Richard's "Lucille" (the same riff that would later power Roy Orbison's "Oh, Pretty Woman").

Feld also gave Domino a three-day break near his home—he missed the Birmingham, New Orleans, and Memphis shows. But it was the absence of the white singers that prompted a fiery editorial in *The Louisiana Weekly* by Elgin Hychew:

Thumbing through the souvenir program of "The Biggest Show of Stars for 1957" the other evening at the Auditorium, we noted a number of popular ofay stars were missing. . . . It's no secret that Louisiana segregation laws prohibit white and Negro stars from performing together on the same shows. The result was that the thousands who jam-packed the auditorium were shortchanged. It's not the first time, either. It all adds up to one thing: WE NEED MORE NEGROES TO REGISTER AND VOTE out certain rabblerousing, troublemaking Legislators and Congressmen like SENATOR RAINACH and CONGRESSMAN ED-WARD HEBERT who invariably carry on their bigotry and race hate campaigns through the press .. . . Any Negro who wastes his vote on rabblerousers like Hebert and Rainach is a traitor to his race and should be dealt with accordingly.

In Memphis even the white bus driver was banned from watching backstage. After the show, Allen Bloom, Clyde McPhatter, and his valet drove to the next date in Oklahoma. When they stopped at a Little Rock gas station, a policeman, suspicious of a white man traveling with two black men, escorted them out of town. "The Little Rock riots scared the shit out of everybody," says Bloom. "None of us were in the business to change society. We were changing society, but we didn't know it. There's no question that we did a lot to break down racial barriers."

Every night Chuck Berry split like a pretzel as he duckwalked across the stage and shouted, *"Hail! Hail! Rock 'n' roll! Deliver me from the days of old!"* Though Berry didn't talk much, his song "School Day" declared rock 'n' roll's racial deliverance. "On the Fats Domino Show, I think they called it the Biggest Show of Stars, [the color line] was breaking then," recounts Berry. "We'd go in and see the salt and pepper all mixed together." A photographer took a picture of Berry at a Waco, Texas, record store shortly after the Little Rock riots with two dozen white kids, all happily holding up copies of his *After School Session* including "School Day." Rock 'n' roll indeed seemed to promise a change from the days of old.

At the October 2 show in Fort Worth the police tripled security to a dozen cops at the Will Rogers Auditorium to prevent the "race riot" that occurred after Domino's Dallas show in July. With the Little Rock protests in the headlines, the contrasting scene that *The Fort Worth Press* reported was profound: "The house was packed for two performances starring Fats Domino, Negro hepcat. Whites and Negroes sat side by side. There was no attempt to segregate the races."

Everyone at the Big Shows, including the fans, were instigators, as the days of old gave way to the news that both Roy Brown ("Good Rockin' Tonight") and

Chuck Berry ("Roll Over Beethoven") had heralded. "We didn't have time to read the news or watch the news," recalled Niki Sullivan. "We *were* the news."

■ ■ ■

The Soviets shocked the world on October 4 with the launch of Sputnik, the first satellite to orbit the Earth, at a time when U.S. test rockets blew up on the launch pad. As the Big Show artists were inoculated against the Asiatic flu epidemic in San Antonio, another Asian menace loomed like a blinking evil eye in the sky. Headlining an Australian tour with Gene Vincent and Eddie Cochran, Little Richard shocked Aussies with rockin' stripteases. But Richard had reached the zenith of his wild ride. He viewed Sputnik as a sign of God's Judgment. Throwing his diamond rings into Sydney's Hunter River, he pronounced, "If you want to live for the Lord, you can't rock 'n' roll, too. God doesn't like it."

Fats did his part against communism that month by delivering a wobbly introduction to a Civil Defense public service radio show. Announcer Jay Jackson explained that "You and your family can actually contribute to world peace" in between Domino hits. The show exemplified Domino's subversion. He was banned in the nation's capital for threatening the puritanical and segregated American way of life with his riots, yet he *seemed* so harmless and upstanding that the government's Defense Department asked him to be a spokesman to protect America.

Chudd and Domino appeared on the cover of the October 5 issue of *Cash Box,* with a cake frosted with the number "25," signifying the millions of records Domino had sold. The story on Imperial Records exaggerated Chudd's role, even crediting him with supervising the recordings. The writer described him calling his thirty-eight distributors, talking to 100 disc jockeys a month, and flying 100,000 miles a year. But there was no mention of his racial pioneering. Besides making Domino a superstar, Chudd had also hired *three* black department heads (now including West Coast A&R director Ernie Freeman) in a company with barely a dozen employees. In fact, the story ignored the roles of Bartholomew and Eddie Ray, much to their disgust.

Imperial again sold more than a million singles a month from August to November due to Domino's touring and Ricky Nelson's first Imperial record, "Be Bop Baby." But, according to Eddie Ray, Nelson's hits never sold after their initial success, whereas Domino's old hits kept selling, with distributors calling Imperial to request 500 or 1,000 of each record. "I could tell what part of the country Fats was working without looking at his itinerary," says Ray.

Nelson appeared on national TV more than Fats and other black rockers put together. In fact, the black music revolution continued almost invisibly. Another two-bus caravan that month included several artists with New Orleans ties: Mickey and Sylvia, Larry Williams, Joe Turner, Annie Laurie, the Moonglows, Roy Brown, Bo Diddley, Nappy Brown, and Ray Charles. Over a year after Elvis Presley's ascendance, the three major rock 'n' roll package tours were eighty percent black with all black headliners, a fact not noted in the annals of history. As Little Richard forsook his gold lamé and his process for a plain suit, a tight hair crop, and a Bible, radios blasted out his swansong in which he screamed a segregation metaphor to psychotic exasperation: *"Keep a-knockin', but you can't come in!"*

■ ■ ■

"Okay, you're into my thousand," said Domino, clutching a $1,000 bill as he leaned over to throw a pair of dice backstage before a show. Fats usually stayed in his hotel or dressing room, though sometimes he shopped for clothes. "My mind would mostly be on my music," says Fats. "I'd get off the stage, get me some rest, and get ready to go to my next job." But Domino looked forward to the Big Show's swing through California and especially revisiting friends in Los Angeles.

In the Golden State only the October 12 date in San Diego sold out, even though the Everly Brothers became the fifth Big Show act to have a #1 hit since the tour started with their parody of American puritanism, "Wake Up Little Susie." The threat of Sputnik perhaps had parents demanding homework instead of rock 'n' roll. Allen Bloom blamed local promoters, who were "more interested in listening to the show than promoting," though fans never turned out in California like elsewhere.

There were changes in the show. In another prearranged move, Irvin Feld replaced the black acts the Bobbettes, the Spaniels, and Johnnie and Joe with Eddie Cochran, Buddy Knox, and Jimmy Bowen, beginning with the October 15 show at the Shrine Auditorium in Los Angeles. While in L.A., Domino had a good time, as he apparently began an affair that would later lead to a paternity suit.

In fact, Fats now closed the first set partly so he could have more time to enjoy himself. A second show ended well after midnight for teens with curfews. "The show was so long people got tired," explains Paul Williams. "A lot of times he'd come on and people'd be leaving. He was 'Fats Domino the Great,' so he changed places." The tour was now the greatest rock 'n' roll touring show of all time, with several future Rock and Roll Hall of Famers who had amassed twenty-two *Billboard* #1 hits between them. Shows in northern California did better: $11,600 in San Jose, $9,000 in Sacramento, $18,500 in San Francisco, and $13,000 in Oakland.

Backstage at the Frisco show, Phil Everly separated his brother Don from an embrace with a fan he'd talked to in Los Angeles, telling her that Don was married. Though some female fans just wanted a star fuck, she had taken a bus and was dressed for a formal date, leading to Phil's reaction. In fact, Sharon Sheeley was the classic "Sweet Little Sixteen" fan, who had met Ricky Nelson by feigning car trouble in front of his home and managed to meet Elvis at L.A.'s Knickerbocker Hotel; she would later become Eddie Cochran's girlfriend. Phil and Paul Anka consoled her afterward, walking her to the bus station. Crying about her foolishness on the way home, Sheeley turned her sadness into a song for Ricky Nelson. The result, "Poor Little Fool," became Lew Chudd's first #1 pop hit on Imperial the next year.

The Big Show artists relieved tension in various ways on the marathon tour. In Seattle, Allen Bloom took Irvin Feld to a house, telling him that the always-feuding LaVern Baker and Clyde McPhatter had had a fight. Feld walked into a surprise birthday party with the Big Show cast. Eddie Cochran bathed in a bathtub full of beer. One of the Everlys dove into a table-sized cake. At the Big Show in Moscow, Idaho, on October 28, the musicians got revenge on Paul Anka for his bratty attitude and practical jokes like hiding Buddy Holly's guitar and knocking out microphone plugs. Backstage, LaVern Baker told Anka she was going to make him a *real* member of show business. Musicians ripped off his clothes as she smeared blackened cold cream all over him. Then she split two feather pillows over him. The musicians howled. Anka was finally officially "black"—*tarred and feathered.*

With the addition of the Diamonds of "Little Darlin'" fame in early November, the proportion of white stars increased to nearly half. Blacks rode in the front of the bus, so that the white bus driver would let them off at their hotel first. While on the bus, Chuck Berry led sing-alongs with the driver's microphone coiled inside an acoustic guitar. Some parodied the absent headliner. The diminutive singers Frankie Lymon and Paul Anka slept in the luggage rack. In the back, Eddie Cochran shivered from the Asiatic flu. Feathers flew from pillow fights. Verbal barbs also darted through the bus. LaVern Baker, preening like a diva with her maid Dorene and her white poodle Tweedlee Dee, tried to insult Buddy Holly as "a one-hit artist."

On November 10, Herbert Hardesty and Paul Anka walked down the mean streets of Detroit with overcoats to deflect the chill. Anka had indeed become a regular member of the troupe. Sometimes the small teen hung underneath the overcoat of a musician sneaking him into a black hotel. After their show at the Fox Theater, Domino gave Anka his own initiation into Detroit's nightlife, beginning at Al Green's Flame Show Bar, where LaVern Baker and Johnnie Ray had started.

The Big Show ran into trouble in Boston on November 15. Irish policemen kicked out two dozen kids for dancing and arrested a dozen others. Municipal Court Chief Justice Elijah Adlow later blasted rock 'n' roll as he dismissed five of the teens arrested as having paid "sufficient penalty with the [$3] high cost of admission."

Three days later, Anka introduced the Big Show musicians to his parents in his hometown of Ottawa. The Ankas threw a party at La Conda, their Italian restaurant across from the Canadian Parliament. The musicians laughed inwardly as they complimented the Ankas on their son, who showed off his new Cadillac with a built-in 45 rpm record player.

As the Big Show buses rolled past snowy fields, David Somerville of the Diamonds asked Buddy Holly, "How long do you think this rock 'n' roll can last?" Holly softly replied, "I'll give it a year at the outside."

Friendships had developed. Holly would present the Everlys with songs. In return, they gave him Boudleaux Bryant's "Raining in My Heart," while Paul Anka gave him the flipside, Holly's final hit, "It Doesn't Matter Anymore." Both songs would feature orchestral strings—back in Vancouver, Holly had confided to disc jockey Red Robinson that he'd "prefer singing something more quieter anyhow."

"Liquor's here!" shouted LaVern Baker, holding up two bottles of Jack Daniels, "and if ya'll don't drink it, we'll have to turn it back in!" Even at their closing party, the musicians broke barriers—the post-tour celebration in Richmond, Virginia, on November 24 was at a nightclub that had never allowed blacks. A tipsy Domino tried to sign an autograph for Allen Bloom. He signed a $100 bill "To Liberace," but messed up. He crumpled the bill and threw it down. After five or six bills, he finally got it right.

Three days earlier the Big Show had filled the Brooklyn Paramount Theater to the rafters. *Look* magazine sent a photographer, Charlotte Brooks, to do a photo shoot on Domino. She snapped Fats fanning himself with $1,000 bills and submitting to a tailor's tape measure. She took scores of photos of him but only took a few shots of LaVern Baker and Paul Anka. Newspaper headlines and stories about the Big Show likewise mentioned Domino's name almost exclusively. Though the others would become legends, Domino already was one.

■ ■ ■

There was a frenzy of activity at Imperial Records that month. Adding to the sale of millions of Domino and Ricky Nelson records, Chudd's arranger Ernie Freeman scored a top five hit with a cover of Bill Justis's "Raunchy." "I couldn't answer the phone anymore," says Chudd. "We had about five companies pressing records. Boy, that was a hell of a time. I took the family to Honolulu for two weeks."

Soon after the Big Show, Domino's musicians started receiving offers. Lee Allen began his solo career, recording for Herald and Ember Records in New Jersey. His Big Show finale, now titled "Walkin' with Mr. Lee," would become a hit on *American Bandstand*. The Diamonds hired Herbert Hardesty and Tenoo Coleman to play on their records. The group's manager, Nat Goodman, would record a whole album of material with Hardesty and other New Orleans musicians the next January.

On December 11, *Jamboree* premiered in Hollywood. Though Fats headlined the film, the riff-rocker he performed, "Wait and See," peaked at #23. Since he replaced the retired Little Richard in the film, Jerry Lee Lewis acquired "Great Balls of Fire," which the film's musical director Otis Blackwell co-wrote for the soundtrack. The song exploded the Louisiana pianist's rising star.

That month, *Billboard* reported that five youths were sentenced to twenty months in prison in Czechoslovakia for playing rock 'n' roll. Columbia Records' producer Mitch Miller called rock 'n' roll records "the comic books of music," while Sammy Davis, Jr., said he'd "commit suicide" if rock 'n' roll was here to stay. Unable to find sponsors, *The Nat "King" Cole Show* was broadcast for the last time on December 17. It would be nearly a decade before blacks again starred in U.S. television shows.

On a chilly December morning, Dave Garroway, of *Today* show fame, stood at the New Orleans corner of Rampart and Canal that Domino had sung about in his first record and presented the city's musical talents, including Mahalia Jackson, on his *Wide World* television program. Reggie Hall brought his seven-year-old nephew, Antoine Domino, downtown to play drums for the show, just as the boy's father was on his way to New York City.

■ ■ ■

A cold wind blew down Broadway. A line of teens stretched around an entire city block from the New York Paramount at Broadway and 43rd Street. Beginning at 5:30 A.M., teenagers stood in the bluesy fifteen-degree weather. Cars jammed the streets, honking in the gridlock. Over the next twelve days, some 20,000 rock 'n' roll fans lined up every day. Many would not make it in—the Paramount held only 3,400. Police on steam-snorting horses patrolled the lines from the first show at nine A.M. The Paramount marquee showed the reason for the commotion:

IN PERSON ALAN FREED AND
HIS HOLIDAY OF STARS ON STAGE
FATS DOMINO JERRY LEE LEWIS
EVERLY BROS. BUDDY HOLLY
CRICKETS DANNY & JUNIORS
PAUL ANKA LEE ANDREWS & HEARTS
SHEPHERD SISTERS LITTLE JOE DUBS
THURSTON HARRIS TEENAGERS
JO ANN CAMPBELL TWINTONES TERRY NOLAND
ALAN FREED'S R'N'R ORCH
on the screen "IT'S GREAT TO BE YOUNG"

There was so much traffic on the streets that Domino's musicians had to walk from their hotel to the Paramount every day. Then they needed a police escort to get through the mob of kids around the theater. With the high demand for tickets, *The New York Times* on December 28 reported that the price of the show was quickly raised from $2 to $2.50, and the movie, *It's Great to Be Young,* was cut short or omitted so that another show, the sixth, could be run before two A.M.

Jerry Lee Lewis thrilled the crowds with his explosive performances. "Jerry Lee Lewis was burning up the place, playing his ass off," says Dave Bartholomew, who joined Domino's band for the shows. "He was so electrifying, with [simulated] fire coming out of the piano. He was standing and walking all on the piano." Though Lewis was unquestionably a sensation, thirty-five years later a book, *Great Balls of Fire,* made statements, soon spread like bad rumors, that Freed made Lewis the closing act and even changed the marquee to make him the headliner. However, those on the show, including Jerry Allison and Joe Mauldin of the Crickets, Joe Teri of Danny and the Juniors, and Domino's band members deny that any such thing happened. "When we worked with Jerry, Fats always closed the show," says Bartholomew. "Fats had 22–23 hits. He was such a force that all the people wanted to see him. Jerry couldn't match him so far as popularity in recordings."

According to Allison, Fats even kicked his piano stool away in mock imitation of Lewis, though both Domino and Little Richard had been doing that for years. The two Louisiana men, Domino and Lewis, actually became friends. They would soon reprise their "rivalry" on January 8 on Patti Page's television program, *The Big Record.* Ironically, Lewis, who received yet another huge benefit from Little Richard's retirement when he replaced him on Freed's show, at the time told *Melody Maker,* "I've no special favourites today except Little Richard and Fats Domino."

Buddy Holly and the Crickets, fresh off an Ed Sullivan appearance and riding their new hit "Peggy Sue," actually played some encores. To Domino, though, the shy Texan seemed almost invisible. "I don't remember nothin' too much about Buddy Holly," says Fats, "but I know I worked with him."

To the *Variety* reviewer, the teenagers responding to the musicians' call stole the show: "The more histrionic of them scream, some organize groups that sway to and fro and nearly all of them rhythmically clap their hands and stomp their feet."

The incredible New York Paramount shows were the apex of several rock 'n' roll careers. The show broke the Paramount's one-day record with $32,000 in tickets and altogether grossed more than $300,000—$148,000 of which went to pay for the music and the musicians, with $28,350 alone going to Domino.

Fats *had* to close the show, as his band led the grand finale. Many of the artists got back on the stage to sing and clap to "When the Saints Go Marching In." The kids clapped and stomped as Bartholomew, his crooked trumpet blaring, led Domino's band in a second line parade. "We'd be watching the balcony shake," declares Phil Everly. "I thought it was going to come down."

The shows that Domino headlined that year had grown progressively "whiter." Alan Freed, once the champion of black rockers, now featured five consecutive white acts after Domino, whose presence gave the show meaning:

One of the original r&b titans still ruled. As the *Variety* reviewer put it, he "sometimes provide[d] a sense of logic to the proceedings."

Fats had achieved an amazing appeal that transcended his music. Though he was an r&b icon, his audience was now more white than black. He was respected for his jazz and blues roots, and yet adored by teenagers who loved the simple fun of his beat. Even adults loved his rocking renditions of pop songs. On December 26, Domino was again named the *Down Beat* "Rhythm & Blues Personality of the Year," beating out Ray Charles and Elvis Presley. It was the forth year in a row that Fats was named the top r&b artist. He had headlined the greatest shows in the short history of the music, whatever it was called, but it was a fleeting moment. Rock 'n' roll's early frenzy had reached its peak.

A scene at the Paramount crystallized the moment. Among the horde of swaying, screaming teens, a group in the upper level hung three bed sheets from the balcony. The first unrolled, revealing one giant word: "FATS." The second one read "DOMINO." The third added "FOR PRESIDENT."

"Be My Guest"
Chapter 12

(1958–1959)

"They tried to kill rock 'n' roll. They didn't succeed."

—Lew Chudd

"We expect to have the biggest year in our history in 1958." Many could have made that statement. Churches enjoyed the largest membership increase since 1950. Wham-O took an idea from a bamboo calisthenics ring and sold 30 million plastic hula hoops. Drive-in theaters cashed in on a new teenage rite, increasing to 4,000 nationwide. But Lew Chudd, who made the prediction in January, had reason for optimism. Domino had just enjoyed an incredible year, and Ricky Nelson had the #2 single and the #1 album entitled *Ricky*—a smoochable cover portrait with a record inside.

At the same time Chudd was concerned about Domino's slide from the top of the charts at the beginning of 1957 to merely mortal top 30 hits at year's end, though he stated in *Billboard*, "You should cool off like he has." Domino's singles were still selling by the half-million, and he still appeared on TV and in movies. But, with the burgeoning teen idol trend, black rockers, including Fats, soon struggled.

Domino was still missing shows. His band played in Lake Charles, Louisiana, in mid-January, but police broke out fire hoses to blast the rioting crowd when Fats failed to show. The district attorney swore out a warrant for his arrest.

Late in the month, Domino records began flying off the racks in El Paso, Tucson, Phoenix, Cheyenne, and Denver, indicating the westward roll of the Fat Man. Road manager Lew Freedman rode in the front seat of the station wagon with the band and sometimes relieved Herbert Hardesty at the wheel.

Fulfilling a promise to Rosemary, Domino flew home in the midst of the tour to play a benefit for her Methodist church before heading to Los Angeles.

After an appearance at the 5-4 Ballroom, Fats and his band recorded Chris Kenner's "Sick and Tired" in a two-song session on February 4 at Master Recorders that was a heartening return to his r&b roots.

But for every genuine rocker which hit, the entertainment industry generated a ton of unadulterated schlock—Domino performed "I'm Walkin'" and the title song in the movie *The Big Beat,* which premiered that month in Detroit, but the only other rocking act in the grade Z movie was the Del Vikings, a rare integrated vocal group.

With the release of yet another pop-sounding Domino single—"Yes, My Darling"—Bill Doggett suggested in *Billboard* that Fats had gotten away from his "authentic, New Orleans blues kick." "I warned him not to let anybody try to make a white artist out of him," said Doggett. "But maybe they made him too refined, because his records don't get played as much as they used to be."

Domino's records had indeed softened, largely due to the insistence on pop crossover records by Lew Chudd, who was seemingly blind to the fact that several of his star's biggest hits were his booming rockers. Still, as a *Melody Maker* story titled "One Day I'll Come to Britain" suggested, Domino rocked as hard as ever in live performances. "The most important thing about my music is the beat," said Fats in the article, noting Earl Palmer's drumming behind artists like Little Richard and Thurston Harris. It would be a decade before Domino actually traveled to England, but it would be a lot longer before the contributions of New Orleans' unsung musicians would be recognized as a driving force behind rock 'n' roll.

The ongoing war against rock 'n' roll continued. The Massachusetts Public Health Department condemned it as the cause of an increase in both VD and JDs—venereal disease and juvenile delinquents—a charge that Alan Freed promptly rebutted. NBC radio banned rock 'n' roll. St. Louis radio station KWK finished its "Record Breaking Week" with disc jockeys playing rock 'n' roll records and then smashing them. Contradicting the American anti-rock "Communist plot" theorists, the Moscow press likewise condemned the music.

Freed started his first "Big Beat" tour, headlined by Jerry Lee Lewis, Chuck Berry, Buddy Holly, and Frankie Lymon, but it crashed head-on with Irvin Feld's Biggest Show of Stars for 1958, starring Sam Cooke, the Everly Brothers, Clyde McPhatter, and Jackie Wilson in March. The stiff competition and a recession hurt both shows. Another tour featuring the Midnighters, the "5" Royales, Bo Diddley, Etta James, and Little Willie John, threw in the towel after a week. Domino had had enough of the eighty-day backbreakers, and turned down such offers. Luckily for him, as it turned out.

Dick Clark tried to book Domino for his prime-time program, *The Dick Clark Beechnut Show*. Lew Chudd cajoled Fats into appearing for Clark's union-scale wages, though Eddie Ray was still "nervous as hell" to see if the unpredictable star would show up. But on Saturday, March 29, Domino appeared live on Clark's show with his band from the Little Theater on West 44th Street in Manhattan. He performed live for nearly a third of Clark's half-hour program and brought the house down with a stomping barrelhouse medley of hits. "To have Fats Domino was a major coup," says Clark, "because you didn't see him on television a lot."

That week, Fats headlined an Apollo show hosted by WWRL disc jockey Tommy Smalls with the silky Flamingos, the poignant Spaniels, the soulful Dells, and the irreverent Coasters, who left the crowd laughing with their impressions of hillbillies. *Variety* called Domino's performance "raucous yet appropriate."

■ ■ ■

Rock 'n' roll suffered several major blows that spring.

In late April, Elvis Presley was inducted into the army after he had filmed scenes for *King Creole* in New Orleans. Though the movie featured the singer's finest acting, it also echoed Hollywood's whitewashed "birth of jazz" travesties. Blacks were only seen in tiny, uncredited parts, including Bartholomew's Imperial artist, Blanche Thomas, who appeared with Presley in the opening French Quarter scene as a seafood peddler lip-synching the song "Crawfish." The film's producers also inserted ersatz New Orleans jazz into songs that ripped off rock 'n' roll recorded a few blocks away—"Hard Headed Woman" was a blatant reworking of "Long Tall Sally" with a lame Dixieland break.

More than a dozen fans were injured at Alan Freed's Big Beat show on May 3 at the Boston Arena. The fracas was no more violent than Domino's many riots, but Freed's legion of enemies pounced on the controversial deejay. It was the beginning of the end of Freed, who was charged with inciting a riot. As Freed's Big Beat tour and Irvin Feld's Big Show both fizzled, Dick Clark canceled his first planned tour.

On May 6, Lew Chudd testified before the Interstate and Foreign Commerce Committee of the Senate, the first witness in hearings that were a shill for politically connected ASCAP publishers aimed at BMI's alleged monopolistic practices. Chudd claimed he didn't pay attention to which organization published his hits. "I got away with murder, I guess," says Chudd. "BMI took the r&b market by the throat. That made ASCAP real mad. They tried to kill rock 'n' roll. They didn't succeed."

Another witness, r&b writer Winfield Scott, saying that he was disturbed by the negative aspersions against music "which is closely associated with the Negro people," put things into perspective:

> Rock 'n' roll, rhythm & blues or "race" music, speaks in terms that have reached all people, not only nationally, but internationally. I don't pretend to know whether people would be better or worse on a steady diet of Cole Porter or Stravinsky, but I do know that rock 'n' roll is a kind of music which people like very much and which they have a right to hear if they want to.

In late May, English fans booed Jerry Lee Lewis off of an English tour with shouts of "Baby snatcher!" after reporters discovered his thirteen-year-old bride Myra on the tour. In less than a year, the pianist's supernova cooled to a smoldering ember.

■ ■ ■

Domino played Vanderbilt University's "Final Fling" in Nashville on May 16 for an astounding guarantee of $5,000. The Vandy students practiced an enlightened musical policy, also booking Count Basie, Clyde McPhatter, and Bo Diddley. An editorial in *The Vanderbilt Hustler* even compared disc jockeys who burned rock 'n' roll records to leaders of lynch mobs.

A week later, Fats was touring the West Coast when Rosemary gave birth to their seventh child, Adonica, on May 24. Despite his own infidelities, Domino had a jealous streak. In his daily calls to her he always found her at home unless she—understandably for a young wife who was often pregnant and had seven children—was at the doctor's office.

While Domino was on tour, Bartholomew recorded a track on June 14 for Domino's "Young School Girl" with musicians including pianist Allen Toussaint, a future creative force in New Orleans music whose first session had been on Domino's "I Want You to Know."

By June 20, Fats was back on the East Coast, playing on the midway of Palisades Park in New Jersey supported by Dion and the Belmonts (who would soon record a doo wop version of Domino's "I Can't Go On" under the title "Rosalie"). A week later, he headlined an all-star revue at the Regal Theatre in

Chicago. Still, Domino's tours were comparatively rare that year. His new hit, "Sick and Tired," reflected his mood. His musicians collected unemployment or backed other acts. Domino's old adversary Roy Brown briefly employed Buddy Hagans, Jimmy Davis, and Wendell Duconge, whose diabetes and personal problems led him to quit Domino permanently.

In a move sure to please ASCAP, all four songs that Fats recorded on August 15 were ancient standards. Bartholomew instructed the saxes to play pseudo string parts on "Once in Awhile" and hired a female group, the Velvetones, to complete Domino's sentences in "Coquette" like syrupy sirens. Chudd, hoping to find another "Blueberry Hill," had instructed Bartholomew to "sweeten" Domino's sound and Dave followed orders, though he may have thought twice about it. "I think he should have stayed with standards real early on," says Chudd. "Fats could go 'white.' He was a Louis Armstrong of a different era."

A week later, Fats, who was rumored to be looking for a new booking agency, renewed his contract with Shaw Artists for five more years. He also talked to Milt Shaw about future TV appearances and Australian and English tours.

Domino's first album in over a year, *The Fabulous Mr. D,* was surprisingly r&b-oriented, in contrast to the teen ballad-sounding single, "Young School Girl." Lew Chudd promoted them with a two-page ad in *Billboard,* including a public letter to Domino stating that he had sold 47 million records— "40,000,000 records [45s and 78s], 3,000,000 albums and about 4,000,000 EP's"—and was "a household name throughout the world."

Ostensibly things were also looking up in New Orleans. On May 31, the U.S. Supreme Court had upheld Judge J. Skelly Wright's ruling against segregation on public transportation, and the legacy of Homer Plessy and Rosa Parks was finally achieved in the city, though segregationists planted an eight-foot burning cross in the lawn of Wright, who also integrated the city's parks and sporting events that year. Three months later, Governor Earl K. Long dedicated Louisiana State University at New Orleans, which enrolled 200 black students, making it the first fully integrated public university in the Deep South, with a peaceful ceremony that was in profound contrast to the deadly integration riots at other southern universities. Some well-to-do blacks, like Dave Bartholomew, bought homes in the new, all-black Pontchartrain Park subdivision, which boasted a golf course, though one day the bandleader made the mistake of telling his boss during a phone call that he was about to go golfing.

"That's what's wrong with you!" scolded Lew Chudd. "You don't want to work anymore! When you're hungry you can write, but you're not hungry anymore!"

With Ricky Nelson sitting at #1 with "Poor Little Fool," "Young School Girl"'s one-week blip at #92 was unacceptable. Worse, his imitators were outdoing him. Jimmy Beasley's lively "Coquette" trumped Domino's anemic rendition. Warren Storm, a swamp pop singer from Abbeville, beat out versions of the country classic "The Prisoner's Song" by Fats and another imitator, Joe Jones.

Lew Chudd was now so obsessed with white pop that he didn't renew the contracts of the New Orleans r&b artists Smiley Lewis, Roy Brown, Chris Kenner, Chuck Carbo, and Bobby Mitchell, keeping only white rocker Bobby Charles. "Race records were either selling as pop or they weren't selling," says Chudd. In a misguided attempt to garner more adult pop respect, Imperial even released a bizarre album of Domino songs by bisexual nightclub chanteuse Frances Faye.

Fats played Memphis for the first time for blacks and whites in the same building at the Coliseum on September 19, though the crowd was still segregated. Record producers eliminated racial problems by having pop singers sing lightweight black styles. Though Domino was in a slump, his sound was not. Chuck Willis, who had died tragically in April, had started the craze for the Stroll dance with his version of "C.C. Rider," which Afro-Caribbean music scholar John Storm Roberts suggests was based on "the rumba-inflected patterns that Fats Domino had made popular." Jimmy Clanton (managed by Cosimo Matassa) stole the show from Chuck Berry and Bill Haley on Alan Freed's Labor Day show singing "Just a Dream," an adenoidal swamp pop ballad. Bobby Darin found fame with the Domino-styled novelty "Splish Splash." Black pop singer Tommy Edwards simply added piano triplets to his minor 1951 hit "It's All in the Game" for a #1 hit. "One Night," a Smiley Lewis triplet ballad, was transformed by Elvis Presley into a bump-and-grind rocker about a one-night stand. As Domino apparently realized, he didn't need to sound like someone else; he needed to sound *like himself.*

■ ■ ■

On September 22, the day before his next session, Domino, Bartholomew, bassist Frank Fields, and guitarist Ernest McLean worked through the songs they would record, including "Whole Lotta Loving," the kind of lyrically minimalist rocker that Bartholomew scorned. As usual, Fats improvised; when he couldn't think of any more words, he simply smacked kisses or clapped into the microphone. He also wanted to play extended honky-tonk piano solos, which Dave disliked for straying from their formulas.

The next day, Fields arrived first at ten o'clock. He was followed by Bartholomew, McLean, Papoose Nelson, drummer Charles Williams, and saxophonist Warren Bell. Fats arrived promptly at 10:15. Gil Webre, a *Times-Picayune* writer, wrote a feature on the session that was especially notable because of the lack of positive stories about blacks in Southern newspapers.

One sax player didn't show up, so Bartholomew called Clarence Ford. Ford, who hadn't played much lately, couldn't find his instrument. He borrowed a sax and appeared during the rehearsal for "I'll Always Be in Love with You" (a song the Beatles would record on a homemade tape early in their career).

The actual session began when the red "RECORDING" light blinked on. Cosimo Matassa intoned, "Take one."

"Cut," Bartholomew soon ordered. "Fats, you don't sound like yourself." He also asked the drummer to use only his right hand.

Charles "Hungry" Williams waved his left arm—like Tenoo Coleman, whom he had idolized, he was a lefty. Bartholomew had never forgiven Tenoo for running away with the beat on Dave's early recording of "Let the Four Winds Blow." But his replacement, Williams, also astounded musicians with his rapid funk rhythms. With the departure of Earl Palmer, he was now the city's top session drummer.

The group was just finishing take five when Fats turned his head on a word. In Matassa's still-primitive studio, Domino still had to sing and play simultaneously; there were no overdubs. They finally completed the song in take eleven.

After a break, the band recorded another standard, "Margie" (which was later rerecorded for the hit version) and "I Miss You So," both in twelve takes.

While Fats recorded his last song, the next singer scheduled to use the studio walked into Cosimo's office. Sam Montalbano, a Baton Rouge produce salesman who owned the tiny Montel label, brought in a gangly seventeen-year-old, John Fred Gourrier, to record his Fats-styled debut, "Shirley," with the session musicians. It was a transcendent moment for John Fred, who had idolized Domino for years.

"Is that him?" asked the excited teen looking through the studio window.

Fats nailed "Whole Lotta Loving" with its relatively intricate piano parts in just six takes. At two P.M., the reporter asked Domino how he felt.

"Great!" replied Fats. "When things go right I can make records all day."

Afterwards, John Fred walked across the floor covered with wires and drink cans to the folding baffle used as a vocal "booth." He stared in awe at the screen scribbled with the dozens of signatures of those who had recorded at Cosimo's.

■ ■ ■

In October, Louis Armstrong announced that he wouldn't play in New Orleans again until he could perform with his integrated band. Dynamite wrecked the integrated Clinton High School in Little Rock. *Variety* noted the proliferation of beat poet coffee houses and offbeat comedians in Los Angeles. Riots occurred regularly at Bill Haley shows in Germany.

When Fats again played the 5-4 Ballroom in Los Angeles that month, Bernard Dunn saw the familiar face of Billy Diamond, who was visiting his relatives. They went backstage together to see Domino, who said he wasn't happy with Lew Freedman as manager and invited Diamond to rejoin them on the next tour.

While in L.A., Lew Chudd charged Bartholomew with getting Domino back up the charts. Dave replaced most of Domino's musicians, who, ironically, had previously played on all of his Hollywood-recorded hits. A Master Recorders session on October 30 included Papoose Nelson, Herbert Hardesty, Earl Palmer, Plas Johnson, and bassist Red Callender. Many of the songs they recorded were old standards, but played with an effervescent feel taken from traditional jazz. Domino's recording of the Original Dixieland Jazz Band's 1917 hit "Darktown Strutters Ball" featured playful saxes and a great, growling baritone ending by Johnson. At another session five days later, a revival of "The Saints" featuring Palmer's thumping drums, Domino's exuberant singing, and cavorting saxes, helped revive the parade tradition, which had declined even in New Orleans. Domino's albums were compiled haphazardly from sessions years apart. The fact that Fats never recorded a planned album for Imperial was a great disappointment to Bartholomew and Chudd, though the musically related late 1958 sessions were the next best thing.

With the major exception of Chuck Berry, few black rockers enjoyed a big year in 1958 due to the recession and the rise of the teen idols promoted by Dick Clark and Top 40 stations. African Americans who scored pop hits were once again mostly balladeers or novelty acts. As a white TV star, Ricky Nelson easily overtook Domino in media coverage, appearing on the covers of *TV Guide, Life,* and *Look.* Fats was now Imperial's number two artist in a trend that reflected a return to the white status quo. Still, Chudd's business acumen was confirmed with Imperial's $10 million net profit for 1958, up from $7.5 million in 1957. *Fortune* magazine called Imperial with its fourteen employees the "largest privately owned independent label."

Apparently energized by the challenge of a comeback, Domino started an unusual media blitz to promote "Whole Lotta Loving." He appeared on *The Dick Clark Beechnut Show* on November 8 with whitebread singers the Kalin Twins, Andy Williams, and Gordon McCrae. Clark had to drag Fats from his hotel room to rehearse. He kept a case of Teacher's Scotch for the always nervous Domino. In December, Fats even appeared on *The Buddy Deane Show* in Baltimore, a lily-white teen dance party, which John Waters would parody thirty years later in the movie *Hairspray*.

Domino called Chudd to ask how much "Whole Lotta Loving" had sold. Chudd replied that it had sold almost a million copies. Domino's instincts on the song now seemed justified. Bartholomew, who had doubted the song, later admitted, "That turned out to be a real handclapper. Fats was playing a lot of piano."

Fats appeared again on Dick Clark's show with pop singers Tommy Edwards and June Valli late in the year. Clark pulled cards off of his Top Ten board to reveal the week's hit songs. Teens screamed as he announced Elvis Presley's "I Got Stung" and "One Night," the Teddy Bears' "To Know Him Is to Love Him," the Everly Brothers' "Problems," Duane Eddy's "Cannonball," Conway Twitty's "It's Only Make Believe," Bobby Darin's "Queen of the Hop," the Platters' "Smoke Gets in Your Eyes," and, number one, the Chipmunks' "The Chipmunk Song."

Clark skipped one card and then came back to it. "By Fats Domino, this is number s-e-v-e-n!" The teenagers screamed as Fats appeared, his piano surrounded by white teenage girls in sweaters clapping to the beat. His hands divebombed his piano and his lips smacked kisses, as he delivered a simple message: *"I gotta whole lotta l-o-v-i-n' for you!"*

■ ■ ■

A tragic blow to rock 'n' roll occurred when Buddy Holly, Ritchie Valens, and the Big Bopper, trekking the glacial Midwest on Irvin Feld's Winter Dance Party tour, died in a plane crash on February 3, 1959. Cosimo Matassa, touring simultaneously on the Biggest Show of Stars with his singer Jimmy Clanton, later that night witnessed an auditorium full of teenagers burst into tears at the announcement of the deaths. The next day, Clanton (along with Frankie Avalon) joined the ill-fated tour as a replacement. He boarded the Dance Party bus in Sioux City, Iowa. Near the back, he froze when he saw the guitar case of Holly, whose legend was just beginning. "They talk about Buddy Holly more after he died than they did when he was living," remarks Domino with some understatement.

In the midst of the blustery weather, Fats played the Howard Theater in Washington, D.C., for promoter Sid Bernstein. While Bernstein was checking on the teenagers waiting in the snow to get in, he was shocked to see Domino himself coming out into the cold to greet his fans. "He was the gentlest, most considerate and involved artist that I have ever met," says Bernstein.

Just as the mild-mannered persona of Joe Louis (Domino's childhood hero who later became a friend) provided a bridge for black boxing champions to come, Domino's charm helped save rock 'n' roll, and thus its social change. Hospitality to strangers had been a mythic theme since *The Odyssey* and the birth of Christ. African American music scholar Gerald Early suggests that civilization could be summed up in the word "welcome." Domino had a hit that year with the same title as hotel mogul Conrad Hilton's 1958 autobiography *Be My Guest,* though even hotel chains were slow to integrate. Blacks couldn't achieve equality by tearing down walls or even with laws. Simple courtesy was the proof of true integration.

Herbert Hardesty deliberately drove the band's station wagon to the new motels springing up along new highways. The musicians were often the first blacks ever to stay at the inns. They were also pleased when they entered their first Howard Johnson's restaurant in Indiana, but the true test would come in the South.

During a Texas tour, they ended up at a Lubbock hotel, knowing that it didn't accept blacks. Domino often played in all-white Texas towns, but he didn't *stay* in them. Billy Diamond, who had returned as Domino's road manager, bravely walked in the front door, knowing the humiliation he would receive. He explained the situation to the angry hotel manager, whose attitude changed at the mention of Domino's name. He immediately came out to the Cadillac. Overjoyed at meeting Fats, he made a startling statement: "I'll give you a place to stay. But I can't have you fellas runnin' around, 'cause it'll run our business away." The band members were stunned: *Fats had gotten them in the door.*

In another incident, Herbert Hardesty once lost his way while driving in South Carolina. The band members suddenly found themselves near a KKK rally with a burning cross. A man in a white hood approached and, seeing Domino's name on the station wagon, asked if Fats was in the car. After Hardesty answered "No" and explained the situation, the man simply gave them helpful directions. "Racists loved Fats Domino," later remembered warm-up singer Sonny Jones. "He was the shield." Domino and his musicians knew what it meant for others to open up the hotels. They were not the hellions of rock myth who broke up rooms. Their rebellion was much more subtle and profound; they were breaking *barriers*.

■ ■ ■

On *American Bandstand* on March 6, Dick Clark sat next to Fats at the piano and asked in his milk-and-honey voice, "What brings you to Philadelphia?"

"You!" shot back Fats with a smile. He had just sung a song titled "Telling Lies." He was, in fact, playing that night at the Philadelphia Town Hall.

Clark asked Domino to name his favorite mode of transportation.

"Well, any one, as long as I make my job on time!" laughed Fats.

"You know, that's one of the records that this man has," said Clark, unaware of the irony of what he was about to say. "He very rarely ever misses a date."

Again, Clark surrounded Domino with white teenage girls. With his self-effacing charm, Fats easily fit into Dick Clark's slick world as he lip-synched "When the Saints Go Marching In," but the image that the show projected shortchanged the power of Domino with his band.

"It was a clean-cut, white thing," remarks Herbert Hardesty. "The show had to be so polished. Everybody was down on rock 'n' roll during that time; they was trying to ban it. So Dick Clark, he had to go by the chalk line, you know?"

Lew Chudd issued "The Saints" with a *Billboard* ad calling Domino "The most copied artist recording today." As if to prove the point, Clark soon presented a singer performing Presley and Domino imitations. Clark's wife, Barbara, had discovered the hefty teenager, Ernest Evans, singing a Fats Domino song in a Philadelphia recording studio and accordingly dubbed him "Chubby Checker."

Lloyd Price, then headlining the Biggest Show of Stars, appeared in late March on Clark's *Beechnut Show* with Tab Hunter, Jimmy Clanton, James Darren, and the Chordettes. At Clark's behest, Price sang a cleaned-up version of the old blues warhorse "Stagger Lee" in which Stag and Billy were "nice" to each other. There was no killing in Clark's antiseptic world. Clark had another Louisiana singer, Rod Bernard, eliminate the line *"If it's a sin to really love you, then a sinner I will be"* in his hit "This Should Go On Forever." There was no sinning, either.

At the same time as Price's Big Show opened across town, Fats headlined Alan Freed's Easter week show at the Fabian-Fox Theater in Brooklyn with Jackie Wilson, Bobby Darin, Duane Eddy, Dale Hawkins, Larry Williams, and many others.

Teenage girls squealed for a handsome teen, Fabian, with talents unapparent to others. Unlike Dick Clark, Alan Freed and Irvin Feld featured teen idols sparingly, though Freed helped a string of white Louisiana teens influenced by Domino—Bobby Charles, Johnny Ramistella (whom Freed renamed "Johnny Rivers"), John Fred, Frankie Ford, Rod Bernard, and Jimmy Clanton, who was also at the Easter show.

One of Domino's late-morning appearances was delayed. The kids inside the theater soon began stomping and yelling, *"WE WANT FATS!"*

Back at their hotel, Domino's musicians had missed their wake-up call. The six musicians flew down the elevator and out of the hotel. They ran the fifteen blocks to the theater. Then they fought through the hordes of fans lined up for the shows.

Freed paced backstage, smoking nervously. He was a man of contradiction—an egotistical idealist, a capitalistic revolutionary, a dour cheerleader. With the Boston riot charge still hanging over his head, he now drank heavily. He begged Domino to play with his orchestra, including Sam "The Man" Taylor and King Curtis. Fats steadfastly replied that he couldn't play without his band.

Finally, the band arrived. Though Domino was himself often late, his musicians couldn't get away with it. He later fined them $25 each, though he bought them new shoes with the money. Still, they appreciated him standing up for them.

Freed finally announced Domino to a blizzard of screams. Despite the many young lions and paper tigers, *Variety* reported that Domino still ruled:

Closing turn is Fats Domino and his orch., strong fave with the younger set, doing such numbers as "I'm in Love Again" and "Blueberry Hill." Domino has no trouble making the kids jump into the aisles, but the stern-lipped cops with their blinding flashlights soon get the youngsters back in their seats, but it is only momentarily before they are high jumpin' again.

In between performances, the young fans mobbed the band members as well as the stars for autographs when they went outside. Herbert Hardesty cashed in on the success of the Freed show, recording a session in New York for Federal Records with Domino's band and jazz pianist Hank Jones.

During the all-day shows Fats invited musicians backstage for a drink or to dig into his home cooking in his dressing room. He was especially friendly to the Louisiana musicians, Dale Hawkins and Jimmy Clanton. Even Bobby Darin, a Domino fan who would soon become a Sinatra-styled nightclub singer, couldn't resist getting a piano lesson from Fats between shows.

March 30th was the best one-day gross ever for the Fabian-Fox, though the total haul of $167,000 was disappointing. Still, it was Freed's last truly great show.

■ ■ ■

In April, Lew Chudd echoed Domino's offer to melt down the Cold War three years earlier. He pledged to trade Domino and Ricky Nelson singles for records by the two top Soviet artists. At the same time, Louisiana-born pianist Van Cliburn astonished the world by winning Moscow's Tchaikovsky piano competition.

The first Grammy Awards were announced in May. The nominees for "Rhythm & Blues" (ironically now a more respected term than "rock 'n' roll," for which there was no category) bizarrely included Nat "King" Cole, Harry Belafonte, Perez Prado, Earl Grant, and the Champs. One anonymous record executive sniped that any r&b list "without artists like Fats Domino, Ray Charles, Clyde McPhatter, etc. has no relevancy to the actual record business." As if paying penance for their Promethean role in bringing black fire to white America, Domino, Chuck Berry, and Little Richard would never even be nominated for a regular Grammy. The top honors went to songs rooted in European balladry—"Volare" and "Tom Dooley."

On May 18, *Billboard* reported that Sam Phillips of Sun Records (who stopped recording black artists after Elvis hit) had bought two easy-listening radio stations. He was throwing in the towel on rock 'n' roll. "[The kids] got tired of the ruckus," declared Phillips.

Also that month, a shocking legislative hearing was televised live from the Louisiana State Capitol in Baton Rouge. A jowly, white-haired man, Governor Earl K. Long, ranted against racist scare tactics to aghast Louisiana legislators (in a scene later dramatized by Paul Newman in the movie *Blaze*). Filled with pep pills and whiskey-laced grape juice (which he drank from a Coke bottle), a shaky Long declared at one point, "You gotta recognize that niggers is human beings!"

Though he peppered his speeches with such incongruous phrases, Long was the only major southern politician to champion black voting rights. His opponents, New Orleans' mayor Chep Morrison and Willie Rainach, conspired to skewer Long on the race issue. With Rainach's cronies purging Long's African American constituents from voter rolls, the governor was forced to defend them. Following his two-day rant, his wife had him briefly committed to a mental hospital, effectively ending his governorship. Any white southerner who publicly supported blacks *had to be crazy.*

■ ■ ■

Orange sunshine stung bleary eyes as deejays at the first national Disc Jockey Convention woke up in Miami hotel rooms, on private boats, or even in Cuba after wild parties on May 31. The jocks' eyes were also hurt by a headline about the convention in *The Miami Herald:* "BOOZE, BROADS AND BRIBES." In March, New York disc jockey Martin Block had told WNTA-TV newsman Mike Wallace (later of *60 Minutes* fame) that payola was "like a headwaiter's tip." Though Block was a pop deejay and major record companies plugging pop had proffered the convention high life, payola was curiously soon twisted into ammunition against rock 'n' roll.

Lew Chudd consistently denied that he paid payola, but New Orleans was a party city with a reputation wilder than Miami's. According to Ken Rogers, who was then the program director of WQXI in Atlanta, Chudd invited him to New Orleans, "where all expenses were paid and a good time was had by all."

In mid-June, Rogers, as part of his trip, witnessed the latest Domino session. At Cosimo's studio, Fats chanted a childlike wooing line—*"I want to walk you ho-ume"*—over and over, intimately, almost hypnotically, into a microphone as Papoose Nelson echoed each line with his guitar. Bartholomew wanted horns to answer the vocal, but Domino, who took the sole writing credit on the song, insisted on Papoose's guitar. Like other songs primarily written by Fats, Bartholomew would call "I Want to Walk You Home" "one of the worst," though it would become Domino's biggest hit in years. After many mistakes, Fats finally came to the end of a good take, but ruined it at the last second by asking, "How does it sound?" A cursing sound was heard, as Bartholomew stomped out of the control booth.

Domino was "a pain in the ass to record," recalls Cosimo Matassa. Fats often made a kingly entrance into the studio with his valet and his chauffeur carrying a case of Teacher's Scotch and two gallons of pigs' feet. His personality likewise took on a rude edge when he was drinking. He once placed an IRS tax refund check for $95,000 on his piano to annoy the other musicians. Despite his own mistakes, Fats might curse them when they messed up. He sometimes missed sessions altogether, leaving Bartholomew and the band waiting for hours. Chudd ascribed Domino's intransigence partly to jealousy of Ricky Nelson. "He didn't want to record," says Chudd, "and I had to go to the Union in New York and force him. He thought the label should be one-track—Fats Domino. He didn't even appreciate Dave."

The relationships had changed. Though he was still soft-spoken, Fats had reached a rare level of stardom and was no longer as deferential to Chudd and Bartholomew. But he had good reason to be wary of their attempts to change his music. The artificially pop-styled recordings suggested by Chudd, with instrumental tracks recorded by Bartholomew while Fats was on the road, had led to Domino's chart slump, whereas his biggest hits were simple rockers that Fats had written and played by himself or on tour before recording them live in the studio, often with his own band. Domino increasingly felt—with fresh justification in view of his new self-styled hits which Bartholomew disdained—that only he truly knew his own sound.

Though Fats rarely went into the studio that year, he achieved an even better average than in 1955, when over half of the twenty songs he recorded became chart hits. Of the six songs Fats recorded in 1959, four made the top 40, including two top 10 hits, "I Want to Walk You Home" and "Be My Guest."

■ ■ ■

Domino's dark moon face filled more than half the TV screens in America on Sunday, June 28, on *The Record Years,* a highly rated Dick Clark special. Fats shouted his willingness to *"rock 'n' roll all night"* in "I'm Ready," joining Little Richard's "Ready Teddy," Shirley and Lee's "Let the Good Times Roll," Roy Brown's "Good Rockin' Tonight" (and, later, the Showmen's "It Will Stand") in New Orleans' proud lineage of rocking anthems.

In the background, Domino's musicians emphasized the beat. Bartholomew, Hardesty, Ford, and Hagans—their horns slung over their shoulders like rifles—simply clapped vigorously. The camera panned back to show Papoose thrashing his guitar, Jimmy Davis thumping his bass, and Tenoo bashing his drums. They rocked the house in another scintillating live television performance.

The message that Fats delivered was important, if not critical. Teen idols resembling shellacked puppets dominated popular music. Clark's other guests—Stan Freberg, the McGuire Sisters, Stan Kenton, Les Paul and Mary Ford,

Fabian, and Johnny Mathis—were virtually antithetical to rock 'n' roll. To demonstrate their musical "diversity," Clark had each perform a verse of "Mary Had a Little Lamb."

There was little rocking heard in 1959 outside of Domino and his heirs—Lloyd Price, Wilbert Harrison, Phil Phillips, and Frankie Ford. Buddy Holly was dead. Elvis was in the army. Little Richard was in Bible School. Jerry Lee Lewis was washed up. Chuck Berry soon would be in jail. Just as Domino had outlasted his early r&b contemporaries, he now stood virtually alone among the great rockers.

"I'm Ready" became a classic, later covered by the Band, Elton John, the Beatles, Keith Richards, and Bruce Springsteen. Though it was actually co-written by Tin Pan Alley writer Al Lewis (one of the writers of "Blueberry Hill") and originally recorded by Bobby Darin on a demo record, Fats bellowed the song with such conviction that people actually believed he didn't like phone calls and couldn't read. "Fats made things his own," remarks Cosimo Matassa. "Even on little frothy tunes whipped up in the studio, the phrasing and delivery was always *Fats*. It's an amazing singularity I think most artists would *die* for. *That fantastic uniqueness.*"

■ ■ ■

In July, two U.S. soldiers were killed in Vietnam. Billie Holiday died not long after an arrest for heroin possession. Alan Freed's final film, *Go, Johnny, Go,* with Jimmy Clanton, Chuck Berry, Jackie Wilson, Ritchie Valens, and Eddie Cochran, contrasted with Dick Clark's first, *Because They're Young,* in which he played a teacher at an all-white school where juvenile delinquency was crashing the prom.

Though rock 'n' roll was increasingly putting on a white mask, Fats and other black rockers were still affecting race relations. Domino's universality was obvious in his record sales. Imperial promotions man Eddie Ray made a point of checking the jukebox of every grease pit and truck stop he visited in his travels. As expected, he always found Domino records. Carl Perkins confirmed the infiltration of segregation's outposts. "In the white honky-tonks where I was playin' they were punchin' 'Blueberry Hill,'" said Perkins, "and 'I Want to Walk You Home.' White cats were dancin' to Fats Domino."

Conflicts over integration overshadowed the growing racial ties. A familiar headline after a Domino show in Denver—"Race Riot Wrecks Fats Domino

Dance"—obscured the fact that the fights started at the Rainbow Ballroom after a white woman and a black man began dancing together.

In fact, a new wave of African American singers was poised to again rearrange popular music. In New Orleans, artists including Irma Thomas, Benny Spellman, Ernie K-Doe, Aaron Neville, Jessie Hill, and Allen Toussaint lined up at the WYLD radio studio to audition for the new Minit Records label that would soon spearhead the new New Orleans rhythm & blues. In Memphis, Chicago, and Detroit, gospel-fired r&b, which soon would become known as "soul music," was in its infancy, ignited that summer by twin-peak volcanic gospel-rooted call-and-response hits—"What'd I Say" by Ray Charles and the Isley Brothers' "Shout."

"I Want to Walk You Home" became Domino's first r&b #1 in over two years in September, neatly cashing in on a similarity to Wilbert Harrison's Domino-styled smash "Kansas City," while the classic b-side, "I'm Gonna Be a Wheel Someday," blasted from the car radios of cruising teens that summer. The song began three years earlier, when Roy Hayes, a Cajun clerk at a drug wholesaler in Baton Rouge, wrote the title on a packing slip as a swipe at his boss. Hayes recorded a demo of "Wheel" for Bartholomew, who produced a twangy version by local r&b singer Bobby Mitchell in 1957. A year later, Bartholomew's studio musicians streamlined the song for Domino like a new Cadillac, with gliding guitars by Justin Adams and Ernest McLean, nifty bass figures by Frank Fields, plus handclaps and shouts.

Domino's "I'm Gonna Be a Wheel Someday" was a personal declaration of independence—an especially potent statement coming from a black man—and inspired people everywhere. Future presidential candidate Patrick Buchanan adopted it as his personal theme song in his youth, as did his ideological opposite, Louisiana political consultant James Carville, who masterminded the first presidential campaign of Bill Clinton in 1992 and later wrote, "When you're toiling out there, particularly when you're not winning, you dream of being a wheel someday, dream of being somebody."

■ ■ ■

In October, Congressman Oren Harris began hearings on the TV quiz show scandal. Smelling blood, ASCAP suggested to Harris that music payola was a conspiracy to "suppress genuine talent and to foist mediocre music upon the public." Harris announced that there would be hearings on payola in early

1960. New York, the only state with a commercial bribery law, started a payola investigation, subpoenaing ten record companies, including Imperial.

Late in the month Domino had a new hit, "Be My Guest." A nineteen-year-old fan, Tommy Boyce, had waited for six hours at a Los Angeles hotel to present the song to Fats, who changed both the lyrics and the music. The song not only symbolized Domino's subversive form of social integration, it also would have a far-reaching musical influence, most obviously launching Boyce's songwriting career, which would be capped by several million-selling songs for the Monkees.

When Fats sang "Be My Guest" on *American Bandstand* on November 10, Dick Clark himself was worried—he was scheduled to see the head of ABC-TV the next day to answer "the payola question." Witch trials were held in the press, as radio stations fired deejays.

Though Alan Freed's inciting-to-riot charge was dropped in November, he then jumped from the frying pan into the fire. ABC decided to use him as a scapegoat to save its sacred cash cow, Dick Clark. ABC's flagship WABC-television and radio stations both fired Freed for refusing to sign an affidavit swearing that he had never taken payola, though the network let Clark write his own statement. Standing amid sobbing teens, Freed's last words on his television show on November 27 were "I know a lot of ASCAP publishers who will be glad I'm off the air."

By December, the payola hysteria reached Red Scare proportions. *Variety* noted that radio stations were "switching away from the more raucous rock 'n' roll platters to more melodic material. . . . [T]he finger of suspicion is more likely to be pointed now at a disc jockey who is spinning a 'far out' brand of rocking music."

There was a similar mob mentality in the Louisiana governor's race, which degenerated into racist one-upsmanship, inflamed by ultra-segregationist candidate Willie Rainach. Though he began his singing career as a Jimmie Rodgers imitator recording risqué blues, Jimmie Davis was now all Jesus 'n' cream. He reassured whites by singing "The Old Rugged Cross" and a classic song that he claimed to have written, but reportedly only bought the copyright for, "You Are My Sunshine." His opponent, Mayor Chep Morrison, capitulated to the hate politics when the Davis camp labeled him "the NAACP candidate."

On December 21, Chuck Berry's lucky escapes ran out when police arrested him for bringing an underage Apache girl from El Paso to be a hostess at his Club Bandstand in St. Louis. He was charged with violation of the Mann Act—transportation of a female across state lines for immoral purposes—the same "White Slavery" law that had been used nearly fifty years earlier to jail another rebellious black man, boxing great Jack Johnson, when no white man could best him.

■ ■ ■

As the decade ended, Domino had reemerged to produce a string of two-sided rockers. Against all odds, he had rolled along like Ol' Man River, rocking the country for ten years, with sixteen records hitting #1 or #2 in the r&b charts, nine top 10 pop hits, and more than fifty chart songs, a total that no other rocker, including Elvis, approached. While others put on the *Sturm und Drang* of revolt, Domino had led a revolution that, as his song "Blue Monday" suggested, was workmanlike, tearing down walls not all at once, but brick by brick.

The "Be My Guest" 45 picture sleeve showed Fats standing like a concert pianist beside a white baby grand with its top raised. It seemed like a parody of Van Cliburn, who had repledged America's allegiance to Old World music by winning the Tchaikovsky competition. But Fats, to paraphrase the now fallen Chuck Berry, was still "telling Tchaikovsky the news." For a decade, he had broken barriers, freed minds and bodies, and brought people together in the egalitarian New Orleans tradition. As Fats sang in "Be My Guest," *"I'm the king, but you can wear my crown."*

Folklorist Alan Lomax remarked on the cultural shift in *Variety* at the end of the year: "Rock 'n' roll is opening the door to America's genuine traditional music and freeing it from its longtime domination by European culture." After he recorded icons like Jelly Roll Morton, Leadbelly, and Muddy Waters, Lomax fled the Red Scare to collect folk music in Europe for much of the 1950s. He returned to the United States in 1959 and marveled as teenagers danced to black rhythms on *American Bandstand*. "Rock 'n' roll is an extension of jazz and blues and it's being kicked around the same way jazz and blues were in their early days," said Lomax. "The record business has turned America into a musical democracy."

L.A. bandleader Johnny Otis added, "Democracy, one of the most important things taught (but not necessarily practiced) in our schoolrooms, was manifesting itself in the ballrooms. A spontaneous integration occurred. Rock 'n' roll audiences became integrated."

The children led. Reflecting on the rise of r&b in early 1956, *Billboard* had editorialized, "It was, of course, the kid with the 89 cents in his pocket who cast the deciding vote." America's youth, who had little or no political power, caused a tidal wave in music and lifestyles with their economic power. They were ruled not by a king, but by a different drummer. Despite setbacks to rock 'n' roll, they accomplished something that no other generation had before, something that would shake the world—the integration of American culture.

In the next decade, America would be ripped apart from the inside. The country's most crucial struggles were not with Red herring foreign enemies, but with disenfranchised Americans, who in the new prosperity were no longer willing to conform to strict barriers against their lives, liberties, and pursuits of happiness. The Supreme Court school integration ruling and rock 'n' roll were their reveille calls. Those defending the status quo railed against integration protesters and Reds under the bed, but they were unprepared for a youth revolt that simply by evoking positive passions was, slowly but surely, turning American culture inside out. The 1960s would erupt with the profound problems that separated people. America was not a melting pot blending into a WASP ideal but a cauldron of cultures that was about to boil over. In a phrase that would be made famous by men representing both extremes—Malcolm X and George Wallace—the chickens were coming home to roost.

"Walking to New Orleans"

Chapter 13

(1960)

"A poor boy. You know, he never forgot he was poor. He built a house in a black neighborhood. He could have gone anywhere at that time."
—LEW CHUDD

"TWO, FOUR, SIX, EIGHT! WE DON'T WANNA INTEGRATE!"
—CHANT HEARD AT TWO SCHOOLS NEAR DOMINO'S NEW HOME IN LATE 1960

"Did you hear that?" asked Domino's bass player Jimmy Davis, turning to his band mates in Domino's new station wagon, an airport limousine that sat twelve. In early 1960, they were waiting outside a dance hall before a show in Breaux Bridge, Louisiana, a dusty stop between Baton Rouge and Lafayette. Herbert Hardesty was sitting in a car romancing one of his girlfriends, Ruby Bocage, a light-skinned Creole from Lafayette. Some young white men were milling around the cars. Davis had heard one of them say, "Do you see that nigger in that car with that white woman?"

Racial tensions had been exacerbated in Louisiana by the recent governor's race won by Jimmie "You Are My Sunshine" Davis on a segregationist platform. The musicians hurried inside to tell Domino about the situation as the whites walked up to Hardesty's car and demanded to know what he was doing with a white woman.

"She isn't white," replied a startled Hardesty.

"Yeah, she's white! You ain't got no business with a white woman."

"Look," said Hardesty, becoming concerned. "Why don't you just cool it?"

A policeman drove up. He nodded to Hardesty's girlfriend, whom, by sheer luck, he knew personally. "Hi, Ruby. What's this all about?"

The rednecks babbled their beef.

"You stupid fools," replied the policeman. "She's not white; she's colored." His presence defused the situation. The couple went into the club.

Backstage, Herbert upbraided his band mates for leaving him outside. But a rattled Tenoo shot back, "Man, don't you ever do that to us again! Don't ever! Man, all of us could have been dead!"

As the band warmed up, Billy Diamond headed through the white crowd to the club's office to collect Domino's money. He was stopped by a thug in the audience who held a knife to his stomach. Diamond, who had narrowly dodged a KKK ambush while touring in South Carolina with Shirley and Lee, was scared.

Again, a policeman intervened: "Hey, the man has to go through here."

After the show, the policeman escorted Hardesty and his girlfriend to Lafayette, where he also lived. The others packed their instruments into the station wagon. Billy Diamond turned the key, but the ignition just clicked. Something was wrong. They looked around, worried that the toughs were forming a mob.

Some young white fans, seeing the hood of the station wagon up, offered to help. Together, they pushed the car to a nearby Billups gas station. The attendant discovered that the distributor cap was missing. Since it was too late to buy one, he took the cap off of his own car. They left town with a police escort.

Domino and his band received a more friendly reception in nearby Lafayette. In his dressing room, he greeted Cajun singer-songwriter Bobby Charles. "Man," said Fats, "I recorded your song the other day. I wish I'd known that you would be here, I'd-a brought a copy for you to hear." Domino had recorded Charles's "Before I Grow Too Old" on February 10. Seeing that Charles was upset that he couldn't hear the recording, Fats invited him to New Orleans.

"I don't have a car. If I'd go, I'd have to *walk*," Charles replied, as sudden inspiration hit him. Riding home to Abbeville after the show with some friends, Charles borrowed a pencil and paper and in fifteen minutes wrote "Walking to New Orleans" for Domino. The song expressed the eternal yearning that Fats felt for his place of birth. It would come to symbolize the year, as his hometown, his home itself, and even his home life would—for better or worse—all be in the news.

■ ■ ■

Headlines reflected the growing civil rights movement. In February, four black students sat at a segregated Woolworth's lunch counter in Greensboro, North Carolina. Similar sit-ins spread throughout the South. That spring, 1,000 black students sang the national anthem on the steps of the old Confederate Capitol in Montgomery, Alabama, while others picketed the White House.

To young blacks, Domino seemed less relevant in the wake of civil rights insurgency and the rise of soulful and sexy singers like Jackie Wilson, James Brown, Ray Charles, Sam Cooke, and Brook Benton. His anemic new hit, "Country Boy," became his first single in five years to fail to make the r&b charts. At the same time, pop artists were turning Domino's piano triplet sound into musical wallpaper—triplets were heard in Brenda Lee's #1 hits and even in the taffy-sweet orchestral hit "The Theme from a Summer Place" by Percy Faith.

Following a week of sold-out Apollo shows featuring the adenoidal Roy Brown–style cries of Jackie Wilson, Fats played the Harlem landmark during Easter week to half-empty seats. Unlike the Catholic-raised Domino, soul singers grew up singing gospel music in church. The passionate fire that Brown had ignited in rhythm & blues over a decade earlier now burned in voices that cooed, hollered, and soared, though the primary musical element that Fats triumphed—rhythm—was also still strong.

Domino's band was bolstered in 1960 by the return of the big sax man, Lee Allen, while guitarist Ernest McLean replaced the perennially troubled Papoose Nelson. Allen, who had played the solos on a handful of Domino hits, displayed an intense power and showmanship that raised the musicianship of the entire band.

Saxophonist Clarence Ford was Domino's bandleader. He woke up the musicians, told them which uniforms to wear, and gave them their schedule. He even reminded Fats what keys his songs were in. The versatile Ford played baritone, tenor, and (on "Mardi Gras in New Orleans") even clarinet. Someone watching Ford carrying all of his instruments backstage at the Apollo once asked Billy Diamond how many salaries he was paying Ford. The most Ford would earn over the next decade was $275 a week; his small raises would not keep up with the cost of living, as he had to pay for his own hotel room, which rose from $50 to $100 a week over the years. As featured soloists, Hardesty and Allen received more money. Dave Bartholomew would receive up to $1,000 a night for his "guest appearances." For the others, the pay was, as Ford put it, "a turkey for me and a weenie for you."

The wild spirit of early rock 'n' roll had largely disappeared. Heavy-handed congressional hearings on payola—with a strong racial undercurrent—began on February 2, the day after Barrett Strong's "Money" entered the pop charts. Chuck Berry was convicted of violation of the Mann Act in a trial that would be thrown out for racial prejudice, though he would be tried again. In England Eddie Cochran was killed and Gene Vincent was injured in a car wreck. Elvis Presley ended both his army stint and any vestige of rebellion when he filmed a TV special with Frank Sinatra. Alan Freed and other deejays were soon charged with commercial bribery.

After he finally made it to New Orleans, Bobby Charles sang "Walking to New Orleans" for Domino, who changed some words, notably adding the self-referencing line *"Now ain't that a sha-ame!"*

Bartholomew rehearsed the song with his rhythm section in his small studio on Claiborne Avenue. He asked session guitarist Justin Adams, "Can you come up with something to give it the feel of walking?" Adams picked his guitar and settled on a tick-tock lick. Ernest McLean, Bartholomew's other guitarist, followed his lead.

Later, at Cosimo's studio, Domino sang the song with a heartfelt vocal. At home that night, Bartholomew listened to the tape until two A.M. He wasn't satisfied. He thought of adding strings, perhaps recalling the Drifters' odd mix of African-rooted improvised passion and European orchestration, "There Goes My Baby," or even "The Theme from a Summer Place." He called Matassa, who contacted an arranger named Whitey Bush from the local symphony. Bartholomew wrote a simple lead arrangement for Bush, who he thought might try to overembellish the song. Still, he didn't know if the public would accept Fats with violins.

■ ■ ■

Domino stood proudly in front of his Fleetwood Cadillac and his brand-new pink tile and yellow brick house as a photographer took pictures. *Ebony* magazine, which loved displaying the lifestyles of rich and famous blacks, sent a writer to New Orleans to report on the mansion. A year earlier, Fats had bought two shotgun houses for $19,000 at the corner of Marais and Caffin, a few blocks from his old home, and his $200,000 dream home emerged amid the poverty of the Ninth Ward. For a time, two security guards patrolled the premises. Domino was wealthy—one of the few African American millionaires—and his home now reflected that fact. Visitors walked into the split-level house through a terrazzo-floor entrance inlaid with dominos. Above the Scandinavian-style living area was a twenty-four-foot ceiling and a balcony. An all-white music room downstairs was dominated by a baby grand piano. Gold records covered the walls.

The *Ebony* photographer took pictures of Fats serving drinks to his old friend Rip Roberts and to the house's architect at a bar imbedded with silver dollars beneath a painting of a European street. Though a few Ninth Ward residents resented Domino's ostentatious lifestyle, more took pride in the success of their favorite son. Fats invited his friends, like struggling Imperial bluesman Smiley Lewis, to see his new home. Often Rosemary or Fats cooked for their guests.

Outside, a tour bus filled with Chicago high school students stopped by during the photo shoot. Fats signed autographs while his son, ten-year-old Antoine, strummed a guitar and sang the Falcons' protean soul hit "You're So Fine."

The house quickly became a New Orleans landmark, a popular and conspicuous stop for tourists. An intermittent stream of fans knocked on the door to meet Domino. Fats didn't mind the fans, but Rosemary, who refused to pose for the *Ebony* photographer, couldn't stand the constant invasion of her privacy. In truth, she hated the new house and the dramatic change in her lifestyle.

"When you marry at a young age," says Rosemary, "you really don't pay attention to fame. We knew poverty in the '30s with the WPA. When my first daughter was born he wasn't doing great. I was living with my mother, washing clothes on a washboard, and if I had to, I'd do it again."

The longing to come home that Domino had expressed years earlier in "Goin' Home" and "Rose Mary" took a stronger turn in world-weary songs like "I've Been Around" and the unreleased "Walking to New Orleans." His surprisingly unsuccessful new single, "Before I Grow Too Old," exposed Domino's dilemma. He had been touring heavily for a decade. Now, at age thirty-two, he sounded fatigued, as if he had trouble convincing himself to keep traveling and partying. Bartholomew exulted in the song's big band crescendo, but Domino's vocal, straining to reach a high note, gave the song emotional resonance. It reflected the primary conflict in his life: Fats loved his home life in New Orleans, but, in a sense, the road was also his home, and the pleasures of the rock 'n' roll highlife were hard to resist.

■ ■ ■

To prove that rock 'n' roll was not dead, Dallas radio station KLIF staged a show with Domino, Jimmy Clanton, Brenda Lee, Frankie Ford, the Champs, and Roy Orbison. The four-hour "April Shower of Stars" also included the stars from TV's *Hawaiian Eye* in a variety act. The concert broke all records in the Dallas Municipal Auditorium, with officials calling the crowd "the most orderly in years."

While in Dallas, Domino told a KLIF disc jockey about his experiment with strings on "Walking to New Orleans." Fats himself was doubtful about the strings fitting "with my style." However, Bartholomew's gamble paid off. The record became a #6 pop hit and a #2 r&b hit in the summer of 1960. In its unadorned state without strings, the song was poignant, but the strings added the sense of a warm Southern breeze echoing Domino. "Walking to New Orleans" summed up his love affair with his hometown. "When I go away, I've still got home on my mind," says Fats. "The whole band is like that. New Orleans is a good place for everything. It's a good place to stay, for food, and for kind treatment. The people never turn you down here."

Racial tensions were, however, making blacks less sentimental about New Orleans. The City Council had even passed an ordinance prohibiting whites in black nightclubs without floor-to-ceiling partitions. There were picket lines outside at Dryades Street businesses that failed to hire black employees. In the French Quarter, segregation laws prohibiting blacks there were now enforced—Ernest McLean was once nearly arrested for taking a break on the sidewalk during a session at Cosimo's. On May 16, Judge J. Skelly Wright fired a shot that would exacerbate the tensions when he ordered the Orleans Parish School Board to integrate the first grade by the fall.

Though Domino was honored that year as one of the first stars on the Hollywood Walk of Fame in Los Angeles (where he made his final appearance at the 5-4 Ballroom in June), he strove to stay near to his home and his roots. In July, he played for his local black fans at Lincoln Beach. While he then took a break, some of his musicians joined Bartholomew's band on a two-week tour with Sam Cooke.

Fats missed a scheduled session at Cosimo's on July 18. But, instead of leaving the musicians hanging, he called Bartholomew, asking him to record a strong rhythm track to contrast with the slew of string-laden ballads he recorded after "Walking to New Orleans." Tenoo started beating out a rhythm that built up steam like a chugging locomotive. The horns even blew like a steam whistle at the end. Fats later listened to the tape and strung together blues-based words to the powerful beat: *"Hel-lo, Josephine, how do you do . . . "*

■ ■ ■

There was great irony in Domino's session on August 6, his thirteenth wedding anniversary. The recordings included the standards "You Always Hurt the One You Love" and "It's the Talk of the Town." Five days later, Rosemary filed for a legal separation. When she did, it was front-page news in *The Louisiana Weekly*.

Domino's years on the road, his drinking, and his philandering had taken their toll on his marriage. He had lost much of the closeness he had once enjoyed with his wife. Through her attorneys, Rosemary even charged her husband with cruelty. Her suit alleged that Fats embarrassed her in public, accused her of being unfaithful, failed to show affection to her or the children, withheld the use of his four cars, and left home without telling her good-bye or leaving any money. Rosemary asked for the use of the previous Domino residence at 1723 Caffin Avenue (to which she returned) and the impressive alimony of $2,500 a month. It was the first lawsuit in New Orleans in which a black man's income was listed at more than six figures.

Rosemary quickly withdrew the suit on August 15, telling the court that she had reconciled. "It wasn't nothin' too much," Domino says of the brief separation. "I didn't know what it was all about." Still, Rosemary, who had rarely stood up for herself before, opened his eyes to her viewpoint.

Jet magazine tried to smooth over the damage to Domino's reputation, which had been squeaky clean to most observers. Rosemary was clearly unhappy in her very public new surroundings. The bottom line was that she wanted to be alone, both with her children and with her husband. The *Jet* story featured pictures of Fats playing piano for Rosemary, doting on his children, and showing a visitor around as Rosemary glowered for the camera. Domino stated that it was always hard for a wife when her husband was in show business and that he couldn't make $100,000 a year staying in New Orleans. "I'd be less of a man," said Fats, "if I didn't try to provide the very best of everything for my wife and children."

Rosemary's mother, Rita Hall, played the peacemaker in bringing the couple back together. She was a very religious woman who attended the African Methodist Episcopal church. Her intervention perhaps prompted Fats to take both his family and his religion more seriously, as he perused his Bible often thereafter. But the very Catholic-oriented lyric in "Before I Grow Too Old" about enjoying sin and then repenting would come back to haunt him again and again.

Domino's next record, the overtly sentimental "Three Nights a Week," had lyrics—*"Three nights a week, you're gone"*—that sounded like they came directly from Rosemary's lips—though "three weeks a month" more accurately described her husband's absences from home. It hit the charts soon after they reconciled.

■ ■ ■

Segregationists still knew better than anyone that the popularity of black rock 'n' roll was a threat to their cause. On August 1, Albert Jones, director of the "segregation cabinet" of the Mississippi State Sovereignty Commission, wrote to Governor Ross Barnett in an "ultimately unsuccessful" attempt to prevent an interracial dance featuring Domino. That month Fats also canceled a show at the Convention Center Dome in Virginia Beach when he discovered that a rope was going to segregate dancers.

Still, Domino recorded two more evocative Southern anthems with strings. "Rising Sun" was a hymn to the languid lifestyle of his childhood. Music writer Hank Davis calls "Natural Born Lover" "a white man's widescreen Technicolor version of the blues superimposed on a black man's backporch lament."

In New Orleans both black and white college students "sat in" at segregated Woolworth's lunch counters. Mayor Chep Morrison, still with eyes on the prize of the governorship, took a hard line, repeatedly arresting the protesters.

On October 25, Fats appeared on *American Bandstand,* playing "Walking to New Orleans" and "My Girl Josephine," three days after performing at Radio City Music Hall for Merv Griffin's *Saturday Night Prom* on NBC. Domino's whip-cracking rocker "Josephine" blasted through the fluff on the pop airwaves that fall. It would later be recorded by Jerry Lee Lewis and a host of British groups, including Them with Van Morrison. Fats also heard another hit on the radio that he had turned down—"You Talk Too Much" by Joe Jones. Domino's brother-in-law, Reggie Hall, had written the song and offered it to Fats two years earlier. Disc jockeys dedicated the song to Fidel Castro and Nikita Khruschev following their outbursts at the United Nations, but the sentiment was also soon applicable in New Orleans.

■ ■ ■

"TWO, FOUR, SIX, EIGHT! WE DON'T WANNA INTEGRATE!" shouted a gauntlet of white women, who spit and threw eggs at three black girls entering McDonough 19 school, three blocks from Domino's home on November 14. Not far away, U.S. marshals escorted a six-year-old black girl with pink bows on her pigtails, Ruby Bridges, to the William J. Frantz School in a scene later immortalized by Norman Rockwell. The four girls' nationally televised walks to integrate New Orleans' public schools gave new meaning to Domino's "Walking to New Orleans."

Governor Davis and the legislature repeatedly tried to kill school integration but were trumped at every turn by Judge J. Skelly Wright, who by now had a twenty-four-hour police guard. Mayor Morrison, the local newspapers, and others opposing integration stood by as rabid segregationists started a crisis unseen since the Little Rock riots.

The next night, more than 5,000 whites gathered at a segregation rally in Municipal Auditorium on the land where a century earlier blacks had celebrated the end of slavery at Congo Square. As vendors sold Confederate flags, the crowd screamed, "SEND 'EM BACK TO AFRICA!" Schoolchildren, half of them in blackface, paraded onstage to kiss each other. Plaquemines Parish boss Leander Perez incited the mob with a foaming diatribe about "Congolese" and "burrheads" raping white women.

The next day, segregationists sent out 2,000 white teenagers to riot in downtown New Orleans. The boys surrounded the mayor's office and the School Board. After they were dispersed by fire hoses, they randomly vandalized property and attacked blacks. Although the mayor was quick to arrest peaceful lunch counter protesters, his police stopped few rioters until that night when blacks met the white gangs. Scores were injured, and 250—mostly blacks— were arrested. New Orleans, long considered an island of relative tolerance in the South, was that week compared to Nazi Germany. But city fathers soon realized that integration protests were bad business in a city that depended upon tourism. By December, both businessmen and teachers called for surrender to the dreaded integration.

Domino was touring the Northeast and missed the uproar, but the segregationists didn't forget about him. During the protests, Allen Toussaint was jarred by a crude sign that exposed the internal conflict: "SEND ALL THE NIGGERS BACK TO AFRICA—EXCEPT FOR FATS DOMINO."

■ ■ ■

Fats also missed a visit from Bobby Charles, who had a new song titled "Little Rascal." It was raining in Philadelphia when Domino received an instrumental tape of the song from Bartholomew, and he wrote a lyric that reflected both the weather and the dark times back home, the majestically solemn "It Keeps Rainin'."

The success of the Cajun songwriter inspired others to visit Domino. In December two white men from Mississippi sat in a car outside of Domino's Marais Street mansion. Rosemary had told them that her husband was not home. When Fats drove up in his Cadillac, the men got out of the car. One of them, Jimmy Donley, carried a guitar. He asked Domino to listen to his songs.

Fats ushered the men into his home. They admired Domino's luxuries, particularly the twenty framed gold records. Donley strummed his guitar and sang heartfelt country songs with a bluesy feel that impressed Fats. The clincher was "What a Price," a ballad that Donley sang with an anguished vocal. He wanted to sell his song outright, but Fats insisted, as Harrison Verrett had instructed him a decade earlier, that he take royalties. However, Donley was a simple man who could not see beyond the sunset. His name would not even appear on the song, as he sold his share to a Reverend Jack Charles Jessup.

At a session on December 28, Domino recorded "What a Price." Except for the chorus and the first couplet, Fats rewrote the lyrics, which reflected the other side of "Before I Grow Too Old" for Domino, who now tearfully—and with obvious regret—proclaimed how he stopped his rambling and gambling to keep his love.

Fats seemed to be working out both emotional and musical tensions in the session, which was capped by a grinding boogie version of Louis Jordan's 1946 humorous ode to misogyny, "Ain't That Just Like a Woman." Lee Allen even blew a solo tribute to "Chattanooga Choo Choo." Having recorded ballads for months, the band's relief was evident. Bartholomew shouted, "It sounds good!" at the end. All four songs they recorded—"It Keeps Rainin'," "What a Price," "Ain't That Just Like a Woman," and "Fell in Love on Monday"—became top 40 hits.

On the last day of the year, Ernest McLean and Billy Diamond traveled to California with their wives. The Golden State's job opportunities, dramatic landscape, and endless sunshine reflected the nation's youthful optimism after the election of John F. Kennedy almost two months earlier. New Orleans session musicians like McLean hoped to work for L.A. record companies. But blacks were leaving Louisiana primarily because of the racial unrest that was rocking their state.

Domino was home for the holidays, but his home was not the same.

(1961–1962)

> *"To them times you start Fats Domino and playin' them type of*
> *people. So from then on the music start to drift [to] the reggae."*
> —BOB MARLEY (IN *The Bob Marley Story* DOCUMENTARY)

"*FATS DOMINO! FATS DOMINO!*" Brilliant sunshine flashed through an ocean of blue sky in Jamaica in early 1961. On narrow dirt roads between simple white shacks, islanders thronged Domino's limousines. Fats waved to the fans, taken aback by the adulation. He was beginning to realize that he had influenced music worldwide, as his hit "Let the Four Winds Blow" would soon suggest.

Walter "Papoose" Nelson had rejoined the band. Instead of agreeing to Ernest McLean's demand for a pay raise, Fats had bailed "Pappy" out of jail. In a way, the Domino band was Papoose's family, as he was now sadly estranged from his own relations because of his drug habit. "He was just a good-hearted cat," writes Mac "Dr. John" Rebennack in his autobiography, "who happened to be strung out." Harrison Verrett, along with lawyer Charles Levy and his wife, also accompanied Domino for the tropical tour.

On January 31, the entire Domino entourage smiled for a photograph upon their arrival at the Montego Bay Airport for the tour, which was booked by Jamaican impresario Stephen Hill. The photo and a story appeared on the front page of nation's major newspaper, *The Jamaica Gleaner,* the next day.

The Caribbean had always been tied closely to New Orleans. Beginning in the late 1940s, Jamaican workers traveled to Louisiana to work in the sugarcane fields. The migrant workers were soon hooked on r&b. They brought home records that became objects worshiped for their soulful spirit rhythms.

Jamaicans sometimes picked up New Orleans radio stations. Local disc jockeys also played r&b records on portable sound systems at weekend dances, notably dancehall originator Tom "The Great" Sebastian, who hooked ska great Prince Buster on Domino. Sailors brought disc jockey Count Matchuki r&b records from New Orleans every three weeks. Another dancehall producer, Clement "Coxsone" Dodd, traveled to New Orleans himself to buy records. The deejays tried to hide the identity of coveted records in order to protect their own little musical monopolies, but everyone knew Domino, who became a Jamaican icon. Even Dave Bartholomew (who did not make the tour) was revered for his skanking 1957 masterpiece of jungle wisdom, "The Monkey Speaks His Mind."

A Jamaican musical revolution had begun in the late 1950s. Guitarist Ernest Ranglin, the primary arranger on early ska sessions (including Bob Marley and the Wailers' first hit), states flatly, "The ska rhythm was derived from the shuffle and boogie beats from New Orleans that were so popular in local dance halls." In particular, Domino's "Be My Guest" from 1959 had a "sprung" boogie beat (similar to that of "She's My Baby" a decade earlier). Musicologist Charlie Gillett later noted the similarities between "Be My Guest" and ska in a *Rolling Stone* review, commenting that the guitar plays "4/4 time while the drummer bashes on the off-beat." The rhythm would become the foundation of ska. In fact, Sam Cooke and his band, who toured Jamaica and the Caribbean in July 1960, heard "Be My Guest" everywhere they went. As Peter Guralnick writes in his Cooke biography *Dream Boogie,* it was "the one song you heard on every radio station and in the repertoire of every local group."

Jamaican devotion to Domino was also obvious in a Kingston nightclub called the "Fats Domino Beer Garden" in the late 1950s, Al T. Joe's *record de plume* "Jamaica Fats," in the album *Millie Small Sings Fats Domino,* and in a group called Justin Hind and the Dominoes. Not long after Domino's tour, fourteen-year-old James Chambers would sing a vocalese version of "Be My Guest" before a huge crowd at a boy scout camp. Under the name "Jimmy Cliff," he soon performed Domino songs in the Kingston talent show *Opportunity Knocks.* "I used to sing all Fats Domino songs," says Cliff. His early hit, "Miss Jamaica," reflected the sound and lyric of "Be My Guest." There were many Jamaican covers of Domino songs from the 1950s to the end of the millennium. If Domino's r&b was a major part of rock 'n' roll, it was the sine qua non of ska. In the documentary *The Bob Marley Story,* Marley indicates Domino's dominant influence and simulates playing piano triplets. In the

Stephen Davis Marley biography, the singer began a list of his influences with the statement: "My earliest influence in music comes from Fats Domino time."

One night, after Domino finished playing a show at Carib in Kingston, he made a royal entrance at another club, King's Lawn, in a simple white short sleeve shirt adorned with drawings of calypso dancers. Fats drank and listened to the popular local singers, Prince Buster and Derrick Morgan. He got up to jam with the band, playing Buster's favorite song, "Going to the River."

"Jamaican artists always tried to sing like him," says Morgan (who titled his hit "Fat Man" in homage to Domino), "'cause we always liked his stuff. 'Be My Guest,' that was a really 'ska' style, so we got all those rhythms from him, too. It was a powerful influence in recording Jamaican music—Fats Domino, Smiley Lewis, Professor Longhair, Louis Jordan, all those type of mans. Fats was the number one."

At out-of-the-way clubs like the Carrot and the Glass Bucket, renegade "rude boys" with unkempt hair heckled Charles Levy, the only white in the club, who stood at the back with Billy Diamond. "They wanted to kill Levy," says Diamond. "They called him 'the devil' in Spanish Town." Levy and his wife hurried back to New Orleans before the others.

■ ■ ■

Back in his new home, Fats stood behind the huge bar fixing a drink for Jimmy Donley and his wife, Lillie Mae. Donley, a country man with greasy curls and rolled-up jeans, brought Fats some fish he had caught. Domino's marital problems paled next to those of the Donleys. Jimmy, a heavy drinker, often took out his temper physically on Lillie Mae, who would leave him before reconciling to a new love song he wrote for her. But the Donleys' good times together were also reflected in a song he wrote for Fats, "Rockin' Bicycle."

As Donley played Domino some songs, they heard another tune playing outside. Domino's children rushed in, yelling, "Ice cream! Ice cream!" Fats went to his safe against the wall and pulled out silver dollars for each child to go to the ice cream truck. In later years, in an echo of the penny pitching at Domino family parties in Vacherie half a century earlier, Fats would come home from Las Vegas and throw handfuls of silver dollars on the floor for his children to grab.

On another occasion, Lew Chudd and his wife, Bette, traveled from Los Angeles to see Domino's mansion. Fats, however, didn't show up. Rosemary cooked the Chudds a dinner of shrimp Creole for them as her children shuffled in and out. Chudd was convinced that Fats was trying to give him ulcers.

Domino suffered more domestic problems in late February when a Los Angeles woman filed a paternity suit for a child born on June 30, 1960. The woman stated in the suit that she had had sex with Domino since October 1957. The threat of the suit had perhaps been a hidden reason behind the separation filed by Rosemary.

Fats told *Jet,* which publicized the suit, that he'd "never been anything but a friend to the young mother" and would fight the suit. Sam Cooke had reportedly settled a similar suit for $5,000. Instead, following advice from Charles Levy, Domino dealt with it bizarrely by avoiding L.A.—the location of his record company, movie and TV studios, and his favorite concert stop. "I could've gotten him out of that," says Lew Chudd. "She would've settled for $5,000, but Levy didn't think I could get him off. Fats lost about three movies and a couple of television shows on that."

In March, seventy-five black Mardi Gras organizations—all except Zulu—again canceled their balls to protest the racial clashes over integration. There was even racial tension in a Domino session that month, as Bartholomew did not appreciate having to arrange three songs by Jimmy Donley and Pee Wee Maddux. "I had to do all the music," says Bartholomew. "So they were trying to hound in on two black men. They got quite a few things that Fats and I had put back on the shelf."

■ ■ ■

In April 1961, the Soviets shocked the world again by putting the first man into space, while Fidel Castro routed Cuban expatriates at the Bay of Pigs. But an American musical virus was, in turn, infiltrating the USSR, bringing truth to Domino's prediction that the Russians would dig the rock 'n' roll beat. Sailors imported forbidden rock 'n' roll records, which were bootlegged onto the only available vinyl—x-rays displaying ghostly bones. The fact that teens defiantly treasured the wretched "rib records" proved their passion (as later dramatized in the movie *Red Hot*). Rock 'n' roll was also spread in other surreptitious forms behind the Iron Curtain. In one example, a postcard showing the Central Committee building of the Communist Party in Byelorussia had a spindle hole in the middle; the recipient placing the card on a record player would hear a sound definitely not heard in the halls of the Committee—crashing drums and Fats Domino singing hello to Josephine! In the port city of Riga in Latvia the first known Soviet rock band, the Revengers, formed in 1961 with a lead singer nicknamed "Saintsky," since his favorite song was the New Orleans anthem "When the Saints Go Marching In." The spirit of freedom that had its roots in Congo Square was now reaching the outposts of human oppression, whether in the Soviet Union or in South Africa.

Domino headlined The Biggest Show of Stars for 1961, which opened on April 2 at the Uline Arena in Washington, D.C. Backstage, Chubby Checker laughed about his record "The Twist." "It's bigger than big!" he exclaimed. *"It's bigger than life!"* Two other Big Show acts had #1 hits—the Shirelles ("Will You Love Me Tomorrow") and the Drifters ("Save the Last Dance for Me"). Ben E. King, who had recently quit the Drifters, sang "Spanish Harlem" and the just-released "Stand by Me." Bo Diddley, the Shells, and Chuck Jackson rounded out the bill.

At a time when southern police regularly arrested Freedom Riders on segregated buses, Irvin Feld's Big Show buses again brought black music to racially mixed crowds. In a *Jet* article, booking agent Bob Astor suggested that business was down for package shows during the racial turmoil because parents withheld $3 admission fees from teens to keep them away from black shows.

Discrimination was not confined to the South. At a roadside diner in Topeka, Kansas, a woman asked the stars if they were traveling or staying—she didn't serve blacks unless they were moving on. Tour manager Allen Bloom told off the witless waitress as the musicians exited. "We talked a lot about civil rights," says Bloom, "but we weren't crusaders. There was a lot of biting your upper lip. There were problems with hotels here and there."

Both Fats and Bo Diddley cooked while on tour using similar spicy recipes, since the Chicago guitarist's mother had been a New Orleans native. Domino fed his band, and Bo sold food to the other acts so they could avoid segregated restaurants. "He's kicks!" says Fats of Bo Diddley. "I don't know if he exactly plays rock 'n' roll, but he's comical with it. He came to work in a hearse." Bloom considered the Chicago bluesman's maturity "a calming influence." But he still had to keep an eye on Fats to keep him on schedule. He occasionally traveled in Domino's Cadillac and watched the star drink heavily and gobble pigs' feet.

■ ■ ■

That spring New Orleans music again blasted out of every radio. Domino's "It Keeps Rainin'" was rising on the charts. Joe Barry (Barrios), who, like Bobby

Charles, was a Cajun from Abbeville, imitated Fats's thick vocals in his hit "I'm a Fool to Care." Bartholomew's producing heir apparent, Allen Toussaint, achieved the first New Orleans r&b #1 pop hit with "Mother-in-Law" by Ernie K-Doe. Toussaint also arranged Domino-inspired hits by Clarence "Frogman" Henry, the #2 pop hit "I Like It Like That" by Chris Kenner, and "Ya Ya" by Domino's former schoolmate, Lee Dorsey.

In two June sessions, Fats recorded "Let the Four Winds Blow," previously recorded by Bartholomew, Bobby Charles, and Roy Brown. The band sizzled with popping drums, washboard guitar licks, and breezy horns. The song was quickly released and rose to #15 pop and #2 r&b. *Million Sellers by Fats,* a collection of recent hits, became his first album since 1957 to make the charts.

Billboard listed Fats among the "Hottest Singles Artists" that month as he began a western tour in Texas. The tour grossed $83,091, with takes ranging from $2,000 in Laramie, Wyoming, to $11,900 in Albuquerque, New Mexico. Domino toured the Northwest and even out to Hawaii, but California was shockingly absent from his itinerary, apparently due to his concern over the paternity suit.

In September Ray Charles played the first totally integrated show in the Memphis Auditorium as "Hit the Road, Jack" climbed to #1. Domino played a similar show at New Orleans' Municipal Auditorium in a benefit on September 24 for St. Mary's Academy School before a still segregated—but now almost all white—audience; Mayor Vic Schiro would soon refuse Martin Luther King, Jr., use of the auditorium, which would not be fully integrated until July 1963.

The next month Domino's shows ranged from a prison rodeo in Huntsville, Texas, to a package show co-headlined by Brenda Lee in Pittsburgh. On October 23, Fats appeared on *American Bandstand* performing "Let the Four Winds Blow" and "What a Party." The next day, Herbert Hardesty used two Domino guitarists on a solo recording session for Federal Records in Cincinnati. Domino had hired session guitarist Roy Montrell to back up the unpredictable Papoose, who sang on one of Hardesty's records, a triplet ballad titled "It Must Be Wonderful." Though he was filling in temporarily, Montrell would soon become an integral part of the Domino band.

Domino's new recordings again seemed autobiographical. On November 6 in Camden, New Jersey, Fats recorded two tributes to his home—the Hank Williams Cajun anthem "Jambalaya" and "Do You Know What It Means to Miss New Orleans," which could have been his theme song. The current hit, "What a Party," was likewise Bartholomew's homage to Fats, including the lyric—*"Big fat piano man he sure could play!"* Recorded in an earlier partying session at Cosimo's, it featured ragtag percussion and drunken shouting as it celebrated the rockin' revelry that Domino had kept going for over a decade.

"What a Party," "Jambalaya," and "You Win Again" all kept Fats in the top 30, but all was not well. *The Louisiana Weekly* even pronounced, "Fats Domino is flopping miserably as a box office attraction in different spots. In places that normally held several thousand, Fats has been able to lure only several hundred."

The fact that the size of Domino's audiences was slipping was painfully obvious to his entourage, but most notably to his brother-in-law, Harrison Verrett, who mentioned it to William Russell and Ralph Collins of the Tulane University Jazz Archives at his home on Jourdan Avenue that year. The researchers chronicled Verrett's career as a jazz sideman until he mentioned that he taught piano to his brother-in-law, Fats Domino. Taken by surprise, the jazz historians asked, "Who?" Harrison pointed out Domino's heavy-set mother Donatile, sitting on her porch at the house next door, and then recounted his protégé's road from childhood to success. His voice broke as he admitted that Domino's crowds were down. Since Verrett never had children, Antoine Domino, Jr., was his pride.

Russell comforted him, noting that Domino's success would carry him the rest of his life, even though he wasn't "number one."

"He'll make it," agreed Verrett. "I mean, he'll make enough. Made famous, a little fella."

■ ■ ■

In January 1962, Domino again toured with two guitarists, this time two brothers, Walter "Papoose" Nelson and Lawrence "Prince La La" Nelson, who was enjoying an r&b hit with "She Put the Hurt on Me" on AFO Records. AFO, or "All For One," was a cooperative record label formed by black New Orleans musicians who were tired of not receiving royalties from hits. Though the artists included at least one white, Mac Rebennack, AFO was a forerunner of black co-ops to come.

Prince La La posed for an amazing publicity photo in robes and a headdress attended by two black princesses clad in leopard skins and feathers in an African outfitting foreshadowing the voodoo "Night Tripper" regalia of Rebennack's alter-ego, Dr. John. Though "black pride" was not yet a familiar cry, African roots were resurfacing in unexpected ways. American and Jamaican calls for civil rights paralleled the African independence movement, including protests against apartheid in South Africa, where both blacks and whites revered Domino.

Luckily, in light of some of the places that Domino played, La La didn't wear his African garb on tour. The current tour included a performance in the all-white town of Rogers, Arkansas, which for years had posted worn-out signs at the bus depot, train station, and highways telling blacks don't "let the sun set on you in Rogers." Police Chief Hugh Basse used every policeman in the area to patrol the theater that Domino was playing. Afterwards, the promoter asked the band if they wanted to eat before they left town, with the emphasis on *leave town*. La La, likely incensed over the obvious racism in the town, got into an argument with Papoose that night and quit. But the next day, in Joplin, Missouri, the band heard that they were the news—"Fats Domino played in an Arkansas town that hasn't had any Negro musicians in 40 years."

Domino's new album was titled *Twistin' the Stomp*. Chubby Checker's "The Twist" hit #1 again in early 1962. Hank Ballard, whose "Work with Me, Annie" ignited the first r&b sex scandals, now indirectly started a more widespread subversion of America's puritanical ethic, as Checker's close copy of his song had everyone twisting. Beamed nationwide by *American Bandstand,* the Twist sparked a new wave of righteous protest, as WASP daughters shook their booties. Even white adults began swiveling in the sexually ostentatious African tradition—like "the hideous gyrations" condemned by the New Orleans bishop in 1786. According to Eldridge Cleaver in *Soul on Ice,* "The Twist was a guided missile, launched from the ghetto into the very heart of suburbia," with whites finding "a sense of freedom they had never known before." Indeed, Nancy Friday, the author of several books on sex, declares that the Sexual Revolution for her began when adults started twisting at New York's Peppermint Lounge. Domino had helped kick off that physical liberation with his hard-driving rhythms. Fittingly, Checker's name was a tribute to Domino, just as the *"thrill on the hill"* chorus of Ballard's "Let's Go, Let's Go, Let's Go" was taken from the sexy refrain in "Blueberry Hill."

■ ■ ■

On February 20, 1962, John Glenn became the first American to orbit the Earth. As he bulleted around the planet, he remarked that he saw the lights of New Orleans from his capsule, Friendship 7.

A week later, as New York City prepared for Glenn's tickertape parade, Domino also headed to New York for an appearance on *The Ed Sullivan Show*. The band members arrived in Harlem at their regular haunt, the Hotel Theresa at five A.M. on Tuesday—Mardi Gras day back home in New Orleans. After sleeping most of the day, Papoose called Billy Diamond, who, like Domino, was staying at the Sheraton Hotel downtown. Papoose wanted his pay. Billy told him he would pay everybody when they went to rehearse for the Sullivan show.

Ten minutes later, Fats called Diamond, telling him to pay Papoose his $300.

It was raining when Billy headed for Harlem. As he drove the bus up to the Theresa, he saw Papoose standing with a man and a woman holding an umbrella. "Man," said Papoose, flashing an electric smile as he took his money, "I'm gonna kill myself or eat me some steaks out of this world!" Diamond knew that the guitarist was more likely in the midst of a drug deal with the couple beside him.

The next morning, February 28, was Ash Wednesday. Diamond drove to the Theresa to pick up the band. When Papoose didn't answer his knock, the bell captain opened the door. They found the guitarist lying askew on the bed with one shoe on and a needle in his arm. He was cold, dead from a heroin overdose at age twenty-nine.

Some of the band members broke down and cried at the news of Nelson's death. Fats told Billy, "Do what you gotta do."

Diamond called the police. After taking Papoose's possessions down to the bus, he called his father to break the news. Then he made arrangements to fly the body back home. He also had to consider the repercussions. Ray Charles had been arrested for drug possession in November and canceled his Ed Sullivan appearance. A drug scandal that both damaged Domino's reputation and canceled a Sullivan appearance could be a disastrous double blow. Accordingly, Diamond today claims that he bribed a *Jet* writer to report that Nelson died of a heart attack.

Finally, Diamond had to find a new guitarist. He called Ernest McLean, who declined the offer. He then fell back on Roy Montrell, who flew from his home in Scotlandville above Baton Rouge to New York, not imagining that his relationship with Domino would last a tumultuous seventeen years.

■ ■ ■

Ed Sullivan presented Domino and his band to millions of viewers on Sunday, March 4, four days after Papoose Nelson's death. Domino pounded out a rumbling "Jambalaya" on a stage with giant dominoes standing like prehistoric monoliths around him. On his right, the saxmen—Buddy Hagans, Clarence Ford, Herbert Hardesty, and Lee Allen—swayed and riffed in unison. In the back, Jimmy Davis plucked his stand-up bass. Roy Montrell sat on a stool like a wooden Indian and strummed his guitar. On Domino's left, Tenoo slapped his drums. Bartholomew stood in front blowing his crooked cornet. The ensemble looked like a remnant of the big band era compared to the pompadoured teen idols and Barbie-doll girl singers who now dominated pop music.

Despite Domino's smile, his face seemed swollen. His eyes were barely visible as he squinted into the lights. He broke into the plaintive Hank Williams classic, "You Win Again," and then concluded with a rousing "Let the Four Winds Blow." Bartholomew blasted out a squealing climax on his trumpet.

Backstage, Sullivan asked Domino the burning question of the day: "Would you play a segregated show?"

"Sure," replied Fats with a guileless grin. "I'd play for anybody." Domino lived for music and generally did not mix politics with his idealistic view that music made people happy and brought them together. After all, he was usually right.

■ ■ ■

Six days later friends and family of Walter "Papoose" Nelson in starched white shirts, black jackets, and Sunday dresses assembled at the Blandin Funeral Home at Ursuline and St. Claude. An informal group looked on, including Tulane University student Beth Bagby, who was writing a story on jazz funerals for *The Tulane Hullabaloo*. Fats and his band were still on tour and missed the funeral.

Pallbearers carried out a white coffin covered with garlands. The crowd walked solemnly to a nearby church as a jazz band played "Nearer My God to Thee." At the church, the crowd let the family members pass—Walter Nelson, Sr., and his wife Edna, Papoose's brothers Lawrence and Warren, and his four sisters. Earline, the guitarist's widow, led his four children into the funeral home. A heavy-set black woman in a nurse's uniform finally ushered in two men who carried flower-covered styrofoam replicas of Papoose's guitar. Outside the church, people gathered in anticipation of the joyful second line parade. The crowd spilled across the street and into the corner bar.

After the service, pallbearers placed the coffin in a hearse. The sight of family members emerging dazed or sobbing uncontrollably from the church quieted the raucous crowd. The jazz band in front of the hearse struck up "Just a Closer Walk with Thee," and the procession began. Hearing the band, people left their houses to join the second line of band followers as they proceeded block by block.

A light rain began to fall on the second-liners bobbing to the rhythm with their umbrellas. On North Claiborne, the crowd parted to "Let the body loose," as the hearse proceeded on the distance to the cemetery. They began shouting *"Hey! Hey! Hey!"* as the band struck up "When the Saints Go Marching In." The crowd danced as the rain fell steadily. Many made their way to the Caldonia, the hole-in-the-wall club near Congo Square where both Papoose's musical career and his addiction had started. The lyric of the New Orleans standard "The Junker's Blues" that Domino had once sung had indirectly come back to haunt him: *"That usin' junk, partner, is gonna be the death of you."*

■ ■ ■

On April 14, Domino recorded the fast boogie number "Dance with Mr. Domino," which, as "Domino Twist," he would perform live for decades. Fats was in a good mood, laughing in the studio. He didn't know that it was his last Imperial session.

Five days later, Domino began The Biggest Show of Stars of 1962 tour at the Municipal Auditorium in Norfolk, Virginia. He co-headlined a tour of twenty-four cities with Brook Benton that included Gene "The Duke of Earl" Chandler, Bruce Channel, Don and Juan, and the Impressions. The tour was again supposed to be all black, but Irvin Feld was shocked to find out that Bruce Channel (who had the #1 hit "Hey Baby") was white. Still, the show played to mixed audiences all over the country.

Domino was riding two hits with Hank Williams songs, but the thunder of his own country crossover, which he had begun many years earlier, was soon stolen by Ray Charles's massive #1 hit of Don Gibson's "I Can't Stop Loving You," with a choir of white girl singers swathing Charles's soulful vocal like cotton candy.

In May, President Kennedy ordered 5,800 troops to Southeast Asia in the same month that *The Freewheelin' Bob Dylan,* with the antiwar anthems "Blowin' in the Wind" and "Masters of War," was released.

The Big Show did mediocre business, as Benton, with his suave mature persona, never attracted as many teenagers as his hits would indicate. And Domino was finally, as Allen Bloom puts it, "on the downside of the mountain." The tour ended in Houston on May 20. Though Irvin Feld would book dates with the Beatles and the Rolling Stones in 1964, he continued to promote all-black tours headlined by Chuck Berry, James Brown, Stevie Wonder, and Wilson Pickett until 1967, when, in a P. T. Barnum-esque ceremony at the Coliseum in Rome, he and his brother Israel became the owners of Ringling Brothers and Barnum and Bailey Circus.

In his new single, "My Real Name," Fats again self-mockingly sang about his name and his weight, as he had in "The Fat Man." Ironically, he faced a real identity crisis on June 5 when he went to obtain a passport. An officious immigration officer made him sign his name as it appeared on his birth certificate. Antoine Domino, Jr., was shocked to discover that a confused registrar had written his name down as "Anthony Domino, Jr." thirty-four years earlier. Now he wasn't even sure of his real name. In his new single "My Real Name," Fats again self-mockingly sang about his name and his weight, as he had in "The Fat Man." Ironically, he faced a real identity crisis on June 5 when he went to obtain a passport. An officious immigration officer made him sign his name as it appeared on his birth certificate. Antoine Domino, Jr., was shocked to discover that a confused registrar had written his name down as "Anthony Domino, Jr." thirty four years earlier. Now he wasn't even sure of his real name. Just four days later, he lost another pillar of his identity when his beloved mother-in-law, Rita LePage Hall, died after a long illness. Fats soon performed "My Real Name" and the ominously titled "Nothing New (Same Old Thing)" on *American Bandstand,* but even Dick Clark couldn't save the record, which only reached #59. Domino needed a new direction. With his slipping career, his characteristic dread of the unknown, and his fear of flying, he was apprehensive as he clutched his stranger's passport and boarded an airplane flying across the Atlantic Ocean for his first European appearance.

■ ■ ■

"Au Zoo!" "Le Domino Circus!" In July, a few jazz purists heckled as Fats took the stage in his appearance at the Antibes Jazz Festival in Juan-les-Pins, France, including the Clara Ward Singers, Dizzy Gillespie, and Jimmy Smith. A writer in the French magazine *Jazz Hot* complained that Fats had a $4,800 watch and didn't know who Thelonius Monk was, but the fans *loved* Domino. Dave Bartholomew, blowing his Dizzy Gillespie–style bent cornet, led the band second-lining through the crowd. Fats even ran into his old friend Dennis "Big Chief" Alley, who, incredibly, just happened to be on leave with the marines on the Riviera.

England's *Melody Maker* sent music writer Robert Houston to review the show. He snootily reported that Domino's appearance was "very entertaining and the crowd loved every minute of it. But it was not jazz festival material." He met Domino as he was leaving and asked him when he'd make a British tour.

"I'd love to come to Britain," replied Domino. "And now that I'm getting more used to airplanes, I think I'll make it soon."

In October as the Cuban missile crisis was threatening world destruction, Domino returned to Europe to tour France, Belgium, the Netherlands, and Germany with English promoter Don Arden. In Paris, Domino's concert, including blues acts Willie Dixon and Memphis Slim, drew 16,000 fans to the Palais-des-Sports. After Roy Montrell sang a Ray Charles song, Fats played ten songs and ended with "When the Saints Go Marching In." Bartholomew and Lee Allen led a second-line parade that whipped the crowd into a frenzy. Fats came back to perform a nine-song encore. Then, in his unassuming way, he signed autographs directly from the stage.

This time a British writer came back home with a rave review, reporting that Domino's "in-person performances are superior to anything he has done on record, and what a fantastic bunch of musicians he has in his orchestra."

The musicians loved the attention that the Europeans gave them. At the hotels, they had to leave their shoes in front of their doors. Inside their rooms the band members got acquainted with the very friendly women who hung around after the shows. Despite the strange surroundings, for the first time Domino's musicians were thrilled to breathe free air without a hint of racial prejudice. It gave them a rush that made them even higher than the fine wine they were drinking.

The band arrived in Hamburg on October 27 for two shows at the Star-Club. As in other seaports, Hamburg received rock 'n' roll from sailors importing records in their duffel bags. Parents called it "Hottentotten" music (another jungle reference—to the African "Hottentot" tribe), but the music thrilled young Germans, who heard it on the American Armed Forces Network. Since 1960 Liverpool bands like the Beatles had played in Hamburg's red-light district, where rocking was undiluted by European tastes for light pop.

In 1962 Horst Fascher, a boxer-turned-bouncer at Hamburg clubs, began managing the Star-Club, a former movie theater in the Grose Freiheit district that featured rockers like Jerry Lee Lewis, Gene Vincent, and Roy Orbison. Teens were allowed in the club before ten, but the late crowd included sailors, neo-Nazis, strippers, pimps, and transvestites. Waiters recruited from the

Hamburg boxing academy kept order with truncheons, heavy boots, and tear gas guns. The club's owner, Manfred Wessleder, had contacted Don Arden to book Domino's first club appearance in Europe.

At noon, Fascher sent five Mercedes sedans to pick up Domino at the train station and offered everyone German beer. Discovering that Domino and his band had been up all night, Fascher feared they might not be able to play both shows. He spiked the band's Johnny Walker whiskey, German beer, and goulash with the pep pills that the British groups swallowed to keep going all night long.

Domino's warm-up bands were two then obscure Liverpool groups, the Searchers and Gerry and the Pacemakers, both of whom proudly had their pictures taken with him. Domino came on at nine o'clock and marched through his hits to the crowd's delight. "Fats was the best act we played with at the Star-Club," declares John McNally of the Searchers. "He was fantastic and so was his band."

At the conclusion of the first set on the second night, minors under age eighteen were forced by curfew to leave, but Fats didn't stop playing until 10:20. His midnight set didn't stop until 1:45 A.M. The exhausted crowd ebbed away. Few stayed to hear the British groups play late sets, but Fats and his band were wired by the pills and ready to party all night. Fascher closed the doors and called a strip club to send over girls. The musicians each ended up with a bottle and a girl. Domino was still jamming at five A.M.

At six A.M., the phone rang. A frantic Don Arden informed Fascher that Domino had only two hours to catch a plane.

■ ■ ■

The tour was a great success, both in terms of publicity and money. But on the way back from Europe, Domino stopped in New York and instructed Billy Diamond to cash his hefty tour check at the Chase Manhattan Bank.

"We're goin' to Las Vegas next week," said Fats. "Let's go there *now*."

"Fats," pleaded Billy, "I gotta send the money for the tax and for Levy."

"Damn Levy," insisted Domino. "Let's go."

Fats and his entourage headed to the gambling mecca, where he hit the craps tables. With his checkered suit, a lacquered flattop, and diamond-studded fingers wrapped around a shot of scotch, he may have thought he had the slick look of a gambler. But, to the casino employees, he looked like a sucker.

Diamond eventually gave him all of the money they had earned from the tour, and Domino lost it all. Then he borrowed money from Phil Long at the California Club and kept losing.

Finally, the casino made a phone call to Lew Chudd. The manager told Chudd that the Flamingo Hotel was holding Mr. Domino until Imperial Records sent a six-figure sum to pay for his gambling debts.

A shaken Chudd woke up Charlie Newton at the Bank of America, who opened up early to give him stacks of cash. Former Murder, Inc., hit man Bugsy Siegel founded the Flamingo fifteen years earlier and mobsters still ran the hotel. The situation was very serious; Siegel himself took two bullets in the head for unpaid debts.

"He went wild that night," says Chudd. "So I came to Vegas and gave him money. He couldn't leave, because they held him up, either *or else*. You don't kid with those boys. That was the day before they cleaned the Mafia out of there."

Charles Levy was angry at Diamond, who lost his license as a bonded money courier for letting go of the cash. "Levy was very bitter about it," says Billy. "He got so he blamed me for Fats losing his money."

Even as Domino struggled to maintain his faltering stardom, he had found a new demon that would afflict him.

"I lost $180,000 the first two weeks I worked there," recalls Fats, "and at that time I wasn't making but $6,500 a week. But I had record money and I paid it off with that. . . . I was a country boy who didn't know no better."

■ ■ ■

At the end of the year, the jaunty rocker "Won't You Come on Back" became Domino's first single to totally miss the charts since 1954. At the same time, Little Richard secretly recorded three Domino songs with his ex-group the Upsetters. In New York, Alan Freed pleaded guilty to payola. The Tornadoes became the first British group to have a U.S. #1 hit with "Telstar," an instrumental tribute to the first trans-Atlantic communications satellite. Just over a year later British beat groups steeped in American rhythm & blues, like the ones Domino had met in Hamburg, would roll that music back across the ocean like a tidal wave.

"Red Sails in the Sunset"

Chapter 15

(1963–1966)

"We'd always liked him. He's marvelous; we sang a song with him."
—JOHN LENNON, ON MEETING
FATS DOMINO IN NEW ORLEANS IN 1964

"They damn sure did hurt us. The Beatles had everybody on the run. They had taken over the world."

—DAVE BARTHOLOMEW

"Fats Domino Breaks with NAACP Policy" read an Associated Negro Press story out of Philadelphia in mid-January. Fats allegedly said that he had lost thousands of dollars from boycotting segregated shows. Domino's music had once brought the races together, but now his fans were predominantly white. "You can't blame him for playing the all-white audiences," says Billy Diamond, "'cause they were his support, even in New Orleans. We *had* to play the white clubs."

Though his boss was seemingly apolitical, Herbert Hardesty insists that Domino was no Uncle Tom, as on a personal basis he would "tell anybody what he thinks about them." Indeed, Fats had refused to play shows when blacks were kept out, when they were segregated, or when they weren't allowed to dance.

In the grand scheme of things, rhythm & blues or rock 'n' roll was a shout of *freedom.* Civil Rights workers recognized that fact when they rewrote rockers as protest songs. SNCC (Student Nonviolent Coordinating Committee) leader and future NAACP chairman Julian Bond even wrote a poem to roll over Walt Whitman in a new vision of America:

I, too, hear America singing
But from where I stand
I can only hear Little Richard
and Fats Domino
But sometimes,
I hear Ray Charles
Drowning in his own tears
or Bird
Relaxin' at Camarillo
or Horace Silver, Doodling
Then I don't mind standing a little longer

"There's plenty of anecdotal evidence," Bond, who is today chairman of the NAACP, says, "that southern segregated rock 'n' roll shows (and eventually integrated ones) in the '50s exposed white youth to black America for the first time—as did the music over the radio—and if the introduction was to a romantic and stereotyped notion of who black people were, I believe it helped prepare them for the civil rights movement then yet to come."

Blacks could take pride in Domino's success, but he was playing for everybody. "I didn't even worry about segregation," says Fats. "Whoever showed up to hear me, I'd go ahead and play. I never had no problem and the people came."

In order to clarify Domino's stand, *Jet* magazine interviewed him in the office of attorney Ernest "Dutch" Morial, the Creole leader of the local NAACP. Morial, the first black graduate of Louisiana State University Law School, would later become New Orleans' first African American mayor. Domino told the *Jet* reporter that he had always supported the NAACP and the boycott, and he noted his new proud marching anthem, "When I'm Walking (Let Me Walk)." A denial of the ANP story appeared in *The Louisiana Weekly* as Fats headed for Las Vegas.

Domino spent most of his time in Las Vegas cooking, playing piano, watching television, and talking to old friends like Paul Gayten. He quickly became a well-loved Vegas fixture. Still, the smell of prejudice affected his early days there. Clarence Ford ran into Paul Anka, his former traveling companion on the Big Show in 1957. Anka now tried to ignore Ford, who looked the singer in the eye until he blushed. Lee Allen had a similar encounter with Louis Prima's bandleader, Sam Butera, a friend who had jammed with Allen in many saxophone battles in New Orleans. When Butera failed to visit Domino's early shows, Allen went over to raise hell and ensure that he and Prima's band members made the next show.

Domino's musicians did not stay in the hotel, but in the inexpensive Flamingo Capri Motel behind it. Jimmy Davis and Buddy Hagans cooked for them in the kitchenettes. The musicians played all night and slept most of the day. Some of their wives stayed in Vegas and enjoyed shopping and playing the slot machines. The musicians discovered that they could play onstage, but they couldn't mingle with the casino clientele. "Damn sure was segregated," says Dave Bartholomew, who led the band periodically, "but we didn't feel it. We just did what we was told, that was all."

There was disturbing news on March 21, as the body of Domino's friend and songwriter, Jimmy Donley, was found slumped over the steering wheel of an idling car in Gulfport, Mississippi; he'd committed suicide from carbon monoxide poisoning. Next to him was an open Bible, a picture of his estranged wife, and the lyrics of his song "I'm to Blame" with a note: "for my wife Lillie Mae Donley." Songs like "Born to Be a Loser" (later the title of his biography) led even *Jet* to eulogize him as a "tragically prophetic blues belter." Domino's "What a Price" would remain Donley's most lasting legacy.

■ ■ ■

The April 6, 1963, issue of *Billboard* announced that Domino had signed with ABC-Paramount Records. His defection from Imperial had been brewing since the beginning of the year, when Rick Nelson ended his association with Imperial and signed with Decca. To Lew Chudd, Nelson's departure was one of good riddance; in fact, he gave the singer a $400,000 lump sum of royalties as a parting gift to screw up his taxes. He didn't try to re-sign him primarily because Rick's father, Ozzie, had been so difficult. And he still didn't think much of Nelson's talent. "Fats sold three times the records Ricky did during that period," claims Chudd.

Fats had intended to re-sign with Imperial, but he heard rumors that Chudd was selling out after Nelson's departure. Domino asked him if he was going to sell Imperial. Chudd's cryptic reply "Who's gonna buy it?" made Fats uneasy. Then Charles Levy demanded that Chudd pay him $25,000 to persuade Domino to re-sign. When Chudd refused, Levy told Domino not to renew his contract because Chudd was going to sell out *after* he signed. "I wouldn't sign," says Domino, "'cause I didn't want to be with anyone else but

Lew Chudd during that time. But he didn't really tell me he was sellin' it—he didn't say he *was* and he didn't say he *wasn't*."

Soon after Domino signed with ABC, Chudd likewise sent him a vindictive $495,000 lump sum of Imperial royalties. "I don't think he's got the money he made," says Chudd. "You're talkin' about millions that Mr. Levy took a good part of. He used Fats beautifully."

Domino traveled to Nashville where veteran country producers Felton Jarvis (later Elvis Presley's producer) and Bill Justis tried to give him a more commercial pop sound, as ABC had with r&b singers like Ray Charles and Lloyd Price. On April 21, Fats began two weeks of sessions at Philips Studio. On the first day, he recorded the single "There Goes My Heart Again."

Domino stayed in his motel with a rented piano to compose, though it wasn't a scene conducive to creativity—fans hung out at both the motel and at the studio. Sam Clark, ABC's president, flew down from New York to greet him. Brenda Lee, a huge Domino fan, also dropped by the studio.

On May 1, Fats recorded "Red Sails in the Sunset" and the instrumental "Song for Rosemary," both of which he would play for decades in concert. Domino's recording of Chris Kenner's "Land of 1,000 Dances" the next day would, ironically, have the most monetary impact of any of his ABC recordings. Fats acquired half of Kenner's songwriter credit simply by recording it. Two months later, Kenner's version finally hit the *Billboard* charts. The song became one of the most covered rockers of the late '60s, including hits by Cannibal and the Headhunters and Wilson Pickett. It was, however, the famed tribal chant—*"Naaaah nah-nah nah-nah"*—added by Frankie "Cannibal" Garcia (who received no writer's credit) that really sold the song, which would pay Domino hefty royalties.

On May 11, ABC-Paramount advertised "There Goes My Heart Again" with a full-page ad in *Billboard*. Though it and other ABC singles were very popular in Europe, it made only a disappointing #59 on the U.S. pop charts. The sound of the record suggested the problem. Fats was nearly drowned out by his accompaniment, and the change in his environment likewise overwhelmed him; without Bartholomew and his familiar musicians he was immediately adrift.

■ ■ ■

In August, Lew Chudd sold Imperial Records. *Billboard* reported on August 24 that Avnet Electronics, which had acquired Liberty Records two years earlier, bought Imperial and its publishing for more than $2 million. Liberty president Al Bennett would head both companies, and he retained Bartholomew and Eddie Ray.

Despite the departure of his major artists, Lew Chudd had considered his options to the bitter end. But now he saw the many hassles of the record business rising like an insurmountable mountain. "If Fats hadn't left, I would have stayed in business," says Chudd. "There was something that Fats had that I liked, and that kept me goin'. But when Fats left, I said, 'To hell with it!' After all the years that I fought for Fats! He coulda kept goin'."

Chudd tried to ensure that his beloved label would continue as a distinct company. In fact, Imperial soon had hits by two Louisiana r&b artists, Irma Thomas and Johnny Rivers, though they recorded in L.A. Chudd's hopes were dashed, though, when Bob Avnet sold both record companies back to Bennett and then committed suicide. New Orleans' rich musical heritage in the catalog of Imperial, Minit, and Aladdin (which Chudd had acquired) was now owned by a man whom Chudd considered a racist southerner and whose best-selling artists had been—at best—slick pop acts like Bobby Vee, the Ventures, Jan and Dean, and the Chipmunks.

Bartholomew quit when Bennett insisted that he move to Los Angeles, though, at Chudd's suggestion, Dave worked briefly for Gene Norman of GNP-Crescendo Records. Chudd went back to radio, buying into several radio stations.

The sale of Imperial was the end of an era. Not only did it signify the end of the heyday of Los Angeles's postwar independent record companies, it was also a devastating blow to New Orleans' influence on popular music.

To his credit, Lew Chudd was the most prominent record company owner to strongly promote ethnic diversity during the civil rights era—both by recording a world of different musical styles and by hiring black executives. Through the music of Domino, Bartholomew, and Toussaint, Chudd reshaped popular music with the joyful rhythms of New Orleans. He also pioneered country music's crossover to pop with Slim Whitman. With Ricky Nelson he made the finest records by any "teen idol" and fully exploited television to sell rock 'n' roll. Imperial was for a time the leading independent record company in America, with the two best-selling rock 'n' roll stars after Elvis Presley. When Lew Chudd quit the music business, one of the titans had truly left the scene.

Two months later, Domino's "Red Sails in the Sunset" made the top 40. His ABC album, *Here Comes Fats Domino,* also charted. But they were merely shooting stars in the twilight of Domino's incredible run on the hit parade.

In late November, as the bittersweet sound of Dale and Grace's "I'm Leaving It All Up to You" (a swamp pop ballad that Domino would occasionally perform) topped the pop charts, televisions in bars and hotel rooms in Las Vegas transfixed everyone with news of President Kennedy's assassination. With all of the shows canceled, Vegas was strangely dark as the neon lights dimmed in mourning.

Though the small Flamingo Lounge may have been a humbling venue for any other "king" of rock 'n' roll, Domino had always loved being close to his fans. The five or six months he spent yearly in the Nevada casino circuit, including a month each in Reno and Lake Tahoe, gave him a safe haven. With his train of hits finally grinding to a halt, his audiences on the one-nighter circuit were now hit and miss.

Domino was surrounded by temptation. His gambling bug was so bad that he sometimes played the dice tables from one performance to the next. Instead of changing his sweat-soaked clothes in between shows, he went straight from the gambling tables to the stage. Rumors abounded that the Mob had Domino under its thumb; that he had to play the Flamingo just to pay off his gambling debts. But Fats claims that he never borrowed more than $8,000, a week's pay.

Though Fats enjoyed Las Vegas, he was always looking homeward. On his last night, he often performed early so he could catch the first flight home. When asked how he liked Vegas, Domino once replied, "I like it in one way, but the other way I don't. They hook you over there—me just like everybody else, I guess."

Domino still toured heavily, and on a snowy off-night in Washington, D.C., he and a friend, music entrepreneur Bill Boskent, visited Mr. Rand's Rock 'n' Roll Club. Fats heard one of his biggest fans, Big Al Downing, a hefty black man, performing with the all-white Poe-Kats band. Downing, who grew up in Oklahoma, had been inspired to play piano when he heard Domino records on WLAC in Nashville. Fats even joined Big Al at the piano. Downing, who considered the meeting "the thrill of my life," would soon co-write several songs for Domino.

On January 19, 1964, fans shouted for Domino at the Belvedere Club in Houma, Louisiana. Michael Vice, a sixteen-year-old Cajun, was going to see his idol. After receiving Domino 45s for Christmas in 1956, he soon told his mother that he wanted to one day play in Domino's band. On the way to the show, he heard "I Want to Hold Your Hand" by the Beatles, but he wasn't impressed because the song didn't have the essential r&b horn section—Vice was an aspiring saxophone player.

Though Houma was only an hour away from New Orleans, Fats was an hour and a half late. Still, he played a superb show. He signed autographs and then performed another set. But only two of the songs were current ABC recordings. Like that other sensation of 1956, fishtail car fins, Domino was finally "out."

That month Domino recorded more sessions in Nashville, featuring Boots Randolph and some New Orleans musicians: Herbert Hardesty, Roy Montrell, pianist James Booker, and drummer Clarence Brown. On a remake of "The Fat Man," Booker played Domino's signature piano runs, while session musician Charlie McCoy played a real harmonica in place of Domino's original mouth harp solo. Hardesty grabbed a bit of glory when his sax instrumental, "Fats on Fire," became the next album's title track. At the sessions, Domino joked about his gambling losses. A reporter present turned the conversation into a headline: "Famed Rock 'n' Roller Says He Lost 70G's in Las Vegas," noting that though Fats wore jewelry, he was "no longer king of rock 'n' rollers."

In February, Domino was back at the Flamingo. He was getting to know Vegas celebrities like Ella Fitzgerald, Count Basie, and Harry James. The man who he really wanted to meet, though, was Nat "King" Cole. Fats sent gift pots of New Orleans–style red beans and rice to Cole. Finally, a valet took him to meet Cole in his room. After only an hour in his company, Domino felt like he had known Nat for years. He offered him a song, "Lonely Man." Sadly, their friendship would be short-lived, as Cole soon developed lung cancer.

A more enduring bond began when Elvis Presley, taking a vacation in Vegas, stopped by to see Domino, one of his favorite singers. They sat down together for a drink after the show. Elvis was not exactly the king of rock 'n' rollers either after the Beatles played *The Ed Sullivan Show* on February 9, 1964.

■ ■ ■

ABC-Paramount issued *Fats on Fire* with a ludicrous photo of Fats in a fireman's jacket boarding a fire engine. Domino's picture in a "Nashville F D" fireman's hat also appeared in a full-page *Billboard* ad plugging "I Don't Want to Set the World on Fire." The irony of the album's title was compounded by a note on the cover—"Recorded: 1964"—apparently to reduce confusion with Imperial re-packages and perhaps to remind some fans that Domino was still recording at all.

Reflecting his fall from the charts, Domino only co-headlined the Supersonic Show of Stars tour that spring with Jerry Butler, in a tour that also included the Drifters, the Impressions, Barbara Lewis, Gene Chandler, Major Lance, Patti Labelle and the Bluebelles, Gene Chandler, Sam and Dave, Bob and Earl, and Atlanta deejay Gorgeous George as MC. On a later package show, Fats was finally second-billed, though not to another singer. The Jackie "Moms" Mabley Show, headlined by the queen of black comedians, also included Mary Wells, the Impressions, Rufus Thomas, Jackie Wilson, "Little" Stevie Wonder, and "dirty old man" comedian Red Foxx. But Domino still earned a healthy $2,000 a night guarantee, plus fifty percent of the gross ticket admissions.

America exploded with violence that summer of '64. Fats had had a premonition of the carnage the previous June when he canceled a show for a black audience in Lexington, North Carolina, after a race riot in which one man was killed. Three civil rights workers were murdered in Mississippi the week before President Johnson signed the Civil Rights Act on July 2, 1964, outlawing discrimination in employment and accommodations. Race riots broke out that summer in New York, New Jersey, Chicago, and Philadelphia.

Domino also had an omen of his own personal tragedies when he was in Cincinnati early in 1963. The display goods of a casket-makers' convention—coffins of white, of black, of polished metal and polished wood—surrounded him as he walked through the auditorium that he would play that night. After seeing the disturbing scene, Fats went to his hotel piano and wrote an instrumental that he dedicated to his wife—"Song for Rosemary."

On one trip to Las Vegas Harrison Verrett lost control of Domino's band bus down a steep stretch of Route 66 in the snow-topped mountains outside of Flagstaff, Arizona. Verrett brought the bus to a screeching stop against the mountain, but he was so shaken that he would never drive for his beloved brother-in-law again.

Domino's father, Calice, who was still working at the New Orleans Fairgrounds, was trampled by a horse. Gangrene set in and his leg was amputated. The bed-ridden patriarch, who had handed down his love for music to his youngest son, didn't last long, dying on July 13, 1964, at age eighty-two.

On September 8, Fats recorded a strong ABC session in Camden, New Jersey, co-arranging the session with Bartholomew. The songs included Al Downing's "Heartbreak Hill," which in the past would have become a major hit. A week later, Domino met with the four major reasons his new records didn't climb the charts.

■ ■ ■

The Beatles were not just on fire in 1964, they were *nuclear*. On Wednesday, September 16, New Orleans' mayor, Vic Schiro, a bald, mustachioed Italian American, presented them with the keys to the city at a press conference before their show at Tad Gormley Stadium in City Park. The Fabs were in top form. "What do you think about topless bathing suits?" asked the local press. George Harrison dryly replied, "We wear them all the time."

The new kings of rock 'n' roll wanted to meet Domino, whose protégé, Clarence "Frogman" Henry, opened the tour for them. He agreed to arrange a meeting. Henry's manager and former Shaw Artists agent Bob Astor had booked the concert. He called up Fats, and they went to the show together. When Domino's Cadillac got hung up in the traffic, Astor attracted the attention of a policeman, who guided them through the confusion to a small trailer behind the stage where the besieged Beatles had found refuge.

"'ello, Mr. Domino," said Ringo Starr as he opened the door.

In the trailer George Harrison and John Lennon strummed unplugged guitars. They all serenaded Domino with an impromptu version of "I'm in Love Again." Fats joined in.

Domino's sparkling fingers put Ringo's rings to shame. Paul McCartney was particularly impressed by his huge star-shaped watch, which was encrusted with diamonds. Harrison was charmed by his sweet nature, as Domino modestly deflected their compliments.

Afterwards, Astor asked Domino what the Beatles said to him. Fats replied, "They were talkin' so fast I barely understood 'em!"

Domino watched as 13,000 girls screamed. Police tackled scores of them as they desperately dashed across the field to reach their idols. "I want to thank everybody for coming, including the football players!" said McCartney, before launching into Little Richard's "Long Tall Sally." The Beatles had won a fan in Domino; they impressed him both personally and musically. "Everything they wrote I liked," says Fats.

The Beatles and the Rolling Stones both admitted Domino's influence from their early days. Though Domino's idiosyncratic songs, with his unique vocals, piano, and horns, were difficult to cover, several British acts tried, including the Animals, the Searchers, the Dave Clark Five, Wayne Fontana and the Mindbenders, Them (with Van Morrison), and Georgie Fame. Even Eric Clapton's first band, the Roosters, performed Domino songs.

Ironically, the British Invasion suffocated Domino's airplay. Two of his better ABC singles that year, Howard Harlan's "Sally Was a Good Old Girl" and "Heartbreak Hill," actually stopped at #99.

Even as the English groups seemed to have "Anglicized" America, it was, in fact, the other way around. Though the faces were whiter than ever, the "Invasion" was prime evidence that African American music was taking over the world. Many of the British groups even ended their shows with call-and-response rockers like "Shout." Concurrent with the British boom, soul music and uptown r&b styles led by Motown, all influenced by New Orleans r&b, became popular.

White American groups also borrowed black idioms. In the "Northwest Sound," groups like the Wailers, the Kingsmen, and Paul Revere and the Raiders played rhythm & blues (including much New Orleans r&b) in a crude style that would later be labeled frat rock, garage rock, or punk rock. In L.A., the Righteous Brothers and Johnny Rivers led early "blue-eyed soul" music. Similarly high-powered white r&b sounds emerged from Detroit (Mitch Ryder and the Detroit Wheels) and New York (the Young Rascals).

Musicologist Charles Keil noted a trend that would continue into the future.

> It is simply incontestable that year by year, American popular music has come to sound more and more like African popular music. The rhythmic complexity and subtlety, the emphasis on percussive sound qualities, the call-and-response pattern, the characteristic vocal elements (shout, growl, falsetto, and so on), blues chromaticism, blues and gospel chord progressions, Negro vocabulary, African American dance steps—all have become increasingly prominent in American music.

The Twist was replaced by even blacker styles with go-go girls (and guys) dancing, even on network television shows, as Keil wryly observed:

> How long will it be before someone compares [rock 'n' roll television] programs like *Hullabaloo* and *Shindig* to the West African puberty rites they so closely resemble? I suspect that a West African villager viewing *Hullabaloo* for the first time would be delighted to see that Western men and women have at last cast aside the disgusting and lascivious practices of embracing, hugging, shuffling, and grappling in public and have adopted the vigorous, therapeutic pelvic exercise that has always been the pride and joy of his community. Each woman dances for herself

and with the other women. Each man demonstrates his strength, agility, and endurance. The musicians are unflagging in their support, though their rhythms are crude by West African standards, and a good time is had by all.

There was a strange, distorted reflection taking place, as British groups brought r&b back to America. The Animals' "House of the Rising Sun," a bluesy (guitar) triplet ballad about a brothel in New Orleans adapted from Bob Dylan's version of the old folk blues, inspired Dylan to rock. Producer Tom Wilson (who later electrified Simon and Garfunkel's "Sounds of Silence") recounts putting "a Fats Domino early rock 'n' roll thing on top of what Dylan had done [with 'House'], but it never quite worked to our satisfaction." Still, in September 1965 Dylan and the Hawks (later known as the Band) appropriately rehearsed Domino's electrifying "Please Don't Leave Me" in Woodstock, New York, prior to their historic tour of England. Writers have also cited Domino's influence on minor Dylan songs. But Dylan didn't play dances. His followers considered themselves the cognoscenti of rock, as he became the key shamanistic figure leading rock 'n' roll away from its tribal call-and-response roots toward its own class system.

■ ■ ■

In January 1965, Domino hammered out eight songs for his third ABC album, *Getaway with Fats Domino,* at Cosimo's. He would perform "Man, That's All" (a rewrite of Roy Milton's "Information Blues" later known as "Another Mule") for decades. Despite an appearance that month in the first hour-long episode of *Shindig,* Fats soon left ABC-Paramount, which brought him musically back to the turn of the century with his final ABC single, "Let Me Call You Sweetheart"/"Goodnight Sweetheart."

New Orleans was still struggling with integration. American Football League players stayed at the Roosevelt Hotel before an All-Star game that month. Though the hotels were now integrated, the French Quarter was not. Several night clubs turned the African American players away. A racist bar manager even pointed a pistol at Ernie Ladd of the San Diego Chargers. The blacks consequently refused to play in the game, which was moved to Houston. Music promoters and conventioneers likewise canceled stays in New Orleans due to segregation, which was proving an expensive habit for a city that desperately wanted professional sports, music festivals, and conventions.

Still, school integration began taking hold in Louisiana and in the South after President Johnson tied its implementation to federal aid.

Memphis was another city that had long fought integration. Even with all the great blues, r&b, and soul acts who had recorded for the local Sun, Hi, and Stax labels, not one black had ever appeared on the long-running local TV music show *Talent Party*. In fact, originally named *Dance Party* and hosted by deejay Wink Martindale, the show changed its name and format rather than accede to demands that the teenage dancers be integrated. Beginning in 1964, Elvis Presley's close friend and disc jockey, George Klein, hosted *Talent Party*. Klein felt he needed a major star to break the color barrier, so he approached Domino after a show at Ellis Auditorium and mentioned their common friends—producer Felton Jarvis and, of course, Elvis. Finally, he asked Fats if he would appear on his show. "Fats was a little apprehensive," recalls Klein. "Black acts hadn't done much TV in the South."

"Fats," said the disc jockey, giving it his best shot, "you'll be the first black to ever do the show and it would really open the door for other black entertainers."

"I'd be the first, huh?" replied Fats, who took a liking to the smooth-tongued announcer. He smiled and said, "C'mon, let's go!"

Klein picked up some liquor for Fats on the way to the studio. Again in his own unassuming way, Domino paved the way for others. "He did four songs and an interview," remarks Klein, "and in the mid-sixties that just opened the door for integrating the show."

■ ■ ■

With Fats taking several weeks off at a time, Billy Diamond took a job at the 5-4 Ballroom. He and Lee Allen didn't like Charles Levy's insistence that they now pay for their flights to New Orleans. Levy even went to Vegas and effectively took away Diamond's job as road manager. That was the final straw for Billy, who began managing the 5-4, one of the few South Central L.A. businesses untouched by the devastating Watts riots later that year. Allen also quit and went to work in a California aircraft factory.

Domino hired more new musicians than ever. The replacements included saxophonists Nat Perrilliat and Gary Bell, trumpeters Tommy Turrentine and Alvin Alcorn, and guitarist Edgar Blanchard. The most significant new member in the long run was a skinny saxman named Walter Kimble, who had started with Huey Smith and the Clowns in the late 1950s. He was playing on the session for the funk classic "It Ain't My Fault" by drummer Smokey Johnson (who would also later join Domino) when Fats came by Cosimo's and hired him for a trip to Lake Tahoe. Kimble's jolly clowning would help lighten up Domino's shows for over two decades.

In the spring of 1965, Shelby Singleton of Mercury Records flew to New Orleans to talk to Domino and Bartholomew. Mercury signed Domino, along with Jerry Lee Lewis and Chuck Berry. The label's commercialization was not as heavy-handed as ABC's, though it was not as successful, either.

Domino was now flying, though not without trepidation. On one flight to Vegas, Singleton told him he wasn't going to die until his time. "I ain't worried about it being my time," replied Fats. "Suppose I'm sittin' next to a guy and it's *his* time?"

During a four-week stand at the Flamingo, Domino recorded a live album in June. Mercury A&R man Ed Townsend, a former r&b balladeer who would later co-write Marvin Gaye's "Let's Get It On," produced the album. He found Domino's suite in the hotel by inhaling the thick aroma of the chittlins that Fats was cooking.

Townsend produced the first Mercury single in a Vegas studio located near a railroad track. During "I Left My Heart in San Francisco," a train's rumbling ruined a good take. The train might have been preferable, though, to the heavy violins and girl singers added later. The live album *Fats Domino '65* fortunately showed Fats in powerful form in a strong antidote to his many overproduced studio records.

But all was not well in Vegas. Fats was still gambling heavily. With Billy Diamond gone, union dues were neglected. Once, the Flamingo accused the band members of dodging their tab. Mob goons held them hostage until Fats paid the bill.

Things were even worse at home, as Hurricane Betsy flooded New Orleans on September 9, 1965. The Lower Ninth Ward was hit the hardest, with snakes swimming in seven-foot water. The Industrial Canal levee between Florida and Claiborne broke, unleashing a torrential deluge. To this day black Ninth Ward residents still insist that city officials intentionally blew up the levee (as they had with the Mississippi levee in a 1927 flood) to divert flood waters away from white residential and business areas. Domino's extended family from Jourdan Avenue tensely weathered the storm with Rosemary, who had to take care of her children, including her five-month-old final child, Antonio, on the second floor of their home.

Domino left his band in Detroit and flew home. He took a boat to his house, which still had several feet of water in it. A photo later appeared in *Jet* of Fats sitting shirtless at his white baby grand piano as water lapped at his feet. Though he lost cars, musical equipment, and other valuables, Domino was only truly concerned about his family. He took them to stay in a house downtown on Poland Avenue.

Harrison Verrett, who was suffering from lung cancer after decades of smoking, stayed in Domino's home while it was being refurbished. On October 13, he died while his *frère* was in the midst of another Vegas stint.

■ ■ ■

The darkness continued in 1966.

Mercury proposed that Domino record an album about the South and New Orleans. *Southland U.S.A.* was scheduled for release in March 1966, but Domino was intransigent, later stating, "They were rushing me, not giving me a chance." Perhaps to help persuade Fats to record, Mercury printed up a few album covers with a childlike drawing of the United States filled in with a picture of moss-draped Louisiana cypress trees in the enlarged southern half.

Domino didn't record much for the album. Over thirty years later, only a couple of unfinished songs emerged from the Mercury vaults. Fats sang the Domino-Bartholomew composition "I Had the Blues for New Orleans" accompanied by a sympathetic bass, a tambourine, a tremolo guitar, and ghostly background vocals.

In New Orleans, artists were still enjoying soulful hits that updated Domino's legacy. Lee Dorsey's "Working in the Coal Mine" added a funky beat to the basic rhythm-over-drudgery message of "Blue Monday." Aaron Neville's "Tell It Like It Is" was a triplet ballad that sloganized the unveiling of black emotions.

Though Domino still lived in the Ninth Ward, his fame and fortune had separated him to a degree from his family. Only one of his brothers, Lawrence, stayed really close to him. He visited Fats often and sometimes sang his songs when Fats came by the old homestead on Jourdan Avenue.

On Wednesday morning, April 27, Lawrence wandered up to the house of one of the few white families left on Tennessee Avenue. The woman who lived there, the wife and mother of policemen, later claimed that Lawrence, apparently intoxicated, attempted to enter the house, even bashing her door with a piece of concrete. The woman pulled out a gun and shot him. The bullet entered his gut and exited out of his back. Lawrence Domino, a husband and father of three children, died forty-five minutes later at Charity Hospital.

The Dominos thought there was more to the story. There were rumors that Lawrence had had an affair with the woman. "We couldn't find out nothin'," says Fats glumly. "I know he didn't have to break into no house. He didn't need no money."

In August, Domino played a stint at the Village Gate in New York with Art Blakey's Jazz Messengers. The jazz drummer became a friend and admirer of Tenoo during the shows. Fats included songs that reflected his mood: "He's Got the Whole World in His Hands" and "Trouble in Mind."

Domino had been through a rough period. After leaving Imperial, his two-year stints with ABC and Mercury quickly went sour. Since Papoose's death, he had also endured the deaths of his beloved mother-in-law, his father, his brother, Jimmy Donley, and Harrison Verrett. In June 1966, Milt Shaw of Shaw Artists died of a heroin overdose at age thirty-nine. In September, Duke "Poppa Stoppa" Thiele, the disc jockey who was key to Domino's discovery and initial success, finally succumbed to an illness that had kept him bedridden for a decade.

In October, Domino went to the home of Overton "Smiley Lewis" Lemons on Freret Street before a tour. The formerly hefty singer was in bed, withered from stomach cancer. Lewis had recently married his longtime love, Dorothy Ester Lemons, after his first wife finally gave him a divorce.

Smiley's lifelong friend, Dave Bartholomew, had written songs for him ("I Hear You Knocking," "One Night," and "Blue Monday") that in some way reflected his hard life. The songs brought great success to others, but not to Lewis. Bartholomew grieved both for his friend and for his own ailing wife Pearl, who had called him when he was performing with Domino in Las Vegas to reveal that she had leukemia.

Fats was shocked to see the once-powerful singer's pathetic condition. He prayed with him. That night, he kept a promise to call Lewis from Chicago. "When I came back he was gone," says Domino. "When I think of Smiley Lewis, I think of 'Blue Monday.' That's the one I really like, because it tells a story."

■ ■ ■

There were finally some rays of hope at the end of the year.

On December 5, the Los Angeles County Superior Court dismissed the dormant paternity suit against Domino, though Fats continued to avoid the city.

Just as the Beatles quit touring, they graced the cover of an English magazine that bemoaned the fact that Fats had never been to England. The writer pleaded, "Can't some enterprising promoter do something about it?" The Beatles' manager, Brian Epstein, likely noted the article. He celebrated New Year's Eve with George Harrison at Annabel's, a London restaurant, after signing Domino to a contract that day. After a decade of trying, British fans would finally see The Fat Man.

"One for the Highway"

Chapter 16

(1967–1970)

"With the press conference over, he had his picture taken with a beaming Fats Domino, who, Elvis insisted to cynical reporters, had been a tremendous influence on him and should be considered the real king of rock 'n' roll."

—Peter Guralnick in *Careless Love: The Unmaking of Elvis Presley*

An egg flew through a jeering crowd at some Everly-esque harmonizers singing "Be-Bop-A-Lula." It hit a gaunt singer, Robin Gibb. Rockers, the leather-jacketed British '50s fanatics also known as "Teddy Boys," were out in force when Fats Domino played the Saville Theatre in London for a week beginning March 27, 1967. They gave the opening acts a brutal reception. On stage, the Bee Gees, billed as "Australia's Number One Group," made their disastrous British debut a month before their first hit, "New York Mining Disaster 1941," singing 1950s rock 'n' roll and "Puff the Magic Dragon." The rockers likewise booed the attempts at vintage rocking by Gerry and the Pacemakers.

Finally, everyone cheered as the curtain rose in the gloomy auditorium and horns shouted Domino's arrival. Suddenly there was a reverent hush. Domino's diamonds glittered like stars as he recalled a night on Blueberry Hill.

As Fats began his booming barrage, fans danced in the aisles. They were overwhelmed by the exuberant power of his band—Chuck Berry and Little Richard had used British bands when they toured. *Record Mirror* later stated that Domino "made today's Stax-Tamla-Soul stars seem like frantic amateurs." On "Let the Four Winds Blow," Buddy Hagans and Clarence Ford switched saxes. Reviving old routines, Hagans put his sax between his legs, while Herbert

Hardesty lay on his back, blasting away on the floor. Skinny saxman Walter Kimble started his own one-man second line, spinning on one foot and dancing. All during the show, a group of swarthy West Indians hollered out requests for "Be My Guest." Fats obliged by performing the ska progenitor.

Finally, Domino pounded the piano with both arms as the horn section second-lined around the stage to "When the Saints Go Marching In." Returning to a slow blues, Fats bumped the piano across the stage with his famous girth. He had started performing the piano-bumping finale in Las Vegas, but not on stages as wide as the Saville's. A couple of rockers jumped up on the stage and raised Domino's hands up in triumph as he finally made it across and wiped his brow.

"LET'S HEAR IT ONE MORE TIME FOR T-H-E F-A-T M-A-N, FATS DOMINO, FROM NEW ORLEANS, U. S. A.!!"

Enraptured fans scrambled under the falling curtain to shake Domino's hand. "It was all I could do not to leap onto the stage myself and hug him," wrote Virginia Ironside in *The Daily Mail.* Even a blue-nosed jazz and blues purist like Paul Oliver pronounced the show a "breathless, exhilarating experience." Struggling for superlatives, *Record Mirror* added a mind-boggling accolade: "Unless Brian Epstein brings Elvis Presley here he will never score a musical triumph as this again." Domino's greatest tribute, though, occurred when Paul McCartney took time off from recording *Sgt. Pepper* to attend one of the shows.

When David Griffiths of *Record Mirror* asked Domino why it took him so long to make it to England, Fats put the blame on his management (meaning Charles Levy), though his own reticence was just as likely. He added that he no longer feared flying. According to Domino, he *had* to tour to pay for a still extravagant lifestyle: $15,000 a month for home expenses and three or four new cars every year.

Domino hired two new musicians for the trip. Wallace Davenport, a highly respected New Orleans trumpeter, filled in for Bartholomew, who stayed home with his wife, Pearl, who died on April 20. Clarence "Juny Boy" Brown, who had worked with the Hawketts, Willie Tee, and Allen Toussaint, replaced Tenoo Coleman. It was Domino's first tour since 1951 without Tenoo, who had a fear of flying.

Erudite British writers and fans plied Domino's band members with more informed questions than they had ever heard before. The writers especially recognized the superb musicianship of Hardesty, Davenport, Perrilliat, and Ford.

On Domino's last night at the Saville, scores of rockers climbed up on the stage to dance next to him in a grand finale. With no security problems, the scene was like a second-line parade 2,000 miles from home. After a short English tour, Domino headed for Germany, and then back to New York and Las Vegas.

In June, *Sgt. Pepper* and the Monterey International Pop Festival rang in the psychedelic era. However, the Summer of Love was not so sunny. In July, inner-city riots in Detroit and Newark left sixty-nine people dead. Brian Epstein's death in August 1967 not only represented the beginning of the end of the Beatles, it also preempted a proposed return for Domino, who would not travel to Europe again for six years.

Domino and Bartholomew entered Cosimo Matassa's new Jazz City studio at 738 Camp Street in September. Fed up with the major record companies, Domino made recordings using his band plus a few session players for Bartholomew's Broadmoor label. Two decent singles, "Work My Way Up Steady" and "Wait 'Til It Happens to You," appeared just as Broadmoor's distributing company, Cosimo Matassa's Dover Records, was folding. Not surprisingly, they failed to sell.

▋▋▋

In reaction to the excesses of psychedelia and nightmarish news headlines, Bob Dylan, the Band, the Byrds, the Beach Boys, and the Beatles and so on all went back to roots music. Paul McCartney wrote "Lady Madonna," which echoed the piano sound and recitation of weekdays in "Blue Monday." Ironically, another hit emanating from radios in the spring of 1968, Georgie Fame's "The Ballad of Bonnie and Clyde," similarly featured the piano intro and stomp of Domino's workingman's anthem.

Fats had enjoyed a homecoming in the last year at Al Hirt's Bourbon Street club, where he would play regularly for the next two years. Hirt, then part owner of the new professional football team the New Orleans Saints, occasionally played trumpet on Domino's closer, "When the Saints Go Marching In," the team's theme song.

The best news for Domino, though, was his signing with Reprise Records on March 8, shortly after his fortieth birthday. The label's co-owner, Frank Sinatra, had once railed against the "cretinous goons" of rock 'n' roll, but with talk of a 1950s revival, Reprise now tried to revive the recording careers of both Domino and his wilder cohort, Little Richard.

Richard Perry, a curly-haired Brooklynite who would later become a major pop producer, took charge of the sessions. He hired crack session musicians, including drummers Earl Palmer and Hal Blaine, pianist and bassist Larry Knechtel, guitarist Eric Gale, and sax player King Curtis. Longtime Domino fan Randy Newman arranged the horns. The first Reprise single, "One for the Highway," with "Whole Lotta Loving"–type piano by New Orleans pianist James Booker, was released in May to a strong *Billboard* review, but meager sales.

One song that Domino and Perry agreed on was "Lady Madonna." The first time that Fats heard the song he declared, "That song fits me." Richard Perry later told him that the Beatles wrote it for him. Domino was apparently a significant influence on Paul McCartney's piano style, as musicologist Walter Everett notes that "the only precedent for Paul's bass-heavy piano in 'Good Day [Sunshine]' comes from Fats Domino." In fact, McCartney admits, "'Lady Madonna' was me sitting down at the piano trying to write a boogie-woogie thing. It reminded me of Fats Domino for some reason, so I started singing a Fats Domino impression." Perry recorded the basic track for the song in Los Angeles, using session pianist Larry Knechtel. He flew with the tape of the track to New York where Domino was staying. The problem was that Fats didn't *feel* the lyric. One day, Perry walked into Domino's hotel room and found him singing along with the Beatles' "Lady Madonna" in his bathrobe. Fats excitedly told him that he finally saw the light, because he had a daughter named Donna, referring to his youngest girl, Adonica.

On July 31, Fats enjoyed a triumphant return to New York City, drawing 7,000 fans to two shows that also featured B. B. King (prior to his pop breakthrough with "The Thrill Is Gone") at the Schaefer Music Festival. Lillian Roxon called the show "the Brooklyn Paramount all over again in Central Park." *Billboard* labeled it "a resurrection." During a year that included more race riots, the assassinations of Martin Luther King, Jr., and Robert F. Kennedy, Vietnam protests, and riots at the Chicago Democratic Convention, any distraction from the news was welcome.

Domino's "Lady Madonna" made the top 30 in many cities, but, like the album *Fats Is Back,* it stalled at the bottom reaches of the charts nationally—a disappointment to a man had who once dominated the hit lists. For the first time in years, though, Fats received airplay and press coverage. Jann Wenner of *Rolling Stone* gave the album a rave review. Wenner's enthusiasm even spilled over into his ultra-rare interview with Phil Spector, who proclaimed, "I could make giant records with Fats." Years later Fats said that he liked the album, but

Domino lip-synchs "When the Saints Go Marching In" to a group of white schoolgirls on *American Bandstand* on March 6, 1959. Domino was able to fit smoothly into Dick Clark's mostly whitebread world, yet there was always an underlying current of subversion in his music (courtesy of Dick Clark Productions).

This line drawing was a promotional advertisement for Dick Clark's highly rated ABC-TV special, *The Record Years*, on June 28, 1959. The show traced the history of popular music in the 1950s. Rock 'n' roll was on the run at the time—Elvis Presley, Little Richard, Jerry Lee Lewis, Buddy Holly, and (soon) Chuck Berry were missing in action. And Clark's other guests—(left to right surrounding Domino at the piano) Stan Freberg, the McGuire Sisters, Johnny Mathis, Stan Kenton, Fabian, and Les Paul and Mary Ford— were virtually antithetical to rock 'n' roll. That night Fats Domino and his band beat out a scintillating and crucial live message: *"I'm ready, willing, and able to rock 'n' roll all night!"* (author collection).

Domino standing in front of his new mansion in the spring of 1960 in the impoverished Lower Ninth Ward area of New Orleans, where he grew up. The house received a lot of attention, especially after Fats sang his anthem to his hometown, "Walking to New Orleans," that year. But his wife, Rosemary, at first hated the big new house (courtesy of Antoine "Fats" Domino).

A frequent early visitor at Domino's new home was Mississippi songwriter Jimmy Donley, a soulful country singer who wrote Domino's "What a Price" and other songs with a tragic bent before killing himself in 1963. Left to right: Anola Domino, Fats, Adonica Domino (peeking between the men), and Jimmy Donley (courtesy of Michael Ochs Archives).

Domino in Jamaica in February 1961. As Bob Marley admitted, Domino's music was a heavy influence on ska, the forerunner of reggae. Left to right: (unknown), Buddy Hagans, (unknown), Clarence Ford, Herbert Hardesty, Lee Allen, Tenoo Coleman, Papoose Nelson, Byron Lee (whose ska band the Dragonaires opened the show), Domino, Jimmy Davis (photograph by Gil Kong).

Fats signing autographs from the stage after a show in Paris in October 1962 during his first large-scale European tour. Fats and his musicians, who played six nights in a row at the Palais des Sports Olympia, were thrilled to discover that his European fans loved them just as much, if not more, than American fans (courtesy of Antoine "Fats" Domino).

The Fats Domino entourage preparing to board a plane in Hamburg, Germany, to continue their European tour on October 9, 1962 after playing two wild nights at the Star-Club. Left to right: Lee Allen, Jimmy Davis, Billy Diamond, Domino, Bartholomew, Herbert Hardesty, Clarence Ford, Bernard Dunn, Tenoo Coleman, Roy Montrell, and Buddy Hagans (courtesy of Antoine "Fats" Domino).

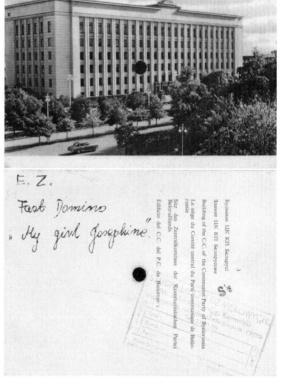

In 1956 Domino had jokingly offered to show the Russians the rock 'n' roll beat. In fact, young Russians heard records smuggled in by sailors and copied them on x-ray vinyl disks called "rib records." Similarly, the music was bootlegged onto plasticized postcards with spindle holes, like this postcard showing the Building of the Central Committee of the Communist Party of Byelorussia, which, when placed on a record player, blasted out real party sounds—crashing drums and Domino shouting out, *"Hello Josephine!"* (author collection).

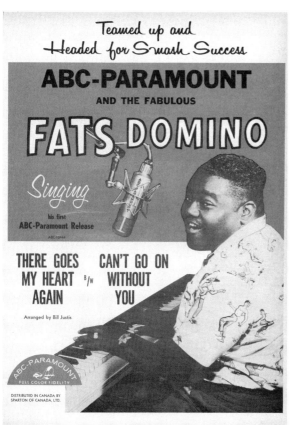

Domino left Imperial for ABC-Paramount in April 1963. There he achieved his last top 40 hit, "Red Sails in the Sunset," in the fall of 1963, stretching his incredible chart run from 1950 to the arrival of the Beatles. Fats is wearing a calypso dance shirt that he had bought in Jamaica two years earlier (author collection).

The Beatles meeting Domino, one of their idols, in New Orleans on September 16, 1964. The Fabs serenaded Fats with their version of "I'm in Love Again" and he joined in. Photograph by Curt Gunther (courtesy of London Features International).

Legendary "lost" Domino album, *Southland U.S.A.* In 1966 Mercury Records printed up covers for this album, hoping that Domino would finish it, but apparently he only recorded a few tracks for it (courtesy of Jos Aussum).

Program book for Domino's first British appearances—his triumphant Saville Theatre shows in London promoted by Brian Epstein in late March and early April 1967. Paul McCartney took a break from recording *Sgt. Pepper* to see the show, which was also the U.K. debut (after living in Australia) for the Bee Gees, who were booed (author collection).

Domino in front of Big Ben in London (courtesy of Antoine "Fats" Domino).

Fats and Nat "King" Cole, circa 1964. Domino became friends with many celebrities in Las Vegas over the nearly two decades he played there; Cole, who died the next year, was a particular favorite (courtesy of Herbert Hardesty).

Around 1968 Antoine Domino III (left) traveled with his father to Las Vegas, where he met stars like Ella Fitzgerald (center) (courtesy of Antoine "Fats" Domino).

Elvis Presley met Domino many times in Las Vegas and always wanted to hear Fats play "Blueberry Hill." Before Presley returned to live performance at the International Hotel on July 31, 1969, he sought advice from Domino about playing in Vegas. After the International concert, Presley presented Domino to journalists as a huge influence on him, as seen here (courtesy of Antoine "Fats" Domino).

Fats in the studio with Richard Perry, 1968. Domino's version of the Beatles' "Lady Madonna" and the album *Fats Is Back*, both produced by Perry, provided a minor comeback in 1968, though no follow-up album appeared (courtesy of Michael Ochs Archives).

The remains of Domino's station wagon after a crash on May 27, 1970 that killed bass player Jimmy Davis and permanently injured sax players Clarence Ford and Buddy Hagans, who would never play shows with Fats again (courtesy of *Natchitoches Times*).

Fats played his first New Orleans Jazz Festival appearance on the *S.S. Admiral* steamboat in an April 24, 1975 show headlined by B. B. King and featuring special guest Allen Toussaint. Left to right: Domino, (unknown), King, and Lee Allen (who had recently returned to Domino's band). Note the fashions of the time (courtesy of Antoine "Fats" Domino).

Paul and Linda McCartney visit Domino and Bartholomew backstage after a show at the Palais des Sports Olympia Theater in Paris in March 1976. Left to right: Roy Montrell, Dave, Paul, Fats, Rip Roberts, Jr. (Domino's valet), and Linda. Montrell would play a major role in Domino's band in the 1970s before his death in 1979 (courtesy of Antoine "Fats" Domino).

Domino pounding his piano, preparing to rock it across the stage in his dramatic nightly finale at the New Victoria Theatre in London in March 1977 (photograph by John Goldman, courtesy of Gina and Peter Goldman).

Domino, Clint Eastwood, and Bartholomew playing for the elk in the shadow of the Grand Teton Mountains near Jackson Hole, Wyoming, 1980. Fats would appear in Eastwood's *Any Which Way You Can* lip-synching "Whiskey Heaven," which became a small country hit (courtesy of Antoine "Fats" Domino).

Domino's great band of the 1980s. Left to right sitting: Jimmy Moliere, Clarence "Juny Boy" Brown, Joseph "Smokey" Johnson, Reggie Houston, Carlton "Frog" McWilliams. Left to right standing: Herbert Hardesty, Walter Kimble, Lee Allen, Erving Charles, Fred Kemp, Dave Bartholomew, and Thomas "Mac" Johnson (courtesy of Herbert Hardesty).

The Imperial Records reunion—Domino and Rick Nelson during their tour together, 1985 (courtesy of Antoine "Fats" Domino).

Fats thanks Vernon "Dr. Daddy-O" Winslow, the father of New Orleans r&b radio, for introducing him at the New Orleans Jazz Festival in April 1987 (photograph by author).

Domino demolishes a piano—and keeps playing—at the July 1987 International Festival du Jazz in Juan les Pins, France. New Orleans Jazz Festival director Quint Davis, who booked the show, is in the background behind Domino (courtesy of Jos Aussum).

The legends of rhythm & blues reunite as friends. Charles Brown, Domino, and Hank Ballard meet at the Hyatt Regency Hotel lounge during the New Orleans Jazz Festival in May 1988 (photograph by author).

Domino in Ultrasonic Studios in New Orleans in 1992 recording his Christmas album (photograph by author).

SEE ROCK 'N' ROLL HISTORY....

Flying Music Presents •• **FIRST TIME EVER TOGETHER IN CONCERT** ••
BORN TO ROCK 'N' ROLL
•**SHEFFIELD ARENA**
Wednesday 17th May
B/O 0114 256 5656
Tickets £19.50 & £24.50
Chuck *Little* *Fats*
BERRY • RICHARD • DOMINO

....IN THE MAKING

The Born to Rock 'n' Roll show at Sheffield, England, on May 17, 1995 was rock 'n' roll history in more than one way—besides uniting the black fathers of rock 'n' roll, it was also the final tour date of Domino's career. Weakened by a bout with pneumonia, Fats was unable to finish the show and unhappy with promoters and touring in general (author collection).

President Bill Clinton and his wife Hillary presenting Domino's oldest child, Antoinette, with the award for the National Medal of the Arts for her father on November 5, 1998 at the White House—Fats didn't feel like getting out of his house that day (photograph by David Lind).

Dave Bartholomew rejoins Domino's horn section for the New Orleans Jazz Festival in their fiftieth-anniversary year together. Left to right: Bartholomew, Herbert Hardesty, Elliot "Stackman" Callier, Michael Vice, Reggie Houston, and Roger Lewis (photograph by Paul Harris).

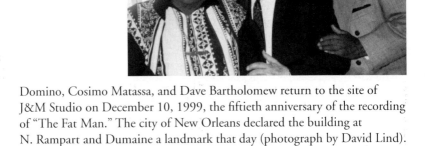

Domino, Cosimo Matassa, and Dave Bartholomew return to the site of J&M Studio on December 10, 1999, the fiftieth anniversary of the recording of "The Fat Man." The city of New Orleans declared the building at N. Rampart and Dumaine a landmark that day (photograph by David Lind).

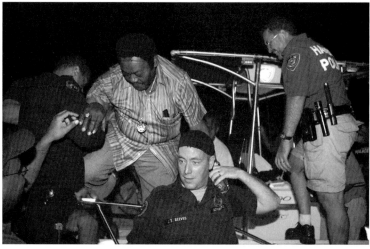

Domino is helped off a New Orleans Harbor Police boat by Officer Earl Brown (left) and NOPD SWAT Officer Trevor Reeves (right) at the St. Claude Avenue Bridge on Monday, August 29, 2005 after Hurricane Katrina had passed through New Orleans that day. Photograph by Alex Brandon (courtesy of *The Times-Picayune*/Newhouse News Service/Landov).

The Domino family's Marais Street home after Hurricane Katrina. Notice the second-story balcony with graffiti reflecting rumors of Domino's loss in the storm and open blinds from the night that the family members stepped from the balcony onto a New Orleans Harbor Police Boat (photograph by author).

Though his homes were destroyed, Domino's piano still stands proudly (photograph by author).

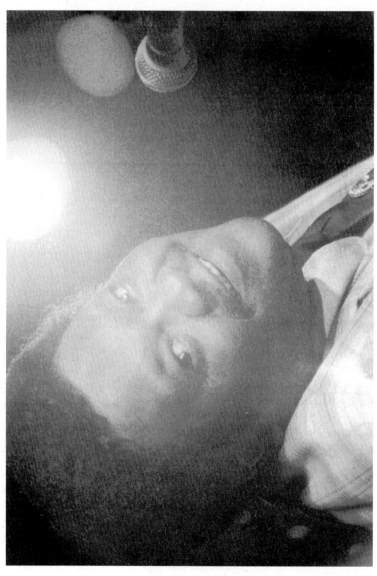

"People don't know what they've done for me," says Antoine "Fats" Domino. "They always tell me, 'Oh, Fats, thanks for so many years of good music.' And I'd be thankin' them before they're thankin' me." (photograph by David Lind).

added pointedly, "I just tried to write songs that stuck close to the rhythm. I don't like too much instrumentation on a record. It covers my voice. I like the words to be clear."

Curiously, the next two Reprise singles were also Beatles covers—"Lovely Rita" (which Fats could relate to his late mother-in-law, Rita Hall) and a rollicking reading of "Everybody's Got Something to Hide Except for Me and My Monkey," which John Lennon proudly called "a great version." All of the hype did little for his record sales. Fats was indeed back, but primarily in live performances.

In November, Richard Nixon defeated Hubert Humphrey for the presidency. The third-party candidate, George Wallace, feeding on racist passions inflamed by burning inner cities, received ten percent of the vote.

■ ■ ■

One night at Al Hirt's Bourbon Street club, Domino called someone up from the audience to join him on the slowly revolving stage. Pat Boone, whom Domino had never met before, sat down beside him on the piano stool. Fats pointed out his largest ring, proclaiming that Boone bought him the ring with his hit of "Ain't That a Shame," which they then sang together.

In February 1969, Domino went into the restaurant business with his namesake "New Orleans Style" Fried Chicken franchise, in a building with a truncated pyramid roof at 3440 South Claiborne. He celebrated the grand opening with his birthday bash including 400 prominent locals in the revolving bar at the top of the International Trade Mart and music by his old friend Charles Brown. Despite Domino's in-person appearance at the opening, free copies of his latest 45, and his face beaming from atop the restaurant, it did about as much business as his records had lately and folded within a year's time.

Two months later, on April 14, Domino, Little Richard, and Jerry Lee Lewis appeared with their pianos seemingly stacked on top of each other in the Monkees' bizarre TV special, *33 1/3 Revolutions Per Monkee*. The appearance confirmed the mainstream emergence of the '50s "rock 'n' roll revival." Fats headlined all-star shows again, though now they were "oldies" shows. One show in Anaheim in June presented a huge array of acts, including the Drifters, the Coasters, and the Shirelles. At the end, Domino and his eight-piece band plowed through their classic repertoire. Peter Johnson wrote in the *L.A. Times* that "Fats Domino salvaged an otherwise dismal" show.

Though few New Orleans acts besides the Meters now scored national hits, the walloping beats of Motown and the piano triplets of the Beatles' "Oh! Darling" and Sly and the Family Stone's "Hot Fun in the Summertime" echoed the city's rhythms. Randy Newman's *12 Songs* album laid bare Domino's influence on his piano shuffles. "Swamp Rock" records by Creedence Clearwater Revival, Tony Joe White, Dr. John, and others likewise revived the funky bayou rhythms, thick patois vocals, and Louisiana mythos that Domino had made famous.

■ ■ ■

Domino's shows at the Flamingo were now a continual party, with fans, friends, and stars stopping to pay their regards. After one show, Fats was relaxing backstage with a drink when his valet Raymond Allen whispered in his ear.

Dressed in black, a godlike Elvis Presley walked in. He shook Domino's hand and soon told him the reason he was there. He was about to return to live performances in Vegas, where he had endured his only major flop in 1956. Presley wanted to talk to Fats because he was—as Domino recalls—"depressed." Fats, the one rock 'n' roll regular in Vegas, reassured Elvis that he would do fine.

The meeting solidified a strong bond between the singers, who were both shy, modest, and reclusive. Fats would play "Blueberry Hill" for Presley whenever they met in Las Vegas. In turn, Elvis introduced Fats from the stage as "an inspiration to me when I started out in the business" when he appeared at Presley's shows. Elvis even sat at the piano to imitate Domino's most famous playing in a medley of "Lawdy Miss Clawdy" and "Blueberry Hill."

On July 31, in between the Moon landing and Woodstock, Presley returned to performing before an invitation-only crowd of stars, including Domino, at the International Hotel in Las Vegas. The audience included celebrities like Cary Grant, Ann-Margret, Paul Anka, Pat Boone, Wayne Newton, Petula Clark, Carol Channing, Burt Bacharach, Henry Mancini, Dick Clark, Sam Phillips, and others, but it was Domino who appeared by Presley's side at a press conference after the show. To reporters, Elvis was the returning king and the gnomish black man next to him was a comparatively quaint figure of nostalgia. But Presley again indicated the significance of rhythm & blues to reporters who would not listen when he told them that he considered Domino the real king of rock 'n' roll.

■ ■ ■

On Friday, January 9, 1970, Domino walked onstage at New York's Fillmore East in a glittering silver jacket with matching shoes. He was headlining a two-night concert with Ike and Tina Turner and Cuban percussionist Mongo Santamaria. Unfortunately, Domino's station wagon with three band members and all the instruments didn't arrive the first night, leaving five musicians to improvise on borrowed instruments over a bad sound system. A *Billboard* writer panned the band's "overlong instrumentals." But *The New York Times* reviewer, aware of the problems, gave Fats the headline and added, "Mr. Domino's songs have become a landmark in this emotional music, and it was good to hear them done, even under less than ideal circumstances."

That year, Newport Jazz Festival director George Wein began producing the New Orleans Jazz Festival and Heritage Fair. Wein, who felt unwelcome earlier because Mayor Schiro objected to his bringing his black wife, sought to break down such racial barriers. He staged concerts at Municipal Auditorium and a fair at the adjacent Beauregard Square featuring a celebration of Louisiana music, culture, and food that recalled its early history as Congo Square. Mardi Gras Indians, whose chants and rhythms reflected the strong preservation of African culture, appeared in costume outside of carnival season for the first time. To the shock of downtown shoppers, they paraded from Canal Street to the Square. But Domino would not appear at the Jazz Festival for years because, as Wein's assistant, Quint Davis, puts it, "We were just a tiny little festival."

Following other band members, Herbert Hardesty moved west and quit the band. He made his home in Las Vegas, where he joined the house band at the Hilton and played with the likes of Wilson Pickett, Little Richard, and B. B. King.

Clarence Ford, Domino's bandleader, was now also his primary saxophone soloist. He, Buddy Hagans, and Jimmy Davis were the only regular band members now left from the 1950s. The portly trio roomed and hung out together.

Domino's current trumpet player, Teddy Riley, also quit as the band headed back to Vegas. Riley left the band because Fats was getting rid of his bus. He didn't want to travel in a station wagon, because he "had too many close calls in cars."

■ ■ ■

The band's latest trip to Las Vegas started on Tuesday, May 26. Charles Levy had replaced Domino's old bus with a brand-new 1970 Ford station wagon, which the band members were supposed to drive slowly for the first 500 miles to break it in. Clarence Ford told the driver, Jimmy Davis, to wake him up when he got tired. Buddy Hagans and temporary guitarist Ramon Estrada fell asleep in the backseat. As instructed, Jimmy drove slowly, but the tedium took its toll. After a couple of hours, he became drowsy. The car began weaving on the highway.

At 2:15 A.M. Wednesday, May 27, 1970, the station wagon crossed the center line for the last time at the Mill Street intersection with Highway 1 near Natchitoches, Louisiana. An oncoming trailer truck driver swerved to avoid a head-on collision. The driver wore a pin testifying to his fifteen years of safe driving.

With a horrifying scream, the car plowed into the side of the trailer. The impact knocked the two front pairs of the truck's tandem wheels into a ditch. The truck driver was uninjured, but an avalanche of steel I-beams and building materials from his trailer flattened the station wagon. There were no skid marks: Jimmy Davis didn't brake.

Later, struggling through a dark nightmare, Clarence Ford heard his own voice whispering, *"I'm gonna die."* Something was against his neck. He couldn't move right or left. He thought of his impending demise and passed out.

Then Ford awoke when he heard Davis saying, "Somebody gotta help us!"

"Who's gonna help us out here in the middle of nowhere?" asked Ford, the words ringing in his ears. He again lost consciousness.

He awoke again to a grinding sound. Somebody was sawing the twisted metal of the crushed station wagon with a hacksaw. Ford heard the ominous words "Not much we can do for him." Highway patrolmen and medics were gazing at Jimmy Davis, who was now still. They cut three musicians out of the crumpled wagon and took them to waiting ambulances. The fourth, Estrada, wriggled out of the backseat and fell asleep in a police car. Clarence's hip and ankle were smashed. Buddy Hagan's pelvis was crushed. Jimmy Davis was dead.

The ambulances sped Ford and Hagans to the nearest major hospital, seventy-five miles away in Shreveport. Estrada went to the Natchitoches Hospital. The hospitals had only recently integrated. The staff at the Schumpert Hospital treated Ford and Hagans royally. A few years earlier, the musicians might have bled to death.

Buddy Hagans had his pelvis broken in nine places. A helicopter flew him to New Orleans. Ford headed home in an ambulance. On the way, the car had three flat tires. Ford had to lie outside on the side of the road while the driver found another spare.

Back in New Orleans, the bedridden Clarence Ford subconsciously knew that his best friend Jimmy Davis was dead, though no one had told him that. Jimmy's death didn't hit him until he saw a photo of Fats kneeling by open coffin of Jimmy Davis on the front page of *The Louisiana Weekly*. He broke down and cried like a baby.

■ ■ ■

Death was ripping America apart. The Charles Manson murders and the Hell's Angels killing at the Rolling Stones' show at Altamont put a deep chill on Woodstock euphoria. There was news that in Vietnam, soldiers had massacred civilians in My Lai. Just as the U.S. invaded Cambodia, Mississippi police shot fourteen blacks at Jackson State, killing two, while National Guard troops shot and killed four student protesters at Kent State. Eighteen-year-olds, who had finally won the right to vote, proved every day in Vietnam that they were old enough to die for their country.

Domino's tragedy occurred a month after the musical death knell signaled by the breakup of the Beatles, who for years remarkably rang the lost chord between egalitarian African American music and self-conscious European-rooted aesthetics. But now rock 'n' roll splintered into opposing camps and a more cynical "maturity." The music, which had achieved an amazing cross-cultural physical and emotional freedom, now was again firmly divided between black and white, between "high brow" and "low brow," as ethnocentrism and egocentrism again triumphed. The music's tribal vibration turned to isolation. Dances became concerts. Rock 'n' roll songs that had ignited instantaneous call-and-response reactions gave way to albums that were the rock equivalents of symphonies and diaries—or self-indulgent jamming and macho posturing that was truly rebellion without a cause. The golden equilibrium of mind, body, and soul that had held together a generation was no more, a musical death that Don McLean would appropriately eulogize the next year with "American Pie." The Beatles' breakup would reflect the fate of rock 'n' roll in microcosm: The whole was greater than the sum of its parts.

Domino had lost the remainder of his 1950s band. Clarence Ford and Jimmy Davis had joined him shortly before Lennon met McCartney in 1957. Buddy Hagans had started with him eleven years before that. "We were supposed to be the slowpokes," says Ford, "but we were the nucleus of the band. Even though you see the pretty outside, under that hood, that's what got it going. And we were like that."

Fats had also lost his best friends in the band. He took comfort in prayer. As Dave Bartholomew says, "From then on it was a different band."

"New Orleans Ain't the Same"

Chapter 17

(1970–1979)

*"People tried to get me for the rock revival shows. Every time they
had one, they wanted me along. They figured I had something to
do with it."*

—Fats Domino

Incredibly, a week after the car wreck that devastated his band, Domino appeared in fine form in the Flamingo Hotel's Driftwood Lounge. Herbert Hardesty, who temporarily rejoined Fats, helped him put together a makeshift band with some Vegas musicians. A *Variety* reviewer, oblivious to the change in the band, reported that "Domino has his rocking rampage without letup."

Fats was still working the second-tier fame of nostalgia, playing an intermittent stream of one-nighters, including appearances for college audiences along with his casino shows. He still wore $200,000 worth of jewelry, drove a Rolls Royce, and had a share in a chain of chicken franchises. He told a *Newsweek* reporter that he had been a millionaire before, and he might be one again, but that it didn't matter. He started each show with "Blueberry Hill" and finished with two fingers in a "V" that signified peace, not victory.

A long-haired youth approached Domino while he was talking to the reporter at the Flamingo's bar. Fats obligingly signed his draft card. A lady asked him why he didn't record anymore. He explained that he was still recording, she just hadn't heard him.

In fact, relations between Domino and his record company Reprise were strained. A month before the wreck on April 16, 1970, Maria Tynes, the co-author of Domino's next overproduced single "New Orleans Ain't the Same," had acted as an agent for him by writing Mo Ostin of Warner Brothers–Reprise to tell him that Fats was "extremely unhappy" with producer Richard Perry. Moreover, she did not appreciate Ostin contacting Atlantic Records' founder Ahmet Ertegun about producing Domino, since Fats had been choosing songs with a producer named Fred Smith, who recorded instrumental tracks in Los Angeles in June 1970. Domino later overdubbed his vocals in Las Vegas— apparently since he still refused to set foot in L.A.—for half a dozen songs including "Raindrops Keep Fallin' on My Head" and the aforementioned latest tribute to Domino's hometown.

Indeed, both Domino and New Orleans were going through changes. With white flight to the suburbs, the central city was now half black. Moon Landrieu, the only state representative to have voted against segregationist bills a decade earlier, had been elected mayor with a heavy black vote. In September 1970 there was a shoot-out between police and Black Panthers who were protesting living conditions in the Desire Housing Project in the area where Domino began his rise to fame at the Hideaway and Club Desire. Now he rarely played at home at all.

Domino's band had likewise changed. He'd added Fred Kemp and Frederick Sheppard on sax and former Huey Smith bandleader Roland Cook on bass. Walter Kimble, Nat Perrilliat, Clarence Brown, and Roy Montrell were now his veterans.

Fats relied more than ever on his new bandleader, Roy Montrell. Born in New Orleans on the day after Domino, Montrell was a longtime session guitarist who had also recorded a great rhumba rocker, "That Mellow Saxophone," for Specialty in 1956. His passion was for modern jazz, but after he flew up to New York City to help out Fats and the band after Walter "Papoose" Nelson's death in 1962, Montrell had signed on full time with Domino. He was Papoose's successor as both a fine musician and a troublemaker, but he also possessed a wicked streak. His nicknames were "Nose" (due to his prominent facial appendage) and "The Devil." The musicians considered him a genius musically and intellectually, but they learned to watch their backs around him. He took malicious joy in tricking people, especially Domino, taking Papoose's old con game—pawning guitars and then extorting money from his boss—to an extreme. And Montrell not only had a heroin habit, he apparently also dealt the drug to other musicians. Still, Domino was impressed by his musicianship, his knowledge, and his persuasive words. "He wouldn't go anywhere without Roy," says Domino drummer Joseph "Smokey" Johnson. "Him and Roy used to get into it, but that was his man."

With his old friends gone, Domino was increasingly isolated within the band. He sometimes sat by himself when he waited in airports, hotel lobbies, or dressing rooms. He offered drinks and food to the younger musicians, seemingly just so they would talk to him or play cards. Domino's longtime sidekicks Bernard Dunn and Raymond Allen were now his only regular companions.

It was perhaps no wonder that Domino grabbed at a ghost from his glory days who appeared in Vegas one night. A graying Lew Chudd sat at a table in the audience with his long-haired and heavyset nineteen-year-old son, Andy. In recent years, Chudd had seen Domino once in New Orleans, but, as Chudd recalls, "We had a couple of drinks too many, and that's where it parted."

Andy Chudd, an aspiring musician, wanted to follow in his father's footsteps by managing Domino. With the '50s revival, he thought he could help Domino make a major comeback. Over drinks at the Flamingo he told Fats that he would settle for a less-than-standard manager's fee of five percent—and ten percent if he made him over $500,000 a year. Domino, who'd regretted not staying with Imperial, considered Lew Chudd's moneymaking acumen when he agreed to the deal.

But no man could truly control Domino—or his musicians, who were now more unruly than ever. Saxophonist Charles Neville, who would later gain fame in the Neville Brothers, briefly joined Domino in a darkly comic episode that revealed the hold of hard drugs then within the band. According to Neville, he had been scoring heroin both in Harlem and in New Orleans and dealing it to some of Domino's musicians. Accordingly, Roy Montrell asked him to join the band on their next trip to Las Vegas. One station wagon now carried the drug users in Domino's band and the other ferried the drinkers. After running out of dope, the druggers pawned their instruments upon arriving in Vegas. As usual, Montrell planned to hit his boss up for drug money.

But Domino, who carried a strongbox full of extravagant jewelry, was now very security conscious—likely realizing his junkie musicians might steal anything to score drugs. His valet Raymond Allen held a handgun at Domino's chained hotel door when Montrell showed up; Allen actually used the pistol the next year in a Miami hotel to wound a burglar he caught stealing pocketfuls of golden baubles with the name "Fats" engraved on them. Sometimes a pistol butt even stuck out beneath Domino's jacket when he bumped his piano at his show finales.

Failing to get his money, Montrell split for Reno. In the meantime, the other musicians, with their instruments in hock, had to make do. Nat Perrilliat borrowed Herb Hardesty's sax and Clarence Brown borrowed the drum set used by the band of the other Flamingo star, Billy Joe Royal. To make extra money for drugs, Neville took a job washing dishes in the hotel kitchen. Neville sometimes filled in on solos for Perrilliat, who was so apparently stoned that he began nodding off. Before Montrell returned with money to get their instruments back, the musicians actually walked off with the Royal drum set and the cymbals of Ed Thigpen (the drummer of another nearby headliner, Ella Fitzgerald) and pawned them for more dope! "We had the band jackets," explains Neville, "and in those days a black person could kinda be invisible if he looked like he belonged. We were some terrible characters, some of the shit we did." Neville ended up making a drug connection in the Flamingo's kitchen with some musicians and stayed after Domino left to live high in Vegas for a time.

As usual, the drug situation soon took a far grimmer turn. Jimi Hendrix and Janis Joplin had made headlines with their drug deaths in the fall of 1970, but Domino had been losing band members to heroin since 1954.

Tenor saxman Nat Perrilliat had played with many of the great New Orleans r&b stars since the mid-1950s. He was a fixture in Allen Toussaint's sessions and the city's finest modern jazz saxophonist, a mainstay of the AFO Combo and the Ellis Marsalis Quartet. But even after joining Domino in 1965, he still drove a taxicab to support his family. He was bitter about his situation and apparently found some solace in drugs. After a show in January 1971 in Lake Tahoe, he collapsed, falling into a six day-coma before his death on January 26, reportedly of a brain hemorrhage, at age thirty-four. Perrilliat's friends blamed drugs, Roy Montrell, and even Domino. New Orleans arranger Harold Battiste, distraught over the death of his talented friend, blamed all three in one interview with British writer John Broven. "He was out there on the road with Fats Domino, which he didn't deserve, a musician of his caliber," railed Battiste. "It was like putting John Coltrane in John Lee Hooker's band! . . . It's just not fair and that's what killed him."

■ ■ ■

Flashing lights shouted the 1950s Rock 'n' Roll Revival all up and down the Vegas strip—FATS DOMINO, LITTLE RICHARD, THE PLATTERS, THE DRIFTERS, and THE COASTERS. Vegas was changing from an organized crime capital to a corporate hotbed of mushrooming mega-hotels and gaudy casinos. The Flamingo, though, was still run by knuckle-breaking goons with names like Rocko and Louie. Under Andy Chudd's guidance, Domino's fee increased to $10,000 a week. Chudd also "babysat" Domino in an effort to cure him of his gambling habit.

Late at night, a parade of stars came by to see Domino. He became friends with Bill Cosby, Liberace, Johnny Cash, and Muhammad Ali. Fats was also on a first-name basis with such jazz legends as Lionel Hampton, Ella Fitzgerald, Duke Ellington, and Count Basie. Elvis Presley still stopped by Domino's shows, though Dave Bartholomew, who still played occasional stints with Domino's band and had written Presley's "One Night," somehow always missed him.

While Domino was more popular than ever in Vegas, his Warner-Reprise Records contract was in jeopardy. In December 1970 the record company had informed him that he had recorded only twenty-four of the ninety-six songs required in the first four years. To fill the void, Reprise purchased the masters of Domino's Broadmoor material for a proposed album called *Fats,* which was subsequently canceled in the United States but released on a very limited basis in Europe in February 1971. Ironically, at the same time, Domino's name was shouted on radios by his fans Van Morrison (in "Domino") and Dave Edmunds (in his version of Dave Bartholomew's "I Hear You Knocking"), while Elton John released his Domino homage, "Honey Roll."

Charles Levy wrote Warner-Reprise on March 15 agreeing that Domino should record with their staff producer Joe Wissert. He insisted, though, that if the resulting record did not produce a top 100 hit, his client should be given his release.

■ ■ ■

Fats boldly a wore matching crimson suit and shoes on April 14, 1971, as TV talk show host Mike Douglas gushed about the sixty-five million records that The Fat Man had sold. When Douglas asked how many children he had, Fats hesitated before coyly replying, "My wife's got eight" to some snickers. Belying his usual aversion to interviews, he kept the crowd rolling with laughter at his sly remarks. He then proceeded to play a rousing rendition of "The Fat Man."

Back in New Orleans that month, the highlight of the Jazz Festival was the rediscovery of Professor Longhair. Though George Wein's first two festivals at Congo Square lost money, his vision would take hold the next year when the festival moved to the Fairgrounds Racetrack, where Domino's family had worked for decades. Louis Armstrong, who had been scheduled for the festival, was gravely ill in a New York hospital. Peter Davis, the first mentor of both Armstrong and Dave Bartholomew, died that month at age ninety-one. After Armstrong's death in July, the city fathers of New Orleans's planned to dedicate a park to him in the nine-block Tremé area—a poor but culturally rich black slum around Beauregard Square, which the city had bulldozed a decade earlier.

Now more than ever, Domino carried the mantle of New Orleans' musical legacy. Fortunately, he was feeling a new energy and losing weight. Under doctor's orders, he and Raymond Allen began exercising when he played Harrah's in Reno. After Fats finished his shows in the early morning hours, they headed out at five A.M. to walk for miles in the mountains. Afterwards, they came back to the Mapes Hotel and had breakfast, showered, and slept until showtime.

Fats powered his way through his hits every night, setting a hard physical pace for his younger band members by playing nonstop and expecting them to keep up. With more modern jazz musicians in the band, "Jambalaya" and "Let the Four Winds Blow" often lasted seven minutes, with multiple solos. He hired Joseph "Smokey" Johnson as a second drummer, since Clarence "Juny Boy" Brown (whose second nickname was "Mule" because of his kicking beat) occasionally wore out under Domino's intense rocking. The musicians had to be ready for anything, including early songs from Domino's vast repertoire that they didn't know. New musicians like Johnson, guitarist David Douglas, and baritone saxophonist Roger Lewis joined the band on stage with no rehearsal. Fats heard every note that they played and would tell them later if they missed one. "Fats can hear a fly piss on cotton," says Johnson.

Domino's musicians *still* faced discrimination. On occasion, a southern hotel manager refused to rent them rooms. The musicians tried to avoid confrontations, but, like his father before him, Andy Chudd wouldn't put up with racists. He told the manager off, saying, "If you don't give us these rooms, we don't play, and the promoter's gonna sue your boss." The manager slapped the keys on the desk.

By August 1971 Mo Ostin of Warner Brothers asked his assistant Don Schmitzerle in a memo, "What's happening with Fats?" The sessions with Joe Wissert had not materialized. Ostin added that "Leiber and Stoller are still interested in cutting him, and I know we were going to contact [Allen] Toussaint." But Domino would no longer record with the company, which by December sent him his official release, allowing him to seek other offers.

That same month, on December 30, Domino's mother Donatile passed away. Lew Chudd, who had offended Dave Bartholomew when he had failed to attend his wife's funeral, flew to New Orleans for the services. Paying his respects at her coffin, he was amazed by how much she had resembled her famous son.

■ ■ ■

In the dark expanse of Madison Square Garden, Fats Domino drove 22,000 baby boomers and their children wild at Richard Nader's eighth Rock 'n' Roll Revival show on February 4, 1972, which included Bo Diddley and Chubby Checker. "That was one of the biggest natural highs of my life," recalls Andy Chudd of the evening. "New York always loved Fats Domino," says Nader, who still ranks Domino as second only to Chuck Berry in crowd response at his shows. Moreover, adds Nader, the other rockers felt a unique affection for Domino: "A lot of the other acts, like Chubby Checker, wanted to meet Fats, to know him." The 1950s revival even made the covers of *Life* and *Newsweek*. The old rockers were cashing in big time. A Nader show inspired Rick Nelson's comeback hit "Garden Party." Similarly, at a London oldies concert, Berry recorded his only pop #1 hit, a dirtier version of Bartholomew's risqué novelty "My Ding-A-Ling."

Accordingly, Motown signed Domino that June. Andy Chudd worked out a contract with attorney Robert Holmes and Motown executive Suzanne de Passe for a proposed old-time rock 'n' roll label. By late summer, though, the deal had fallen through, as Berry Gordy's production of the Diana Ross movie about Billie Holiday, *Lady Sings the Blues,* went over budget, and the label was scrapped. Motown paid Domino $10,000 to terminate the deal.

Late in 1972, Fats grinned when a chambermaid at the Fontainbleau Hotel in New Orleans mistook him for his son. Domino, who was playing the lounge there, had slimmed down to the 200 pounds of his theme song and wore a modest Afro—Andy Chudd had also persuaded him to stop flattening his thinning hair. Fats was so used to Vegas hotels that for these shows he even stayed in a hotel room in New Orleans to get some peace and quiet. When asked about his former band members, he commented cryptically, "A couple of 'em got killed, a couple of 'em died."

In fact, Domino's ex-band members hobbled around New Orleans like disabled veterans of a forgotten war. At the 500 Club, on the cobbled tourist flytrap of Bourbon Street, Clarence "Frogman" Henry employed three of the Fat Man's former musicians—drummer Tenoo Coleman, bassist Lawrence Guyton, and saxman Clarence Ford. Guyton still couldn't close his hand from his injury in the 1956 Fayetteville riot. Like Buddy Hagans, Ford still limped. Frogman was so close to Domino in sound that Ford sometimes imagined that he was still in the old band.

Domino's fine alto saxophonist, Wendell Duconge, who for years waited tables in the Fairmont Hotel, had drowned the sorrows of his failed musical career and personal life in alcohol, a bad habit for a diabetic. After he lost his job in 1969, his life went steeply downhill. Pianist Edward Frank was shocked to see the once handsome sax player reduced to a dirty bum on Derbes Street. On Christmas Eve 1972, Duconge, having developed cirrhosis of the liver, suffered a gastrointestinal hemorrhage and died alone at Charity Hospital at age forty-nine. His death certificate under his real name, "Emmett Fortner," achieved his goal of anonymity with nearly every item stamped "UNKNOWN." Unclaimed, his remains were turned over to the Louisiana State Anatomical Board. The lips that aspired to jazz greatness, the lungs that blew sensuous solos, and the eyes that saw the discrimination, riots, and glory of Domino's early days were now anonymous fodder for medical students.

Two months later, Cornelius "Tenoo" Coleman promised to take L.A. musician Billy Vera to see Frogman Henry. They had just played a show with Bartholomew's band at the Fountainbleau Hotel. The drummer, who had amazed scores of musicians on the road with Domino, impressed one more. As he was talking, Tenoo's eyes rolled and his head fell on the table. Not knowing him well, Vera figured that he had had too much to drink. Bartholomew took Tenoo home to his wife. There, at age forty-four, he collapsed again and died of a stroke on February 20, 1973.

■ ■ ■

Domino primped in his room in the Flamingo Hotel before a show in January 1973. He sprayed his Afro and doused himself with cologne. Raymond Allen helped him put on his jewelry and a pink-sequined coat. Fats played with his dog, read the Bible, and had a drink. Andy Chudd and Allen accompanied him to the stage like two bulky bodyguards. The Vegas routine was captured on film for a movie titled *Let the Good Times Roll* after Shirley and Lee's classic hit. The other oldies artists were filmed in arenas in Detroit or Long Island, New York, but Richard Nader, the movie's coproducer, wanted Domino badly enough to film him separately.

The movie was the last major dealing between Domino and Andy Chudd, who had achieved his goal in raising Domino's income and profile, though he failed to revive his recording career. The young manager never saw eye to eye with Charles Levy, who didn't want the upstart derailing his gravy train, especially when Chudd attempted to audit Domino's income (something that the Internal Revenue Service eventually did). Like his father, Andy Chudd thought that the pianist's trust in Levy was misplaced, but Fats continued to listen to the old lawyer.

As usual, Domino's finances were a shambles. When he got paid in cash (as much as $8,000 a day), Chudd had to chase his percentage. Even though he and the Associated Booking Company had deduction orders with the casinos so they would receive their commissions directly, Domino still owed them money. Like Allen Bloom fifteen years earlier, Chudd sometimes even had to track Fats down when he went missing. When he could no longer afford to run his office on Wilshire Boulevard in Hollywood and pay his secretary, he parted ways with Domino.

In April 1973, English rhythm & blues enthusiast John Broven visited New Orleans for the purpose of writing a book on the city's woefully neglected r&b pioneers. Ironically, Dave Bartholomew, who was also enjoying the oldies revival, and his band opened for Domino at the Fontainbleau. Broven was shocked that he could reserve a table next to the star's piano two hours before showtime, when in England there would be "queues half way across London." With fond memories of the 1967 Saville Theatre shows, Broven was unimpressed with the new band.

In his review of the show, Broven suggested that Herbert Hardesty had quit because the horn section wasn't up to par. In fact, family ties and a contract with the Hilton Hotel kept the great saxophonist in Las Vegas. Besides rockers, he was thrilled to play with the great pop vocalists—Tony Bennett, Ella Fitzgerald, Sarah Vaughan, and even Frank Sinatra when Hardesty toured with Count Basie's band.

■ ■ ■

Soon after Broven's visit, Domino finally returned to Europe. On April 27, 1973, at the start of his first European tour in six years, a bomb threat unnerved Fats. The show was delayed at the Carlton Theatre in Dublin, where the Irish Republican Army had blown up a taxicab the day before and the musicians heard gunfire in the streets, a sound that reminded them of the street violence in New Orleans. After a police squad searched the venue, the concert went on as planned.

The next night, at the Hammersmith Odeon in London, Domino dressed like a wedding cake, with a white jacket, a pink tie and pants, and a frosting of diamonds. The show started with some jazzy jamming by his band. Some who had seen the 1967 English shows were disappointed—other than Roy Montrell and Walter Kimble, they did not recognize the musicians. Tenoo's onetime pupil Walter Lastie filled in on drums. Three jazz saxophonists, Fred Kemp, Maurice Simon, and Roger Lewis, played the solos. "How the hell Fats picked that band, I don't know," says Tom Stagg, an expatriate Englishman living in New Orleans who served as Domino's road manager on the tour. "They reminded me of the AFO [modern jazz] Band." There were further grumblings about Domino's relatively short set.

Still, most fans loved Domino's return. "Fats Domino produced the most satisfactory show I've yet seen from a major Fifties rock idol," wrote Richard Williams in *Melody Maker.* "Unlike Chuck, he wasn't cynical or saddled with a poor backing band; unlike Jerry Lee, he didn't want to sing country ballads; unlike Little Richard, he wasn't carried away by his own divinity." A highlight occurred at the Odeon when Domino saw Professor Longhair, who was then beginning his first tour of Europe, at the wings of the stage. Temporarily stunned, Fats paused his usual nonstop show to nod at his old friend.

Glam rockers Elton John and David Bowie (who in the '50s made "Blueberry Hill" his first-ever record purchase) also paid their respects backstage in London, but Domino didn't know the flamboyant newcomers. "Fats would *accept* you as a friend," says Tom Stagg. "You could not *become* his friend. He was a very shy person. If anybody was too boisterous he would back off. A very sincere, very friendly, very God-fearing person, and absolutely genuine: there is no side to him; he's either miserable or he's happy, but he's always Fats."

In August 1973, *Let the Good Times Roll,* starring Chuck Berry, Little Richard, Fats Domino, Bill Haley, Bo Diddley, and Chubby Checker, premiered in the same month as the classic *American Graffiti.* The movies were a needed bright spot of cheer in the gloom caused by the Watergate hearings and the bombing of Southeast Asia.

However, there was also a 1950s stereotype created for mass consumption in fantasies like *Happy Days* and *Grease.* The mythos ignored the paranoia and racial strife of the '50s—whitewashing the decade as a virtually all-white theme park of endless malt shops, leather-clad greasers, and high school dances. Ironically, *Happy Days* actor Ron Howard frequently quoted the "Blueberry Hill" line *"I found my thrill"* in a sexual context that few now associated with

Domino, even though Fats, similar to Jimi Hendrix making love to his guitar, figuratively humped his piano at every show. The pasteurized '50s rock 'n' roll fantasy land was ruled by a commercialized image of Elvis Presley, who was mythologized as the Creator-King of Rock 'n' Roll.

Amazingly, myopic rock histories reinforced such myths, as if white rockers had dominated early rock 'n' roll. Fortunately, John Broven's classic survey of New Orleans r&b, *Walking to New Orleans (a.k.a. Rhythm & Blues in New Orleans)*, featuring Domino on the cover, appeared in 1974. The burgeoning success of the New Orleans Jazz Festival and artists like Domino, Professor Longhair, Allen Toussaint, the Meters, and Dr. John, also raised the consciousness of the city's music. Soon rock histories—notably *The Rolling Stone Illustrated History of Rock & Roll* (1976)—at least started mentioning New Orleans' vast rock 'n' roll legacy.

In the meantime, Domino had signed with Atlantic Records, which soon discovered his intractable nature. In early 1974, Fats was touring Japan when *Rolling Stone* reported that Atlantic would record him in New Orleans with Allen Toussaint or in Nashville with Jerry Wexler. The sessions never materialized. Instead, the label, whose bosses Ahmet Ertegun and Jerry Wexler had coveted Domino in the 1950s, ironically accepted and released a live album he had recorded at the 1973 Montreux Jazz Festival with his atypically jazzy band.

An *Ebony* feature article on Domino that spring focused on the more than $2 million that he had lost gambling. He sometimes introduced his version of "Stagger Lee" saying, "This is a song about two men who love to gamble—and I make three." Domino's musicians could attest to his gambling. Roger Lewis watched him lose $75,000 shooting craps between shows in Lake Tahoe. Bartholomew saw him drop $100,000 in a night. Out of concern for his family, though, Domino was curbing his habit. "I now walk right by the tables; I don't even see 'em anymore," Fats told *Ebony*. "For me, they don't exist."

The article featured family portraits of Domino and his eight children—again without Rosemary. Two of his sons attempted to follow him into music. Antoine III, who was nicknamed "Brother," performed his dad's hits and more modern sounds for years on Bourbon Street. Anatole would briefly play with the band Windjammer. Domino said that he'd like to build a church in New Orleans bringing together people of different faiths—like himself and Rosemary. He still called her daily when he was on tour.

Continuing the changing of the guard in Domino's band, his brother-in-law Reggie Hall began accompanying him on his tours. Hall took calls from promoters and began negotiations for shows. He demanded contract riders on all of the band's transportation, rooms, and concert requirements. The intense demand for Domino in Europe drove up his asking price everywhere. An old friend, Rip Roberts, Jr., the son of Domino's first booking agent, also began working for him. The burly ex-football player replaced the ailing Raymond Allen, though Bernard Dunn still handled the primary duties of valet and paymaster. Domino finally appeared as part of the New Orleans Jazz Festival in April 1975 on a cruise on the SS *Admiral* steamboat in a concert with B. B. King and Allen Toussaint.

In August, Fats and Elvis were scheduled together at the Hilton Hotel in Las Vegas. However, a paunchy Elvis was acting strangely. He took squirt guns and doused his band on stage. Comedian Bill Cosby replaced the ailing Presley.

The next night, a man handed a note to drummer Smokey Johnson that read "You're fired." As the band started the show with "I'm Walkin'," Fats sensed that something was wrong. He looked around to find Bill Cosby, grinning like a Cheshire cat, at the drums. The comedian waved back. Domino stood up and started a standing ovation for him.

One night in Evansville, Indiana, the inevitable happened. During the finale of Domino's show at the Executive Inn, the band played "The Saints" and "Sentimental Journey" as he slammed his body into a baby grand piano, pushing it across the stage. His manhandling of pianos was the most obvious manifestation of the strength that his musicians knew he possessed.

This night, the piano veered toward the stage's edge. Between clowning and waving a handkerchief, saxman Walter Kimble indicated the distance to the edge to his boss with his hands after each blast from the band. He motioned to Fats to stop.

Domino gave the piano one more push. The front wheel came off the stage and the piano began a slide. People sitting at the front row tables were seemingly unaware of the danger as the piano teetered off the stage. Fats tried to hold onto the keyboard as it suddenly went vertical, like the *Titanic,* taking him down with it. He yelled "Roy!" as he fell on the floor by the wreckage.

Montrell jumped down and helped his boss back onto the bandstand. People stood up and gave him an ovation, as if the spectacle were part of the show. Shaken, Domino retreated to his dressing room. For the next set, Montrell sang the hits.

■ ■ ■

Airborne above an endless blue ocean on a flight to Australia in October 1975, Domino's band broke into "Mardi Gras in New Orleans." Led by Dave Bartholomew on trumpet, they entertained the passengers to lighten up the marathon journey. The tour featured a rearranged band, also including Lee Allen.

There was great respect for Bartholomew within the band, though he sometimes belittled Domino's musicians or waved the blank check that Fats paid him in front of them. Still, he worked the band into shape like a football coach, even rehearsing them while on the road. Though Bartholomew always wanted star recognition, his arguments with Fats were mostly congenial spars over food. "Dave's always been a good bandleader," says Domino. "He strictly took care of business."

Lee Allen again brought his megawatt saxophone solos to the band. Fats called Lee "Long Tall Sally," while Lee affectionately called Fats "Short Fat Fanny" or "Big Chief." Domino—and the crowds—loved Allen's powerful sound.

Domino played venues ranging from giant tents to the Sydney Opera House. While down under, he told an interviewer that he was on a steak, toast, salad, and grapefruit juice diet. He said his favorite current song was the revival of Scott Joplin's ragtime piano classic "The Entertainer." His favorite television shows were *Let's Make a Deal, The Price Is Right, Name That Tune, Cher,* and *Kojak.*

Before the last Australian show in Melbourne on October 12 a local traditional jazz band met them at the airport. Bartholomew, wearing a white leisure suit, started blowing his trumpet. Smokey Johnson borrowed a drum. Walter Kimble led an impromptu parade waving a handkerchief. Fats walked up in a pink suit and just laughed. A local writer, Dr. Pepper, commented: "The Fats Domino Band really showed what music is all about—acoustic music, the music of the streets, the music that does not rely on a million watts but on two hundred years of tradition."

In March 1976, Domino again went to Europe in a tour booked by Patrick Malynne, an English agent. A reissue of "Blueberry Hill" made the British charts. While on tour Fats revealed plans to record, stating that he liked country music, which "tells a true story and it's got soul." The songs that he reportedly recorded included Roy Acuff's "Wabash Cannonball." In turn, many country artists recorded Fats Domino songs, including Hank Williams, Jr., who returned Domino's compliments to his father with a hit of "Ain't That a Shame." Mid-1970s hits by country-based artists like "I Can Help" by Billy Swan and "Wasted Days and Wasted Nights" by Freddy Fender likewise swam in Domino's swamp pop gene pool.

The musicians were shocked to find that they hadn't escaped prejudice in London. Herbert Hardesty (who returned to Domino's band between tours with Tom Waits), Dave Bartholomew, and Lee Allen went shopping at Harrod's department store, which the Irish Republican Army bombed fifteen months earlier. After Hardesty looked at jeweled watches procured from locked cases, the legendary trio was met downstairs by security police with gas masks and guns who interrogated them apparently just because they were black.

The musicians loved touring Europe, though, where they were usually treated like rajahs. In contrast to the rules that Charles Levy had instituted against women on the tour bus in the 1960s, the band members' European girlfriends met them at the airports and rode across the continent with them on the band bus. Domino sometimes rode along so he could play cards for small stakes with the others, though at other times he found himself alone at the back of the bus.

In Paris at the Olympia Theatre, Fats performed an ABC-Paramount single that was popular in Europe, "When I'm Walking." After the show, Paul and Linda McCartney visited with Domino and Bartholomew backstage. When Fats played a television show in the Netherlands, fans danced on the stage. The Dutch fans were perhaps the most fanatical of all of Domino's followers, though he drew strong crowds everywhere. At an ice rink in Guttenberg, Switzerland, he reportedly drew more than Frank Sinatra earlier at the same venue.

Domino and Bartholomew were indeed recording together again. At Cosimo Matassa's Camp Street studio, James Booker again played on the sessions. A photo of Domino, Bartholomew, and Matassa appeared in the playlist of radio station WNNR in June announcing "a new album under the St. Philip Music company label," which would be "released in August." The album never appeared.

■ ■ ■

Besides the lack of new record releases, Domino would soon have to confront several other ongoing problems.

In December 1976, Domino used a newspaper interview to defend himself against a lawsuit filed by a nightclub owner in the New Orleans suburb of Metairie. The previous February, he had ended a stay at the Five Star Theater (a club previously known as "The Crash Landing" built in an old airliner) after playing only three of twenty-four shows, claiming laryngitis. The club owner sued Fats, charging that he and his band members were intoxicated. "I've got too much pride," claimed Fats, "too much respect for audiences to ever let myself get in that position."

The suit and the resulting bad publicity caused Domino's blood pressure, which he monitored himself, to rise. It didn't help that he sang a Schlitz Beer commercial and in print ads he touted "The Domino Theory of Drinking Teacher's Scotch": "The Fat Man's theory is that once you down a Teacher's Scotch, a second one will soon follow in its place. And maybe a third. Sometimes even a Fifth."

On the other hand, Domino's throat problems were well known. He had a rider in his contract that allowed him to turn off the air conditioning in clubs if it gave him a sore throat. Rip Roberts, Jr., made up a concoction of "goose grease" with honey, lemon, and vinegar to soothe Domino's sore larynx.

In Las Vegas, corporate conglomerates that had bought up the hotels started closing the lounges that had been a major source of revenue for Domino for fifteen years. The decline of Domino's stays in Nevada casinos was offset by his burgeoning European and American tours, and his impressive performances at the New Orleans Jazz and Heritage Festival. In the spring of 1977 he played for the first time for a crowd of several thousand at the New Orleans Fairgrounds where he had once worked briefly as a stable boy. More than anything else, the Jazz Fest would help reconnect Domino with his hometown over the next two decades.

The normally quiet Rosemary brought up another problem. After bearing and caring for eight children, she had attended the YWCA business school to help her husband. She audited his finances and finally opened his eyes to Charles Levy, who not only still had power of attorney over Domino, he reportedly even had some of Domino's possessions, including cars, in his own name. "Levy messed us out of a *lot* of stuff," says Fats. "Just before he died [in 1980], I found out what was goin' on. If anything had happened to me, my wife had to go through him. Boy, he was *something else.*"

One man who continued to manipulate Domino was Roy Montrell. Someone in a unique position to know the guitarist was his German girlfriend, Ulrike Sprenger, who began what she calls "the wildest unbelievable love affair" with Montrell in 1973 when she was a teenage reporter for the Dutch magazine *Muziek Express* attempting to get a Domino interview. Though Montrell was reportedly abusive to his girlfriends, Sprenger was special to him. He even flew her to New Orleans to meet his wife! He told Sprenger, "When I'm gone, she's gonna be your best friend."

"He was not even a man," says Ulrike (Sprenger) Mazakowski. "He was beyond anything and everything. He was charismatic and magnetic. He made people love to work for him. He was so brilliant. He always got money out of Fats. He was the Mind, the Brain. Roy always talked for Fats. He called for Roy whenever he needed anything like negotiating a record contract."

For a time, Sprenger was naïve about Montrell's furtive drug habit, though band members joked about his "golden arms." She once had to carry him leaning on her shoulders to a show in The Hague. "He became a different person when he was loaded," she says. "He became The Devil."

When Montrell failed to get money from Domino, he would sometimes play out of key or strike sour notes on stage, but such instances were rare. When on one occasion Fats left his band in New York for a flight home without leaving drug money, Montrell told the diminutive sax player Fred Kemp to jump in a cab to try to catch him. The dubious Kemp complied, only to discover when he arrived at LaGuardia Airport that someone had called in a bomb threat on the plane, which was delayed for a search, allowing Kemp to get cash from Domino.

The younger band members sometimes joked that Fats was "The F.B.I."—Fat, Black, and Ignorant—behind his back, though they depended on his largesse. Drummer Smokey Johnson worked his own scam: He quit Domino six times in order to demand a salary increase each time Fats needed his services.

Once in Vegas Montrell told Johnson that he was going to see "Doughbelly," another band nickname for Domino. They walked into the hotel suite where Fats was lying on his bed. Roy told him in his raspy voice that he needed money for his children. Domino knew better and said so. When Montrell insisted, Fats shot back, "Fuck your children!" At that Montrell dove onto the bed and began wrestling with his boss. They went at each other with years of pent-up resentment over their mutual dependency—rolling, punching, and poking. Domino jerked Montrell's tie in an attempt to choke him, but it was a clip-on tie that came off in his hands. Fats looked at the tie and then back at Roy poised above him. They both broke out laughing. As usual, Montrell got his money.

■ ■ ■

At a Richard Nader oldies show in Madison Square Garden on October 14, 1977, Domino opened with the dramatic piano flourish of "Blueberry Hill," which he dedicated to the recently deceased Elvis Presley. Even in the last year of his life, Presley had pushed aside his pianist to play the song flawlessly after years of personal lessons from Domino. Starting with his ace, Fats, as Smokey Johnson recalls, "tore that whole place up." Chuck Berry had demanded to close the show, but Domino drove the crowd wild, climaxing with a bump-and-grind of his piano to the edge of the stage as Bartholomew led the horns in a parade. "The place was going crazy," declares Nader. "I'm talkin' about 20,000 people!" "Fats Domino was every bit as exciting as he always has been," reported Robert Palmer in *The New York Times,* "and the reason is that his music has always been deeply rooted in his native New Orleans. . . . [Chuck Berry's] performance was an anticlimax after Mr. Domino."

That fall, Domino's friend, Ernest "Dutch" Morial, was elected the first black mayor of New Orleans. Across the country, African American mayors were elected in Detroit, Los Angeles, and Washington, D.C. President Jimmy Carter appointed blacks to more federal positions than ever before. *Roots,* Alex Haley's story of his own African heritage, beat out *Gone with the Wind* for the highest one-night TV audience that year, with more than eighty million viewers. Throughout the '70s, blacks became increasingly visible in shows like *Sanford and Son, The Jeffersons,* and *Good Times.*

Though Domino had once been perhaps the most popular black entertainer in America, now, twenty years later, he was more popular in Europe. Still, the most successful rock act of 1977, Fleetwood Mac, would pay homage to him by recording "Blue Monday." In fact, pianist Christine McVie had started her rock 'n' roll career after her brother bought a Domino music book. Her father had wanted her to become a concert pianist, but, as she says, "unfortunately for him, I discovered Fats Domino."

The next year, the *Saturday Night Fever* disco of Domino's onetime warm-up act, the Bee Gees, ruled the airwaves. The disco beat echoed New Orleans' bass drum with a robotic dancing thump that gave release to the body, but not to the collective soul, as in the parade tradition. Narcissistic dancers looked for splintered reflections in flashing mirror balls. Fats, the past master of the big beat, hated disco: "I'd never play it. The stuff's too loud. Way too loud. I don't even like to hear it."

Nonetheless, the title song of Domino's first new studio album in a decade in 1978 featured a mild thumping beat. *Sleeping on the Job* was released late in the year in Europe with a photo of Fats napping on his piano. Domino produced the album at Allen Toussaint's Sea-Saint Studios with musicians including Lee

Allen, Fred Kemp, Roy Montrell, Smokey Johnson, and bassist Erving Charles. "Sleeping on the Job," written by his old friend Bill Boskent, was "Record of the Week" on BBC Radio One and led to several television appearances in Europe.

The album's highlights included a sweet version of Domino's 1953 favorite "The Girl I Love," a churning workout on Avery Parrish's "After Hours" in a medley with Ivory Joe Hunter's "I Almost Lost My Mind," and "Just Can't Get New Orleans (Off My Mind)." With a funky beat provided by Smokey Johnson, the latter was a reminder that the city's rhythms had always been the best dance music.

Before a European tour in the spring of 1979, an ailing Bernard Dunn sadly gave up his place beside Domino that he had occupied as chauffeur, bodyguard, valet, and road manager since the death of Melvin Cade in 1952. He handed his ragged briefcase to Rip Roberts, Jr., who accepted it with tears in his eyes.

Now Fats had lost both of his most faithful traveling companions, Bernard Dunn and Raymond Allen. Dunn soon entered Veterans' Hospital, where he died of cancer in September. Allen, who suffered from emphysema, would continue to see his former boss and neighbor, who cooked for him regularly into the next century.

Domino drew fanatical European crowds for the fourth year in a row. "The people loved *all* American music," says Fats. "They might be more crazy than in the '50s over there." In an interview with John Broven, English promoter Patrick Malynne claimed credit for the European success, declaring that Domino was "the top-paid American act in 1979."

The tour ended in the Netherlands. After a show in Utrecht, the tour bus traveled to Amsterdam. The band arrived at the Sonesta Hotel on Saturday, May 16. Roy Montrell and others met with a man from the local drug trade. The dealer laid out a line of purple dots, claiming that they could kill an elephant. Montrell took one, crushed it, and snorted it. He grew impatient when he didn't get an immediate rush. He melted another of the rocks, injected it, and went back to his room.

Saxophonist Roger Lewis, who witnessed the scene, later called Montrell's room. A groggy Montrell growled that he was all right. Nearing showtime, Lewis called again but received no answer. He went down to Montrell's room and found his girlfriend, Ulrike Sprenger, with a basket of laundry knocking on the locked door. He offered to help, but she refused.

In the past year Montrell had taken up residence with Sprenger in Hamburg. He was perhaps turning over a new leaf, as the last several months had been both blissful and, according to her, largely drug free. That may have been one reason why the potent Amsterdam drugs finally hit him so hard.

Reggie Hall and Patrick Malynne were the last to leave for Domino's show. When Montrell failed to answer his door, the hotel manager let them into his room. They walked past the distraught Sprenger into a scene eerily like one seventeen years earlier with Walter "Papoose" Nelson, the man whom Montrell had replaced. Roy was lying dead on the floor of the bathroom with a syringe nearby.

Domino's musicians were about to take the stage when they heard the news. David Douglas switched from bass to guitar and the warm-up band's bass player filled in for him. Starting two hours late, Domino numbly played the show.

"We knew he had an overdose," comments Roger Lewis, "'cause we knew what he did. But the thing that tripped me out, when we was driving there, he said, 'If I die, let me die in Amsterdam.' I'm not saying the man foreseen his death, because he should have known not to shoot that much dope. So maybe he committed suicide, 'cause he'd been shootin' drugs a long time, bro."

Seeking solace after Montrell's death, Ulrike Sprenger used his plane ticket to fly to New Orleans. There she attended her first jazz funeral parade—Montrell's. As he had predicted, she became friends with his wife Edna Montrell, living with her for a time before marrying another of the city's jazz guitarists, Steve Mazakowski, and becoming a professional New Orleans pianist herself.

Some memorialized Montrell, like Nat Perrilliat, as a brilliant musician who could play anything. Others said that "The Devil" had finally gotten his due.

Domino had heard the same bad news before. "Papoose and Roy was the two best guitar players I had," says Fats. "And they both died the same way. I was *used* to them. But I just kept on playin'."

Chapter 18

"Whiskey Heaven"

(1979–1987)

"Retire? Are you kidding? No, I hope to play music as long as I live because I love it. Music has been almost 100% of my life. All my problems, any kind of worries I have, go away. . . ."

—FATS DOMINO

In the fall of 1979, Domino heard a hard rock version of "Ain't That a Shame" booming out of the radio. Cheap Trick's hit of the song was logical in a sense, as the quartet was influenced by both punk and glam rock—Joe Jackson performed the song and T. Rex recorded it. Andy Chudd, now a music promoter in Salt Lake City, presented an Imperial gold record of "Ain't That a Shame" to Cheap Trick when they played a concert there. In 1974, John Lennon finally recorded "Ain't That a Shame" in a version that nearly became his follow-up 45 to "Stand by Me." Paul McCartney, who listed Domino's version as one of his ten favorite records, would record it twice. In 1999, National Public Radio would name "Ain't That a Shame" one of the 100 greatest American songs of the century. In 2002, it would enter the Grammy Hall of Fame.

The cover versions were a reminder that hard rocking virtually started with Domino. Other modern rockers, including Jonathan Richman, Alex Chilton, and Richard Hell surprisingly played Domino songs. Likewise, rock critic Richard Meltzer compared the "dumb" minimalism of the Ramones to Domino, who had long foreshadowed their nonstop, virtually nonspeaking, viscerally rhythmic, self-effacing tribal rocking. Nick Cave paid similarly ambivalent tribute in his song "King Ink": *"What a wonderful life, Fats Domino on the radio!"* Secondary influence was soon heard in the ska craze that swept England, including Madness, a group that actually began as a '50s revival band playing Domino songs.

As the new decade began, the third seat of a concert uniting New Orleans pianists Tuts Washington, Allen Toussaint, and Professor Longhair remained empty, as "Fess" sadly died just before the show and the release of his first real album, *Crawfish Fiesta* (including a wildly idiosyncratic version of Domino's "Whole Lotta Loving"). Longhair often saw Fats when he visited his former drummer, Jessie Hill, who lived next door to Domino. They talked about religion and, of course, music. Longhair spoke of his European tours and played the piano for Fats. "He was just startin' to get big, I think, before he passed," says Domino.

Similarly, Roy Brown, who also enjoyed a brief touring comeback, would shout out the good rockin' news one last time in his birthplace at the New Orleans Jazz Festival a year later—less than a month before his heart gave out after a performance at his home in California.

With the rising success of the Jazz Fest, New Orleans was slowly beginning to recognize its musical birthright beyond jazz. In 1980, Louis Armstrong Park was finally dedicated on the site of Congo Square. That year marked the debuts of a radio station (WWOZ) and a magazine (*Wavelength*) devoted to local music. Tipitina's nightclub became a shrine to Longhair. Record companies reissued classic recordings and recorded new albums with neglected r&b greats.

One night in April 1980, music again echoed off the murky waters of the Mississippi River. Fats Domino was playing the *Riverboat President* with the Neville Brothers and Dr. John. There was a delay before Domino started. He refused to go on until the boat re-docked in order to pick up his daughters. Afterwards, the party went on deliriously.

Dave Bartholomew conducted the crowd with his arms as Fats caressed all the different ways to sing *"I want to walk you home."* With one hand waving a hanky and another on his hip, Walter Kimble ended the song with a flirting call: *"I WANNA WALK DAVE BARTHOLOMEW HOME, HONEY!"* The crowd roared.

Kimble, who introduced Fats each night, had now been with him for fifteen years, the longest unbroken period of any band member. Before that he had toured with Huey Smith and the Clowns, Bobby "Blue" Bland, Little Richard, Ray Charles, and B. B. King. Kimble danced with a handkerchief, an umbrella, a yo-yo—and even with a hard hat with a flashing red light on top—in a throwback to his slapstick performances with the Clowns. To him, "moonwalking" was a dance they used to perform called "the slop." Those who didn't appreciate his clowning—like a man in Vegas who once pushed him down—

were oblivious to the New Orleans tradition of revelry from which Domino's music sprang. Kimble also took some of the spotlight pressure off of Fats, who smiled at the skinny saxman bobbing with an umbrella. "People used to come *to see him!"* laughs Domino.

While Domino played, another old friend was confined to a Veterans Hospital bed. Living on his army pension, the portly Buddy Hagans had tended his garden and his chickens while leaning on a cane. He still stayed in the small Flood Street home where he and Antoine Domino had first practiced together thirty-four years earlier. "I used to go see him all the time when he couldn't work," says Fats. "Me and Buddy were the first two. I know we started that." On June 5, 1980, Hagans died at age fifty-seven from a combination of prostrate cancer, diabetes, and kidney failure.

■ ■ ■

Clint Eastwood, who had always been a Domino fan, saw Fats in Las Vegas that year and talked him into appearing in his next movie, *Any Which Way You Can.* On June 30, Domino recorded the song "Whiskey Heaven" for the movie in a Las Vegas session produced by Snuff Garrett. The movie's producers paid three L.A. studio guitarists—Tommy Tedesco (acoustic), Billy Walker (electric), and J. D. Mannis (steel)—stratospheric studio rates to accompany Domino's musicians. They entered the studio at one P.M. and waited two hours for Domino to arrive after flying in from the previous night's concert in St. Louis. "There were no charts or lead sheets to the song we recorded," wrote Tedesco (a veteran of Phil Spector's much more formal wall-of-sound sessions) in his *Guitar Player* column afterwards, "we simply sat and listened to Fats, and learned the tune." After three hours of recording, Garrett played the song over the phone for Eastwood, who was pleased.

Domino soon filmed his part for *Any Which Way You Can* wearing a cowboy hat in the tourist town of Jackson Hole, Wyoming. His musicians were supposed to appear in the film, but Bartholomew insisted that they instead rehearse for a European tour, much to their disappointment. Eastwood hauled a white grand piano into the prairie brush on the plains of the purple Grand Teton Mountains for promotional photos. Fats, still wearing the hat, played "I Want to Walk You Home" while Eastwood and Bartholomew watched. They laughed when they saw that several elk were attracted to the music. Then they went out for some barbecue.

Domino soon flew to Europe, where he started a riot at his first show in Lisbon. On a tour booked by Jazz Festival producers George Wein and Quint Davis, the excited Portuguese fans rushed the stage and threw chairs. "People went *nuts,*" says Davis. "It had the whole dynamic tension, energy, and excitement of when rock 'n' roll was born."

Davis noted before the tour that Domino's tour baggage was unmanageable, including a dozen hanging bags with suits. Two huge metal trunks contained thirty pairs of colored shoes. Davis discovered that the shoes were mounted on a false bottom hiding contraband cooking equipment that Fats sneaked into hotel rooms—notably, a faulty-looking hotplate held together with paper clips. After Davis bought him a new 220-volt hotplate, Fats fed the touring troupe late at night.

The next-to-last show of the tour was at the Montreux Jazz Festival, where Domino appeared with an eclectic lineup including Dizzy Gillespie, Art Blakey, Van Morrison, Santana, Elvis Costello, and the Boomtown Rats.

Returning home, Domino released *Fats Domino 1980,* a poorly repackaged version of *Sleeping on the Job,* on his own "FD" label. It included a new single, "If I Get Rich," which made light of Domino's gambling habit.

One morning while Domino was riding around New Orleans, he saw his album covers in guitarist Earl King's record store window on Dryades Street. He and his driver, singer Curley Moore, picked up some vodka and stopped to offer King an unusually early libation. King, who had seen Fats impress Dew Drop Inn owner Frank Painia with rolls of $1,000 bills in the 1950s, now watched him ostentatiously lay out checks totaling $350,000. The conversation turned to the deaths of New Orleans guitarists, including Roy Montrell. King had hit upon a very sore spot.

"Let's go, Curly," said Domino. "Earl just mentioned three dead people in one sentence." Understandably, Fats didn't want to talk about death. Superstition had also always been strong in the voodoo capital of New Orleans. On one occasion, a woman lit a candle—the usual lighting in voodoo ceremonies—next to Domino's piano in Las Vegas while the band jammed on "Jambalaya." As soon as he saw the candle, Fats left the bandstand.

In November 1980, Ronald Reagan won the presidency. That month, thirty years after Domino had popularized piano triplets, they were heard on the radio in John Lennon's hit "(Just Like) Starting Over," shortly before his senseless murder.

The Clint Eastwood movie *Any Which Way You Can* became a huge hit, debuting in a record 1,560 theaters in December and grossing $70 million. The success of the film contributed to a small hit for Domino, "Whiskey Heaven," his second single in a row to celebrate his vices. Perhaps the best example of Domino's classic triplets and warm vocals since his Imperial days, it made the country charts in late December, peaking at #51. Bartholomew suggests that Domino could have become a country artist, "but he didn't really want to do that."

■ ■ ■

Adoring throngs of schoolchildren greeted Domino with gifts upon his arrival at an Amsterdam airport in April 1981. The city became his European home, the base from where he traveled to his shows all over the continent. Fats often went shopping in the Dutch capital, buying dozens of suits and brightly colored shoes. Best of all, the hotels there didn't mind him cooking.

In other hotels, the management wasn't so happy to have Domino practice his spicy culinary skills. In an upscale Munich suite, he stuffed towels under the doors and opened the windows so that the heavy aroma of his Creole cooking wouldn't awaken the elite guests' nostrils. As Fats cooked a tomato stew in the bathroom, Rip Roberts and Domino's Dutch agent, Jos Aussum, went out for bay leaves. Upon returning, they found a murderous scene, with tomato splattered over the white walls. "Goddamn!" exclaimed Aussum. "Fats, did you kill a pig in here?"

Fats, with his black glasses poised on his nose, looked up from reading his Bible. "Well, just make sure it's clean in the morning!"

Largely due to the attrition within his band, Domino employed several new musicians during the late 1970s and early 1980s who filled in ably, including guitarists Teddy Royal and Jimmy Moliere; baritone saxophonist Reggie Houston; trumpeter Thomas "Mac" Johnson; drummer Herman Ernest; and bass players Carlton "Frog" McWilliams and Erving Charles.

With Herbert Hardesty and Dave Bartholomew in and out of the band, Lee Allen provided stability, acting, as Mac Johnson puts it, as "the workhorse." Allen enjoyed a busy year in 1981, recording his own album and playing on both an LP by the Stray Cats and on the breakout debut by the Blasters, with whom he toured for over a decade. He even filled in briefly on the Rolling Stones' fall U.S. tour, appropriately blasting out the raucous solo in "Brown Sugar," the Stones' paean to New Orleans miscegenation. Allen was so popular in Europe that at one show Domino was shocked to see the first three rows of fans wearing Lee Allen T-shirts.

As suggested by his impassioned solos, Allen was a man who lived life full throttle, with a voracious appetite for music, women, smoking, golfing, and drinking. Allen once drank so much that he passed out on the toilet during intermission at a show in Monte Carlo. On another night the big man leaned conspicuously against an amplifier all night and barely played a note.

Domino's band was now dominated by drinkers. Allen, Walter Kimble, Clarence Brown, and Smokey Johnson grabbed the best bottles of alcohol from Domino's dressing room as soon as they arrived backstage. They began drinking hard liquor early in the morning. When the bars stopped serving alcohol at two A.M. in Dallas, Kimble once walked two miles to get a case of beer all for himself. When his doctor warned him not to drink any more beer, he took up vodka. "Everybody used to be drunk on the fucking gig!" declares trumpeter Thomas "Mac" Johnson.

Their boss hardly set a good example, as he still drank beer, wine, and scotch heavily. During one show in The Hague, Domino imbibed so much that he sang only one song and played instrumentals for the rest of the night. On another occasion in Vienna he refused to get out of bed and nearly missed a plane to England. But Domino also chided Lee Allen for being drunk on the bandstand. According to guitarist Jimmy Moliere, "Lee Allen kinda showed Fats what he looked like."

▪ ▪ ▪

"What do you want me to play?"

"BLUEBERRY HILL!" shouted the crowd.

Domino's white suit and finger rings gleamed, sweat dotted his plump face. Teasing the audience, he honored a lone request for "I'm Gonna Be a Wheel Someday." The *Riverboat President* again plied the dark Mississippi as Domino played a March 1982 fund-raiser for Mayor "Dutch" Morial. Finally, the crowd squealed as they found their thrill in his piano trill. As usual, Domino enraptured the audience. Gary Esolen in the local *Gambit* newspaper wrote, "I think you could make a silent film of his performance and it would be deeply moving." Another riverboat show similarly stunned a British observer a month later. "I was reduced for the first and only time in my life, to tears of disbelief," wrote Paul Harris in a *Now Dig This* review. "In fact, I avoided seeing Fats' show at the Jazz Fest the next day as I was convinced that it could only be an anti-climax after this experience."

There were a series of firsts in 1983—the first American woman in space, England's first female prime minister, the first black Miss America, and the first television-made black music superstar, as Michael Jackson's *Thriller* became the best-selling album in history after he broke through MTV's race barrier. Jackson became the first black artist to simultaneously reign as king over both black and white popular music since Domino had achieved that feat over twenty-five years earlier.

A bad sound system and an invasion of Teddy Boys onto the stage at the Royal Festival Hall in London dampened the beginning of Domino's European tour in July. Though he had none of his legendary '50s musicians with him on the tour, Fats demanded more money during a European recession. With ticket prices up, the crowds were down.

Later that month, Domino flew to Washington, D.C., to record at Bill Boskent's studio with local musicians. The eight songs included a revamped "Ain't That a Shame" without horns.

After a November 1983 show at the Royal Albert Hall in London, Robert Plant, who had sung "Blueberry Hill" on early Led Zeppelin tours, jammed backstage with Fats on an upright piano. In fact, Plant's hit "Tall Cool One" would display a notable similarity to Domino's "I'm in Love Again."

Domino's profile rose considerably in 1985 and 1986. He appeared on *Late Night with David Letterman* and in commercials. Still, he didn't want to simply sing "Blueberry Hill" as a nostalgia act. He turned down most TV offers, including invitations from Johnny Carson, Smokey Robinson, and Dick Clark, who even visited Fats at home to try to persuade him. Domino, who was cooking gumbo, insisted on calling Clark's wife to ask if her husband could stay over and eat. Fats took him to a local bar to meet his friends but then gently turned down Clark's offer. Domino likewise turned down virtually all interview requests, including several attempts to film documentaries about him. He was simply a very private man.

On May 1, 1985, Domino and Cajun fiddler Doug Kershaw recorded a session at Ultrasonic Studios in New Orleans. Fats stomped his piano and Kershaw played fiddle on "My Toot Toot," a novelty written by Lake Charles zydeco musician Rockin' Sidney. For once, Fats jumped on the cover version bandwagon (as did John Fogerty, who even filmed a video with Rockin' Sidney). Domino made his first U.S. video for the song, which included appearances by Louisiana Governor Edwin Edwards as his chauffeur and *Kung Fu* star David Carradine.

"My Toot Toot" was a high-water mark in popularity for zydeco, which rode the Cajun food craze (popularized by both the Jazz Fest and New Orleans' 1984 World's Fair) to spread its fiery mix of r&b and brash accordion riffs worldwide. The Edison of zydeco, accordion wizard Clifton Chenier, had toured with Fats in 1956 and later recorded several of Domino's songs under different titles. Rockin' Dopsie, Rockin' Sidney, Queen Ida, and Buckwheat Zydeco also recorded Domino songs. Stanley "Buckwheat" Dural had idolized Fats since age nine, when he learned "Ain't That a Shame" on piano and sneaked in to see him at a Lafayette club.

In July 1985, the same month that Live Aid brought 70,000 fans to Wembley Stadium, a pumping sousaphone and a spattering snare drum signaled the arrival of a new wave in New Orleans rhythm at London's Royal Festival Hall. The Dirty Dozen Brass Band marched onto the stage behind a British Mardi Gras band, including lady second-liners decked out in top hats and leotards.

Domino took a request for "Please Don't Leave Me." He then pummeled his piano and let out a series of *"woo"*s. He followed with a boogie piano assault that astonished the crowd. Bartholomew led a second line around the hall that included Domino's horn players, the Dirty Dozen, the Mardi Gras Band, and their dancers. The scene overwhelmed everyone, including music writer Chris Woodford, who compared it to "something out of a grand opera" in *Now Dig This*.

The Dirty Dozen Brass Band, cofounded by Domino's baritone sax player Roger Lewis in the late 1970s, had sparked a brass band explosion in New Orleans. The group scorched the ears of the Englishmen with their burning fusion of jazz, r&b, and funk. Despite his busy schedule, Lewis always made a point of playing with Domino whenever he could. "Playing with Fats Domino is exciting, bro," explains Lewis, "because the songs are never played the same way."

Others agreed. "Every gig for me is like pulling out a new canvas," says saxophonist Reggie Houston, who filled in when Lewis was playing with the Dirty Dozen. "Domino's music is the hippest shit in the world. It's the big beat. It's New Orleans. It's the world. In a word, like Duke [Ellington] would say, it's good music. I've seen ninety-year-old grandmothers and teenagers dress out in Fifties costumes and sing the songs. When you leave his performance he's gonna give you something you can take with you. You can't fault anybody who gives like that. This is Art."

"You hear in that [Domino] horn section everything from New Orleans street jazz, through blues, r&b, and modern jazz," adds Quint Davis, who booked many of the world's greatest musical artists. "And there are no other musicians in the world that can do that. None."

In the tiny mountainous country of Andorra between France and Spain, Domino played a jazz festival on a high stage. Unfortunately, the stage was not properly secured. Walter Kimble twice told trumpeter Mac Johnson that he felt the stage move, but Johnson scoffed at the frequently inebriated saxophonist. During the pounding refrain of "When the Saints Go Marching In," Smokey Johnson suddenly jumped off of his drums, which collapsed into a widening black hole in the stage. Kimble fell through it, hurting his arm. Finally, Domino's piano tipped over into the chasm. The musicians scrambled to get off the stage, which collapsed into the adjoining dressing rooms.

But the band's harrowing trip through the Pyrenees was not yet over. The musicians arrived at the drawbridge of the medieval walled city of Carcassonne, France, at two A.M. The tour bus was too big to get into the gate, so Fats and the band walked across the bridge with their baggage. The New Orleans musicians stared up at dark gargoyles on an ancient cathedral. Inside the castle, they walked past heraldic crests and paintings of demons to their rooms. Some slept in dungeon cells converted into bedrooms. When Walter Kimble played an Aretha Franklin tape, a bat flew in his window. Everyone kept their doors open and many ended up spending the night together in the hall.

Finally, the band arrived on the glorious beaches of the French Riviera. In the Nice Hyatt Regency Domino brewed a cauldron of cayenne boil and threw in camel-sized hogs' feet. "Fats Domino makes the best pigs' feet you ever wanna eat!" declares Smokey Johnson, who once passed out after eating a pot full of them. "Walk in the front door and you can hear those pig feet back in the pot stampeding!" The smell of parboiled pork permeated the hotel floor and wafted out the balcony toward the beach. A knock was heard at the towel-stuffed door. Two black ladies from St. Louis asked, "Excuse me. Are y'all cookin' pigs' feet?"

■ ■ ■

Domino soon launched a U.S. tour with Rick Nelson, climaxed by a show at the Universal Amphitheater in Los Angeles on August 22, 1985. Nelson's Imperial Records arranger, Jimmie Haskell, recorded the show for album release. He called Lew Chudd's son Reeve to invite the elder Chudd to an Imperial Records reunion, including Domino, Nelson, Haskell, and Dave Bartholomew. Chudd's reply was simple and cold: "When I left the record business, I left the record business. Period." Still, such Domino aficionados as Randy Newman and John Fogerty were there for Domino's first real appearance in L.A. in over two decades.

Following Nelson's set, Domino rocked for over an hour below a painting of a giant blueberry basket in a brilliant performance that would appear in several videos. He capped the night with a barrelhouse version of "I'm Walkin'," as he and Nelson sang a duet on their shared hit. Fats stomped his foot and Herbert Hardesty blew two house-rocking solos. Next to the rhythm master and his rollicking rockers, Nelson looked stiff, but it was a poignant moment in light of events to come.

Some of Domino's musicians flew in Nelson's aging DC-3 airplane previously used by Jerry Lee Lewis. "They put about fifteen gallons of oil on that plane," says Herbert Hardesty, for whom the experience was a flashback to his Black Army Air Corps days. Later that year, on New Year's Eve, the plane crashed just out of Texarkana, killing Rick Nelson and six others in a tragic end for a dedicated rocker.

■ ■ ■

On January 23, 1986, three days after the first national Martin Luther King, Jr. holiday and five days before the Space Shuttle Challenger exploded like a nightmarish cumulonimbus in the Florida sky, Elvis Presley, Chuck Berry, Little Richard, Jerry Lee Lewis, Sam Cooke, James Brown, the Everly Brothers, Buddy Holly, Ray Charles, and Fats Domino became the original ten members of the Rock and Roll Hall of Fame, in a ceremony in the Waldorf-Astoria Hotel in New York City. Billy Joel introduced Domino, thanking him for making the piano a rock 'n' roll instrument. Domino, looking splendid in an all-white suit, later remarked, "I just wish that Elvis, Buddy Holly, and Sam Cooke were here."

The ceremony was the beginning of an impressive year for Domino, culminating in a series of television concerts. That spring his European tour even included a week defrosting Iceland.

On June 4 and 5, Domino performed with Jerry Lee Lewis and Ray Charles at Storyville in New Orleans. The concert was videotaped for a Cinemax special titled *Fats Domino and Friends*. The three pianists ended the show with "Jambalaya." "Mr. Domino plays twinkling, right-hand filigrees like a card sharp riffling the deck," wrote Jon Pareles in *The New York Times*. "No matter what your imagination is," chimed in *People* magazine, "these guys sound even better."

■ ■ ■

"What you say, Killer?" Fats said with a smile as Jerry Lee Lewis strutted like a rooster into Domino's hotel room with a whiskey bottle while on a month-long tour together after the Cinemax show. Fats got a kick out of touring with Lewis, who would play music, including classical pieces, on Domino's hotel piano while they were hanging out together. A heavy drinker himself, Lewis (and occasionally his television) would soon be smashed. Though he and Domino were old friends, America's perceptions of them had altered dramatically over the decades. Lewis's rebellious redneck image paid off in several biographies, one of which became the basis for a movie. His hell-raising attitude translated well to mythic retelling, but Domino's awesome performances still captured audiences unlike anyone else's.

Ironically reviving the exaggerated feuds of the 1950s, Lewis demanded one night to close the show instead of Domino, who still always delivered the concert finale. Surprisingly, Fats readily agreed. After Domino's powerful set exhilarated and exhausted the fans, Lewis was dismayed to watch much of the audience leaving as he took the stage. Still, fans and critics alike were thrilled by the historic double bills. "If Friday night's Fats Domino/Jerry Lee Lewis concert at the Long Beach Theater wasn't the musical event of the decade," wrote Todd Everett in the *Los Angeles Herald-Examiner*, "it's only because that honor remains with last year's Domino/Rick Nelson show at the Universal Amphitheater."

Fats continued a relative flurry of television performances. In August 1986, he filmed a show for the Canadian Broadcasting Company at the World's Fair in Vancouver. In November, he appeared on *Austin City Limits*.

A circle was closed in April 1987 when Domino played the New Orleans Jazz Festival. Vernon "Dr. Daddy-O" Winslow, who had started r&b radio in New Orleans before going into gospel, had recently returned to r&b on a program titled *Wavelength* on WYLD-AM, though he still hosted a gospel radio show and performances at the Jazz Fest Gospel Tent. As the producer of *Wavelength,* I received permission from Domino and Quint Davis for Winslow—instead of Davis—to introduce Domino. I led the elderly legend from the Gospel Tent to Domino's stage. Before a crowd of thousands, Bartholomew introduced

Winslow as "the man who gave us our break." Then Winslow introduced Domino, as he had nearly forty years earlier.

At the International Festival du Jazz in Juan Les Pins, France, that summer, Fats bumped his piano across the stage until the front wheel got stuck in a rut. He popped the piano one more whack, breaking off the front leg. The piano's front end crashed down in a demolition reminiscent of more flamboyant rockers. Fats walked off to screams, and then he returned to play an encore on the shattered keyboard. The fans went wild with delight.

Domino had enjoyed a renaissance with one of the greatest touring shows on earth, featuring a legendary horn section led by Dave Bartholomew, Lee Allen, and Herbert Hardesty. But there were underlying tensions with Bartholomew, who, as always, wanted more recognition. Though he was by far the best-paid band member, Dave wanted billing on the marquees. Domino, who frequently deflected glory or even mocked himself, also neglected the egos of others. Though he often recognized Bartholomew during his performances, he never announced any of his other musicians. As Herbert Hardesty notes, his boss was "just not that type of person." Once in Italy, Fats told Dave in no uncertain terms that the band was his—not Bartholomew's. Quint Davis thought the situation became like "too many cooks in the kitchen and too many chiefs in the tribe."

One day in New Orleans, Domino, Reggie Hall, and Rip Roberts, Jr., sat on a jet preparing to fly to Vegas for a one-nighter at Caesar's Palace. Bartholomew walked in and found his seat across from them in first class.

"What you doin' up here?" Fats asked, ribbing Dave in a weak joke.

Bartholomew was not in a joking mood. He snapped back angrily. When the plane landed, instead of going to the show, he caught a flight to visit relatives in Richmond, California.

On Wednesday, December 9, 1987, opera diva Beverly Sills read from a script she obviously didn't write: "Many of us grew up listening to Huey 'Piano' Smith, Professor Longhair and Ernie K-Doe. . . ." The occasion was the television broadcast of the *Grammy Lifetime Achievement Awards,* which paid tribute to classical violinist Issac Stern, jazz saxophonist Benny Carter, Grand Ole Opry great Roy Acuff, and r&b legends Ray Charles, B. B. King, and Fats Domino. Ray Charles and B. B. King had won several Grammys, but Domino had never even been *nominated.*

Newsman and New Orleans music fan Ed Bradley added, "His music is a reflection of the jazz rhythms he grew up with, coupled with that special warmth and easy-going charm of New Orleans. Even so, it's hard to sit still during a Fats Domino song because of that infectious beat."

A curtain rose. In a splendorous white tuxedo, Fats pummeled a grand piano. Next to him, Dave Bartholomew spit out crooked cornet blasts, as Fats sang "I'm Walkin'." There was not much harmony between the two men, but the musical moment was nonetheless magic. The music tycoons in the audience rose from their seats like hot-air balloons.

"Love You 'til the Day I Die"

Chapter 19

(1988 to 2006)

*"His [Domino's] rich voice and distinctive piano style helped to
define rock 'n' roll, the music that more than any other creative force
in America has brought the races together."*
— PRESIDENT BILL CLINTON, NOVEMBER 5, 1998

A parade strutted through the streets of New Orleans. A jazz band played "The Saints," as second-liners danced with umbrellas and handkerchiefs. As always in the second line, the celebration was bittersweet. It was a jazz funeral for Domino's court jester and superb saxophonist Walter Kimble, who did as much as anyone to popularize the city's parade tradition while touring with Fats. Kimble didn't even think he was that sick. With his irrepressible spirit, he had tried to walk out of the hospital. The nurses took away his clothes. A cold quickly developed into pneumonia. He died on February 28, 1988, at age forty-nine.

Domino couldn't face the funeral of a man who had been bringing joy to his shows for over twenty years. Thankfully, at the same time he celebrated his sixtieth birthday at a University of New Orleans Lakefront Auditorium concert. Allen Toussaint presented him with a giant marzipan piano cake as the crowd sang "Happy Birthday."

Two new band members joined Domino at the show. Fine tenor saxophonist Elliott "Stackman" Callier in effect replaced Kimble. Michael Vice, a Cajun whose love for Domino's music had led him to become a musician (and who, as noted earlier, had first seen Fats in his hometown of Houma, Louisiana, in early 1964), amazingly achieved his over-thirty-year dream of joining his idol's band, filling in on baritone. He became the only white musician to play with Domino for any length of time.

Later in the year, Fats played some high-profile nightclub shows. In August, he appeared in New York City for a week at the Ritz. Jon Pareles wrote in *The New York Times* that "Mr. Domino's songs rolled and swaggered, chuckled and sighed . . . like the sounds of a long-running house party." *Variety* added that Domino appeared "ageless and surprisingly svelte." In October, during a five-week European tour, he stayed for two weeks at the Club Lionel Hampton in Paris.

At the Palaeur Arena in Rome, Fats showed up two hours before showtime on November 17 for a concert with Little Richard, Jerry Lee Lewis, Bo Diddley, James Brown, B. B. King, and Ray Charles. *The Legends of Rock 'n' Roll* concert was broadcast live to hundreds of millions. After a month of touring in freezing weather, Domino was hoarse for the outdoor concert, though he ripped the keyboard fiercely with his festooned fingers on "I'm Ready." Musical director Dave Edmunds tackled the last-minute dilemma of coordinating a ragged grand finale with the legends.

Afterwards, Fats couldn't sleep at his hotel. He and Rip Roberts went down to the airport and sat in the restaurant all night. At the same time, Dave Edmunds and his crew repeatedly watched the videotape of Charles and Domino. Edmunds judged that Fats was the "only one of the 'pioneers' of rock and roll with the uncanny ability to sound exactly the same onstage as on record."

That month, George Herbert Walker Bush defeated Michael Dukakis in a presidential campaign that featured the infamous racial stereotype of the Willie Horton political ad, conceived by Bush's political strategist (and blues guitarist) Lee Atwater. New Orleans–area candidate David Duke, a former Grand Dragon of the KKK, received 150,000 votes for president nationwide and soon became a Louisiana state legislator.

The following spring, the New Orleans Jazz Festival honored Domino with a poster by Richard Thomas immortalizing his 1950s flattop likeness as pop art iconography (just as performers like Grace Jones, Arsenio Hall, and Vanilla Ice were reviving similar coiffures). Wearing a pin-striped suit and a sea captain's hat, Domino appeared at the poster's unveiling ceremony. He said that he only played the Jazz Fest every other year so he would not "wear out his welcome" with hometown fans.

In contrast, European fans never took Domino for granted. Paul McCartney that year paid homage by recording three Domino songs, plus "Lawdy Miss Clawdy," for his *CHOBA B CCCP* ("Back in the U.S.S.R.") album of oldies, which was released at first only in the Soviet Union, indirectly fulfilling Domino's offer to show the Russians the rock 'n' roll beat.

The Cold War was ending, as symbolized by the demolition of the Berlin Wall in November. Rock 'n' roll had long represented freedom to young people in communist countries. Euphoric Germans sang Beatles songs on the Wall's rubble. Keith Richards suggested that "blue jeans and rock 'n' roll" had brought it down.

■ ■ ■

A marquee at the Desert Inn in Las Vegas heralded the pairing of Domino and his namesake Chubby Checker in February 1990. Driving down the Vegas strip, Bruce Springsteen, who had closed his shows with "Let the Four Winds Blow" early in his career, saw the sign and pulled over. Not long after *Born to Run,* the modest Springsteen had met Fats in a Hamburg bar and asked for an autograph. Now he and his girlfriend Patti walked in and sat in a booth next to Domino's old friend Dennis "Big Chief" Alley. Backstage afterwards, someone announced, "The Boss is here!" Seemingly unaware of the modern icon, Fats asked, "Whose boss?" as Springsteen walked in.

In May, Fats canceled another show with Checker in Reno due to high blood pressure. He took the disease seriously. Other musicians, including Tenoo, had suffered strokes. His former warm-up singer, John "Sonny" Jones, had recently died of a heart attack. Domino was cleared, though, for a four-week European tour a month later. Upon returning home, suffering from exhaustion, he checked into a Chalmette hospital near his home for two weeks.

That spring, Representative Peppi Bruneau read the lyrics of Domino's suicide shuffle "Going to the River" before the Louisiana Legislature. Censorship was a hot issue in 1990 with the rise of rap and hardcore rock. Bruneau was ridiculing a bill that proposed outlawing records about homicide, suicide, crimes, and deviance. He suggested such classics would be censored by the bill. Nearly everyone laughed.

In early 1991, Art and Charles Neville of the Neville Brothers inducted Dave Bartholomew into the Rock and Roll Hall of Fame. Dave occasionally played shows with his band, but more often he sat in with the Preservation Hall Jazz Band in his father's Dixieland tradition. Sadly, he and Fats rarely spoke.

In a bit of irony considering his former gambling addiction, Domino played an extravaganza in the Superdome on September 5 to promote the launching of the Louisiana State Lottery. The other acts were Gladys Knight, Huey Lewis and the News, and Vanna White, hostess of one of Domino's favorite shows, *Wheel of Fortune.*

Seven weeks later, New Orleans' second African American mayor, Sidney Bartholomey, declared the second "Fats Domino Day" in the city on October 24 when Domino's first EMI box set was released. Fats made a rare promotional appearance at New Orleans' Tower Records, staying for hours to sign autographs and talk to fans. At the end of the month, he continued promoting the box in New York City at the Bottom Line. "Forty two years after his first record," wrote Peter Watrous in *The New York Times,* "[Domino] is still making music as fresh and vital as ever."

Soon after returning home, Fats began work on a Christmas album at Ultrasonic Studios. He had reason to be reflective. His last remaining brother, Joseph "Tenig" Domino, who had introduced young Antoine to both Rosemary and Billy Diamond, had died after heart surgery on October 27 at age sixty-six. Accordingly, some of the songs revealed Domino's growing spiritual side, as he contemplated his own mortality.

Fats also paid tribute to his friends. Sitting at an electric piano with headphones on, he sang "Blue Christmas" in warm, Creole tones, adding a two-beat parade rhythm to Elvis Presley's hit. Afterwards, he sat at the mixing board and played cards. Domino also recorded another friend's classic that had borrowed his triplet piano sound—Charles Brown's "Please Come Home for Christmas."

In March 1992, EMI announced that it was raising its royalty rate on reissues to ten percent of sales, meaning that the money that Domino and others received from CDs would be greatly increased. Unlike many of their contemporary rhythm & blues artists, Domino and Bartholomew had always collected royalty checks from their songs. That income had increased in recent years from the use of Domino's hits in movies, TV shows, and commercials. Now, with extremely handsome royalty checks coming in, Domino had less incentive to tour.

Saxophonist Michael Vice went to see Domino when he played a Mardi Gras ball at the New Orleans Convention Center. Vice, who hadn't played with the band in a while, hoped to sit in. He walked into the dressing room, where Fats asked him if he had brought his sax. He told Vice that he didn't want Lee Allen, who had been drinking heavily, to go on stage. For Vice, who had joined the band through the help of Allen, it was a heavy blow. Lee Allen would not play with Domino again. While touring the next year with the Blasters, he suffered a seizure. He was diagnosed with the ultimate irony for the mighty sax man—lung cancer.

■ ■ ■

A circle was finally closed on January 28, 1993, when Congo Square officially became a landmark under that name a century after it was renamed for a Confederate general. In a sense, the Jazz Festival, which had started there, re-created the Square's tradition of music, dancing, trading, and feasting.

A month later, at the Endymion Mardi Gras Ball in the Superdome, Domino "warmed up" for the Beach Boys. Outside the Dome, he was held up for not having the proper pass. Instead of pitching a well-deserved star fit, he took it in stride, standing outside his two cars with his entourage for half an hour.

In the dressing room, Fats admitted that he didn't know much about the Beach Boys. However, they certainly knew him. From their teens they had listened to his records on the radio. Amazingly, they had never seen him perform. Upon his arrival, Alan Jardine kneeled before his dressing room door, salaaming with an "I-am-not-worthy" bow. "You don't know what he meant to us, man," he confided.

Brightly colored Mardi Gras floats carrying Hollywood heartthrobs Steven Seagal and John Stamos circled the vast perimeter of the darkened Superdome. Soon, the California group watched in awe as eternal youth did handsprings on Domino's keyboard. He *seemed* younger than the grizzled Beach Boys, who later had young singers hit the high notes for them and women in bikinis prancing around the stage.

In May, a month after playing the Jazz Festival with Fats, Smokey Johnson suffered a stroke that paralyzed his arm. Domino's other drummer, Clarence Brown, was stricken with a totally disabling stroke. It was a double tragedy from which the band would never fully recover. Very few modern drummers could play the driving combination of shuffle and backbeat rhythms that Fats required.

Jerry Wexler of Atlantic Records had boldly predicted in a 1953 *Down Beat* article that Domino's music would still live on forty years later. His prediction became truth beyond his expectations with the 1993 release of *Out of New Orleans,* an eight-CD box set of Domino's complete Imperial recordings on Germany's Bear Family Records. That same year, Wexler's autobiography once again praised those recordings as "Fats Domino's earth-shattering sessions with Dave Bartholomew, the extravagantly talented r&b maestro."

Christmas Is a Special Day, Domino's first major-label studio album since *Fats Is Back* twenty-five years earlier, was released in late 1993 on EMI's The Right Stuff label. Some listeners were disappointed upon hearing Domino's electric piano and religious sentiments, but longtime fans treasured the album.

As the studio engineer, Steve Reynolds, noted, "It's like Fats Domino entertaining you in his own living room."

In view of the tragedies felling those around him, the religious subtext was not surprising. Domino had long attended Catholic masses, but he now gravitated toward a Baptist church in which he was baptized. "The first song I thought about was 'Amazing Grace,'" says Fats. "That's something that the Lord gave all of us."

Domino's influence was still strong. "I'm Walkin'," already a country standby recorded by Hank Williams, Jr., and others, also became a jazz standard. Rock 'n' roll adversary Stan Freberg once joked about the unlikelihood of Ella Fitzgerald singing "the Fats Domino songbook." In fact, Ella became fast friends with Fats in Las Vegas, and her version of "I'm Walkin'" on her 1978 album *Lady Time* kicked off a flurry of over a dozen jazz covers of the song.

Many others also paid tribute. Brian Wilson surprisingly based "Rio Grande," his *Smile*-like slice of Western Americana on his first solo album, on Domino's version of "Along the Navaho Trail." Sheryl Crow's grrl-power version of "I'm Gonna Be a Wheel Someday" would be nominated for a Grammy in 1995. When Elton John (who recorded "I'm Ready") and Billy Joel toured together, they performed a nightly tribute to Domino, Little Richard, and Jerry Lee Lewis. Van Morrison reaffirmed his Domino influences with the "Be My Guest"–styled title track to his *Precious Time* CD (1999) and his revival of "Hello Josephine" in concert. Several ska and reggae acts recorded "Be My Guest," perhaps Domino's most underrated song. His original was appropriately heard in the soundtrack of *White Squall* (1996), a movie about teens sailing the Caribbean in 1962. Reggae artists revived other Domino songs for international hits—Yellowman ("Blueberry Hill"), Bitty McLean ("It Keeps Rainin'"), and Super Cat ("My Girl Josephine").

Super Cat's "ragga" (reggae mixed with rap) hit, which included Domino samples, brought Domino's influence on Jamaican music and the island's influence on hip hop full circle. "Purists may shudder at the thought of such a hybrid," wrote Jim Irvin of *Mojo*, "but if nothing else, it's further proof that rock 'n' roll has enduring properties not even dreamed of by its originators— that its simple, human pleasures continue to romp around the world untroubled by boundaries. That, brothers and sisters, it has truly become the foundation for a global folk music."

To Domino, signifying in the African oral tradition had always been around, from the 1940s raps of Louis Jordan ("Beware") to the 1950s jive talk of black disc jockeys. "I could take some records I heard years ago and make some real good rap songs," says Fats, "but that's not my style."

■ ■ ■

There was more bad news in 1994. Clarence Ford, who added session work on the Christmas album to his thirteen years with Domino, died of a heart attack after a jazz trio gig at the Marriott Hotel on August 9. New Orleans music writer Geraldine Wycoff had recently noted that he was so versatile that he could play "five different jobs in 24 hours, each a different style of music—brass band, traditional jazz, big band swing, r&b and contemporary jazz." In his last years, Ford walked with a cane due to the car wreck injuries that still haunted him. "If I'd go back in Fats' band I'd look for those guys, because, you know, *I dream,*" remarked Ford just a few days before his death. "It's been twenty-something years, but I still have dreams that I'm workin' with 'em, because it's so embedded in my mind."

On October 18, the great Lee Allen, whose supreme sax solos shot through 1950s rock 'n' roll like roaring rockets, also passed away. At Allen's funeral in Englewood, California, Herbert Hardesty at first didn't recognize his friend so withered by cancer. He, Billy Diamond, and Earl Palmer sat together as a jazz band played. "Lee Allen was the greatest saxophone player of all time," says Bartholomew, "the most imitated saxophone player in the world. King Curtis listened to him standing on the side, and he copied Lee. Same with Sam Butera from here. Lee Allen wasn't just a showman, he was *one hell of a saxophone player.*" Domino put up a photo of Allen—as a daily reminder of his friend—next to his telephone.

■ ■ ■

On March 2, 1995, the Rhythm & Blues Foundation presented Domino with the "Ray Charles Lifetime Achievement Award" in Los Angeles. The all-star r&b line-up, including Lloyd Price, Charles Brown, the Temptations, the Supremes, Whitney Houston, Jerry Butler, and Earl Palmer, honored him royally.

Soon afterwards, Fats was hospitalized with pneumonia. His illness came back to haunt him during a three-week tour of Europe. After playing several solo dates, Domino joined forces with Chuck Berry and Ray Charles to play a huge stone amphitheater in Berlin where Hitler had once harangued the masses.

Fats had cooked a pot of gumbo ahead of time at home and managed to get the frozen dish through airport customs to his friend Charles, who still reveled in his good times spent in New Orleans, including many visits to Domino's house.

Unfortunately, it rained in the open-air show, and Fats started getting hoarse. Rip Roberts, Jr., medicated Domino's throat with his mix of honey, lemon, and vinegar, but his voice got worse. Domino also received word of the death of his sister Philomena. The promoters insisted that he finish the tour. Fats didn't care about the promoters, but he didn't want to disappoint his fans.

By the time Domino reached England for a summit on May 17 with Chuck Berry and Little Richard at Sheffield, his throat was shot. He performed a short set, with his voice diminishing to a hoarse whisper. Some in the audience actually jeered as he tried to finish the show. He apologized, telling them that he was doing the best that he could, since he had just recovered from pneumonia. Finally, Domino's friend Jos Aussum came on stage and told him to stop so he wouldn't ruin his throat.

Fats went to a hospital where a doctor told him that his vocal cords looked like "raw meat." Finally, he took a flight home. He spent the rest of the year recuperating. The experience soured Domino on the European promoters. He finally decided that he had had enough of touring.

■ ■ ■

In 1996, four decades after its release, Domino's "Blueberry Hill" made #13 in a poll of the Top 40 Jukebox Singles of All Time. New Orleans music writer Bunny Matthews wrote that the record, which had entered the Grammy Hall of Fame in 1987, was "as vital a component of the nation's jukeboxes as electricity or vacuum tubes." In 2001, the National Endowment for the Arts and the Record Industry Association of America ranked it number 18 in the "Songs of the Century," between Duke Ellington's "Take the 'A' Train" and Kate Smith's "God Bless America."

Several artists had recently reworked "Blueberry Hill." Yellowman had a hit with a reggae version, Jah Wobble (of Public Image Ltd.) made an industrial dub record of it, jazz trumpeter Lester Bowie recorded an "avant-pop" rendition, and Bruce Cockburn (with Margo Timmins of Cowboy Junkies) turned it into a languorous dirge. But Domino held an eternal claim on the song. In the movie *Twelve Monkeys* (1996), Bruce Willis, portraying a time traveler from an apocalyptic future, hears Domino's "Blueberry Hill" on the radio. His eyes water with the revelation of lost humanity revealed in a simple song. "Ah!" he cries, "I love the music of the 20th Century!" Domino's music continued to have that kind of effect on people, even as he retreated from public life.

By the mid-1990s, Domino and Bartholomew had not heard from the even more reclusive Lew Chudd, whose whereabouts were totally unknown, directly in two decades. Both thought that he was dead. In April 1996, though, I managed to locate Andy Chudd, who, at the end of our conversation, revealed—to my shock—that his father might be willing to do an interview. Indeed, Lew Chudd, who was still living in Beverly Hills, was healthy for age eighty-four and surprisingly friendly, with only a shadow of his famed crustiness. For the only time in his life, the great record man related hours of stories of his amazing career. Sadly, the three legends were too proud to call each other. Still, Chudd praised Bartholomew and Domino. "Fats had a beautiful sound," he said. "That thumpin' piano will go down in history."

As if to prove Chudd's point, on September 23, 1996, NASA's Mission Control broadcast the blistering piano and repeated *"woo woo woo"*'s of Domino's "Please Don't Leave Me" to awaken American astronauts and Russian cosmonauts working together on the joined space shuttle Atlantis and Mir space station. The song punctuated the fact that the astronauts were leaving with heartfelt farewells. As Fats had predicted almost exactly forty years earlier, his music crossed all barriers.

Sadly, death continued to call. In January 1997, Domino's forty-four-year-old son Andre was hospitalized with chest pains. A week later, he collapsed at the family home and died. It was an unforeseen tragedy, as shocking as any Fats had suffered. Domino and his family were still close, emotionally and literally. For much of his life, Andre had shared a room with "Brother," Antoine III, who was deeply affected by his death. Domino's youngest daughter, Adonica, now took care of the family's business with her mother, Rosemary, while a grand-nephew, Ronald Domino, helped Fats with his daily needs.

In April, Domino buried his last sibling, his oldest sister, Philonese Verrett, who had given Antoine his love for cooking. Like her sister, she had lived in a run-down home in the Domino family homestead block on Jourdan Avenue until Fats finally had to place her into a nursing home, where she died at age ninety. During the same time, saxophonist Fred Kemp was diagnosed with cancer. Kemp, who had joined Fats after the 1970 wreck, had led the horn section.

He would miss the New Orleans Jazz Festival, which his jazz quartet including Smokey Johnson had opened for two decades.

On Sunday, May 3, 1997, a month before Kemp succumbed to cancer, Domino played his first Jazz Fest show in two years. Without speaking, he blasted through relative rarities like "Poor Me," "What a Price," and "Low Down Dog." "Just like sittin' on the plunger," says festival director Quint Davis, "he *blew* the thing apart. They did a 'Domino Stomp' that was just *screaming*."

Five saxophone players blew up a storm. Elliott "Stackman" Callier wore a white rag tied around his head and blasted several hard-edged saxophone solos reminiscent of the great Lee Allen. The ever-magnificent Herbert Hardesty led the band. "Tenor man Herb Hardesty was the star," wrote Keith Spera in *The Times-Picayune,* "consistently turning in solos that were both creative and in keeping with the rollicking spirit of the piano-driven vocals." Hardesty was still Domino's right-hand man, his one remaining standby. He always delivered his classic saxophone solos with fresh passion. And he and Fats had always shared a mutual respect and friendship. "When you play with someone for fifty years," says Hardesty, "that answers all questions."

Two months later, Domino played a free outdoor July 4th concert at a casino right across the Mississippi River—an impressive nonstop, ninety-minute show that would be Domino's last formal performance for years.

■ ■ ■

On August 6, 1997, Antoine and Rosemary Domino quietly marked their fiftieth wedding anniversary. He was finally—as he promised in a song dedicated to her forty-four years earlier—spending almost all of his time at home. He had even written a new song for her titled "Rose Marie." That they were still together after fifty years was perhaps the greatest "gold record" that he had achieved. "I've been blessed," says Domino of his family. "I was lucky when I got Rosemary. And I've got some fine children. All of them finished school. No problem with none of 'em."

Just before Mardi Gras in 1998, Mayor Marc Morial inducted Fats into the "walk of fame" of the nightclub Tipitina's with Allen Toussaint and the late jazz greats Danny and Blue Lu Barker. Eighty-one-year-old Billy Diamond, who had flown in from L.A. for a Mardi Gras ball, introduced his friend. They joked over who the real "Fat Man" was now. Encouraged by his friends, Fats performed three songs with Toussaint's band: "The Fat Man," "Blueberry Hill," and "Shake, Rattle and Roll."

Domino and Bartholomew received a shared honor when they were inducted into the Songwriters Hall of Fame on June 10 along with Paul Simon, Diana Ross, John Williams, and, appropriately, the late Larry Stock, coauthor of "Blueberry Hill." Allen Toussaint graciously flew up to New York City to accept Domino's award. Bartholomew made the trip with family members. Just a month earlier, he had played his own rousing Jazz Festival gig showcasing his album *New Orleans Big Beat,* featuring his finest solo recordings since his 1950s Imperial 45s.

"Lew Chudd sold my publishing catalog so many times I needed a road map to find it!" joked Bartholomew. "When they sent me checks they forgot to put the zeroes on them!" He finished on a serious note: "Fats and I were a great team. And you, ladies and gentlemen, made us part of the American Dream."

Exactly one week later, Lew Chudd suffered his sixth and final heart attack, dying at home in the arms of his son Reeve at age eighty-six. He received little acknowledgment of his place in music history in the press, though Bartholomew's last sentence was the only elegy he really needed.

As the millennium ended, Domino retreated to his blue heaven. His grandchildren came by to see their "Pa-pa." He stayed home and watched TV, occasionally tinkering on his piano. He cooked for his friends that came by, sending pots of pigs' feet and chittlins to his youngest son Antonio's restaurant.

Domino even turned down a reported million-dollar offer to tour Europe. He was weary of the road. He suffered from arthritis in his shoulders, but his health wasn't the only reason he didn't tour. He didn't feel he could control the younger musicians without his veteran bandleaders. The fact that his close confidant Rip Roberts, Jr., was himself hobbled by a bad leg also contributed to his reticence. Nothing illustrated Domino's reclusion more than events in late 1998.

Under a tent in the Rose Garden of the White House on Thursday, November 5, the president of the United States, Bill Clinton, presented the National Medal of the Arts to honor actor Gregory Peck, folk singer Ramblin' Jack Elliott, scholar Henry Louis Gates, Jr., and others. The president's personally selected favorite, though, was not there. In 1992, when he was running for president, Clinton had played "Heartbreak Hotel" on saxophone on *The Arsenio Hall Show.* But while shaking hands after a campaign stop in New Orleans he told me that he would love to play sax with Domino, mentioning "I'm Walkin'." Now, at the end of a nightmarish year of scandal, he found a small respite from his troubles in presenting the awards, including one for Domino. Clinton received laughs with the song title shtick that Fats had been using for decades: "When I heard he couldn't make the ceremony, I thought, 'Ain't that a shame!'"

Back at home, a not-exactly-ailing Domino told an Associated Press reporter, "Who wouldn't want to meet the president? I just love him. I think his wife is a great lady. Like my wife—I've been married over 50 years. Got one of the greatest wives in the world." Even the president couldn't get Fats out of his home when he didn't feel like leaving. There was a certain symmetry to the fact that President Clinton awarded the nation's highest cultural medal to Antoine Domino, Jr., who had failed to advance past the fourth grade at the poorest of the black schools in New Orleans, in absentia to his oldest daughter, Antoinette, a teacher. Clinton spoke about Domino's music bringing America together in words that rang with unusual clarity in the ongoing cultural wars. Later, Fats said he could relate to the president: "They tell me he liked my music. Well, anytime he comes here, I'd like to go see him. One thing I like about him, regardless of what happened, he kept goin'."

■ ■ ■

In the fiftieth-anniversary year of his recording career, Domino was more active than he had been in years, playing several local concerts, including a free outdoor show for the grand opening of Harrah's Casino in October. The 1999 Jazz and Heritage Festival also marked the brief reunion of Domino and Bartholomew after a twelve-year separation. Quint Davis set the show up with a newspaper interview including both of them at his Storyville District nightclub.

The reunion was front-page news in *The Times-Picayune* on the day of their joint Jazz Fest appearance. Bartholomew strutted onstage with the band including Herbert Hardesty. Cosimo Matassa, Earl Palmer, and Billy Diamond watched from backstage. They were all marking at least fifty years with The Fat Man.

Domino was periodically in the studio recording "Rose Marie," his newest song about his wife ("he must be crazy," laughed Rosemary upon hearing about the song). He also worked on another song with the same self-mocking humor as his first hit, reminding people, *"I'm alive and kickin'!"*

In the fall of 1999, I began an effort to dedicate Cosimo Matassa's J&M Studio building, the New Orleans birthplace of both rhythm & blues and rock 'n' roll, as a historic landmark on the fiftieth anniversary of the recording of "The Fat Man," with help from WWOZ radio cofounder Jerry Brock, *Offbeat* magazine, the Louisiana Music Commission, and several donors for a plaque. Though "The Fat Man" predated the crossover of rock 'n' roll by five years, rock legends acknowledged its significance: John Lennon had placed Domino's debut at the beginning of rock 'n' roll; Robbie Robertson recorded the song on its thirtieth anniversary for the movie *Carny;* John Fogerty said that it should be considered a rock 'n' roll standard like "Jailhouse Rock"; even Lou Reed admitted that, as one of the first records he ever bought, "The Fat Man" inspired him to rock.

On December 10, Domino, Bartholomew, and Matassa all returned to North Rampart and Dumaine, where exactly fifty years earlier they started a musical revolution. Like Sun Studios in Memphis, the building that had housed Matassa's J&M Studio had been used by several businesses since its heyday. Still, the architectural grandeur of the building was undiminished. Inset before the front door like a Roman mosaic for the ages was a terrazzo circle inscribed with the words "J&M Music Shop."

Dressed in a striped shirt and an engineer's cap, Fats shook hands with his partner, saying, "Thank you, Dave."

"Thank *you,* Antoine," replied Bartholomew. "If it don't be for you, I'd still be eatin' grits and greasy meat!"

The plaque commemorating the greats that had recorded at J&M, including Papa Celestin, Paul Gayten, Annie Laurie, Roy Brown, Professor Longhair, Lloyd Price, Joe Turner, Ray Charles, Shirley and Lee, and even Jerry Lee Lewis (who made his first amateur recording with Matassa in 1951), was unveiled. New Orleans and Louisiana officials representing the mayor and governor declared the day "Rock 'n' Roll and Rhythm & Blues Founders' Day." Allen Toussaint, Ernie K-Doe, Harold Battiste, and Frankie Ford also attended. The crowd cheered news that the Rock and Roll Hall of Fame had inducted legendary drummer Earl Palmer, though—to this day—no such honor has been accorded to Cosimo Matassa or to the man who literally started everybody rocking, Roy Brown. Just as with Domino, Bartholomew, and Palmer, it's very safe to say that rock 'n' roll as we know it would not have existed without them.

Reflecting on the day, Domino stated, "It means everything. Fifty years ago I made my first record and I'm still livin', thank God; we're all still livin'. And all I can say is thank God, it means so much."

Across the street from Congo Square, where all the music began, another circle was closed that day as Matassa wiped tears from his eyes. Local TV station WDSU even produced a short documentary, which ended with Fats softly playing and singing "Walking to New Orleans," as Dave echoed him with a muted trumpet.

"From December 1949 when we made 'The Fat Man,' we never looked back," Bartholomew once reflected. "From that day on, he always had a hit record. He's just like the cornerstone—you build a new church and lay the cornerstone, and if the church burns down, the cornerstone is still there. I think Fats Domino will be here to the end of time."

■ ■ ■

Less than a week after Keith Richards jammed with Sheryl Crow on "Ain't That a Shame" at a New York club, Fats again wowed a huge Jazz Fest crowd in May 2001, in a concert that would be filmed for a DVD titled *The Music of Fats Domino*. One English fan compared the show to Domino's legendary Saville Theatre performances. *The Times-Picayune* declared, "Fats Domino refuses to age." In an impassioned review in *The Austin Chronicle,* Raoul Hernandez described the concert's climax, with Domino "playing intently, like he's never played a piano before, and in this ten-minute interlude, the miracle of New Orleans comes to life with the life-affirming vigor of pure, unheralded joy."

Domino spent his seventy-fifth birthday at home on February 26, 2003, receiving calls from dozens of well-wishers. Even then, one call was tragic, as his longtime musician Erving Charles, Jr., the finest bass player that he had ever employed, died that day of a heart attack at age sixty-one, a year after a stroke had paralyzed his left hand. On April 9, Domino's longtime drummer Clarence "Juny Boy" Brown died of cancer a decade after the stroke that had disabled him.

Rip Roberts, Jr., often joked that Fats had "killed two or three bands." "A lot of people come and go," reflects Domino. "So I figure, whatever happens, the Lord giveth and the Lord taketh. All I want is my health and strength. And the Lord gave me that." Tragedy had long haunted Domino, but his music always represented the duality of life in the African American tradition with its dance-defying deliverance from the blues.

On ultra-rare occasions Fats still leaves his house for an appearance. In recent shows he has acknowledged that he was reaching the end of his career by performing a subdued "Before I Grow Too Old" (a song that, under the title "Silver and Gold," provided an elegant elegy for former Clash frontman Joe Strummer on his final album *Streetcore*). Each Domino performance is a precious reminder of the joy that he brought to the world for over half a century.

"He's the Count Basie of rock 'n' roll," states Quint Davis. "Fats is like a big steam engine and he's pumpin' and drivin' that train. It's fantastic that this music is vital, vibrant, and alive to this day, and he's still great. In New Orleans music, I would rank him 1-A with Louis Armstrong. And then Mahalia, Fess, and a pantheon of other people, but Louis Armstrong and Fats Domino infected, infused, informed, and changed the music of the whole world."

■ ■ ■

For all of the tragedies that Domino had endured, at age seventy-seven he was faced directly with the greatest devastation New Orleans—and America—had ever witnessed on August 29, 2005, as Hurricane Katrina approached. Despite calls from friends and relatives urging him to get out of the city, Antoine and his family had determined to try to weather the storm. Early that Monday morning the waters in the Lower Ninth Ward began to rise rapidly. "The water didn't seep in," says Domino's daughter Adonica, "it *poured* in." Ernest "Box" Fontenot, Domino's drummer for more than a decade and a close friend, carried his boss on his back through waist-deep water to the "big house" next door. Another friend, Leary Hughes, helped the family members carry valuable items to the second-story master bedroom. Besides Antoine and Rosemary, their children "Brother" (Antoine III), Anatole, Andrea, Anola, and Adonica all took refuge upstairs, along with Anola's husband Edward, their three children, and Andrea's husband, Charles Brimmer, a onetime r&b singer. There in the yellow brick Marais Street house the fourteen waited and watched neighbors and dogs climbing onto roofs nearby.

Amazingly, the Katrina they experienced was not a storm, but an apocalyptic flood. Many had heard thundering sounds before the torrent began, and while some imagined (as they had thirty years earlier after Hurricane Betsy) that the city might have blown up the Industrial Canal levee to save the downtown area, others thought that a massive barge crashed against the levee until it finally broke through above the North Claiborne Avenue Bridge, where it ended up on Jourdan Avenue. In any event, an angry river of water tore through the levee not far from the old Domino homestead. Before noon the water was up to the chandelier downstairs. Still, the Dominos were not too worried. "The Lord wasn't ready for me yet," says Fats.

That night the New Orleans Harbor Police piloted a twenty-two-foot Boston Whaler boat in floodwaters as deep as twelve feet through the pitch darkness of the Lower Ninth Ward, shining a spotlight anywhere they heard people calling out from rooftops. The boat would rescue some 200 people that night. Around nine o'clock, the craft, piloted by Cpl. Robert Lincoln and navigated by Sgt. Steven Dorsey, who had grown up in the area, *docked* at the Domino home; the second-story outside balcony that Antoine Domino had built forty-five years earlier now served as a berth to step down into the boat riding on the eight-foot waters surrounding their house. The family loaded into the large boat and traveled to the first staging area at the St. Claude Avenue Bridge and then by truck to the Superdome, which was still relatively quiet late that night. Later the next day a National Guard armored truck and a bus took them to the Assembly Center in Baton Rouge, where they accepted accommodations from Louisiana State University quarterback JaMarcus Russell, the boyfriend of Domino's granddaughter Chantel. By Friday morning the family headed to Texas, where Domino's daughter Antoinette and his son Antonio were waiting for them. Antonio booked them all hotel rooms in Arlington, where they watched the ongoing aftermath of Katrina on television.

The nonstop news coverage had tried to follow the fate of Fats Domino, the most famous person who had been "missing" during the storm, yet communication was difficult and the word of Domino's rescue was not known until the Thursday after Katrina. Hundreds of other New Orleans musicians, including Dave Bartholomew (who went to see relatives in California), were likewise displaced, their homes ruined. Television programs for hurricane relief all paid strong tribute to the city's grand heritage—and especially to its musicians. At the coda of two such benefits on consecutive nights, Dr. John and Neil Young performed their passionate versions of "Walking to New Orleans."

A month later, Domino finally returned to New Orleans. Surprisingly, he took the destruction all in stride, as he walked through his ruined homes, finding a few muddy gold records (out of the nearly two dozen he once had) and his grand piano, broken and upended. His homes and his beloved Lower Ninth Ward neighborhood were gone, so Antoine calmly moved to a new home across the Mississippi River from New Orleans. "Whatever goes up," says Domino with a smile, "gotta come down some kinda way."

■ ■

In the spring of 2006, Fats prepared for his appearance at the New Orleans Jazz Festival, which honored him with a smashing poster of the great pianist by James Michalopoulos that captured both the blues underlying both New Orleans and Domino's music with its rocking, visceral ecstasy. He was a perfect symbol for the city. After all, who better personified the survival of New Orleans and its music than Antoine "Fats" Domino?

To emphasize the point, Domino finally released a new album—making many of the songs that he had been working on in the last decade available on a CD titled *Alive and Kickin'*—initially released by the Tipitina's Foundation (www.tipitinasfoundation.org) for the benefit of New Orleans musicians. A beautiful new Domino song on the CD, "Love You 'til The Day I Die," not only confronts his own mortality, it summarizes his attitude toward his family, his fans, and his hometown.

"I never thought about no music," says Domino with typical modesty. "It's just something I guess the Lord gave me. A lot of people went to a conservatory school of music and say they can't play the simple things I play. I don't know if I changed music or not, but that's how I liked it, and that's what I stuck with.

"People don't know what they've done for me. They always tell me, 'Oh, Fats, thanks for so many years of good music.' And I'd be thankin' them before they're thankin' me!

"I try to keep a light beat and pleasant words to say in all my songs. That's part me and you know I love New Orleans, so I can do nothin' but New Orleans.

"I don't think New Orleans will ever die—just take some time and we'll get it back together. I think it'll be all right. . . I know I ain't goin' nowhere."

Acknowledgements

In the course of over twenty years, I have been indebted to far too many people to thank. But let me try.

First of all let me thank my dear friends—Dennis Dolbear, without whom I would have never have had a chance to write; Jason Kruppa, my personal art director, interview engineer, and "saxophonist;" Warren Loyd, my research assistant and stalwart supporter; Haydee and Steve Ellis, two of the finest people anywhere—especially Haydee, a graceful Southern belle and a Domino confidant without whom I could not have finished this; David Lind, a true Domino fan (the man who nominated Fats for the 1998 National Medal of the Arts) and a fine photographer; and Jerry Brock, a rock of musical information, assistance, and advice. My utmost thanks also to Peter Guralnick, an endless source of wisdom, a literary inspiration, and a prince of a man.

Then there are those who helped immensely, especially in the early days of this project, and helped lay the foundation of what was to come—Tad Jones, John Broven, Walter Brock, Robert Vernon, Collin Escott, Dave Booth, Robert Leslie Dean, Alan Warner, Peter Preston (and his late brother Denis Preston), Richard Weize, Walter DeVenne, Sheldon Harris, Michael Ochs, and Galen Gart. Other music friends who have helped include Bruce Raeburn, Jeff Hannusch, Jos Aussum, Andy Chudd, Jim Dawson, Steve Propes, Peter Grendysa, Ben Sandmel, Steve Rodolfich, Andy Schwartz, Gregory Hagans, Eric Leblanc, Bill Bentley, Marv Goldberg, Bill Griggs, Norman Robinson, John Jackson, Michael P. Smith, Peter Jason Riley, Charles Murrell, Paul Harris, Andy Unterfurtner, Cor Lahnstein, Brian Smith, Willem te Wechel, Paul MacPhail, Eddie Hillman, and Charlotte Brooks, who took such great photos. For help with the Domino influence on ska, I am indebted to Michael Turner and especially David Katz, who kindly shared excerpts from his rare run of primo interviews with Jimmy Cliff, Prince Buster, and Byron Lee from July 2002 and made helpful suggestions.

Those whose writings or editing instructed me, inspired me, or constructively infuriated me include, Professor Herbert Rothschild, Nik Cohn, Nick

Tosches, Charlie Gillett, John Broven, Jeff Hannusch, David Fricke, Connie Atkinson, Jan Ramsey, Lisa Chase, Ben Schafer, and Michael Lydon. Special thanks to my agent Erin Hosier, who has stood by me, kept me going with kind words, and edited me as well.

All of my work would have been lifeless without those who kindly allowed me to interview them, sometimes at great length. I was very lucky to obtain the conversations of which I am most proud—my very rare interviews with the triumvirate at the core of this book: Antoine "Fats" Domino, Dave Bartholomew, and Lew Chudd. I am likewise happy that some of the New Orleans musical greats that I interviewed became friends—notably Herbert Hardesty, Earl Palmer, Cosimo Matassa, and Billy Diamond.

Other New Orleans and Louisiana musicians who shared their memories with me included Justin Adams, Johnny Allan, Lee Allen, Hiram Armstrong, Danny Barker, Charles Burbank, Robert "Catman" Caffrey, Bobby Charles (Guidry), Jimmy Clanton, Charles Connor, Wallace Davenport, Freddie Domino, Salvador Doucette, David Douglas, Champion Jack Dupree, Herman Ernest, Frank Fields, Clarence Ford, Frankie Ford, Edward Frank, John Fred (Gourrier), Paul Gayten, Shirley Goodman, Lawrence Guyton, Reggie Hall, Roy Hayes, Clarence "Frogman" Henry, Reggie Houston, Walter Kimble, Earl King, David Lastie, Roger Lewis, Joseph "Smokey" Johnson, Plas Johnson, Thomas "Mac" Johnson, John, "Sonny" Jones, Walter Lewis, Ernest McLean, Carlton "Frog" McWilliams, Curtis Mitchell, Frank Mitchell, Jimmy Moliere, Oliver Morgan, Charles Neville, Charles "Honeyboy" Otis, Frank Parker, Lloyd Price, Tommy Ridgley, Huey "Piano" Smith, Allen Toussaint, Alvin "Red" Tyler, and Michael Vice.

I also talked to many other Domino associates, friends, and fans: Raymond Allen, Dennis "Big Chief" Alley, Jos Aussum, Bill Boskent, Andy Chudd, Reeve Chudd, Quint Davis, Adonica Domino, Rosemary Domino, Doris Hagans, Jimmie Haskell, Pee Wee Maddux, Edna Montrell, Charles Murrell, Rip Roberts, and Rip Roberts, Jr.

Some of the greats of rhythm & blues, rock 'n' roll, and other genres I was thrilled to converse with included Jerry Allison (The Crickets), Hank Ballard, Charles Brown, Ruth Brown, Red Callender, Herb Cox (The Cleftones), Sonny Curtis (The Crickets), Bill Doggett, Lalo Guerrero, Dale Hawkins, Harold Lucas (The Clovers), John McNally (The Searchers), Matthew McQuater (The Clovers), Joe Mauldin (The Crickets), Derrick Morgan, Bill Pinkney (The Drifters), Johnny Rivers, David Sommerville (The Diamonds), Niki Sullivan

(The Crickets), Joe Teri (Danny and the Juniors), Ed Townsend, Paul Williams, Brian Wilson, Harold Winley (The Clovers),

There are many others who, through their memories, contributed to the story: Bill Archer, Samuel Z. Arkoff, Jerry "The Geator" Blavat, Allen Bloom, Julian Bond, Ellis Bourgeois, Boo Butt, Dick Clark, Bill Clinton, Isadore Crump, Ben DeCosta, Henry Domino, Sgt. Steven Dorsey, Ronald Dumas, Henry Faggen, Horst Fascher, Clarence Hamann, Ted Jarrett, Eugene Jones, Kay Martin, George Mayoral, Ulrike (Sprenger) Mazakowski, Larry Myers, Richard Nader, Bill Randle, Eddie Ray, Abraham "Bunny" Robyn, Art Rupe, Jim Russell, Shelby Singleton, Eugenia Steib, Tex Stephens, Martha Thiele, Sylvia Weinberg, John Woods.

I hope to continue to research New Orleans music, rhythm & blues, and rock 'n' roll, and I would like to hear comments from readers, including additional information and corrections for future editions of this book—and possible future projects on New Orleans rhythm & blues and Little Richard. You can write the publisher or e-mail me at neworleansrhythmandblues@yahoo.com. I am also planning a website at neworleansrhythmandblues.com.

Finally, I must thank the man who made it all possible—and I mean it all, starting with the music itself—the great Antoine "Fats" Domino, who honored me by taking me into his very kind good graces over twenty years ago. Still, I think this book is as objective as possible—after all, Fats never really cared about interviews, documentaries, or even his biography. But, in spite of his seeming indifference to his own history, he has remained a true giant of a man in every way, and, I'm proud to say, a friend.

Notes

PROLOGUE

ix **While many thought.** . . CNN, 9-3-05.

x **My friend Stevenson.** . . Palfi titled his Allen Toussaint documentary *Songwriter: Unknown*, reflecting the fact that most people did not know who Toussaint was, despite the fact that they knew his songs. After Palfi's death, friends and fans were uniting in an effort to help his daughter Nell in any way to complete her father's work. See The Mudcat Café Forum, "Obit Stevenson Palfi, RIP (December 2005)" http://www.mudcat.org/thread.cfm?threadid=87302& messages=4#1629457.

xi **In the fall.** . . Hearst-Metrotone Newsreel, 9-26-56.

xii **In fact, Presley.** . . Horine, Don, "Portland Teenagers Frenzied Over Elvis," *Portland Journal*, 9-3-57, reprinted in Rijff, Ger, *Long Lonely Highway: A 1950's Elvis Scrapbook*, Pierian Press, Ann Arbor, MI, 1987, 62. Presley repeated similar sentiments: "Rock 'n' roll has been around for many years, it used to be called 'rhythm & blues'" (*Elvis Presley's Newsreel Interview*, 9-22-58) and "The colored folks been singing it and playing it just like I'm doin' now for more years than I know. They played it like that in the shanties and in their juke joints, and nobody paid it no mind 'til I goose it up. I got it from them" (*Charlotte Observer*, June 26, 1956).

xii **Boone, then an.** . . *Charles Grodin*, CNBC, 7-11-95.

xiii **The song even.** . . Ibid.

xiii **Even the Rock.** . . The program book for the inaugural Rock and Roll Hall of Fame induction gave Domino an incorrect birth date. For over a decade, Domino's bio on the Hall of Fame's website was second shortest (only to that for the Coasters). It read in its entirety: "The first ambassador of New Orleans rock 'n' roll, Domino collected 23 gold singles and sold 65 million records, more than any other '50s-era rocker except Elvis Presley. His boogie-woogie piano style complemented his easygoing rhythm and blues vocals on 'The Fat Man,' 'Blueberry Hill,' 'Blue Monday,' 'Ain't That a Shame' and 'I'm Walkin'.' His last big hit, 'Walking to New Orleans,' came in 1960." In 1999, the fiftieth anniversary of Domino's recording career, this blurb was finally replaced by a more substantial bio, though the accompanying timeline gave him a different incorrect birth date before it was corrected (Hill, Michael, "Inductees and Nominees: Fats Domino," *The First Annual Rock and Roll Hall of Fame Foundation, Inc. Induction Dinner*, Queens Group, Inc., Long Island City, NY, 1986; http://www.rockhall.com).

xiii **Domino's music, like.** . . Peter Guralnick apparently crystallized this critical appraisal, which would appear in the majority of Domino bios thereafter, when he wrote He did not threaten the established order" and similar sentiments in his essay on Domino in the *Rolling Stone Illustrated History of Rock & Roll*, which was edited by the writer who would write *Flowers in the Dustbin*. Miller, Jim (ed.), *The Rolling Stone Illustrated History of Rock & Roll* (Revised), Random House, New York, 1976, 45.

xiii **This disregard reached...** Miller, James, *Flowers in the Dustbin: The Rise of Rock 'n' Roll 1947–1977*, Simon and Schuster, New York, 1999, 102.

xiii **In 2002, the...** *Q Special Edition, 100 Songs That Changed the World*, December 2002, 39.

xiv **As Dave Bartholomew...** *Sunday Morning with Charles Kuralt*, CBS-TV, 9-23-84.

xv **Just as journalists...** There is an amazing Paul Whiteman short film from 1930 titled *The King of Jazz* that ends with a gathering all of the ethnic groups who supposedly contributed to the creation of jazz. Virtually every group is represented *except* African Americans.

xv **After one such...** The full Presley quote was "A lot of people seem to think I started this business. But rock 'n' roll was here a long time before I came along. Nobody can sing that kind of music like colored people. Let's face it: I can't sing it like Fats Domino can. I know that." ("What You Don't Know About Elvis Presley," *Tan*, 11-57, 31, 75).

xv **That statement's popularity...** Roach, Joseph, *Cities of the Dead: Circum-Atlantic Performance*, Columbia University Press, New York, 1996, 71.

xvi **A year before...** King, Jr., Martin Luther, "Transforming a Neighborhood into a Brotherhood," Address to NATRA, 8-11-67, quoted in Ward, *Just My Soul Responding*, 232.

xvii **But, in fact...** Sheff, David (G. Barry Golson, ed.), *The Playboy Interviews with John Lennon and Yoko Ono*, Playboy Press, New York, 1981, 50.

CHAPTER 1: A DIFFERENT DRUMMER

1 **"The most important...** Grevatt, Ren, "One Day I'll Come to Britain," *Melody Maker*, 3-11-58, 2.

1 **Historian Jerah Johnson...** Hirsch, Arnold R., and Joseph Logsdon (eds.), *Creole New Orleans: Race and Americanization*, Louisiana State University Press, Baton Rouge, 1992, 57.

2 **In 1786, the...** Macdonald, Robert, John Kemp, Edward Hass (eds.), *Louisiana's Black Heritage*, Louisiana State Museum, New Orleans, 1979, 25–26.

2 **One New England...** Kmen, Henry A., *Music in New Orleans: The Formative Years, 1791–1841*, Louisiana State University Press, Baton Rouge, 1966, 227.

2 **Increasingly, Congo Square...** Latrobe, Benjamin, *Impressions Respecting New Orleans*, Columbia University Press, New York, 1951, 49.

3 **In 1866, a massacre...** See James G. Hollandsworth, *An Absolute Massacre: The New Orleans Race Riot of July 30, 1866*, Louisiana State University Press, Baton Rouge, 2001.

4 **After the war...** Ennis, Philip H., *The Seventh Stream: The Emergence of Rocknroll in American Popular Music*, Wesleyan University Press, Hanover, CT, 1992, 136.

4 **Ellison later wrote...** Ellison, Ralph, *Living with Music: Ralph Ellison's Jazz Writings* (2001), Modern Library, New York, 129.

4 **Vernon Winslow, an...** Berry, et. al., *Up from the Cradle of Jazz*, 66.

5 **Elvis Presley first...** Presley later again displayed his allegiance to Brown in the fevered cries of "Heartbreak Hotel," which were apparently influenced by Brown's apocalyptic 1950 r&b #1 "Hard Luck Blues" (Gillett, *The Sound of the City*, 148).

5 **Though the debate...** See Tosches, Nick, *Unsung Heroes of Rock 'n' Roll*, Charles Scribner's Sons, New York, 1981, 6-7 for many of the rocking songs recorded in the wake of "Good Rockin' Tonight."

5 **In addition, as...** They noted Brown's vocal influence on Clyde McPhatter, B. B. King, Little Richard, Elvis Presley, Jackie Wilson, Junior Parker, Bobby "Blue" Bland, Chubby Checker, "and countless others" (Gillett, *The Sound of the City*, 148; Harris, *Living Blues*, Spring 1982, 54; Palmer, *Rolling Stone*, 7-9-81, 52).

5 **In his essay...** Ventura, *Shadow Dancing in the USA*, 133.

5 **Even Langston Hughes...** Hughes, Langston, "Jazz: Its Yesterday, Today, and Its Potential Tomorrow," *New York Age*, 7-28-56.

6 **Afterwards, Jordan told...** Julian, Lorraine, "Louis Jordan's Last Words Thrill Crowd— His Music Sends 'Em," *Louisiana Weekly*, 12-4-48, 14.

6   **Amazingly, it even became.** . . . Some edited versions of "Saturday Night Fish Fry" cut out the verse about the *"big, fat piano man."*
6   **Johnny Otis, who.** . . Finnis, Rob, "Little Richard," *Little Richard: The Specialty Sessions*, Specialty Records, Hollywood, 1989, 9.
6   **Echoing John Lennon's.** . . Doerschuk, Bob, "The Rock Piano Story: From Boogie to B. Bumble," *Keyboard*, 2-82, 52.
6   **Likewise, Charlie Gillett.** . . Gillett, *The Sound of the City*, 44. Note: this statement is deleted from the later editions.
6   **"We started what.** . . Foose, Jonathan, and Tad Jones, unpublished interview with Dave Bartholomew, 9-23-81.
7   **"New Orleans, as.** . . Watrous, Peter, "Fats Domino's Old Tricks Made New," *New York Times*, 11-9, 1991, Entertainment section, 13.
7   **"Be-bop didn't have.** . . Dance, Stanley, *The World of Swing: An Oral History of Big Band Jazz*, DaCapo, 2001, 248.
7   **But, as British scholar.** . . Fairclough, *Race and Democracy*, xviii.
7   As Peter Shapiro, *Turn the Beat Around: The Secret History of Disco*, Faber and Faber, New York, 2005, 90-91.
9   **As session guitar.** . . Gillespie, Lex, Producer Notes Q & A, *Let the Good Times Roll*, http://www.goodtimesroll.org/shows/producer_notes.shtml
9   **Texas singer-songwriter Butch.** . . Ventura, *Shadow Dancing in the USA*, 156.
9   **Indeed, both John.** . . Wenner, Jan, *Lennon Remembers: The Rolling Stone Interviews*, Popular Library, New York, 1971, 100; Seay, David, *Mick Jagger: The Story Behind the Rolling Stone*, Birchlane Press, New York, 1993, 16.
9   **"It is the.** . . Ventura, *Shadow Dancing in the USA*, 147.
9   **But Richard's shout.** . . (author interview: Charles Connor).
10 **African American scholar.** . . Spencer, Jon Michael, *The Rhythms of Black Folk*, Africa World Press, Trenton, NJ, 151–152.
11 **"The musicians and.** . . Egerton, John, *Speak Now Against the Day: The Generation Before the Civil Rights Movement in the South*, University of North Carolina Press, Chapel Hill, 1995, 538.
11 **A Mississippi circuit.** . . Baker, *The Second Battle of New Orleans*, 228.
12 **Young rock 'n' roll.** . . Turner, Victor, *From Ritual to Theater: The Human Seriousness of Play*, PAJ Publications, New York, 1982, 44–45.
12 **John Lennon once.** . . Wenner, Jan, *Lennon Remembers*, 100.

CHAPTER 2: "SWANEE RIVER BOOGIE"

13 **But the first.** . . Oubre, Elton, J. *Vacherie: St. James Parish History and Genealogy* (2nd ed.), Oubre's Books, Thibodaux, LA, 2002, 77, 84.
14 **In January 1811.** . . Thrasher, Albert, *On to New Orleans! Louisiana's Heroic 1811 Slave Revolt*, Cypress, New Orleans, 1995, 48–66.
14 **St. James Parish.** . . State of Louisiana, Parish of St. James Court Records, 1855, in St. James Parish Historical Society, Cultural and Heritage Center Museum.
15 **The first known.** . . Schexnayder, R. V., *200 Years of Descendants in South Vacherie African American Family Lines, 1800's to Present*, SchexDumas Ancestry Series, Vol. V, Gretna, LA, 2003.
15 **That same year.** . . St. James Parish Census, 1880, 1890; St. James Parish Conveyance Records, 1860; (author interview: Freddie Domino).
15 **Plantation owner.** . . St. James Parish Census, 1900; (author interview: Freddie Domino).
15 **Shortly after the turn.** . . St. James Parish Census, 1910; (author interviews: Ronald Dumas, John Woods).
16 **The area had.** . . Lower Ninth Ward Neighborhood Profile, City of New Orleans, Ernest N. Morial, 5-78.

17 **It was in.** . . . Domino's birth certificate incorrectly places the birth at "2301 Jordan Ave.," listing Gustave Domino's mailing address. It also incorrectly lists Antoine as "Anthony Domino, Jr.," his father as "Anthony Domino," and his mother Donatile as "Domithilda" (Birth Certificate for Anthony Domino, Jr., Parish of Orleans and the City of New Orleans, 3-14-28).

19 **Born on February.** . . Russell, William, and Ralph Collins, interview with Harrison Verrett, 8-10-61, Vertical Files, Hogan Jazz Archives, Tulane University, New Orleans.

20 **The Lower Ninth.** . . Slim, Almost, "The Many Careers of Lee Dorsey," *Wavelength*, 8-82, 12.

20 **The iceman's daily.** . . J. Skelly Wright, the native New Orleanian who as a federal judge would make many crucial civil rights rulings favorable to blacks in the city, made his first black friend with a boy who delivered ice to his Camp Street home each day. Baker, *The Second Battle of New Orleans*, 92–93.

23 **Robert "Buddy" Hagans.** . . Vernon, Mike, "Domino Men: Clarence Ford and Robert 'Buddy' Hagens [sic]," *Jazz Monthly*, July 1967, 56. Jones, Tad and Richard B. Allen, Clarence Ford: Interview, Hogan Jazz Archives, Tulane University, 12-10-75.

26 **Word of Domino's.** . . Alonzo Rockford Lewis built his pavilion with money he made from selling voodoo charms and rheumatic oils. The "mojos" and other charms sold in New Orleans held a continuing sense of awe and power for blacks. Lewis became infamous after the FBI sent him to prison in 1934 for mail fraud and "voodoo extortion." He reportedly sent a threat to a man in Texas who owed him money: "I buried a seed in the cemetery, and when it rots, your heart will rot with it!" Wright, Earl M., "A. Rockford Lewis Victim in Gun Mishap," *Louisiana Weekly*, 8-27-60, 1–2.

27 **On May 15.** . . Book of Membership Dues, American Federation of Musicians, Local 496, New Orleans, 5-15-48.

28 **Roberts and Brown.** . . Broven, John, "Roy Brown: Part 1: Good Rockin' Tonight," *Blues Unlimited*, 3-4-77, 11; (author interview: Billy Diamond).

29 **Roberts paid the musicians.** . . Jones, Tad, unpublished interview with Rip Roberts, 5-14-79.

CHAPTER 3: "HIDEAWAY BLUES"

31 **"There is no.** . . Gundersen, Edna, "At Jazzfest, Musical Flavors for Every Taste," *USA Today*, 4-23-99.

31 **For decades, blacks.** . . Ironically, a year after Williams's play *A Streetcar Named Desire* debuted on Broadway in 1947 for a successful two-year run (leading to the highly acclaimed 1951 movie and Marlon Brando's breakthrough stardom), the Desire Streetcar was replaced by the Desire Bus Line on May 30, 1948, in part of what later turned out to be a conspiracy between bus and tire manufacturers to boost their businesses at the expense of the economical and efficient city trolley system. In 2000 plans began to restore part of the Desire Streetcar Line.

32 **On Saturday, January.** . . "Red Hot Show at Club Desire Wows College Crowd," *Louisiana Weekly*, 1-29-49.

33 **The song was.** . . Saxon, Lyle, Robert Tallant, and Edward Dreyer, *Gumbo Ya-Ya: A Collection of Louisiana Folk Tales*, Bonanza Books, New York, 1945, 461.

34 **Winslow even planned.** . . Dr. Daddy-O, "Boogie-Beat Jive," *Louisiana Weekly*, 8-20-49.

35 **Famed blues pianist.** . . "Blindfold Test: 'The Fat Man,'" *Jazz Journal*, 10-61, 5.

35 **Lewis was the.** . . For unknown reasons, Lew Chudd's mother, Reva (Samuels) Chudd, gave birth to him in Toronto, Canada.

35 **He also had.** . . "An Ear for Money," *Fortune*, 11-58.

36 **The ambitious Chudd.** . . Collier, James Lincoln, *Benny Goodman and the Swing Era*, Oxford University Press, New York, 1989, 128–129; Firestone, Ross, *Swing, Swing, Swing: The Life and Times of Benny Goodman*, Norton, New York, 1994, 106–107, 120–127;

Crowther, Bruce, et al., *The Big Band Years*, Facts on File, New York, 1988, 72. There is scant documentation of Lew Chudd's early life, including his radio and his big band promotion careers. His sons, Andy and Reeve, themselves were unable to discover much about it and *never met his family*. However, Andy does recall that on one trip to New York in the 1950s, Gene Krupa greeted his father as an old friend.

36   **But the advance. . .** Passman, Arnold, *The Deejays*, Macmillan, New York, 1971, 73–74.

36   **Though white bandleaders. . .** Hennessey, Thomas J., *From Jazz to Swing: African American Jazz Musicians and Their Music, 1890–1935*, Wayne State University Press, Detroit, 1994, 133.

40   **As Aaron Bell. . .** Dance, Stanley, *The World of Duke Ellington*, Da Capo, New York, 1970, 204.

41   **Billed as "America's. . .** *Louisiana Weekly*, 11-17-45.

42   **The idea for. . .** The first Poppa Stoppas were (now) unknown WJMR announcers; Winslow and Henry "Duke" Thiele, who became the first well-known Poppa Stoppa, never worked together on the show. For more on Winslow, see Hannusch, Jeff, *I Hear You Knocking*, 119–126 and Berry, Jason, et. al., *Up from the Cradle of Jazz*, 65–70.

44   **On that very. . .** Winslow, Vernon, "Guest Column: What Happened to 'Poppa Stoppa'?" *Louisiana Weekly*, 12-4-48, 14.

44   **On the Monday. . .** Fairclough, *Race and Democracy*, 56–59, 138.

45   **Jordan became enraged. . .** Julian, Lorraine, "Louis Jordan's Last Words Thrill Crowd—His Music Sends 'Em;" *Louisiana Weekly*, 12-4-48, 14.

45   **Jordan issued an. . .** "Louis Jordan Issues Ultimatum, 'Will Play No Jim-Crow Dates,'" *Louisiana Weekly*, 1-1-49.

45   **In February 1949. . .** "62 to Appeal 'Interracial Party' Verdict" and "Artists to Buck N.O. Jim Crow," *Louisiana Weekly*, 2-12-49, 1; "63 Negroes, 6 Whites Held in Raid of Club," *Louisiana Weekly*, 2-19-49, 1.

46   **He told his. . .** As Peter J. Silvester writes in the boogie-woogie history *A Left Hand Like God*, Morton's bass-line likely influenced a longer variation of the riff popularized by boogie pianist Jimmy Yancey. Played on guitar, Yancey's riff was heard in the 1948 #1 race hit "Long Gone" on Miracle Records by Sonny Thompson and even in the 1949 country hit "Blues Stay Away from Me" by the Delmore Brothers (Silvester, Peter J., *A Left Hand Like God*, Da Capo, New York, 1988, 15, 75).

46   **Atlantic Records, arranger. . .** Gillett, Charlie, *Making Tracks: Atlantic Records and the Growth of a Multi-Billion-Dollar Industry*, Dutton, New York, 1974, 53.

47   **Ahmet Ertegun of. . .** Ertegun has listed the number of copies he initially supplied to the New Orleans distributor as from 5,000 to 30,000 (ibid., 43–44; Ertegun, et al., *What'd I Say: The Atlantic Records Story*, Welcome Rain, New York, 2001, 44).

47   **Even more astounding. . .** Paisant, Ken, "Jam, Jive and Gumbo," *Urchin* (Tulane University magazine) (Vol. XIII, No. 9, circa May 1949), 9.

47   **Long before Alan. . .** Tosches, Nick, *Hellfire: The Jerry Lee Lewis Story*, Dell, New York, 1982, 64–65.

CHAPTER 4: "THE FAT MAN"

49   **"Well, I wouldn't. . .** "Wayne Jones Talks with Fats Domino," *Goldmine*, 2-1-81.

50   **Before Chudd left. . .** The story of Domino's discovery and signing at the Hideaway is derived from the author's interviews with Fats Domino, Dave Bartholomew, Lew Chudd, and Sonny Jones, as well as Shaw, Arnold, *Honkers and Shouters*, Collier Books, New York, 1978, 261; Jones, Tad, unpublished interview with Lew Chudd, 9-3-73; Russell and Collins, interview with Harrison Verrett.

50   **Al Young rallied. . .** (author interview: John "Sonny" Jones).

51   **Though he had. . .** Bartholomew's contract was dated 11-23-49, as noted in the Imperial, Minit and Aladdin Artists File, 8-13-63.

53 **Musicologist Robert Doerschuk. . .** Doerschuk, Robert L., "Improvisational Piano: Fats Domino, Part 1: The Nascence of Rock Piano," *Keyboard*, 4-92, 112.

55 **Though he was. . .** Haas, Edward F., *DeLesseps S. Morrison and the Image of Reform: New Orleans Politics, 1946–1961*, Louisiana State University Press, Baton Rouge, 1974, 68.

55 **With his first. . .** Cyrus, Bernie et al., Fats Domino interview, *Louisiana Homegrown* WCKW-FM, LaPlace, LA, 1993.

55 ***Cash Box* raved. . .** "Jazz 'n' Blues Reviews," *Cash Box*, 1-28-50, 15.

55 **Bartholomew brought Fats. . .** Some discographies have listed Domino's December 10, 1949, recordings as an eight-song "double session," but, in fact, as Vernon Winslow wrote in his column, the second four songs were recorded a month later (Dr. Daddy-O, "Boogie-Beat Jive," *Louisiana Weekly*, 1-14-50, 12).

56 **A caravan departed. . .** Dr. Daddy-O, "Boogie-Beat Jive," *Louisiana Weekly*, 4-1-50.

58 **Accordingly, Dr. Daddy-O. . .** Dr. Daddy-O, "Boogie-Beat Jive," *Louisiana Weekly*, 4-22-50.

59 **Fats omitted the. . .** Klingler, Professor Tom (transl.), Vertical file, Hogan Jazz Archives, Tulane University.

60 **Thus, the saying. . .** Gates, Henry Louis, *The Signifying Monkey: A Theory of African American Literary Criticism*, Oxford University Press, New York, 1988, 222–223.

60 **Slanderously identified. . .** Puckett, Newbell Niles, *Folk Beliefs of the Southern Negro*, Chapel Hill, University of North Carolina Press, 1926, 554.

61 **Johnny Otis, whose. . .** Finnis, Rob, *Little Richard: The Specialty Sessions*, 1989.

61 **In south Louisiana . . . got into me, man. . .** Bernard, Shane K., *Swamp Pop: Cajun and Creole Rhythm and Blues*, University of Mississippi Press, Jackson, 1996, 116–117.

61 **In Kenner, outside. . .** Audience interview with Lloyd Price, Heritage Tent, New Orleans Jazz and Heritage Festival, 5-4-96.

61 **In New Orleans. . .** Murphy, Michael, director, *Make It Funky: The Music That Took Over the World*, Sony Pictures, Culver City, CA, 2005.

64 **Again an Imperial. . .** Broven, *Rhythm and Blues in New Orleans*, 11.

64 **To kill time. . .** Greensmith, Bill, and Bez Turner, "Fess," *Blues Unlimited*, 8-78.

CHAPTER 5: "GOIN' HOME TOMORROW"

67 **In January 1951. . .** Webman, Hal, "Rhythm-Blues Notes," *Billboard*, 1-13-51.

68 **In fact, a. . .** Cyrus, Bernie et al., Fats Domino interview.

68 **Both Vernon Winslow. . .** Dr. Daddy-O, "Boogie-Beat Jive," *Louisiana Weekly*, 1-20-51.

69 **Though he claimed. . .** *Criminal District Court for the Parish of Orleans: State of Louisiana versus Emmett W. Fortner*, 6-17-69.

70 **Walter Charles Nelson, Jr. . . .** Russell, William, and Ralph Collins, interview with Walter Nelson, Sr., Jazz Archives, Tulane University, New Orleans, 10-6-60; Greensmith, Bill, and Bez Turner, "'Fess.'"

70 **While Fats played. . .** Jones, Tad, "Charles 'Hungry' Williams," *Wavelength*, 11-83, 22; Berry, Jason, "Walter Lastie Passes—Death of Jazz Player," *Wavelength*, 3-81, 19.

70 **Mac Rebennack (who. . .** Dr. John (Mac Rebennack), *Under a Hoodoo Moon*, 20–22.

71 **Late that year. . .** Dr. Daddy-O, Boogie-Beat Jive, *Louisiana Weekly*, 11-11-51.

72 **Both Domino and. . .** Domino's new record "You Know I Miss You" featured the refrain *"Lawdy, Lawdy, Lawd-y!"* and Bartholomew's "Lawdy Lawdy Lard" (recorded at the same session as the original "My Ding-A-Ling" in February 1952). Both shortly predated Price's classic.

72 **Art Rupe of. . .** American Federation of Musicians contract for Lloyd Price session 3-13-52; (author interviews: Art Rupe and everyone on the "Lawdy Miss Clawdy" session except for the late Joe Harris). Learning that Rupe followed him to New Orleans, Lew Chudd would later remark, "I caused all the damage, huh?"

73 **As Mac "Dr.". . . .** Dr. John, "The Immortals: Fats Domino," *Rolling Stone*, 4-15-04, 106.

73 **Musicologist Robert Doerschuk. . .** Doerschuk, Robert L. "Improvisational Piano: Fats Domino and the Jigsaw Rhythm Theory," *Keyboard*, 5-92, 115.
73 **Another music scholar. . .** Kamin, Jonathan Liff, "Rhythm & Blues in White America: Rock and Roll As Acculturation and Perceptual Learning" (Ph.D. Dissertation in Sociology), Princeton University, 1975, 63.
74 **Doerschuk concludes that. . .** Doerschuk, "Improvisational Piano."
74 **That April, Fats. . .** Rolontz, Bob, "R&B Notes," *Billboard*, 4-12-52.
74 **Not long afterwards. . .** Hannusch, Jeff, *I Hear You Knockin'*, 139.
75 **But exactly a. . .** "14 Injured in 'Pier Six' Brawl at D'town Dance," *Louisiana Weekly*, 5-24-52, 1; Jones, interview with Rip Roberts.
76 **The owner, Billy. . .** Rolontz, Bob, "Rhythm & Blues Notes," *Billboard*, 8-9-52.
76 **At the same. . .** Lydon, Michael, *Ray Charles: Man and Music*, Riverhead, New York, 1998, 74.
76 **In Mallory's record. . .** Shaw, Arnold, *Honkers and Shouters: The Golden Years of Rhythm and Blues*, Macmillan, New York, 1978, 513.
76 **One deejay who. . .** Ennis, *The Seventh Stream*, 170.
77 **After Randle broke. . .** Enna, Aunt, "Bill Randle's Story: From Cool to Hot to Luke Warm," *Down Beat*, 5-5-52, 8.
78 **Domino was, as. . .** "Thousands Pay Final Tribute As Booking Agent Takes Last Ride," *Louisiana Weekly*, 9-13-52, 1; "Booking Agent Killed in Crash," *Times-Picayune/New Orleans States*, 9-7-52.
78 **As jazz critic. . .** Giddins, Gary, *Riding on a Blue Note*, Oxford, New York, 1981, 108–109.
79 **But social changes. . .** Advertisement: "Another GM Dance: Two Big Bands, Fats Domino/ The Blazers Plus Mary Jo, Thursday October 2, Legion Auditorium," *The Tribune* (Roanoke, Virginia), 9-27-52, 5.
79 **On the day. . .** Baker, Liva, *The Second Battle of New Orleans*, 187.
79 **A month later. . .** Ibid., 189.
79 **But outgoing Governor. . .** Ibid., 191–192.
79 **After the show. . .** (author interview: Curtis Mitchell, Price's pianist).

Chapter 6: "Going to the River"

83 **As early as. . .** Beacham, Frank, *Whitewash: A Southern Journey Through Music, Mayhem and Murder*, Frank Beacham, New York, 2002, 43–54.
84 **Movie stars like. . .** Jung, Maureen, and Jack Rhyne, "Live at the 5-4 Ballroom and Supper Club: Bringing the Blues Back to South Central L.A.," *Living Blues*, 5-6-95, 37.
85 **Tommy Ridgley recorded. . .** Ridgley's record was titled "I'm Gonna Cross That River"; Little Milton's was "Begging My Baby."
86 **Fats originally sang. . .** Hannusch, Jeff, *"They Call Me the Fat Man. . .": Antoine "Fats" Domino: The Legendary Imperial Recordings*, EMI Records, Hollywood, 1991, 21.
87 **In November, Ruth. . .** *Louisiana Weekly*, 11-7-53.
89 **He was only. . .** "3 Domino Sidemen Seized for Dope in Philly," *Jet*, 12-2-54, 55.
89 **Two years after. . .** "Jail Fats Domino Drummer on Weapons Charge," *Jet*, 11-29-56, 61.
90 **Though their acts. . .** Hawkins claimed that he punched Jerry Wexler in the mouth when he demanded he sing the unreleased "Screamin' the Blues" like Domino (Sculatti, Gene, "Screamin' Jay Hawkins," *Other*, 1991 at http://www.rocksbackpages); Darin's first three hits, "Splish Splash," "Queen of the Hop," and "Plain Jane" were in a quasi-Domino style, and, according to Darin's advisor, Harriet Wasser, ATCO "wanted him to do an album in a Fats Domino vein" when she persuaded him to move toward big band pop standards (Wasser, Harriet, "Letters," *Billboard*, 2-7-98, 5); Charles claimed that "one of the cats" at Atlantic suggested that he "listen to Fats Domino and maybe do something on the style of 'Blueberry Hill'" (Charles, Ray, and David Ritz, *Brother Ray: Ray Charles' Own Story*, Dial Press, New York, 1978, 150).

90 **In July 1953...** Wexler, Jerry, "Mainstream of Jazz Is R and B," *Down Beat*, 7-15-53.

91 **He once called...** Hilburn, Robert, "The Hits, the Misses: Atlantic Records Founder Ahmet Ertegun Looks Back on His Storied Career," *The Los Angeles Times Sunday Calendar*, 5-24-98.

91 **Another time he... Atlantic jazz series...** Wexler, Jerry and David Ritz, *Rhythm and the Blues: A Life in American Music*, Knopf, New York, 1993, 114–115.

91 **The Atlantic Records...** Pond, Steve, "Get Down, Ahmet," *Live!* 2-98, 68, 70.

91 **Cracks were suddenly...** Fairclough, *Race and Democracy*, 162–163.

92 **"Politically there was...** Broven, John, *Rhythm and Blues in New Orleans*, 38.

92 **On WGST in...** Smith, Wes, *The Pied Pipers of Rock 'n' Roll: Radio Deejays of the 50s and 60s*, Longstreet Press, Marietta, GA, 1989, 70–71.

93 **The song's infectious...** Dawson, Jim and Steve Propes, *What Was the First Rock 'n' Roll Record?* 139.

93 **As Alan Freed...** Cage, Ruth, "Rhythm & Blues," *Down Beat*, 4-20-55, 41.

94 **"It is common...** Schuller, Gunther, *Early Jazz: Its Roots and Musical Development*, Oxford University Press, New York, 1968, 5.

94 **Bandleader Les Brown...** Brown, Les, "In the Whirl," *Down Beat*, 9-19-56, 45.

95 **Buddy Holly's drummer...** (author interview: Jerry Allison).

95 **His version whitewashed...** Ironically, Turner himself censored some of the words of "Shake, Rattle and Roll" when he performed it live for the *Showtime at the Apollo* television shows around that same time.

95 **Haley, who admitted...** *Bill Haley and the Comets Interview by Red Robinson*, The Great Northwest Record Company, Seattle, 1981.

96 **At Moriarty's, a...** Jackson, *Big Beat Heat*, 81–85; Fields, "Only Human," *New York Daily News*, 3-18-57.

CHAPTER 7: "AIN'T THAT A SHAME"

97 **Seventy-five hundred teens screamed...** *Cash Box*, 1-29-55; Schoenfeld, Herb, "R&B Big Beat in Pop Music," *Variety*, 1-19-55; "Rock 'n' Roll: Freed Ball Takes 24G at St. Nick," *Billboard*, 1-22-55.

98 **Even Freed's biographer...** Jackson, *Big Beat Heat*, 81; *Behind the Music: Alan Freed*, VH-1, 2000.

98 **Even rival deejay...** Smith, Wes, *Pied Pipers of Rock 'n' Roll*, 188.

98 **Freed's congregation was...** Irwin, Theodore, *Pageant*, July 1957.

98 **New York journalists...** "'Rock & Roll' to Get Ofay Theatre Showcasing," *Variety*, 2-16-55.

98 **"Ofay" was black...** *Brewer's Dictionary of 20th-Century Phrase and Fable*, Houghton-Mifflin, Boston, 1992, 445.

98 **A decade earlier...** Jordan only recorded the song on September 20, 1945, in a live remote broadcast from the Café Zanzibar in New York City that was not released commercially (*Rock Before Elvis...*, Hoy Hoy Records, Canada, 1993).

99 **In light of...** "Top Jock," *Time*, 2-14-55.

99 **L.A. deejay Al...** Jarvis, Al, "If They Want R&B Play It, Says Jarvis," *Billboard*, 1-29-55, 58.

100 *Cash Box* **called...** *Cash Box*, 2-12-55.

101 **Musicologist Charlie Gillett...** Gillett, Charlie, *"Fats Domino: The Legendary Masters Series," The Rolling Stone Record Review*, Vol. 2, Pocket Books, New York, 1974, 38.

102 **"All By Myself"...** Domino hits using his two-beat piano included "My Blue Heaven," "Bo Weevil," "When My Dreamboat Comes Home," "I'm Walkin'," "I'm Gonna Be a Wheel Someday," "My Girl Josephine," and "Let the Four Winds Blow."

102 **"Fats got more...** *Dr. John Teaches New Orleans Piano, Vol. 1*, Homespun video, Woodstock, NY, 1995.

102 *Variety* **would later...** "House Reviews," *Variety*, 2-14-68, 58.

102 **Michael Ventura adds.** . . Ventura, *Shadow Dancing in the USA*, 115.

103 **In late March.** . . "R&B's Slip Is Now Showing," *Variety*, 3-30-55, 40.

104 **"'Blue Monday' is.** . . Davis, Hank, *Fats Domino—Out of New Orleans*, Bear Family Records, Hambergen, Germany, 1993, 42.

104 **Clare Boothe Luce.** . . Dawson, Jim, *Rock Around the Clock: The Record That Started the Rock Revolution!* Backbeat, San Francisco, 2005, 121.

104 **Offended also by.** . . "More Crow for Binford," *Variety*, 4-20-55, 7.

105 **An article titled.** . . "Fear of Rock-Roll Nixes Conn. Date," *Billboard*, 6-4-55, 18.

105 **"I tried to.** . . *Charles Grodin*, CNBC, 7-11-95.

105 **"When I first.** . . Joyce, Mike, "Intermission with Fats," *Living Blues*, Nov./Dec. 1977, 19.

106 **At a restaurant.** . . (author interview: Dave Bartholomew).

107 **"The Fats Domino.** . . Letter from Bumps Blackwell to Art Rupe, Specialty Records Files, 9-55.

107 **Dallas promoter Howard.** . . "R&B Cracking Racial Barriers in Southwest Where It's Bigger'n Ever," *Variety*, 7-6-55, 43.

107 **"For those who.** . . Cage, Ruth, "Rhythm & Blues," *Down Beat*, 10-5-55, 18.

108 **Domino next recorded.** . . "Rhythm 'n' Blues Reviews: *Cash Box* Award o' the Week," *Cash Box*, 11-12-55, 30; Chuck Berry concert, Bay St. Louis, Mississippi, 1994.

108 **Fats is almost.** . . Broven, *Rhythm & Blues in New Orleans*, 32.

108 **"I said the.** . . Kolanjian, Steve, "Fats Domino Was Different," *Fats Domino—My Blue Heaven—The Best of Fats Domino*, EMI Records, Hollywood, California, 1990.

109 **Articles in the.** . . "Boundaries Between Music Types Fall; Deejays Spin 'Em All," *Billboard*, 11-12-55, 34. Notably Domino had also won "Best Instrumental Group" in *Down Beat* in May, an award that nicely gave credit to his musicians, though it was apparently a consolation prize, as Domino had only entered the r&b top ten once in the previous year ("Don't You Know"). "*Down Beat'* Institutes Annual Awards in Rhythm, Blues Field," *Down Beat*, 5-18-55, 5, 21.

109 **"He [Domino] was.** . . *Hollywood Rocks the Movies: The Early Years (1955–1970)*, 20th Century Fox, Hollywood, 2000.

109 **He was still.** . . Shaw, Arnold, *The Rockin' '50s: The Decade That Transformed the Pop Music Scene*, Hawthorn, New York, 1974, 7–10; Clayton, Rose, and Dick Heard (eds.), *Elvis Up Close: In the Words of Those Who Knew Him Best*, Turner, Atlanta, 1994, 89–92.

110 **Henry David Thoreau.** . . *Great Books: Walden*, Discovery Channel, 1997.

110 **The top fifteen r&b charts,** . . . *Billboard*, 12-3-55. The seven records by New Orleans artists are taken from the totality of the three top 15 Rhythm & Blues charts that week: Best Sellers, Juke Boxes, and Jockeys. "All by Myself," recorded in Los Angeles, and "Those Lonely, Lonely Nights," recorded in Jackson, Mississippi, both featured New Orleans musicians.

111 **"We had the.** . . Kolanjian, "Fats Domino Was Different."

CHAPTER 8: "MY BLUE HEAVEN"

113 **"The obscenity and.** . . *The History of Rock 'n' Roll: Good Rockin' Tonight*, Warner Home Video, Burbank, CA, 1995.

114 **Though Dave Bartholomew.** . . Hilburn, Robert, "Bartholomew: The Man Behind the Fat Man," *The Los Angeles Times Calendar*, 9-1-85, 52.

114 **"*Down Beat*'s Ruth.** . . *Down Beat '56 Yearbook*, 112.

114 **"We played a.** . . Fats at 65, BBC Radio Special, 1993.

115 **"It just would.** . . Kamin, Jonathan Liff, *Rhythm & Blues in White America: Rock and Roll As Acculturation and Perceptual Learning*, 173.

115 **Domino concluded his.** . . Marsh, Dave, *The Heart of Rock & Soul: The 1001 Greatest Singles Ever Made*, New American Library, New York, 1989, 114.

116 **Presley's TV appearances.** . . *Great Books: The Adventures of Huckleberry Finn*, Discovery Channel, 1994.

116 **"People in the.** . . Smith, Joe, *Off the Record: An Oral History of Popular Music*, Warner Books, New York, 1988, 108.

116 **A *Cash Box*.** . . "Rock and Roll May Be the Great UNIFYING FORCE!" *Cash Box*, 3-17-56, 3.

116 **Not even a.** . . "Negro Zulus Be Prim As Zouaves; Fear Race Tension at Mardi Gras," *Variety*, 2-8-56, 1, 53.

117 **The next day.** . . Baker, *The Second Battle of New Orleans*, 258–262, 274–275; Fairclough, *Race and Democracy*, 199–201.

117 **Enraged by both.** . . newsreel in *The History of Rock 'n' Roll: Good Rockin' Tonight*, Warner Home Video, Burbank, CA, 1995.

117 **Its leader, Asa.** . . Banks, Dave, "Group Seeks to Remove R&B Discs from Boxes," *Down Beat*, 5-2-56, 7.

118 **The New Orleans.** . . Fairclough, *Race and Democracy*, 179, 192, 195.

118 **Lew Chudd had.** . . *Cash Box*, "Los Angeles," 2-18-56; (cover) 1-28-56.

118 **As Mahalia Jackson.** . . Jackson, Mahalia, with Evan McLeod Wylie, *Movin' On Up*, Hawthorn, New York, 1966, 13–14.

119 **Domino ran into.** . . The Hartford State Theater rock 'n' roll concerts were so beneath adult interest and cognition that none of the artists—and not even Alan Freed—were mentioned in the local newspaper stories on the disturbances and their aftermath, though Jimmy Merchant of the Teenagers (in an interview with Marv Goldberg) and Lubbock, Texas, Buddy Holly archivist Bill Griggs, who was then a teenager in Hartford, recalled the shows. Goldberg, Marv, *Marv Goldberg's R&B Notebooks: The Teenagers*, 2001, http://home.att.net/~marvy42/ Teenagers/teenagers.html; (author interview: Bill Griggs); Owens, James M., "Theater Ousts Rock 'n' Roll Called 'Communicable' Ill: Acts As Police Ask for Action,'" *Hartford Courant*, 3-27-56, 1, 3; Mourey, Richard L., "Experts Can't Explain Music," *Hartford Courant*, 3-27-56, 1, 3; "Rock and Roll Ban Studied," *Hartford Times*, 3-26-56, 1; "Keep License but Play Cool, Theater Told," *Hartford Times*, 3-29-56, 1.

120 **The promoters took.** . . Simon, Bill, "Rhythm-Blues Notes," *Billboard*, 4-7-56, 63; 4-14-56; *Cash Box*, 4-14-56.

120 **Or Ruth Brown.** . . McGarvey, Seamus, "This Little Girl's Gone Rockin'—Ruth Brown, Part 2," *Juke Blues*, 12-89, 19.

120 **Domino soon had.** . . (author interview: Herbert Hardesty).

121 **As Bill Simon noted.** . . Simon, Bill, "Rhythm-Blues Notes," *Billboard*, 5-5-56, 51.

121 **Freberg's actual session.** . . Freberg, Stan, *Tip of the Freberg: The Stan Freberg Collection 1951–1998*, Rhino Records, Los Angeles, 1999.

121 **"The rhythm &.** . . "The Honkers," *Let the Good Times Roll* (radio series), PRI, 2002.

121 **Jazz musicians ridiculed.** . . Roberts, John Storm, *Black Music of Two Worlds*, Praeger, New York, 1972, 28.

121 **As Simon concluded.** . . Simon, ibid.

122 **The tour rambled.** . . Hychew, Elgin, "Dig Me!" *Louisiana Weekly*, 4-28-56.

122 **In Memphis the.** . . (Author interview: Harold Winley).

123 **A full-scale.** . . Ward, *Just My Soul Responding*, 113–114; "Dance Ends in Melee," *New York Times*, 5-6-56, 78.

123 **A month later.** . . Bertrand, *Race, Rock, and Elvis*, 181.

123 **During May, the.** . . "State Senators' Credo: Don't Want White Kids Seeing Negro Acts Mixing, *Variety*, 6-13-56, 1, 20; "Rock 'n' Roll Called 'Worm 'n' Wiggle' As Censors Rap 'Delinquent' Beat," *Variety*, 6-6-56, 43; "See R.I.P. Sign on Rock 'n' Roll;" "Rock 'n' Roll: Pros 'n' Cons: The Music Goes On and On," *Variety*, 6-13-56, 51, 58.

124 **On June 23.** . . "Shaw Artists Not for Sale," *Billboard*, 7-7-56, 20.

124 **Traveling to California.** . . McGee, Mark Thomas, *The Rock and Roll Movie Encyclopedia of the 1950s*, McFarland and Co., Jefferson, NC, 1990, 157–160.

124 **On the afternoon.** . . American Federation of Musicians' contract for Antoine Domino session, 6-27-56.

125 **It featured Bartholomew's.** . . The Bartholomew riff was also heard in a related Sun record, Rufus Thomas's "Bear Cat," an answer to Thornton's "Hound Dog," which may also have influenced both Freddie and the Bell Boys' and Presley's versions.

126 **"He had to.** . . Joyce, Mike, "Intermission with Fats," *Living Blues*, Nov./Dec. 1977, 19.

126 **Shortly afterwards, Fats.** . . "2,500 White Teen-agers in Rock and Roll Riot—Fats Domino Escapes Injury," *Norfolk Journal*, 7-56, 1.

CHAPTER 9: "BLUE MONDAY"

127 **Sonny Jones was.** . . "Riot Breaks out at S.J. Dance Hall," *San Jose Mercury*, 7-8-56, 1–2; "Cops Blame Riot on Drinking—2,500 Wreck S.J. Ballroom, *San Jose Mercury*, 7-9-56, 1–2; Engelmann, Larry, "Ain't That a Shame: Thirty Years Ago, America Experienced Its First Rock 'n' Roll Riot," *Los Angeles Times Magazine*, 7-6-86, 6–7; "2,500 White Teen-agers in Rock and Roll Riot—Fats Domino Escapes Injury," *Norfolk Journal*, 7-56; (author interviews: Fats Domino, Herbert Hardesty, Lawrence Guyton, Sonny Jones).

127 **The news reports led.** . . Gleason, Ralph J., "Perspectives: The Fat Man Made a Breakthrough," *Rolling Stone*, 4-12-73, 22; Gleason, Ralph J., "Fats Domino: Not Responsible," *Down Beat*, 9-19-56, 40.

128 **While Domino's July.** . . Simon, Bill, "Rhythm-Blues Notes," *Billboard*, 8-11-56, 65; "Flash: Rock 'n' Roll Dance Is Not a Riot," *Variety*, 8-1-56.

128 **Both Fats and.** . . "So Long" ended radio shows even in Europe on Jack Jackson's "Record Roundup" on Radio Luxembourg (heard by fans as far away as England) in 1956. One Anglo-Indian Domino fan later admitted that he loved "So Long" so much that he bicycled through miles of jungle in India to spend his hard-earned money to listen to it in one of the few cafés in Bombay with a jukebox (Paul Jones's radio show, BBC2, 7-19-03).

128 **In late July.** . . McGee, *The Rock and Roll Movie Encyclopedia of the 1950s*, 160.

128 **In the film.** . . Sterling Holloway (who became the voice of Winnie the Pooh) plays an overaged hipster, while the film's anti–rock 'n' roll matron is appropriately portrayed by Margaret Dumont, the long-suffering foil for the Marx Brothers' anarchic madness.

129 **In an issue.** . . Gleason, Ralph J., "Fats Domino: Not Responsible."

129 **His performance fee.** . . "Fats Domino Rock Awhile; The Money Just Rolls In," *Jet*, 7-56, 60–61.

129 **But some upstanding.** . . Hychew, Elgin, "Dig Me?" *Louisiana Weekly*, 7-21-56.

129 **At the time.** . . Kramer, Gary, "Caution Handicaps R&B LP Production," *Billboard*, 10-13-56.

129 **Traveling back home.** . . "Near-Riot in Houston As Police Nix Dancing by Negroes at R&R'er," *Variety*, 8-15-56, 1, 18; "Fats Domino Wins Own Civil Rights Demand," *Tri-State Defender*, 8-25-56, 12; "Negro, White Fans Protest Houston Dance Ban," *Jet*, 8-30-56, 62; "Scuffles at Houston Dances Cue Move to Ban Desegregation," *Variety*, 9-5-56.

130 **But, in the wake.** . . "R&R Battered 'n' Badgered: Riots Sparking New Crackdown," *Variety*, 7-18-56, 41.

130 **The American Civil** . . . Kaplan, Mike, "Civil Liberties and Rock 'n' Roll: Free Expression at Issue: ACLU," *Variety*, 8-15-56, 49.

130 **Manager Buck Ram.** . . "Rock 'n' Roll, Get Lost; It's Now 'Happy Music' and Buck Ram's Got It," *Variety*, 8-15-56, 49.

130 **Attacks against rock.** . . "Sir M. Sargent on 'Tom-Tom Thumping," *Times* (London), 9-18-56, 5; "Editorially Speaking," *Music Journal*, 2-58, 16:3.

131 *Look* **magazine reviewed.** . . Leonard, George, "The Great Rock 'n' Roll Controversy," *Look*, 6-26-56, 40–48.

131 **When riots broke.** . . "British Rattled by Rock 'n' Roll," *New York Times*, 9-12-56, 40.

132 **On Wednesday, August.** . . Jackson, *Big Beat Heat*, 143–144.

132 **An old school.** . . "Freed Reprises '55 B'klyn Par R&R Click with Plenty of Kids, Cops, Coin," *Variety*, 9-5-56, 48.

133 **After Allen presented.** . . Eddie Silvers had been a stand-out saxophonist with bandleader Paul Williams, notably playing solos for Big Joe Turner and Ruth Brown in the 1955 *Harlem Variety Revue/Showtime at the Apollo* films. He would also appear in the movies *Shake, Rattle and Rock* and *The Big Beat* before leaving Domino in 1957. He later toured with Bill Doggett and Ike and Tina Turner and produced r&b records for Duke and Chess Records, including the hit "Mama Didn't Lie" by Jan Bradley (Pruter, Robert, *Chicago Soul*, University of Illinois Press, Chicago, 1992, 156; Biro, Nick, "R&B Roundup," *Billboard*, 5-11-63, 22).

134 **An article in.** . . Grevatt, Ren, "Rock & Rollers on Standard Kick Reap Fat Loot for Pub-bers," *Billboard*, 9-15-56; Kramer, Gary, "Rhythm-Blues Notes," *Billboard*, 8-11-56, 65.

134 **But few white.** . . "Fats Domino's Rock 'n' Roll Too Much for GI's," *Louisiana Weekly*, 9-29-56, 15; "Rock and Roll Banned: Admiral Acts After Enlisted Men Riot at Newport," *New York Times*, 4:20; "Fats Domino Naval Dance Ends in Rioting," *Jet*, 9-56, 59.

134 **In late September.** . . Hearst-Metrotone Newsreel, 9-26-56. Although Domino's state-ments about rock 'n' roll in the newsreel seem genuine, his pronouncement about Russia was pretty obviously scripted by the filmmaker for a bit of topical humor, especially as Domino makes a further statement about "those Russian bears."

134 **At a time.** . . "Rock and Roll Programs Hit," *Times-Picayune*, 6-4-56, 7.

134 **The cultural war.** . . "Queen's Curiosity Aroused, Her Kingdom Much Upset by Rock 'n' Roll Film," *Variety*, 9-26-56; "Rahs 'n' Raps on Rock 'n' Roll," *Variety*, 9-26-56, 1, 48; Kramer, Gary, "Rhythm-Blues Notes," *Billboard*, 10-13-56; "R&R Has 'Had It' Here, O'Seas Not Hot: ASCAP Top," *Variety*, 10-17-56.

135 **On October 24.** . . Conversation in 8-94 with Lawrence Zwisohn, 20th Century Fox music director, regarding 1956 memos from *The Girl Can't Help It*. Domino lip-synched "Blue Monday" for *The Girl Can't Help It* with seemingly anonymous L.A. musicians, nonetheless including Plas Johnson, a New Orleans expatriate sax player, who had recently recorded one of the first instrumental rock 'n' roll albums. Ironically, he had been the leader of the John-son Brothers, who had laughed at Billy Diamond's band, including Fats, at the Robin Hood club in 1948. He would record saxophone solos for many rock 'n' roll acts, including the Coasters, Larry Williams, and Domino (in late 1958). He would later gain fame for playing cool jazz, notably the saxophone solos in Henry Mancini's "Pink Panther Theme" and in Linda Ronstadt's Nelson Riddle albums (author interviews: Plas Johnson, Billy Diamond).

135 **While in L.A.** . . . (author interviews: Fats Domino, Lew Chudd, Andy Chudd).

135 **Domino's delivery impressed.** . . Cullman, Brian, "Sincerely, L. Cohen," *Details for Men*, 1-93; Kirk, Kris, "As a New Generation Discovers Leonard Cohen's Dark Humour Kris Kirk Ruffles the Great Man's Back Pages," *Poetry Commotion*, 6-18-88.

136 **The success of.** . . Others who recorded "Blueberry Hill" include Pat Boone, Charles Brown, Carl Perkins, Cliff Richard, Brenda Lee, Andy Williams, Slim Whitman, Katie Webster, Bobby Vinton, Duane Eddy, Link Wray, Conway Twitty, Bill Haley, Chubby Checker, Wilbert Harrison, Freddy Fender, Neil Sedaka, Mose Allison, the Everly Brothers, the Walker Brothers, and the Dave Clark Five.

136 **Twenty-five hundred.** . . "Gas Ends Rock 'n' Roll Riot," *New York Times*, 11-4-56, 4:20; "Fats Domino's Band Causes Third Near Riot, *Louisiana Weekly*, 11-17-56; "'Mix of Beat 'n' Booze' Blamed for Tear Gas, Etc., at Domino R 'n' R'er," *Variety*, 11-14-56; (author in-terviews: Fats Domino, Herbert Hardesty, Lawrence Guyton, Ben DeCosta).

137 **Many blue-collar.** . . Those who recorded "Blue Monday" include Buddy Holly, the Crick-ets, Bobby Darin, Wilbert Harrison, Dave Van Ronk, Billy Lee Riley, Frankie Ford, Georgie Fame, Alexis Korner, Ronnie Laine, Dave Edmunds, Delbert McClinton, Randy Newman, Cat Stevens, Dr. John, Huey Lewis, Bob Seger, and Fleetwood Mac.

137 **Indeed, Domino went.** . . "Riot Injuries Don't Stop Fats from Fingering Fine," *Norfolk Journal*, 11-10-56.

137 **In *Invisible Man*. . .** Ellison, Ralph, *Invisible Man*, Vintage Books, New York, 1972, 7–8.

139 **"Fats was superhot. . .** Neville, Art, Charles, Aaron and Cyril and David Ritz, *The Brothers Neville*, Little, Brown and Company, Boston, 2000, 21.

139 **In Lubbock, Texas. . .** Goldrosen, John, and John Beecher, *Remembering Buddy: The Definitive Biography of Buddy Holly*, Penguin Books, New York, 1987, 15.

139 **In San Antonio. . .** Brown, Andrew, *Doug Sahm—San Antonio Rock: The Harlem Recordings, 1957–1961*, Norton Records, New York, 2000.

139 **In Hawthorne, California. . .** (author interview: Brian Wilson).

139 **In the Bay. . .** *Behind the Music: John Fogerty*, VH-1, 1997; Jordan, Scott, "Backtalk: John Fogerty," *OffBeat*, 9-97, 84.

140 **In the Spring. . .** O'Donnell, Jim, *The Day John Met Paul*, Penguin, 1994, 45; Beatles, The, *The Beatles Anthology*, Chronicle Books, San Francisco, 2000 (from *The Mike Douglas Show*, 1972).

140 **Domino likewise gave. . .** White, Timothy, "A Portrait of the Artist (George Harrison)," *Billboard*, 12-5-92; *The Beatles Anthology*, video, Apple Corps Ltd., London, 1996.

140 **Mick Jagger famously. . .** Cott, Jonathan, and Sue Clark, "Mick Jagger," 1968, Editors of *Rolling Stone* (eds.), *The Rolling Stone Interviews*, Paperback Library, New York, 1971, 163. For Domino's refutation of Jagger's claim, see Greene, Bob, "The Car Radio Delivered the Intended Sound," *Jewish World Review*, 9-3-02, http:www.newsandopinion.com/bob/greene090302.asp.

140 **The rhythms and. . .** Seay, David, *Mick Jagger: The Story Behind the Rolling Stone*, Birchlane Press, New York, 1993, 16.

140 **In a statement. . .** Wenner, *Lennon Remembers*, 100.

141 **"At the outset. . .** Dawson, Jim, and Spencer Leigh, *Memories of Buddy Holly*, Big Nickel Publications, Milford, NH, 1996, 14.

141 **"The big man. . .** "Personalities of the Year," *Down Beat*, 12-26-56.

142 **On Tuesday, December. . .** "Review Spotlight on Records (C&W)," *Billboard*, 12-22-56.

142 **"Elvis headed. . .** Johnson, Robert, "TV News and Views," *Memphis Press-Scimitar*, 12-5-56.

142 **That month the. . .** "Europe on the Rocks (and Rolls)," *New York Mirror Sunday Magazine*, 12-56 (quoted in Jahn, Mike, *Rock: From Elvis Presley to the Rolling Stones*, Quadrangle/*New York Times* Book Co., New York, 1973, 44–45).

CHAPTER 10: "I'M WALKIN'"

143 **After *The Ed*. . .** "Mr. Million Records," *Billboard*, 1-5-57, 14–17; "Geo. Liberace's 'Teenage' Deal in Imperial Upbeat," *Variety*, 3-18-57, 44.

143 **In New York. . .** "BMI's 'Rhythm & Blues' Awards," *Variety*, 1-30-57.

144 **Fats was wide. . .** "King of Rock and Roll: Fats Domino Hailed as New Idol of Teenagers," *Ebony*, 2-57, 26–28, 30–31.

144 **At the same. . .** "Fats Domino Spurns New Orleans Club Jim Crow Job," *Jet*, 1-31-57, 65.

144 **Palmer pumped a. . .** Conversation with Bruce Raeburn, Hogan Jazz Archives, Tulane University, 2002.

144 **Bartholomew wasn't satisfied. . .** Kolanjian, "Fats Domino Was Different."

145 **"I'm Walkin'" was. . .** "1956's Top Country and Western Records: C&W Best Sellers in Stores," *Billboard*, 1-26-57, 64; Early, Gerald, *One Nation Under a Groove*, Ecco, Hopewell, NJ, 1995, 80.

146 **Como even joked. . .** (author interview: Ernest McLean).

146 **"They didn't want. . .** Shaw, Arnold, *The Rockin' '50s*, 71.

147 **Backstage at the. . .** Rock historians have been oblivious to Irvin Feld (1918–1984), who should be placed alongside Alan Freed and Bill Graham among the greatest concert promoters in rock 'n' roll history. Apparently Feld had reasons for not telling his own story. After his amazing promotion for over two decades of primarily black musicians—from selling

records to cross-country tours—he and his brother Israel in 1967 bought Ringling Brothers and Barnum and Bailey Circus, which valued a wholesome, family image that apparently precluded reference to his prior association with rock 'n' roll. Although an enlightened entrepreneur, who, against incredible adversity, brought young blacks and whites together all over the country, Feld became known, as the *New York Times* dubbed him, as "The Man Who Saved the Circus"—or, worse, the founder of the world's first college for clowns, (Deckard, Linda, "From Record Store to Concert Promotions," *Amusement Business*, 12-23-91; Gunther, Marc, "The Greatest Business on Earth," *Fortune*, 11-8-99; "From Pitchmen to Proprietors," *Variety*, 1-11-84; Emerson, Marty, "Between You & Me," *International Musician*, 10-84, 4; Ennis, Philip H., *The Seventh Stream*, 9-10, 180–181; Pottker, Janice, *Born to Power: Heirs to America's Leading Businesses*, Barron's, Hauppauge, New York, 1992, 101–103). The latter book gives more reasons why Feld's story has never been told. In her profile of Feld's son Kenneth Feld, heir to the Ringling Brothers empire, Janice Pottker alleged that Irvin Feld was a bisexual and that his orientation contributed to his wife Adele's suicide in July 1958. In a bizarre twist, Pottker in 1999 would, with the help of famed attorney Johnny Cochran, file a lawsuit against Kenneth Feld and his associates for more than $120 million, alleging that they tried for years to ruin her career because of her stories mentioning the rumors of his father's hidden life and her attempts to write a related exposé on the circus (Stein, Jeff, "The Greatest Vendetta on Earth," *Salon*, 8-30-01; LaPeter, Leonora, "The Author Who Would Tell Circus Family Secrets," *St. Petersburg Times*, 1-18-04).

148 **Though, like Bill Randle. . .** (author interview: Herb Cox).
148 **Domino, Bill. . .** (author interview: Bill Doggett); "The Record That Changed My Life," *Musician*, 10-94, 38.
149 ***"Welcome to the. . .*** (author interview: Harold Cromer).
149 **"Domino's Fat $22,700. . .** "Domino's Fat $22,700 in SRO Pitt Pair," *Variety*, 3-4-57.
150 **The black St. Louis. . .** Lonesome, Buddy, "3,500 Shriek for Fats Domino and Other R&R Stars," *St. Louis Argus*, 3-1-57.
150 **"This is a. . .** (author interview: John Fred Gourrier); Gambaccini, Paul, *Paul McCartney: In His Own Words*, Flash, New York, 1976, 9. Others who recorded "I'm Walkin'" include Connie Francis, Cliff Richard, Doug Kershaw, Jimmy McGriff, Tom Jones, the Rebirth Brass Band, Chubby Checker, Nancy Sinatra, Frankie Avalon, Patti Page, Rockin' Dopsie, J. D. Crowe, Bill Haley, and Carl Perkins. (Weinberg, Max, *Max Weinberg Presents Let There Be Drums, Vol. 1: The '50s*, Rhino Records, Santa Monica, 1994).
150 **That winter sixteen-year-old. . .** Selvin, Joel, *Ricky Nelson: Idol for a Generation,* Contemporary, Chicago, 1990, 60, 64.
151 **Coleman's fiery. . .** Suhor, Charles, *Jazz in New Orleans: The Postwar Years Through 1970*, Scarecrow Press, Lanham, MD, 2001, 212.
151 **The word "funky". . .** Ventura, *Shadow Dancing in the USA*, 106.
151 **In fact, James. . .** Rose, Cynthia, *Living in America: The Soul Saga of James Brown*, Serpent's Tail, London, 1990, 47; Payne, Jim, *Give the Drummers Some! The Great Drummers of R&B, Funk & Soul*, Face the Music Productions, Katonah, New York, 1996, 21–22, 55.
152 **In Los Angeles. . .** (author interviews: Allen Bloom, Ernest McLean).
152 **"Oh, you're having. . .** (author interviews: Jimmie Haskell, Lew Chudd).
152 **While in L.A. . . .** (author interviews, Edward Frank, Herbert Hardesty).
153 **Domino's dizzying dominance. . .** Kaplan, Mike, "New Definition of a 'Pop Artist,'" *Variety*, 3-27-57.
153 **Chudd likely envisioned. . .** Jimmie Haskell later recalled producing the entire "Valley of Tears" session with Domino in L.A., though Domino, Bartholomew, and Chudd would all refute that claim (which led discographer Lawrence Zwisohn to incorrectly credit Los Angeles musicians for the "Valley of Tears" session in the Bear Family Fats Domino box set *Out of New Orleans*) (author interviews: Fats Domino, Dave Bartholomew, Lew Chudd, Jimmie Haskell, Lawrence Zwisohn).

154 **With as much.** . . Johnson, Robert, "Fats Not There, But, Oh, What a Show," *Memphis Press-Scimitar*, 3-29-57; "Memphis Show Goes on Sans Fats Domino Who Pleads Illness 11th-Hr.," *Variety*, 4-3-57, 74.

154 **It was perhaps.** . . *Tan*, 7-57, 61.

156 **A huge crowd.** . . "Elvis Presley Mops up 308G in 9 Days; Police, Press Almost Outnumber Kids," *Variety*, 4-10-57.

157 **As fond as.** . . Crenshaw, Marshall, *The Best of Ricky Nelson*, EMI Records, Hollywood, 1986.

157 **"It was a.** . . Chapple, Steve, and Robert Garofalo, *Rock and Roll Is Here to Pay*, Nelson Hall, Chicago, 1977, 47.

157 **Every night, Ann.** . . Ann Cole would perform as a warm-up act on other shows in Detroit with Domino that year; she also sang background on his hit "When I See You," which Paul Gayten played piano on in Los Angeles.

157 **The mojo was.** . . "Domino Unit Fat 18G in Return to Pitt," *Variety*, 4-17-57, 45; (author interview: Allen Bloom).

158 **Walter Brown, the.** . . "BBB Beefs on Domino No-Show," *Variety*, 5-8-57, 1.

158 **In New Haven.** . . Grandjean, Pat, "Burnin' Down the House," *Connecticut Magazine*, 7-00.

158 **At the Big.** . . (author interview: Allen Bloom); Shaw, Greg, "The Paul Anka Story," *Paul Anka Gold*, Sire Records, L.A., 1974; Booth, Dave, unpublished interview with Fats Domino, 1976.

159 **The kid also.** . . Berry, Chuck, *Chuck Berry—The Autobiography* (1987), Harmony, New York, 154.

159 **At the same.** . . Pitts, George, "A Reader Blasts Rock 'n' Roll and Pitts," *The Pittsburgh Courier*, 4-27-57, 22.

159 **Back home Fats.** . . "'Fats' Domino Plays Here Saturday"; Hychew, Elgin, "Dig Me!" *Louisiana Weekly*, 5-18-57.

CHAPTER 11: THE BIG BEAT

161 **Soothing strings were.** . . *The Perry Como Show*, 5-25-57, Video Yesteryear, Sandy Hook, CT, 1985.

162 **A few days.** . . "Fats on Fire," *Time*, 6-10-57, 71.

162 **But even the.** . . "'Outside' Riot in Dallas," *Variety*, 7-24-57, 62. The Dallas concert promoters apparently did not learn their lesson from late March, when twenty-five fans fainted in a similar crush at Domino's Biggest Show of Stars appearance ("Rock 'n' Roll Fans Faint at Fats Domino Show," *Jet*, 4-11-57, 62).

162 **Backstage, Fats talked.** . . "Fats on Fire," *Time*.

163 **As Fats trekked.** . . "New York Beat," *Jet*, 8-15-57, 43.

163 **He began a.** . . "Fats Domino in Hollywood Nitery Hassle," *Jet*, 7-11-57, 58; (author interview: Lew Chudd).

163 **A week earlier.** . . The incident where Chudd invited Domino to have a drink may have occurred on June 1, 1957, when they signed a supplement to Domino's contract (author interview: Jimmie Haskell); Imperial Records, Inc., *Supplement to Contract, Antoine "Fats" Domino, Jr.*, 1-20-62.

163 **Also in June.** . . Bernstein, Sid, "Rock 'n' Rollers No Flash-in-the-Pan; They're 1-Nite Goldmine In-the-Flesh," *Variety*, 6-19-57, 57.

163 **In fact, Domino.** . . "Domino's 104G in 30 Coast Stands," *Variety*, 7-24-57, 62.

163 **A week later.** . . Grevatt, Ren, "On the Beat," *Billboard*, 7-15-57, 95.

164 **The same Sid Bernstein.** . . Bernstein, "Rock 'n' Rollers No Flash-in-the-Pan."

164 **Fats flew to.** . . Grevatt, Ren, "On the Beat," *Billboard*, 7-29-57, 37.

164 **During a stay. . .** (author interviews: Dick Clark and Charles Murrell, a Texas Domino fan who saw or even tape-recorded many of Domino's early national television appearances and still vividly remembers them).
164 **In *Variety* on. . .** "Imperial's Wham $3,162,000 Intake," *Variety*, 8-26-57, 47; "Nelson to Imperial," *Variety*, 8-28-57, 43.
165 **The promoters added. . .** Grevatt, Ren, "On the Beat," *Billboard*, 9-9-57, 64.
165 **Domino's international appeal. . .** Ibid.
166 **There was bad. . .** "Fats Domino Banned in Nation's Capital," *Jet*, 9-12-57, 62; Follard, Edward T., "The Century in *The Post;* Strom's Talkathon," *The Washington Post*, 8-30-99.
166 **The caravan grossed. . .** "Rock 'n' Roll Troupe Rolls Up 21G in Pitt," *Variety*, 9-18-57, 54.
166 **Jack Kerouac's 1957. . .** Ginsberg, Allen, *First Blues—Rags, Ballads and Harmonium Songs, 1971–1974*, Full Court Press, New York, 1975. A "beat" singer, Tom Waits, also has a memory of hearing Domino on the road that year: "I remember once we were on Goodyear Boulevard, about 1957 and a hotrod was idling with us side by side at a red light on an intersection. And there was this guy in it with blonde hair all greased back in a D.A. like a waterfall, and a tattoo, and an I.D. bracelet, shades and a cigarette. He was with his girlfriend and she had black eye make-up on, and they were drinking beer and listening to Fats Domino on the radio. And my dad looked over at me and said: 'If you ever grow a D.A. I'll kill you'" (Hamblett, John, "The Neon Dreams of Tom Waits," *New Musical Express*, 5-12-79).
167 **The fans at. . .** Blakely, Norman, "Fats Domino Interview," CKFH Radio, Toronto, 5-67.
167 **The next night. . .** "'Biggest Show of Stars' Wham 400G 1st 3 Wks.; Drop 'Whites' in Dixie," *Variety*, 10-2-57, p. 59; Grevatt, Ren, "On the Beat," *Billboard*, 9-23-57.
167 **"Diana" received airplay. . .** Jackson, John, *American Bandstand: Dick Clark and the Making of a Rock 'n' Roll Empire*, Oxford University Press, New York, 1997, 92–93.
168 **"It's so great. . .** (author interview: Bill Pinkney).
168 **Three weeks after. . .** On June 30, 1957, Buddy Holly and the Crickets recorded two promo recordings thanking Bill Randle and other (unnamed) WERE disc jockeys for the way they "have played and played" "That'll Be the Day" (Griggs, Bill, *Buddy Holly: His Songs and Interviews*, Bill Griggs/Rockin' 50s, Lubbock, TX, 1995, 60). In fact, *Billboard* first listed the record as breaking out in northern Ohio and Boston (Goldrosen, John, and John Beecher, *Remembering Buddy*, 68). Publisher Murray Deutch claimed that a black Philadelphia deejay named George Woods broke the record, but Dick Clark, a Philly deejay himself, stated, "We added the Crickets' 'That'll Be the Day' to the playlist after it took off in Cleveland" (Dawson, Jim, and Spencer Leigh, *Memories of Buddy Holly*, 30–31). The Everly Brothers have often credited Randle for breaking their first hit "Bye Bye Love" (White, Roger, *The Everly Brothers: Walk Right Back*, Plexus, London, 36; Pollock, Bruce, *When Rock Was Young*, Holt Rinehart and Winston, New York, 1981, 86). Producer Bumps Blackwell stated that Randle turned over Sam Cooke's original A-side, "Summertime," and made "You Send Me" a hit (Bumps Blackwell interview, Specialty Records).
168 **Likewise, before the. . .** "Armstrong's Strong Statement Lauded by Top Negro Figures," *Louisiana Weekly*, 9-28-57, 1.
169 **In Greenville, South. . .** Turner, Harry, *This Magic Moment*, GM Enterprises, Atlanta, 1994, 125. Note: Turner did not use the work "niggers" in his book, though it was implied.
169 **Given the racial. . .** (author interviews: Allen Bloom, Bill Pinkney).
169 **"A lot of. . .** Demaris, David, "Paul Anka Puts It Together His Way," *Parade Magazine*, 2-12-84, 4.
169 **In a preplanned. . .** "'Biggest Show of Stars' Wham 400G 1st 3 Wks.; Drop 'Whites' in Dixie," *Variety*, 59.
169 **Feld also gave. . .** Ibid.; Hychew, Elgin, "Dig Me!" *Louisiana Weekly*, 9-28-57, 14.
170 **In Memphis even. . .** (author interviews: Clarence Ford, Allen Bloom).
170 **Every night Chuck. . .** "Chuck Berry," Editors of *Rolling Stone*, *The Rolling Stone Interviews*, Paperback Library, New York, 1971, 181. The amazing Jimmy Willis photo of

Chuck Berry and the children in the record store can be seen in Woodward, Fred (ed.), *Rolling Stone Images of Rock 'n' Roll*, Little, Brown and Co., Boston, 1995.

170 **At the October. . .** *The Fort Worth Press*, 10-3-57 (quoted in Griggs, Bill, "On Tour with Buddy Holly and the Crickets," *Goldmine*, 2-26-99, 36).

171 **Fats did his. . .** "Stars for Defense" featuring FATS DOMINO (radio public service program record), Federal Civil Defense Administration, 10-27-57.

171 **Chudd and Domino. . .** "The Imperial Story," *Cash Box*, 10-5-57, 18–21.

171 **Imperial again sold. . .** "Imperial's Regal Million-a-Month," *Variety*, 11-20-57, 62.

172 **In the Golden. . .** Grevatt, Ren, "On the Beat," *Billboard*, 11-4-57, 59; "Fats Domino Unit 52G in 4 N. Calif. Dates," *Variety*, 10-23-57, 55.

172 **There were changes. . .** "'Biggest Show of Stars' Wham 400G 1st 3 Wks.; Drop 'Whites' in Dixie," *Variety*, 59.

172 **While in L.A. . . .** *Complaint for the Support of an Infant and to Determine Paternity, No. 0587063: Theron Domino, A Minor, Earnestine Price Robinson, His Guardian Ad Litem, and Earnestine Price Robinson vs. Antoine Domino*, the Honorable Superior Court of the State of California, in and for the County of Los Angeles, 2-21-61.

173 **Backstage at the. . .** Selvin, *Ricky Nelson*, 89.

173 **The Big Show. . .** (author interviews: Clarence Ford, Allen Bloom, Paul Williams, Jerry Allison).

173 **With the addition. . .** (author interview: David Somerville).

174 **On November 10. . .** (author interviews: Herbert Hardesty, Clarence Ford).

174 **The Big Show. . .** "Hub Chief Justice Rocks 5 Taken into Tow After Hot Fats Domino Roller," *Variety*, 11-20-57, 62.

174 **Three days later. . .** (author interviews: Clarence Ford, Allen Bloom, Paul Williams).

174 **Friendships had developed. . .** The songs Holly tried to give to the Everly Brothers, who had to decline because of their contract with Acuff-Rose publishing, were his classics "Wishing" and "Love's Made a Fool of You." Fortunately, he made demo versions of them, which later became posthumous hits in England.

174 **Three days earlier. . .** This Biggest Show of Stars date is previously undocumented on a schedule that is otherwise well-known to Buddy Holly devotees. November 21, 1957, has always been listed as an unknown "open date" on itineraries of the tour (Goldrosen, John, and John Beecher, *Remembering Buddy*, 199). Apparently, the date was filled on fairly short notice with this show at the Brooklyn Paramount, as documented by Charlotte Brooks's magnificent photos of Domino and, in particular, a photo of fans standing in front of the theater with a Big Show poster showing the obvious date and the words "Brooklyn Paramount" barely discernible at the top.

175 **Since he replaced. . .** *Billboard* listed Blackwell as music director and Little Richard—not Lewis—among the film's stars in June. Grevatt, Ren, "On the Beat," *Billboard*, 6-24-57.

175 **Columbia Records' producer. . .** Chapple, Steve, and Reebee Garofalo, *Rock 'n' Roll Is Here to Pay*, Nelson-Hall, New York, 1978, 47.

176 **A cold wind. . .** "20,000 Rock 'n' Rollers Queue for Block in Midtown to Crowd into Holiday Show," *New York Times*, 12-28-57; "185G Rock 'n' Roll," *Variety*, 1-1-57, 1, 47.

177 **Though Lewis was. . .** Lewis, Myra, with Murray Silver, *Great Balls of Fire: The Uncensored Story of Jerry Lee Lewis*, Quill, New York, 1982, 127.

177 **Ironically, Lewis, who. . .** In October *Billboard* reported the stars of Freed's forthcoming Christmas show as Domino, Little Richard, and the Everly Brothers. Grevatt, Ren, "On the Beat," *Billboard*, 10-7-57; Johnstone, Nick, *Melody Maker History of 20th Century Popular Music*, Bloomsbury, London, 1999, 99.

177 **Buddy Holly and. . .** Fats impressed the Crickets and the Everly Brothers with his new minor-chord song, "I Want You to Know." Both Sonny Curtis and Allison (who still plays it) recall Holly's fondness for the song; the Everlys later recorded it. Allison also watched every show and learned things from Domino's drummer Tenoo: "I stole every lick I could put into our kind of stuff."

177 **To the *Variety*...** "House Reviews: Paramount, New York," *Variety*, 1-1-58.
177 **The incredible New...** "185G Rock 'n' Roll," *Variety*, 1-1-57, 1, 47; Grevatt, Ren, "On the Beat," *Billboard*, 10-7-57.
177 **Fats *had* to...** Pollock, Bruce, *When Rock Was Young*, Holt Rinehart and Winston, New York, 1981, 86.
178 **The shows that...** "House Reviews: Paramount, New York," *Variety*, 1-1-58.
178 **On December 26...** "Personalities of the Year," *Down Beat*, 12-26-57, 22.
178 **A scene at...** (author interview: Clarence Ford).

Chapter 12: "Be My Guest"

179 **"We expect to...** Grevatt, Ren, "On the Beat," *Billboard*, 1-27-58.
179 **Domino was still...** "New York Beat," *Jet*, 2-13-58, 63.
179 **Fulfilling a promise...** Grevatt, Ren, "On the Beat," *Billboard*, 1-20-58, 77.
180 **After an appearance...** Domino's hit, "Sick and Tired," would become a minor classic, recorded by Jerry Lee Lewis, Ronnie Hawkins, the Righteous Brothers, Waylon Jennings, Johnny and Edgar Winter, Professor Longhair, Georgie Fame, Lee "Scratch" Perry, Delbert McClinton, Sam Butera, the Searchers, Frankie Ford, Boz Scaggs, Rick Danko, Alex Chilton, the Grateful Dead, and John Fogerty.
180 **But for every...** Outside of the appearances by Domino and Del Vikings, the other movie on the double bill with *The Big Beat*, *The Thing That Couldn't Die* (featuring the same "stars," William Reynolds and Andra Martin) was more memorable.
180 **With the release...** Grevatt, Ren, "On the Beat," 3-24-58, 66. As if to confirm Doggett's claims, a bizarre and *totally untrue* item appeared in *Jet* stating that Domino had recorded twelve romantic ballads with a thirty-six-piece orchestra for an album titled *Fats Digs the Love Bit* ("Rock 'n' Roller Fats Domino Turns Balladeer," *Jet*, 3-13-58, 60). Lew Chudd, who may have spread rumors that Domino was going to play Fats Waller in a movie a year earlier, apparently was the source of another weird rumor that Domino was recording an album titled *One Minute of Time* including "a flock of complete tunes, with vocal by Fats, each of which will have a one-minute duration"—a concept foreshadowing the Residents' *Commercial Album* by twenty-two years (Grevatt, Ren, "On the Beat," *Billboard*, 1-27-58). But the most amazing untrue story—reported seriously by *Variety*—was that legendary film mogul Harry Cohn of Columbia Pictures bought Imperial Records, with Cohn (just weeks before his death) insisting he had a "verbal agreement" with his equally acidic peer, Chudd (author interview: Lew Chudd; "Col Pictures Buys Imperial," *Variety*, 1-29-58, 45).
180 **Still, as a...** Grevatt, Ren, "One Day I'll Come to Britain," *Melody Maker*, March 8, 1958.
181 **That week, Fats...** "House Reviews: Apollo, New York," *Variety*, 4-9, 58, 113.
181 **Blacks were only...** Hychew, Elgin, "Dig Me," *Louisiana Weekly*, 7-12-58.
181 **On May 6...** (author interview: Lew Chudd); "Imperial's Chudd Smacks Smathers Bill, ASCAP; Bevy of Others on Stand in D.C. to Voice Pro-BMI Sentiment," *Variety*, 5-7-58, 55–56; Ward, *Just My Soul Responding*, 120–122.
182 **Domino played Vanderbilt...** Grevatt, Ren, "On the Beat," *Billboard*, 2-17-58, 60; "Fats Here Tonight for Senate Dance; ODK Tappings Set," *Vanderbilt Hustler*, 5-16-58, 1; Ward, *Just My Soul Responding*, 229–230.
182 **While Domino was...** (author interviews: Fats Domino, Allen Toussaint, Cosimo Matassa, Edward Frank, Dave Bartholomew). Strangely, Bartholomew would later deny that he used session pianists on Domino's records, stating flatly, "Nobody played Fats' piano but Fats Domino."
183 **A week later...** "Fats Domino, Show [*sic*] Agency Renew Pact," *Billboard*, 8-25-58.
183 **Ostensibly things were...** Fairclough, *Race and Democracy*, 213, 219; Kurtz, Michael L., and Morgan D. Peoples, *Earl K. Long: The Saga of Uncle Earl and Louisiana Politics*,

Louisiana State University Press, Baton Rouge, 1990, 200–202; Baker, *The Second Battle of New Orleans*, 297–298.

184 **Chuck Willis, who. . .** Roberts, John Storm, *The Latin Tinge: The Impact of Latin American Music on the United States*, Oxford University Press, New York, 1999, 138.

184 **Bobby Darin found. . .** Neil Sedaka's first reaction upon hearing "Splish Splash" was "Oh, that must be the new Fats Domino record. It sounds terrific" (Evanier, David, *Roman Candle: The Life of Bobby Darin*, Rodale, Emmaus, PA, 2004, 45). Darin later admitted that Domino and Ray Charles "opened up my ears to a whole new world, different from anything I'd ever heard until then. They both became major influences . . . " (Darin, Bobby, *Bobby Darin Sings Ray Charles*, Atco Records, New York, 3–62).

185 **The next day. . .** Webre, Gil, "Fats Makes a Record," *New Orleans Times-Picayune, Dixie Roto*, 11-2-58, 12.

186 **Still, Chudd's business. . .** "Smaller Record Firms Spin to Success," *Business Week*, 9-7-57, 49; "An Ear for Money," *Fortune*, 11-58.

187 **Bartholomew, who had. . .** Kolanjian, "Fats Domino Was Different."

187 **A tragic blow. . .** The deep freeze cost another musical great his life when New Orleans bluesman Guitar Slim, a wild and flashy precursor of Jimi Hendrix, died of pneumonia on February 7 in Rochester, New York.

187 **Cosimo Matassa, touring. . .** (author interviews: Cosimo Matassa, Jimmy Clanton).

188 **In the midst. . .** Bernstein, Sid, and Arthur Aaron, *Not Just the Beatles . . .* , Jacques and Flusster, Teaneck, NJ, 2000, 59–60.

188 **African American music. . .** Burns, Ken, *Jazz*, PBS Home Video, 2000.

189 **As if to. . .** Besides Chubby Checker, other singers named in joking tribute to Fats Domino included Skinny Dynamo, Tubby Chess, Round Robin, and Pudgy Parcheesi. Likewise, jazz bass player Jaco Pastorius nicknamed his overweight brother Greg "Massive Monopoly" (Milkowski, Bill, *Jaco*, Backbeat, New York, 1996, 25). Domino's real name "Antoine" was the inspiration for the name of author Antwone Fisher (Fisher, Antwone, *Finding Fish*, HarperTorch, New York, 2002, 226).

189 **Clark had another. . .** Bernard, Shane K., *Swamp Pop*, 29.

190 **At the same. . .** Other acts on the 1959 Alan Freed Easter show included Larry Williams, Jo Ann Campbell, the Impalas, Thomas Wayne, the Mello Kings, the Cadillacs, Bobby Freeman, and the Skyliners.

190 **Freed finally announced. . .** "House Reviews—Fabian's Fox, Bklyn," *Variety*, 4-1-59, 62.

191 **During the all-day. . .** (author interviews: Jimmy Clanton, Dale Hawkins, Raymond Allen).

191 **March 30th was. . .** Jackson, *Big Beat Heat*, 232–233.

191 **In April, Lew. . .** *Variety*, 4-15-59.

191 **The first Grammy. . .** "R&B, Jazz and LP Execs Quizzical on Naras (Disk 'Oscar') Nominations," *Variety*, 3-25-59, 57.

191 **On May 18. . .** Asbell, Bernie, "Sam Phillips Notes: R&R Fading but Imprint Permanent," *Billboard*, 5-18-59, 4.

191 **Also that month. . .** Kurtz and Peoples, *Earl K. Long*, 205–212.

192 **In March. . .** "DJ Payola: Like Headwaiter's Tip," *Variety*, 3-25-59, 57.

192 **Lew Chudd consistently. . .** Correspondence from Ken Rogers, 7-2-01.

192 **Like other songs. . .** Kolanjian, "Fats Domino Was Different."

192 **Domino was. . .** Broven, John, *Rhythm and Blues in New Orleans*, 16; (author interviews: Frank Fields, Cosimo Matassa, Dave Bartholomew, Lew Chudd).

194 **"I'm Ready" became. . .** The Beatles recorded a snippet of "I'm Ready" twice in the *Let It Be* sessions. Sulpy, Doug, *Get Back: The Unauthorized Chronicle of the Beatles' Let It Be Disaster*, St. Martin's Griffin, New York, 1999, 215, 217; Bruce Springsteen performed the song live in a medley with Domino's "Let the Four Winds Blow." Cross, Charles R., and the editors of Backstreets Magazine, *Backstreets: Springsteen: The Man and His Music*. Harmony, New York, 1989, 174.

194 **Though it was. . .** Conversation with Colin Escott, 1993. Rockabilly singer Ersel Hickey stated in an interview with Escott that he was offered "I'm Ready" on a demo sung by Bobby Darin, who recorded many such demos for Don Kirschner's music publishing concerns. Al Lewis and Sylvester Bradford, the writers of "I'm Ready," also wrote Little Anthony and the Imperials' hit "Tears on My Pillow."

194 **Carl Perkins confirmed. . .** Flanagan, Bill, *Written in My Soul: Rock's Great Songwriters Talk About Creating Their Music*, Contemporary, Chicago, 1986, 19–20.

194 **A familiar headline. . .** "Race Riot Wrecks Fats Domino Dance in Denver," *Jet*, 8-13-59, 56.

195 **Future presidential candidate. . .** Kunen, James S., "Patrick Buchanan," *People*, 8-29-88; Matalin, Mary, *All's Fair*, Simon & Schuster, New York, 1995, 8. "I'm Gonna Be a Wheel Some Day" apparently also inspired the dreams of a young boy born in New Orleans' Ninth Ward exactly forty-five years to the day after Domino—Marshall Faulk, who grew up in the desolation of the Desire Housing Project area where Domino started his career, and, after years of struggling (including a job selling popcorn in the Superdome), became one of the National Football League's premier running backs. Saraceno, Jon, "Faulk Hits the Big Time," *USA Today*, 9-6-94.

195 **In October, Congressman. . .** "Dot, Imperial, & Liberty Prexies Aid N.Y. Probe," *Variety*, 11-23-59, 55.

196 **By December, the. . .** "Jocks Brushing 'Rock' for Class," *Variety*, 12-2-59, 1.

196 **His opponent, Mayor. . .** Haas, Edward E., *DeLesseps S. Morrison and the Image of Reform*, 247.

197 **Folklorist Alan Lomax. . .** Gross, Mike, "U.S. Now a 'Musical Democracy' As Result of Disk Spread: Lomax," *Variety*, 3-25-59, 58.

197 **L.A. bandleader Johnny. . .** *Los Angeles Sentinel*, 6-23-60, 4A.

197 **Reflecting on the. . .** "Editorial: R&B Spreads Wings," *Billboard*, 2-4-56, 54.

CHAPTER 13: "WALKING TO NEW ORLEANS"

199 **"Did you hear. . .** (author interviews: Ernest McLean, Herbert Hardesty, Billy Diamond).

201 **Saxophonist Clarence Ford. . .** (author interviews: Clarence Ford, Billy Diamond); Jones, Tad, and Richard Allen interview with Clarence Ford.

202 **After he finally. . .** Charles sang his original lyric to "Walking to New Orleans" with the alternate line *"I hope you understand"* on his *Wish You Were Here* album (Stony Plain/Rice 'N' Gravy Records, Edmonton, Alberta, 1995). The recording, which features an ultra-rare guest vocal by Domino on the final chorus of the song, was reissued on the two-disc *Last Train to Memphis* (Rice 'N' Gravy Records, Bogalusa, LA, 2004).

202 **Domino stood proudly. . .** "Fats Domino's 200,000 Home," *Ebony*, July 1960, 115, 118–120.

204 **To prove that. . .** *Billboard*, 5-28-60.

204 **The record became. . .** Radio was awash in New Orleans anthems that year. Less than a year after Johnny Horton's #1 hit "Battle of New Orleans," the lilting "Walking to New Orleans" contrasted with the raucous, New Orleans r&b-influenced sounds of Freddie Cannon's "Way Down Yonder in New Orleans" and Gary U.S. Bonds's "New Orleans." The flipside of "Walking to New Orleans" was a #21 pop hit titled "Don't Come Knockin'," a country two-step number with the orchestral strings imitating fiddles. The lyric could have been Rosemary's message to fans who now tried to knock on her door on a regular basis.

204 **Though Domino was. . .** "History of the Hollywood Walk of Fame," http://www.hollywood .com; conversation with Hollywood Chamber of Commerce, 3-29-00.

205 **There was great. . .** "'Fats' Domino, Wife 'Kiss and Make Up," *Louisiana Weekly*, 8-27-60, 1–2; *Mrs. Rosemary Hall, Wife of Antoine Domino, Jr. Versus Antoine Domino, Jr.*, Civil District

Court for the Parish of Orleans State of Louisiana Division G No. 383-058 with attached Summons, Restraining Order, and Motion to Dismiss, 8-11-60.

205 *Jet* **magazine tried.** . . . "Why Fats Domino's Wife Wanted to Leave Their $200,000 Home," *Jet*, 9-15-60, 58–62.

206 **Segregationists still knew.** . . . Albert Jones letter to Ross Barnett, 8-1-60, Document 21, 1, Hinds County folder, Mississippi State Sovereignty Commission Papers, Jackson; "Nixes Jim Crow Date," *Norfolk Journal*, 8-27-60.

206 **Music writer Hank.** . . . Davis, Hank, *Fats Domino—Out of New Orleans*, 44.

207 **"TWO, FOUR, SIX.** . . . Fairclough, *Race and Democracy*, 234–253; Baker, *The Second Battle of New Orleans*, 389–436.

207 **During the protests.** . . . Palmer, Robert, *Rock and Roll: An Unruly History*, Harmony, New York, 1995, 22.

208 **Charles's success inspired.** . . . Allan, Johnnie, and Bernice Larson Webb, *Born to Be a Loser: The Jimmy Donley Story*, Jadfel, Lafayette, LA, 1992, 210–212; Jimmy Donley's original version of "What a Price" with different lyrics can be heard on Jimmy Donley, *Born to Be a Loser: The Crazy Cajun Recordings*, Edsel Records, Richmond, Surrey, 1999.

Chapter 14: "Let the Four Winds Blow"

209 **"To them times.** . . . *The Bob Marley Story: Caribbean Nights*, Island Visual Arts, New York, 1986.

209 **"He was just.** . . . Rebennack, Mac (Dr. John), with Jack Rummel, 91,

209 **On January 31.** . . . "'Fats D' Here for Concerts," *Jamaica Gleaner*, 2-1-61, 1.

210 **Local disc jockeys.** . . . (Katz, David, interview with Prince Buster, 7-26-02); "Hip to the Jive and Stay Alive!" Turner, Michael, and Mark Gorney, *The Beat*, Vol. 15, #4, 1996, 38.

210 **Guitarist Ernest Ranglin.** . . . Timm, Bob, Ska/Reggae: "Rappin' with Ranglin: An Interview with the Originator of Ska Guitar: From Whence Came the Ska?" http://www.ska.about.com, 2002, 2.

210 **Musicologist Charlie Gillett.** . . . Gillett, Charlie, "Fats Domino: The Legendary Masters Series," *The Rolling Stone Record Review, Vol. 2*, Pocket Books, New York, 1974, 38.

210 **Jamaican devotion.** . . . White, Timothy, *Catch a Fire: The Life of Bob Marley*, Holt, Rinehart and Winston, New York, 1983, 127; Katz, David, *Solid Foundation: An Oral History of Reggae*, Bloomsbury, London, 2003, 51.

210 **Not long after.** . . . Ragogna, Mike, with Dana Smart, *Jimmy Cliff—Ultimate Collection*, Universal City, CA, 1999. "I used to sing all Fats Domino songs," says Cliff in an interview with David Katz. "Fats Domino, Sam Cooke, and Ray Charles were the artists I really loved, and in my mind I thought if I could combine these three people together I could be as good as them all put together. . . So when I went to Kingston to do this *Opportunity Knocks*, I keep singing a lot of Fats Domino songs" (Katz, David, interview with Jimmy Cliff, 7-31-02).

210 **There were many.** . . . Reggae archivist Michael Turner and I have compiled a list of vintage Jamaican versions of Domino songs and myself from which someone will hopefully compile on a CD: "Ain't That a Shame" (Superboys); "Be My Guest" (Al T Joe and Millie Small); "The Big Beat" (Dennis Alcapone—as "Rock to the Beat" or "Number One Station"); "Blueberry Hill" (Ferdinand); "Careless Love" (Beresford Ricketts); "Going to the River" (Prince Buster, Eric Morris, and Monty Morris); "I'm in the Mood for Love" (Heptones) (and Lord Tanamo—as "I'm in the Mood for Ska"); "I'm Walkin'" (Tommy Burton Combo—as "I'm Walking [Yes Indeed]"); "Little School Girl" (Ruddy and Sketto and Lloyd Williams); "Margie" (Blues Busters—as "Marjie"); "My Girl Josephine" (Joe Henry—as "My Darling Josephine") (and Ken Parker—as "Hello My Little Queen"); "Please Forgive Me" (Al T Joe); "Prisoner's Song" (Al T Joe); "Sick and Tired" (Neville Grant) (the Techniques—as "Oh Ba-a-by"; Ken Boothe—as "Oh Baby";

and the Upsetters—as the hit instrumental "Return of Django"); "Sometimes I Won-der" (Jackie Opel); "Telling Lies" (Techniques); "True Confession" (Silvertones); "Valley of Tears" (Al T Joe); "What a Price" (Busty Brown) (and Al T Joe—as "Oh Whatta Price"); "When My Dreamboat Comes Home" (Al T Joe—as "Goodbye Dreamboat"); and "You Done Me Wrong" (Charmers—as "Done Me Wrong").

210 **In the documentary. . .** *The Bob Marley Story: Caribbean Nights.*

210 **In Stephen Davis's. . .** Davis, Stephen, *Bob Marley: The Biography*, A. Barker, London, 1983, 48.

211 **He got up. . .** A photo of Fats at the piano with music producer Duke Reid appears in *Catch a Fire: The Life of Bob Marley* on page 110. According to Prince Buster, Reid's coup in bringing Domino to the club earned Reid great prestige (Katz, David, interview with Prince Buster, 7-26-02). Legendary saxophonist and Skatalites' founder, Tommy McCook, who played upstairs at the Bournemouth Club, later cited playing with Domino on his ré-sumé, possibly in a jam session with Domino that night (Mack, Bob, "Skatalites Founder Sets the Record Straight," *Grand Royal*, #2, 1995).

211 **At out-of-the-way. . .** Early ska band Byron Lee and the Dragonaires opened for Domino on two dates on the tour. In a photograph by Gil Kong from the time, Lee is visible in a bow tie behind Domino, and Tenoo plays on the Dragonaire's drumset. Interviewed by David Katz, Lee recalls that all of Domino's songs "were number one on the charts," citing "Be My Guest," "I Want to Walk You Home," and "the big one" "Blueberry Hill" (Katz, David, interview with Byron Lee, 7-17-02).

211 **Back in his. . .** Allan, Johnnie and Bernice Larson Webb, *Born to Be a Loser*, 212–213; 269–270, 273–277.

212 **Domino suffered more. . .** "Name 'Fats' Domino in L.A. Paternity Suit," *Jet*, 3-9-61, 41, *Complaint for the Support of an Infant and to Determine Paternity, No. 0587063.*

212 **Fats told *Jet*. . .** Robinson, Major, "New York Beat," *Jet*, 3-23-61, 64.

212 **But an American. . .** Troitsky, Artemy, *Back in the U.S.S.R.: The True Story of Rock in Rus-sia*, Faber and Faber, Boston, 1987, 19, 21; postcard "Building of the C.C. of the Commu-nist Party of Byelorussia" with written note "E.Z. Fast [*sic*] Domino 'My Girl Josephine.'"

213 **In a *Jet*. . .** Robinson, Major, "How Dixie Race Tension Is Killing Mixed Shows: The Big Rock 'n' Roll Package a $3 Million-a-Year Casualty," *Jet*, 12-22-60, 56–59.

214 ***Billboard* listed Fats. . .** "Just Completed Another Sensational Top-Grossing Tour," *Bill-board*, 7-17-61.

214 **The current hit. . .** Songwriters Jimmy Donley and Pee Wee Maddux (who later that day sang with Fats on their own song, "Rockin' Bicycle") joined in the background shouting on "What a Party" (author interview: Pee Wee Maddux).

215 ***The Louisiana Weekly*. . .** Hychew, Elgin, "Dig Me," *Louisiana Weekly*, 11-25-61.

215 **The fact that. . .** Russell, William, and Ralph Collins, interview with Harrison Verrett.

215 **Prince La La. . .** The photo of La La with the two African-garbed ladies graces the cover of *Gumbo Stew: Original AFO New Orleans R&B* (Ace Records, London, 1993), which also includes a short history of the AFO Combo.

216 **Luckily, in light. . .** (author interview: Clarence Ford); "Fats Domino Sets Rogers Prece-dent," *Memphis Press-Scimitar*, 1-25-62; "Fats Domino Performs at Biased Arkansas City," *Jet*, 2-8-62, 59. The first Wal-Mart opened in Rogers, Arkansas, that year.

216 **Even white adults. . .** Macdonald, Kemp, Hass (eds.), *Louisiana's Black Heritage.*

216 **According to Eldridge. . .** Cleaver, Eldridge, *Soul on Ice*, Delta, New York, 1968, 197.

216 **Indeed, Nancy Friday. . .** "The History of Sex," The History Channel, 1999.

217 **Accordingly, Diamond claims. . .** A month later *Jet* writer Major Robinson wrote that Walter "Papoose" Nelson "died of a heart attack in a Harlem hotel." Robinson, Major, "New York Beat," *Jet*, 3-22-62, 64.

218 **Six days later. . .** Bagby, Beth, "Negro Jazz Band Funeral Tradition Still Popular," *Tulane Hullaballoo*, 3-23-62.

219 **The Big Show. . .** One columnist noted that Domino's Big Show's Atlantic City appearance "hardly broke even." Young, Masco, "Masco Young's Notebook," *The Carolinian* (Raleigh, NC), 8-11-62, 16.

220 **Ironically, he faced. . .** Passport for Anthony Domino, Jr., issued 6-5-62, reproduced in *"They Call Me the Fat Man . . . ": Antoine "Fats" Domino: The Legendary Imperial Recordings*, EMI Records, Hollywood, 1991; Birth Certificate for Anthony Domino, Jr., Parish of Orleans and the City of New Orleans, 3-14-28. Domino would have his name legally changed to "Antoine Domino, Jr." in December 1968 (Civil District Court for the Parish of Orleans, State of Louisiana, Docket No. 5, No. 486-735, *Anthony Domino vs. James Garrison, Petition for Change of Name*, 12-17-68).

220 **"Au Zoo! Le. . .** *Jazz Hot*, 1962, quoted in Broven, John, *Rhythm & Blues in New Orleans*, 182.

220 **England's *Melody Maker*. . .** Houston, Robert, *Melody Maker*, 7-62, quoted in Preston, Denis, and Peter Preston, *The Fats Domino Story*, Stanford-Le-Hope, Essex, England, 1985, 20.

221 **This time a British. . .** Preston, Dennis, and Peter Preston, *The Fats Domino Story*, 20.

221 **The band arrived. . .** (author interview: Horst Fascher); Miles, Barry, *Paul McCartney: Many Years from Now*, Henry Holt, New York, 1997, 62–63; "The Star Club History," www.center-of-beat.com; Clayson, Alan, *Hamburg: The Cradle of British Rock*, Sanctuary, London, 1997, 71–72, 114.

222 **Domino's warm-up. . .** Several people, notably Domino, Bartholomew, Billy Diamond, and Horst Fascher, recall that the warm-up act for Domino at the Star Club was the Beatles. Fats didn't pay attention to the warm-up bands, but he later took Bartholomew's word that one of them was the Beatles. Fascher's recollection is puzzling, because he places not only the Beatles there that night but also the Searchers, Gerry and the Pacemakers, and Tony Sheridan, apparently getting it half right. W. H. te Wechel, in his authoritative listing of Domino's European concerts, dates two Domino Hamburg shows on October 27 and 28, 1962. At that time the Beatles were in England, performing at the Empire Theatre in Liverpool on October 28. The photos of Domino with the Searchers and Gerry and the Pacemakers are in a German article about Domino, reprinted in the booklet of the Bear Family box set (*Fats Domino—Out of New Orleans*, Bear Family Records, Hamburg, 1993, 61).

223 **"I lost $180,000. . .** Massaquoi, Hans J., "Fats Domino: The Man Who Gambled Away $2 Million Without Going Broke," *Ebony*, 5-74, 157.

CHAPTER 15: "RED SAILS IN THE SUNSET"

225 **"We'd always liked. . .** Giuliano, Geoffrey and Brenda, *Lost Beatles Interviews*, Virgin, London, 1994, 48.

225 **"Fats Domino Breaks. . .** "Fats Domino Breaks with NAACP Policy," *Louisiana Weekly*, 1-12-63, 1; "Losing Moola, Fats Domino Okays Jim Crow Gigs," *Jet*, 1-10-63, 61.

225 **Civil Rights workers. . .** Carawan, Guy, and Candie (eds.), *Sing for Freedom: The Story of the Civil Rights Movement Through Its Songs*, Sing Out, Bethlehem, PA, 1990, 42, 48, 53, 88.

225 **SNCC (Student Nonviolent. . .** Pool, Rosey E. (ed.), *Beyond the Blues: New Poems by American Negroes*, Hand and Flower Press: Lympno, Kent, England, 1960, 44–45.

226 **"There's plenty of. . .** Correspondence from Julian Bond, 3-21-02.

226 **In order to. . .** "Fats Domino Denies Report of NAACP Split," *Jet*, 1-24-63, 65.

226 **Domino told the. . .** Morial also said that he planned to have Domino play a benefit for the local NAACP. It is uncertain as whether Fats held such a concert or not, though he did soon play at least one NAACP benefit in Salisbury, Maryland, for the "Freedom Fund Dance" of the Wicomico County NAACP on April 2, 1963 (Ibid.; concert poster reproduced in *Fats Domino—The Very Best of Fats Domino, 1963–1965*, Varese-Sarabande, 2004).

226 **A denial of. . .** "'Fats' Domino Denies Remarks About NAACP," *Louisiana Weekly*, 1-19-63, 1, 7.

227 **There was disturbing. . .** Johnny and Bernice Larson Webb, *Born to Be a Loser*, 299–300;"Blues Singer's Hits Tell Story of Own Death," *Jet*, 4-4-63, 61.

227 **The April 6, 1963. . .** "ABC-Para Signs Fats Domino," *Billboard*, 4-6-63, 1.

227 **His defection from. . .** Zhito, Lee, "Decca $1 Mil. Gets Rick," *Billboard*, 1-12-63, 1, 8; Rolontz, Bob, "Bids for Young Talent Soar High: Offers Often Hit $50,000," *Billboard*, 1-26-63, 1. Fate soon added injury to the great blows Chudd suffered with the loss of both Ricky Nelson and Domino. Another of Imperial's stars, twenty-four-year-old drummer Sandy Nelson, was riding his motorcycle home from a meeting with Chudd on April 22, 1963, when he ran under a school bus loaded with children (including thirteen-year-old future blues star Bonnie Raitt). Nelson's leg, crushed by the rear wheel of the bus, would be amputated above the knee (Fein, Art, *The L.A. Musical History Tour (Second Edition)*, 2-13-61, Los Angeles, 1998, 92). To scare his adolescent sons away from motorcycles, Chudd took them to the hospital to view Nelson's stump (author interviews: Lew Chudd, Andy Chudd).

227 **Fats had intended. . .** Embree, Jerry, interview with Fats Domino, 1999.

228 **Domino traveled to. . .** "A 1st for Fats: He Makes a Disk in Nashville," *Billboard*, 5-4-63; "The Domino-Sound Bows in Nashville," *Cash Box*, 5-4-63; Ward, Rick, *Fats Domino— Here Comes Fats Domino*, ABC-Paramount Records, 1963. The headline of the *Billboard* story was inaccurate, as Domino had recorded in Nashville in 1952.

228 **In August, Lew. . .** Zhito, Lee, "Liberty Records Buying Imperial Label, Pub Firm," *Billboard*, 8-24-63, 1, 12.

230 **When asked how. . .** Blakely, Norman, "Fats Domino Interview."

230 **Downing, who considered. . .** Cajiao, Trevor, "Oh Babe: An Interview with Big Al Downing, Part 2," *Now Dig This*, 1-87, 24.

230 **On January 19. . .** (author interview: Michael Vice); Vice, Michael, notes on Domino concert, 1-64.

231 **A reporter present. . .** "Famed Rock 'n' Roller Says He Lost 70G's in Las Vegas," *Carolina Times*, 2-1-64.

232 **Reflecting his fall. . .** Poster for Supersonic Attractions' Spring 1964 Show of Stars, Richmond, Virginia, 4-5-64; Jackie "Moms" Mabley Show program book, circa 1964; Contract Carpenter Field House, University of Delaware, 3-12-64.

233 **Fats had had. . .** WDSU-TV, New Orleans, news report, 6-7-63.

233 **The Beatles were. . .** Giuliano, Geoffrey, and Brenda, *Lost Beatles Interviews*, Virgin Books, London, 1994, 48; Slim, Almost, "The Beatles Visit New Orleans," *Wavelength*, 8-83, 13–14; Kane, Larry, *Ticket to Ride: Inside The Beatles' 1964 Tour That Changed the World*, Running Press, Philadelphia, 2003, 125–127; Jones, Max, "Fat Man from New Orleans," *Melody Maker*, 4-67.

233 **Even Eric Clapton's. . .** Forte, Dan, "Eric Clapton: The Eric Clapton Story," *Guitar Player* Online Archives: Eric Clapton, http://www.archive.guitarplayer.com, 7-85.

234 **Musicologist Charles Keil. . .** Keil, Charles, *Urban Blues*, University of Chicago Press, Chicago, 1966, 45–46.

235 **Producer Tom Wilson. . .** Heylin, Clinton, *Bob Dylan: Behind the Shades Revisited*, Perennial Currents, New York, 2003, 173.

235 **Still, in September. . .** http://www.expectingrain.com/dok/olof/1960-69/1965.txt. Ironically, three years later the Newport Folk Festival apparently considered Domino's brand of rock 'n' roll worthy of a folk audience, as Jim Rooney of the Festival invited him to appear for the standard fee of $50 a day, plus accommodations and travel expenses, an offer that Domino declined. Warner Brothers Records Memo, Andy Wickham to Mo Ostin, 12-4-68.

237 **During "I Left. . .** Much better than "I Left My Heart in San Francisco" was the B-side, an incorrectly titled cover of Guitar Slim's "Well, I Done Got Over It" arranged by Roy Montrell. Dave Bartholomew later produced a session in New Orleans including

"What's That You Got," a rewrite of Chris Kenner's "Something You Got" featuring a slurring sax solo by jazzman Nat Perrilliat.

237 **But all was.** . . Letters from American Federation of Musicians to Antoine Domino, dated 8-26-65 to 5-31-66 in American Federation of Musicians file, Hogan Jazz Archives, Tulane University, New Orleans; (author interview: Ernest McLean).

238 **A photo later.** . . "The Week's Best Photos," *Jet*, 9–66.

238 **Harrison Verrett, who.** . . Domino presented Verrett with a Cadillac after the traumatic bus accident. The car, which was lost in Hurricane Betsy, provided an insurance settlement accounting for the sum of $1,615.90 in Verrett's bank account at his death (Civil District Court for the Parish of Orleans State of Louisiana, Division A, Docket 1, No. 441-398, *The Succession of Harrison Verrett*, 10-26-65).

238 *Southland U.S.A was.* . . Griffiths, David, *Record Mirror*, 4-67.

238 **On Wednesday morning.** . . "Deaths," *Times-Picayune*, 4-29-66, 1:2; "Entry Attempt Proves Fatal," *Times-Picayune*, 4-28-66, 1:4.

239 **In August, Domino.** . . "House Reviews: Village Gate, New York," *Variety*, 8-10-66; "Fats Domino the Greatest in New York Club Date," *Billboard*, 8-13-66, 7 (author interview: Herbert Hardesty).

239 **On December 5.** . . Superior Court of the State of California for the County of Los Angeles, D 587068, *Theron Domino, Etc. Et. Al., vs. Antoine Domino*, Declaration of Morton Minikes, 12-5-66.

240 **Just as the.** . . Goodman, Pete, "Fats Domino: Heavyweight of Beat," *Beat Instrumental*, 8-66,15; Munoz, Victor, "A Beatles Index," http://aristoteles.ciencias.uchile.cl/~vmunoz/dates/dec31.html.

CHAPTER 16: "ONE FOR THE HIGHWAY"

241 **"With the press.** . . Guralnick, Peter, *Careless Love: The Unmaking of Elvis Presley*, Little, Brown and Co., Boston, 1999, 353.

241 **"An egg flew.** . . The composite description of Domino's Saville Theatre shows is gleaned from the following: Gibb, Barry, Robin and Maurice as told to David Leaf, *Bee Gees: The Authorized Biography*, Delilah/Delta, New York, 1979, 53–54; Welch, Chris, "Fats Has 'Em Jiving in the Aisles," *Melody Maker*, 4-1-67, 4; Broven, John, *Rhythm and Blues in New Orleans*, 183–184; Cohn, Nik, *Rock from the Beginning*, Pocket Books, New York, 1969, 23–24; Clare, Michael, "'Fats' Domino Stands 'Em on Their Feet in London," *Billboard*, 4-8-67, 24; Papard, Shakin' Tony, "Rock 'n' Roll at the Saville," *Bop Cat*, May/June 67; Preston, Peter, "Fats Domino Shows I Have Seen"; Cook, John, "Fats Domino in Manchester," 4-67.

242 **"It was all.** . . Ironside, Virginia, "Oh Fats I Could Hug You!" *The Daily Mail*, 3-67.

242 **Even a blue-nosed.** . . Oliver, Paul, "Fats Domino at the Saville," *Jazz Monthly*, 5-67, 11–12.

242 **Struggling for.** . . "Fats Triumphs at Saville," *Record Mirror*, 3 67.

242 **Erudite British writers.** . . Pioneering English blues scholar Mike Vernon interviewed nearly all of Domino's band members, publishing short biographies on Clarence Brown, Wallace Davenport, Clarence Ford, Buddy Hagans, Roy Montrell, and Nat Perrilliat from April to July 1967 in *Jazz Monthly*; also see Abbey, John E., and Peter Trickey, "Fats Domino and His Band," *Home of the Blues*, 6-67; Illingworth, David, "Jazz in Britain," *Jazz Journal*, 5-67.

243 **Brian Epstein's death.** . . Van Der Gun, Jos, "Talking With: Fats Domino," *Rockville-International*, 10-72.

243 **Domino and Bartholomew.** . . The information on these recordings, which, for the most part, would not be released in the United States until 2005, is previously unpublished. A double session on September 1, 1967, stretched into the next day and produced "I'm Going

Across That River," "Big Mouth," "It's a Sin to Tell a Lie," and "I'm Going to Help a Friend." It included Bartholomew, James Booker, George French, Clarence Brown, Roy Montrell, Herbert Hardesty, and Edward Frank. On two songs recorded—"Guitar Man" and "Funky Broadway"—Domino apparently did not overdub his vocals. The session on September 2 for "Work My Way Up Steady," "Another Mule," "Lawdy Miss Clawdy," and "Help Me" included the same musicians except Domino is listed and Bartholomew and Frank are not. A session on September 13 that included "[Wait 'Til] It Happens to You," and "When You're Smiling" (along with the unreleased backing tracks for "Always" and "One Rose") included Bartholomew, Perrilliat, French, and Frank, along with Meyer Kennedy (alto), Ralph Johnson (tenor), Wellington McKissick (baritone), Lawrence Cotton (piano), Frank E. West (guitar), and Albert Miller (drums). The session information on "The Lady in Black" and "These Shoes" is not known (American Federation of Musicians File, Hogan Jazz Archives, Tulane University, New Orleans). "Work My Way Up Steady," backed with the Willie Tee–styled "Lady in Black," was featured in a full-page ad showing Domino in a tuxedo in *Record World* on 12-9-67.

243 **Fats had enjoyed. . .** Greene, Danny, "Fats Domino Brings Back Pop Music History at Hirt's," *New Orleans States-Item*, 3-12-68.

244 **Richard Perry, a. . .** Wickham, Andrew, "Phenomenal Fats Domino Is Comin' Back," *Eye*, 10-68, 37, 77.

244 **Domino was apparently. . .** Reising, Russell (ed.), *Every Sound There Is*, Ashgate, New York, 2002, 36.

244 **In fact, McCartney. . .** Miles, Barry, *Paul McCartney: Many Years from Now*, Henry Holt, New York, 1997, 449.

244 **Perry recorded the. . .** Hopkins, Jerry, "Reviews: Tiny Tim—*God Bless Tiny Tim*," *Rolling Stone*, 4-19-69; "Richard Perry," Tobler, John, *Other*, 1982 (at http://www.rocksbackpages.com); Richard Perry interview from BBC files.

244 **Domino's "Lady Madonna". . .** A Western Union Telegram from Stanley Chaisson, a Warner Brothers representative in New Orleans, reported on July 24, 1968, "Lady Madonna Fats Domino WTIX Top Pick Hit Responds in One Day Play Looks Like a Winner Says Buzz Bennett P D [program director] WTIX." Besides many others, the record appeared in the following hit lists: "KHJ's Boss 30 Records in Southern California," Los Angeles, 8-23-68; "KYA Radio 1260 Official San Francisco Music Survey," San Francisco, 8-19-68; "WKNR Music Guide," Detroit, 8-29-68; "CKOC 1150 Instant Sound Survey," Hamilton, Ontario, Canada, 8-22-68.

244 **Jann Wenner of. . .** Wenner, Jann, "Review: Fats Is Back," *The Rolling Stone Record Review*, Pocket Books, New York, 1971, 40–42.

244 **Wenner's enthusiasm even. . .** Wenner, Jann, "Phil Spector," Editors of *Rolling Stone* (eds.), *The Rolling Stone Interviews*, Paperback Library, New York, 1971, 272–273.

244 **Years later Fats. . .** Mick Farren (with Chalkie Davies), "Diamonds and Mr. Domino," *New Musical Express*, 4-30-77, 17.

245 **Curiously, the next. . .** Dowlding, William J., *Beatlesongs*, Fireside, Palmer, AK, 1989, 241.

245 **One night at. . .** Pat Boone interview by Charles Grodin, *Charles Grodin*, CNBC, 7-11-95.

245 **In February 1969. . .** Invitation to birthday party celebrating the grand opening of "Antoine 'Fats' Domino's New Orleans Style Restaurants, Inc.," 2-26-69; "Grand Opening, Saturday April 15th: Fats Domino's 'New Orleans Style' Fried Chicken," advertisement in *Times-Picayune*, 3-15-69; "Fans See Fats; Sample Fowl," *Times-Picayune*, 3-16-69; Emery, Joe, "Dig Me," *Louisiana Weekly*, 7-4-70.

245 **One show in. . .** Johnson, Pete, "Fats Domino at Anaheim Center," *Los Angeles Times*, 6-16-69, IV:20.

246 **Dressed in black. . .** Matthews, Bunny, "Fats Keeps Cooking in New Orleans," *Times-Picayune, Lagniappe*, 4-8-83; Jones, Wayne, "Wayne Jones Talks with Fats Domino."

246 **On July 31. . .** Guralnick, Peter, *Careless Love: The Unmaking of Elvis Presley.*

247 **On Friday. . .** Kirby, Fred, "Ike and Tina Turner, Fats Domino, Mongo Santamaria," *Billboard*, 1-24-70; Jahn, Mike, "Early Rock Sung by Fats Domino," *New York Times*, 1-11-70.

247 **Domino's current trumpet. . .** Ridley, Andy, "Teddy Riley," *Wavelength*, 7-88, 23.

248 **The band's latest. . .** "Crash Kills Man at Intersection," *Natchitoches Times*, 5-28, 1970, 1,3; "Bandsman Killed at Natchitoches," *Alexandria Daily Town Talk*, 5-27-70, 1.

249 **Jimmy's death didn't. . .** "Kneeling in Prayer," *Louisiana Weekly*, 6-6-70, 1.

CHAPTER 17: "NEW ORLEANS AIN'T THE SAME"

251 **"People tried. . .** Pepper, Dr., "What Do You Have for Breakfast, Fats?" *Juke*, 10-22-75, 20.

251 **Incredibly, a week. . .** "House Reviews: Flamingo, Las Vegas (Driftwood Lounge)," *Variety*, 6-17-70, 52.

251 **Fats was still. . .** Fats Domino Itinerary, June to December 1970, 5-15-70; "Where Are They Now?" *Newsweek*, 10- 19, 1970, 24; "You Can't Be ON All the Time," article of unknown source, circa 1970.

251 **In fact, relations. . .** Letter from Maria Tynes to Mo Ostin, Reprise Records, 4-16-70.

252 **Fats relied more. . .** Vernon, Mike, "Domino Men: Roy Montrell," *Jazz Monthly*, 6-67; Broven, John, "All for One: Harold Battiste," Blues Unlimited 146, 1984, 11 (author interviews: Roger Lewis, Joseph "Smokey" Johnson, David Douglas, Thomas "Mac" Johnson).

253 **Allen actually used. . .** (author interview: Raymond Allen); "Bodyguard Fires Fats for 'Fats'," uncredited newspaper clipping, 10-11-71.

254 **As usual, the. . .** Battiste, Harold, New Orleans Heritage: *Jazz: 1956–1966,* Opus 43 Records, Los Angeles, 1976, 20–21; Broven, John, "All for One: Harold Battiste," 11.

255 **While Domino was. . .** Letter from Warner Bros. Records Inc. (unsigned) to Antoine Domino, 12-4-70.

255 **To fill the void. . .** In January 1970, Charles Levy sent the 7-1/2-inch master tape of Domino's Broadmoor recordings to Reprise with the comment "I feel quite certain that it will not be a loser, expecially [*sic*] in the foreign market" (letter from Charles A. Levy, Jr., to Morris Ostin, Warner Bros.–Seven Arts Records, Inc., 1-21-70). Mo Ostin bought the tape for $5,000 the next month (letter from Morris Ostin, Warner Bros.–Seven Arts Records to Charles Levy, 2-20-70). In January 1971 the *Fats* album was canceled in a memo, which read, "It has been decided that the Fats Domino album scheduled for a February release will now be on an 'international only' basis" (memo from Don Schmitzerle to "Those Concerned," 1-13-71).

255 **Charles Levy wrote. . .** Letter from Charles A. Levy, Jr., to Don Schmitzerle, Warner Bros. Records, Inc., 3-15-71. Levy stated that he and Domino had tried to work with Richard Perry, who was unavailable on two occasions when Domino took two weeks off. He inadvertently called producer Joe Wissert "Mr. Wizard," in an ironic commentary on who might be necessary to put Domino back in the top 100.

256 **By August 1971. . .** Memo from Mo Ostin to Don Schmitzerle re: Fats Domino, 8-27-71; letter from Edward Mist, Warner Bros. Records, Inc., to Antoine Domino, 12-7-71.

257 **Accordingly, Motown signed. . .** (author interview: Andy Chudd); Van Der Gun, Jos, "Talking With: Fats Domino," *Rockville-International*, 10-72; unexecuted and undated contract, Motown Record Corporation with Antoine Domino, Jr.

257 **Late in 1972. . .** Newlin, Jon, "Fats Domino Comes Home," *Figaro*, 11-11-72, 2, 4.

258 **Domino's fine alto. . .** In 1969, Wendell Duconge, a.k.a. Emmett Fortner, pled guilty to theft of $463.00 in unemployment benefits and received a $300 fine (or a three-month local jail sentence) and a two-year suspended prison sentence with probation (State of Louisiana, Parish Of Orleans, Arrest No. 132745, 11-26, 1969; City of New Orleans, State of Louisiana, Certificate of Death No. 157720008491, Fortner, Emmett, 1-9-73).

258 **Two months later. . .** (Billy Vera, Dave Bartholomew). "C.J. Coleman's Services Friday," *Times-Picayune*, 2-21-73.

259 **In April 1973.** . . Broven, John, "Behind the Sun Again," *Blues Unlimited*, 6-73, 5–6.

260 **Still, most fans.** . . "Caught in the Act: Fats the Way . . . ," Williams, Richard, *Melody Maker*, 5-5-73, 46.

260 **Glam rockers Elton.** . . Sanford, Christopher, *Bowie: Loving the Alien*, DaCapo, New York, 1996, 19.

260 **In August 1973.** . . *American Graffiti* and another film that year, Martin Scorsese's *Mean Streets*, popularized the use of rock 'n' roll in movie soundtracks, which had been pioneered in Kenneth Anger's *Scorpio Rising* (1964) and Scorsese's *Who's That Knocking at My Door* (1968). Scorsese had been inspired to use rock 'n' roll in the latter after seeing two drunks fighting while he heard Domino's "When My Dreamboat Comes Home" in his tenement neighborhood (Martin Scorsese, *Scorsese on Scorsese*, ed. Ian Christie, David Thompson, Faber and Faber, New York, 2004, 28).

261 **In the meantime.** . . "Random Notes," *Rolling Stone*, 1-17-74, 22.

261 **An *Ebony* feature.** . . Massaquoi, Hans J., "Fats Domino: The Man Who Gambled Away $2 Million Without Going Broke," *Ebony*, 5-74, 155–158, 160.

263 **Domino played venues.** . . Pepper, Dr., "What Do You Have for Breakfast, Fats?"

263 **While on tour.** . . Jones, Max, "Fats Life!," *Melody Maker*, 4-3, 1976, 8–9.

264 **Domino and Bartholomew.** . . (author interview Rip Roberts, Jr.); WNNR Playlist circa 6-76; Fats Domino interview, WNOE Radio, New Orleans, 12-26-76.

264 **In December 1976.** . . Dodds, Richard, "Fats Domino Keeps '50s Alive," *Times-Picayune*, 12-19-76, 2:10–11.

266 **At a Richard.** . . Plecas, Bodie, "Fats Domino: He Doesn't Understand That He's a Legend," *Morning Advocate* (Baton Rouge), 2-9-79, Fun Section: 4; Palmer, Robert, "Rock: Nader's Show at Garden," *New York Times*, 10-16-77.

267 **Still, the most.** . . (Liner notes) *Fleetwood Mac—The Chain*, Warner Bros. Records, Hollywood, 1992; Lindsey Buckingham sang "Blue Monday" in an unreleased outtake for the 1982 album *Mirage*.

267 **Domino, the past.** . . Hance, Bill, "Wax Fax," *Nashville Banner*, 4-6-79, 19.

CHAPTER 18: "WHISKEY HEAVEN"

271 **"Retire? Are you.** . . Stafford, John, "I Call It Music with a Good Beat: A Chat with Fats Domino," *Now Dig This*, 5-86, 19.

271 **Paul McCartney, who.** . . Ingham, Chris, "100 Greatest Singles," *Mojo*, 8-97.

271 **The cover versions.** . . Jonathan Richman performed "Hello Josephine" and "Let the Four Winds Blow"; Alex Chilton recorded "Sick and Tired." Richard Hell waxed "I Lived My Life" (originally recorded by Tommy Ridgley as "I Live My Life"), a ballad with a punky attitude. Las Vegas, Viva, "A Whore Like the Rest: Rock Critic Richard Meltzer Repeats Himself," *Exotic*, 3-01. "King Ink," which Cave recorded with The Birthday Party in 1981, became one of his best-known early songs and titled two books (*King Ink* and *King Ink II*) of Cave's lyrics and poetry. Stokes, Allison, "Mad Old Men; They're Still Calling It Madness," *Liverpool Echo*, 12-14-02.

272 **One night in.** . . Boyd, Richard, "Jazz Fest '80: Rockin' 'n' Rollin' on the River," *Times-Picayune*, 4-25-80; *The States-Item*, 4-28-80.

273 **On June 5.** . . Hagans, Buddy, City of New Orleans, State of Louisiana Certificate of Death No. 11915646, 6-12-80.

275 **The city became.** . . "Great Getaways," *Times-Picayune*, 5-1-94.

276 **"What do you.** . . Esolen, Gary, "Standpoint: Fats Domino in His Prime," Gambit, 3-20-82.

276 **Another Riverboat show.** . . Harris, Paul "Hey! Fat Man," *Blues & Rhythm: The Gospel Truth*, 1-92, 8.

277 **Later that month.** . . (author interview: Bill Boskent).

277 **After a November. . .** (author interview: Quint Davis).
277 **He turned down. . .** (author interviews: Fats Domino, Dick Clark).
278 **In July 1985. . .** Woodford, Chris, "The Fabulous Fat Man," *Now Dig This*, 8-85, 30–31.
281 **"Mr. Domino plays. . .** Pareles, Jon, "'Fats Domino and Friends' on Cable," *New York Times*, 7-31-86, C-22.
281 **"No matter how. . .** Jarvis, Jeff, "Picks & Pans: Tube," *People*, 7-28-86, 7.
281 **Ironically reviving the. . .** (author interviews: Thomas "Mac" Johnson, Jimmy Moliere).
281 **"If Friday night's. . .** Everett, Todd, *Los Angeles Herald-Examiner*, 8-31-86.
283 **In a splendorous. . .** "A Whole Lotta Shakin' Goes on As Rock 'n' Roll's Oldies but Goodies Make It to the New Hall of Fame," *People*, 2-10-86, 52.

CHAPTER 19: "LOVE YOU 'TIL THE DAY I DIE"

285 **His [Domino's] rich. . .** National Medal of the Arts Ceremony, 11-05-08, CSPAN video.
285 **A parade strutted. . .** Coleman, Rick, "Walter Kimball [*sic*], #1 on the Second Line, Dies," *Wavelength*, 5-88, 6.
285 **Thankfully, at the. . .** Berry, Jason, "The Fat Man Turns Sixty," *New Orleans Magazine*, 5-88, 6.
286 **Jon Pareles wrote. . .** Pareles, Jon, "New Orleans House Party: Fats Domino Returns," *New York Times*, 8-3-88.
286 **At the Palaeur. . .** Dave Edmunds website.
286 **Wearing a pin. . .** Hannusch, Jeff, "Fats Finds a Thrill at the Fest," *Times-Picayune*, 5-6-89, E:1.
287 **Keith Richards suggested. . .** *Rock and Roll Report*, 9-15-03, http://www.rockandroll report.com.
287 **Driving down the. . .** (author interviews: Dennis "Big Chief" Alley, Herbert Hardesty).
287 **His former warm-up. . .** Jones died on December 17, 1989. Coleman, Rick, "Little Sonny Jones [1931–1989]," *Wavelength*, 1-90, 6.
287 **That spring, Representative. . .** "Rep. Haik Fails on First Try on Dirty Record Measure," Associated Press story, 6-16-90.
288 **"Forty two years. . .** Watrous, Peter, "Fats Domino's Old Tricks Made New," *New York Times*, 11-9-91, Entertainment: 13.
288 **His last remaining. . .** "Deaths: Joseph Domino," *Times-Picayune*, 10-30-91; "Mass of Christian Burial for Joseph 'Te Nag' Domino," 11-2-91.
288 **In March. . .** Bourgoyne, J. E. (compiler), "Domino Royalties Raised," *Times-Picayune*, 3-18-92, A-17.
288 **That income had. . .** Early movie uses of Domino's songs included "I'm Gonna Be a Wheel Someday" in *Return to Macon Country* (1975), "The Fat Man" (performed by Robbie Robertson) in *Carny* (1980), "I'm Walkin'" in *The Blues Brothers* (1980), and "Whole Lotta Loving" in *Diner* (1982). "Ain't That a Shame" evoked youthful angst in *American Graffiti* (1973), *Mischief* (1985) (which also included "I'm in Love Again"), *October Sky* (1999), *Hearts in Atlantis* (2001), and a remake of *Shake, Rattle and Rock!* (1994) featuring the first leading role by Renée Zellweger. "Blue Monday" (as recorded by Bob Seger) was heard in Patrick Swayze's *Roadhouse* (1989). Domino's original version in *This Boy's Life* (1993), starring Robert De Niro, became the rebellious theme song of the young boy in the film played by Leonardo DiCaprio. "Blueberry Hill" titled both a low-budget fifties coming-of-age American movie in 1988 and a Belgian film on the same subject the following year. Domino's "Blueberry Hill" was also heard in *First Born* (1984), *Heavy Petting* (1988), and *Twelve Monkeys* (1996). Besides *My Blue Heaven*, three other Steve Martin films featured Domino songs—*L.A. Story* (1991), *Mixed Nuts* (1994), and *Father of the Bride, Part II* (1995) featured "Ain't That a Shame," "I'll Be Home for Christmas," and "When the Saints Go Marching In," respectively. "I'm Ready" was heard in *Gremlins 2* (1990) and

(performed by Taj Mahal) in *Little Big League* (1999). *Scandal* (1989) included Domino's version of "Jambalaya." *A Rage in Harlem* (1991) featured both "I'm in Love Again" and "Bo Weevil," which was also heard in *Circle of Friends* (1995). *White Squall* (1996) had both "Be My Guest" and "I Want to Walk You Home."

289 **That same year. . .** Wexler, Jerry, and David Ritz, *Rhythm and the Blues*, 96.

290 **Rock 'n' roll adversary. . .** Stan Freberg joked about the unlikelihood of Ella Fitzgerald singing "the Fats Domino songbook" in "The Old Payola Roll Blues" in 1960.

290 **"Purists may shudder. . .** Irvin, Jim, *Born to Rock 'n' Roll* souvenir programme, Flying Music Company, London, 1995, 2.

291 **New Orleans music. . .** Wycoff, Geraldine, "New Orleans Magazine's Fourth Annual Jazz All-Stars," *New Orleans Magazine*, 4-93.

292 **In 1996, four. . .** AMOA Top 40 Jukebox Singles of All Time 1996 Update.

292 **New Orleans music. . .** Matthews, Bunny, "Fats Keeps Cooking in New Orleans," *Times-Picayune/States-Item*, Lagniappe, 4-8-83.

294 **On Sunday, May 3. . .** "Deaths: R&B, Jazz Sax Player Fred Kemp Dies at 55," *Times-Picayune*, 6-9-97.

294 **"Tenor man Herb. . .** Spera, Keith, "Spera's Spin," *Times-Picayune*, 5-4-97.

295 **"Lew Chudd sold. . .** Spera, Keith, "Songwriters' Hall of Fame Gets a Little New Orleans Flavor," *Times-Picayune*, 6-19-98, Lagniappe, 6.

295 **Under a tent. . .** National Medal of the Arts ceremony, 11-05-98, C-SPAN video.

296 **Back at home. . .** McConnaughey, Janet, "Fats Domino to Receive Arts Medal," *The Advocate*, 10-29-98.

297 **Though "The Fat. . .** "Backtrack: Modern Rockers Pick Their Top Ten Hits of the Fifties," *Rolling Stone*, 4-19-90, 128; Fricke, David, "The Music Q&A: Rock's Dark Prince Sets Edgar Allan Poe to Music—But He's Still Jonesing for Fats Domino," *Rolling Stone*, 3-6-03, 29.

298 **From December 1949. . .** *Sunday Morning with Charles Kuralt*, CBS-TV, 9-23-84.

298 **Less than a. . .** Pearlman, Nina, "Crow and Friends Take NYC," http://www.rollingstone.com, 5-1-01.

298 **One English fan. . .** Carter, Howard, "Fabulous Fats," NOLA Live Jazzfest Forum, 5-13-01; Spera, Keith, "Spera's Spins," *The Times-Picayune*, 5-11-01; Hernandez, Raoul, "Live Shots," *The Austin Chronicle*, 5-18-01.

301 **"People don't know. . .** Coleman, Rick, "Fats Is Back!" *Rolling Stone*, 12-12-93, 17.

301 **"I don't think. . .** Pitts. Byron, Interview with Fats Domino for CBS Evening News, Channel 4 "Eyewitness news," WWL-TV, New Orleans, 2-25-06.

Bibliography

These works were key sources for the material used in this book; other sources are cited in the Notes.

Adams, Deanna R., *Rock 'n' Roll and the Cleveland Connection*, Kent State University Press, Kent, OH, 2002.

Allan, Johnnie and Bernice Larson Webb, *Born to Be a Loser: The Jimmy Donley Story*, Jadfel, Lafayette, LA, 1992.

Baker, Liva, *The Second Battle of New Orleans: The Hundred-Year Struggle to Integrate the Schools*, HarperCollins, New York, 1996.

Bashe, Philip, *Teenage Idol, Travelin' Man: The Complete Biography of Rick Nelson*, Hyperion, New York, 1992.

Beacham, Frank, *Whitewash: A Southern Journey Through Music, Mayhem & Murder*, Frank Beacham, New York, 2002.

Beatles, The, *The Beatles Anthology*, Chronicle, San Francisco, 2000.

Bernard, Shane K., *Swamp Pop: Cajun and Creole Rhythm and Blues*, University of Mississippi Press, Jackson, 1996.

Bernstein, Sid and Arthur Aaron, *Not Just the Beatles. . .* , Jacques & Flusster, Teaneck, NJ, 2000.

Berry, Chuck, *The Autobiography*, Harmony, New York, 1987.

Berry, Jason (et al.), *Up from the Cradle of Jazz: New Orleans Music Since World War II*, University of Georgia Press, Athens, 1986.

Bertrand, Michael, *Race, Rock, and Elvis*, University of Illinois Press, Urbana, IL, 2000.

Bodin, Ron, *Voodoo: Past and Present*, The Center for Louisiana Studies, University of Southwestern Louisiana, Lafayette, LA, 1990.

Broven, John, *Rhythm & Blues in New Orleans*, Pelican, Gretna, LA, 1974.

Broven, John, *South to Louisiana: The Music of the Cajun Bayous*, Pelican, Gretna, LA, 1983.

Cable, George W., *The Dance in Place Congo & Creole Slave Songs*, Faruk von Turk, New Orleans, 1974.

Chapple, Steve and Reebee Garofalo, *Rock 'n' Roll Is Here to Pay: The History and Politics of the Music Industry*, Nelson-Hall, New York, 1977.

Chase, John Churchill, *Frenchmen, Desire, Good Children and Other Streets of New Orleans*, Collier, New York, 1979.

Clark, Dick with Fred Bronson, *Dick Clark's American Bandstand*, Collins, New York, 1997.

Clark, Dick and Richard Robinson, *Rock, Roll & Remember*, Popular Library, New York, 1976.

Clayton, Rose and Dick Heard, *Elvis Up Close in the Words of Those Who Knew Him Best*, Turner, Atlanta, 1994.

Cleaver, Eldridge, *Soul on Ice*, Delta, New York, 1968.

Cohn, Nik, *AWopBopaLooBopaLopBamBoom*, Paladin, London, 1969.

Collier-Thomas, Bettye and V. P. Franklin, *My Soul Is a Witness: A Chronology of the Civil Rights Era 1954–1965*, Henry Holt, New York, 1999.

Cotton, Lee, *Shake Rattle & Roll: The Golden Age of American Rock 'n' Roll: Volume I, 1952–1955*, Popular Culture, Ink., Ann Arbor, MI, 1989.

Cotton, Lee, *Reelin' & Rockin': The Golden Age of American Rock 'n' Roll: Volume II, 1956–1959*, Popular Culture, Ink., Ann Arbor, MI, 1995.

Cotton, Lee, *Twist & Shout: The Golden Age of American Rock 'n' Roll Volume III: 1960–1963*, High Sierra, Sacramento, CA, 2002.

Daniel, Clifton (ed.), *Chronicle of the 20th Century*, Chronicle, Mount Kisco, NY, 1987.

Dannen, Fredric, *Hit Men: Power Brokers and Fast Money Inside the Music Business*, Times Books, New York, 1990.

Davis, Stephen, *Bob Marley: The Biography*, A. Barker, London, 1983.

Dawson, Jim, *Rock Around the Clock: The Record That Started the Rock Revolution!*, Backbeat, San Francisco, 2005.

Dawson, Jim and Spencer Leigh, *Memories of Buddy Holly*, Big Nickel, Milford, NH, 1996.

Dawson, Jim and Steve Propes, *What Was the First Rock 'n' Roll Record*, Faber & Faber, Boston, 1992.

Dr. John (Mac Rebennack) with Jack Rummel, *Under a Hoodoo Moon*, St. Martin's, New York, 1994.

Early, Gerald, *One Nation Under a Groove: Motown & American Culture*, Ecco, Hopewell, NJ, 1995.

Editors of Rolling Stone, *The Rolling Stone Interviews*, Paperback Library, New York, 1971.

Editors of Rolling Stone, *The Rolling Stone Interviews, Vol. II*, Warner Paperback Library, New York, 1973.

Editors of Rolling Stone, *Rock Almanac: The Chronicles of Rock & Roll*, Collier, New York, 1993.

Editors of Rolling Stone, *The Rolling Stone Interviews: The 1980s*, St. Martin's, New York, 1989.

Editors of Rolling Stone, *The Rolling Stone Record Review*, Pocket, New York, 1971.

Editors of Rolling Stone, *The Rolling Stone Record Review Volume II*, Pocket, New York, 1974.

Editors of Time-Life Books, *Rock & Roll Generation: Teen Life in the 50s*, Time-Life, Alexandria, VA, 1998.

Egerton, John, *Speak Now Against the Day: The Generation Before the Civil Rights Movement in the South*, University of North Carolina Press, Chapel Hill, 1995.

Ellison, Ralph, *Invisible Man*, Vintage, New York, 1952.

Ellison, Ralph, *Living with Music: Ralph Ellison's Jazz Writings*, Modern Library, New York, 2001.

Eliot, Marc, *Rockonomics: The Money Behind the Music*, Watts, New York, 1989.

Emerson, Ken, *Doo-dah! Stephen Foster and the Rise of American Popular Culture*, Simon & Schuster, New York, 1997.

Ennis, Philip H., *The Seventh Stream: The Emergence of Rocknroll in American Popular Music*, Wesleyan University Press, Middletown, NH, 1992.

Fairclough, Adam, *Race & Democracy: The Civil Rights Struggle in Louisiana 1915–1972*, University of Georgia Press, Athens, 1995.

Fein, Art, *The L.A. Musical History Tour: A Guide to the Rock and Roll Landmarks of Los Angeles*, 2.13.61., Los Angeles, 1998.

Flanagan, Bill, *Written in My Soul: Rock's Great Songwriters Talk About Creating Their Music*, Contemporary, Chicago, 1986.

Gambaccini, Paul, *Paul McCartney: In His Own Words*, Flash, New York, 1976.

Gart, Galen, *First Pressings: Rock History as Chronicled in Billboard Magazine, Volume One–Nine, 1948–1959*, Big Nickel, Milford, NH, 1986.

Gates, Henry Louis, *The Signifying Monkey: A Theory of African-American Literary Criticism*, Oxford University Press, New York, 1988.

Gibb, Barry, Robin and Maurice as told to David Leaf, *Bee Gees: The Authorized Biography*, Delilah, 1979.

Gillett, Charlie, *Making Tracks: Atlantic Records and the Growth of a Multi-Billion-Dollar Industry*, E. P. Dutton, New York, 1974.

Gillett, Charlie, *The Sound of the City: The Rise of Rock and Roll*, Outerbridge & Dienstfrey, New York, 1970.

Ginsberg, Allen, *First Blues—Rags, Ballads and Harmonium Songs, 1971–1974*, Full Court Press, New York, 1975.

Goldrosen, John and John Beecher, *Remembering Buddy: The Definitive Biography of Buddy Holly*, Penguin, New York, 1987.

Griggs, Bill, *Buddy Holly—Day-by-Day, Book Two* (January 1957 to December 1957), Rockin' 50s, Lubbock, TX, 1997.

Guralnick, Peter and Ernst Jorgensen, *Elvis: Day by Day*, Ballantine, New York, 1999.

Guralnick, Peter, *Careless Love: The Unmaking of Elvis Presley*, Little, Brown & Co., Boston, 1999.

Guralnick, Peter, *Dream Boogie: The Triumph of Sam Cooke*, Little, Brown & Co. Boston, 2005.

Guralnick, Peter, *Last Train to Memphis: The Rise of Elvis Presley*, Little, Brown & Co., Boston, 1994.

Haas, Edward F., *DeLesseps S. Morrison and the Image of Reform: New Orleans Politics, 1946–1961*, Louisiana State University Press, Baton Rouge, 1974.

Hannusch, Jeff, *I Hear You Knockin': The Sound of New Orleans Rhythm and Blues*, Swallow, Ville Platte, LA, 1985.

Hannusch, Jeff, *The Soul of New Orleans: A Legacy of Rhythm and Blues*, Swallow, Ville Platte, LA, 2001.

Harley, Sharon, *The Timetables of African-American History*, Touchstone, New York, 1996.

Harris, Sheldon, *Blues Who's Who: A Biographical Dictionary of Blues Singers*, Da Capo, New York, 1979.

Heylin, Clinton, *Bob Dylan: Behind the Shades Revisited*, Perennial Currents, New York, 2003.

Hirsch, Arnold R. and Joseph Logsdon (eds.), *Creole New Orleans: Race and Americanization*, Louisiana State University Press, Baton Rouge, 1992.

Holloway, Joseph E. (ed.), *Africanisms in American Culture*, Indiana University Press, Bloomington, 1991.

Jackson, John A., *American Bandstand: Dick Clark and the Making of a Rock 'n' Roll Empire*, Oxford University Press, New York, 1997.

Jackson, John A., *Big Beat Heat: Alan Freed and the Early Years of Rock & Roll*, Schirmer, New York, 1991.

Johnson, Jerah, *Congo Square in New Orleans*, University of New Orleans, New Orleans, 1995.

Kamin, Jonathan Liff, "Rhythm & Blues in White America: Rock and Roll As Acculturation and Perceptual Learning" (Ph.D. Dissertation in Sociology), Princeton University, Princeton, 1975, 63.

Katz, David, *Solid Foundation: An Oral History of Reggae*, Bloomsbury, London, 2003.

Keil, Charles, *Urban Blues*, University of Chicago Press, Chicago, 1966.

Kein, Sybil, *Creole: The History and Legacy of Louisiana's Free People of Color*, Louisiana State University Press, Baton Rouge, 2000.

Kmen, Henry A., *Music in New Orleans: The Formative Years, 1791-1841*, Louisiana State University Press, Baton Rouge, 1966.

Kurtz, Michael L. and Morgan D. Peoples, *Earl K. Long: The Saga of Uncle Earl and Louisiana Politics*, Louisiana State University Press, Baton Rouge.

Latrobe, Benjamin, *Impressions Respecting New Orleans*, Columbia University Press, Baton Rouge, 1966, 227.

Leadbitter, Mike, Leslie Fancourt, and Paul Pelletier, *Blues Records 1943–1970 "The Bible of the Blues" Volume Two L to Z*, Record Information Services, London, 1994.

Leadbitter, Mike and Neil Slaven, *Blues Records 1943 to 1970: A Selective Discography, Volume One A to K*, Record Information Services, London, 1987.

Liebling, A. J. *The Earl of New Orleans*, Louisiana State University Press, Baton Rouge, 1960.

Levine, Lawrence W., *Black Culture and Black Consciousness: Afro–American Folk Thought from Slavery to Freedom*, Oxford University Press, New York, 1977.

Lewis, Jerry Lee and Charles White, *Killer!*, Century, London, 1993.

Lewis, Myra with Murray Silver, *Great Balls of Fire*, Quill, New York, 1982.

Lydon, Michael, *Ray Charles: Man and Music*, Riverhead, New York, 1998.

Macdonald, Robert, John Kemp, Edward Hass (eds.), *Louisiana's Black Heritage*, New Orleans, 1979.

McGee, Mart Thomas, *The Rock and Roll Movie Encyclopedia of the 1950s*, McFarland and Co., Jefferson, NC, 1990.

Marsh, Dave, *The Heart of Rock & Soul: The 1001 Greatest Singles Ever Made*, Plume, New York, 1989.

Martin, Linda and Kerry Seagrave, *Anti-Rock: The Opposition to Rock 'n' Roll*, Da Capo, New York, 1988.

Miles, Barry, *Paul McCartney: Many Years from Now*, Henry Holt, New York, 1997.

Miller, Douglas T. and Marion Nowak, *The Fifties: The Way We Really Were*, Doubleday, New York, 1977.

Miller, James, *Flowers in the Dustbin: The Rise of Rock 'n' Roll 1947–1977*, Simon & Schuster, New York, 1999.

Miller, Jim (ed.), *The Rolling Stone Illustrated History of Rock 'n' Roll*, Random House, New York, 1976.

Neville, Art, Aaron Neville, Charles Neville, Cyrille Neville, and David Ritz, *The Brothers Neville*, Little, Brown, Boston, 2000.

Osbourne, Jerry, *Elvis Word for Word: What He Said, Exactly How He Said It. . .*, 1999.

Oubre, Elton J., *Vacherie: St. James Parish History and Genealogy* (2nd ed.), Oubre's Books, Thibodaux, LA, 2002.

Palmer, Robert, *Rock & Roll: An Unruly History*, Harmony, New York, 1995.

Palmer, Robert, *A Tale of Two Cities: Memphis Rock and New Orleans Roll*, Institute for Studies in American Music, New York, 1979.

Passman, Arnold, *The Deejays: How the Tribal Chieftains of Radio Got to Where They're At*, Macmillan, New York, 1971.

Pavlow, Big Al, *The R&B Book: A Disc-History of Rhythm & Blues*, Music House, Providence, 1983.

Payne, Jim, *Give the Drummers Some! The Great Drummers of R&B, Funk & Soul*, Manhattan Music, New York, 1996.

Pegg, Bruce, *Brown Eyed Handsome Man: The Life and Hard Times of Chuck Berry*, Routledge, New York, 2002.

Pollock, Bruce, *When Rock Was Young: A Nostalgic Review of the Top 40 Era*, Owl, New York, 1981.

Pomerance, Alan, *Repeal of the Blues: How Black Entertainers Influenced Civil Rights*, Citadel, Secaucus, NJ, 1988.

Pottker, Jan, *Born to Power: Heirs to America's Leading Businesses*, Barron's, New York, 1992.

Preston, Denis and Peter Preston, *The Fats Domino Story*, Stanford-Le-Hope, Essex, England, 1985.

Redd, Lawrence N., *Rock Is Rhythm and Blues (The Impact of Mass Media)*, Michigan State University Press, East Lansing, 1974.

Rees, Dafydd and Luke Crampton, *Rock Movers and Shakers*, Billboard, New York, 1991.

Rijff, Ger, *Long Lonely Highway: A 1950's Elvis Scrapbook*, Pierian Press, Ann Arbor, 1987.

Roach, Joseph, *Cities of the Dead: Circum-Atlantic Performance*, Columbia University Press, New York, 1996.

Roberts, John Storm, *Black Music of Two Worlds*, Praeger, New York, 1972.

Roberts, John Storm, *The Latin Tinge: The Impact of Latin American Music on the United States*, Oxford University Press, New York, 1999.

Robinson, Plater, *A House Divided: A Teaching Guide on the History of Civil Rights in Louisiana* (Second Edition), Southern Institute for Education and Research, Tulane University, New Orleans, 1995.

Rogers, Kim Lacy, *Righteous Lives: Narratives of the New Orleans Civil Rights Movement*, New York University Press, New York, 1993.

Rose, Al and Edward Souchon, *New Orleans Jazz: A Family Album*, Louisiana State University Press, Baton Rouge, 1984.

Roxon, Lillian, *Rock Encyclopedia*, Tempo, New York, 1971.

Ruppli, Michel, *The Aladdin/Imperial Labels: A Discography*, Greenwood, 1991.

Saxon, Lyle, *Gumbo Ya-Ya: A Collection of Louisiana Folk Tales*, Bonanza, New York, 1945.

Scherman, Tony, *Backbeat: Earl Palmer's Story*, Smithsonian, Washington, DC, 1999.

Schexnayder, R. V., *200 Years of Descendants in South Vacherie African American Family Lines, 1800's to Present*, SchexDumas Ancestry Series, Vol. V., Gretna, LA, 2003.

Schuller, Gunther, *Early Jazz: Its Roots and Musical Development*, Oxford University Press, New York, 1968.

Seay, David, *Mick Jagger: The Story Behind the Rolling Stone*, Birchlane Press, New York, 1993.

Selvin, Joel, *Ricky Nelson, Idol for a Generation*, Contemporary, Chicago, 1990.

Shannon, Bob and John Javna, *Behind the Hits: Inside Stories of Classic Pop and Rock and Roll*, Warner, New York, 1986.

Shaw, Arnold, *Honkers and Shouters: The Golden Years of Rhythm & Blues*, Macmillan, New York, 1978.

Shaw, Arnold, *The Rockin' '50s: The Decade That Transformed the Pop Music Scene*, Hawthorne, New York, 1974.

Sheff, David (G. Barry Golson, ed.), *The Playboy Interviews with John Lennon & Yoko Ono*, New York, 1981.

Shore, Michael, *The History of American Bandstand*, Ballantine, New York, 1985.

Silvester, Peter J., *A Left Hand Like God: A History of Boogie-Woogie Piano*, Da Capo, New York.

Smith, Joe, *Off the Record: An Oral History of Popular Music*, Warner, New York, 1988.

Smith, Michael P., *Mardi Gras Indians*, Pelican, Gretna, LA, 1994.

Smith, Michael, *New Orleans Jazz Fest: A Pictorial History*, Pelican, Gretna, LA, 1991.

Smith, Wes, *The Pied Pipers of Rock 'n' Roll*, Longstreet, Marietta, GA, 1989.

Spencer, Jon Michael, *Re-Searching Black Music*, University of Tennessee Press, Knoxville, 1996.

Spencer, Jon Michael, *The Rhythms of Black Folk: Race, Religion and Pan-Africanism*, Africa World Press, Trenton, NJ, 1995.

Suhor, Charles, *Jazz in New Orleans: The Postwar Years Through 1970*, Scarecrow, Lanham, MD, 2001.

Thrasher, Albert, *On to New Orleans! Louisiana's Heroic 1811 Slave Revolt*, Cypress, New Orleans, 1995.

Tisserand, Michael, *The Kingdom of Zydeco*, Arcade, New York, 1998.

Tosches, Nick, *Unsung Heroes of Rock 'n' Roll: The Birth of Rock 'n' Roll in the Dark and Wild Years Before Elvis*, Scribner's, New York, 1984.

Troiktsky, Artemy, *Back in the USSR: The True Story of Rock in Russia*, Faber and Faber, Boston, 1987.

Turner, Harry, *This Magic Moment: Musical Reflections of a Generation*, AGM Enterprises, Atlanta, 1994.

Ventura, Michael, *Shadow Dancing in the U.S.A.*, Jeremy P. Tarcher, Los Angeles, 1985.

Ward, Brian, *Just My Soul Responding: Rhythm & Blues, Black Consciousness, and Race Relations*, University of California Press, Berkeley, 1998.

Weinberg, Max with Robert Santelli, *The Big Beat: Conversations with Rock's Great Drummers*, Billboard, New York, 1984.

Wenner, Jan, *Lennon Remembers: The Rolling Stone Interviews*, Popular Library, New York, 1971.

Wexler, Jerry and David Ritz, *Rhythm and the Blues: A Life in American Music*, Alfred A. Knopf, New York, 1993.

White, Charles, *The Life and Times of Little Richard: The Quasar of Rock*, Harmony, New York, 1984.

White, Roger, *The Everly Brothers: Walk Right Back*, Plexus, London, 1998.

White, Timothy, *Catch a Fire: The Life of Bob Marley*, Holt, Rinehart and Winston, New York, 1983.

Widmer, Mary Lou, *New Orleans in the Fifties*, Pelican, Gretna, LA, 1991.

Widmer, Mary Lou, *New Orleans in the Forties*, Pelican, Gretna, LA, 1991.

Wechel, Willem H. te, *European Concert List* (A complete list of every European Fats Domino concert from 1962 to 1995), 2003.

PERIODICALS AND NEWSPAPERS

The following have been invaluable sources, with individual articles cited in the Notes: *The Austin Chronicle, Beat Instrumental, Billboard, Blues Unlimited, Business Week, Cash Box, Down Beat, Ebony, Figaro, Fortune, The Fort Worth Press, Gambit, Goldmine, Guitar Player, Jamaica Gleaner, Jazz Journal, Jazz Monthly, Jet, Juke, Juke Blues, Keyboard, Life, Living Blues, Live!, The Los Angeles Times, The Louisiana Weekly, Melody Maker, Memphis Press-Scimitar, Mojo, Morning Advocate, Natchitoches Times, New Musical Express, New Orleans Magazine, The New York Times, Norfolk Journal, Now Dig This, Offbeat, Other, Parade, People, The Pittsburgh Courier, Record Mirror, Rolling Stone, San Jose Mercury, The States-Item, Tan, Time, The Times-Picayune, The Tribune, The Washington Post, Wavelength.*

AUDIO

Bartholomew, Dave, *The Big Beat of Dave Bartholomew: 20 of His Milestone New Orleans Productions 1949–1960*, EMI Records, Hollywood, CA, 2002.

Bartholomew, Dave, *The Spirit of New Orleans—The Genius of Dave Bartholomew*, EMI Records, Hollywood, CA 1993.

Bartholomew, Dave, *New Orleans Big Beat*, Landslide Records, Atlanta, 1998.

Brown, Roy, *Good Rockin' Brown*, Ace Records, 2005.

Brown, Roy, *Good Rockin' Tonight: The Best of Roy Brown*, Rhino Records, Santa Monica, CA, 1994.

Charles, Bobby, *Wish You Were Here*, Stony Plain/Rick 'N' Gravy Records, Edmonton, Alberta, Canada, 1995.

Crescent City Soul: The Sound of New Orleans, 1947–1974, EMI Records, Hollywood, CA, 1996.

Doctors, Professors, Kings & Queens: The Big Ol' Box of New Orleans, Shout Factory, Los Angeles, 2004.

Domino, Fats, *My Blue Heaven—The Best of Fats Domino*, EMI Records, Hollywood, CA, 1990.

Domino, Fats, *Out of New Orleans*, Bear Family, Hambergen, Germany, 1993.

Domino, Fats, *The Paramount Years: The Most Wanted Albums*, Disky Communications, Hoorn, The Netherlands, 1996.

Domino, Fats, *Sweet Patootie: The Complete Reprise Recordings*, Warner Brothers, Burbank, CA, 2005.

Domino, Fats, *"They Call Me the Fat Man...": Antoine "Fats" Domino: The Legendary Imperial Recordings*, EMI Records, Hollywood, 1991.

Domino, Fats, *The Very Best of Fats Domino, 1963–1965*, Varese-Sarabande, 2004.

Domino, Fats, *Walking to New Orleans: The Legendary Imperial Recordings, 1949–1962*, EMI, Hollywood, 2002.

Donley, Jimmy, *Born to Be a Loser: The Crazy Cajun Recordings*, Edsel Records, Richmond, Surrey, 1999.

Fats at 65, BBC Radio Special, 1993.

Gillespie, Lex, *Let the Good Times Roll* (radio series), http://www.goodtimesroll.org

Little Richard, *Little Richard: The Specialty Sessions*, Specialty Records, Hollywood, 1989.

Louisiana Homegrown with Bernie Cyrus, Fats Domino Interview, WCKW-FM, LaPlace, LA, 1993.

Rock Before Elvi[Unknown font 2: Palatino Linotype]s. . . [End Font: Palatino Linotype]., Hoy Hoy Records, Canada, 1993.

VIDEO

The Beatles Anthology, Apple Corps Ltd., London, 1996.

Behind the Music: John Fogerty, VH-1, 1997.

The Bob Marley Story: Caribbean Nights, Island Visual Arts, New York, 1986.
CBS Evening News/Channel 4 Eyewitness News (WWL-TV, New Orleans), (Byron Pitts interview with Fats Domino), 2-25-06.
Charles Grodin, CNBC, 7-11-95.
Dr. John Teaches New Orleans Piano, Vol. 1, Homespun, Woodstock, NY, 1995.
Domino, Fats, *Blueberry Hill*, K-Tel Entertainment, 2001.
Domino, Fats, Hearst-Metrotone Newsreel, 9-26-56.
Domino, Fats, *The Legends of New Orleans—The Music of Fats Domino*, Shout Factory, Los Angeles, 2003.
Domino, Fats and Rick Nelson, *Rockin' with Ricky and Fats*, Varese Records, 2003.
The History of Rock 'n' Roll: Good Rockin' Tonight, Warner Home Video, Burbank, CA, 1995.
Hollywood Rocks the Movies: The Early Years (1955–1970), 20th Century Fox, Hollywood, 1970.
Make It Funky: The Music That Took Over the World, Sony Pictures, Culver City, CA 2005.
The Perry Como Show, 5-25-57, Video Yesteryear, Sandy Hook, CT, 1985.
Shake, Rattle and Rock, American International Pictures, Hollywood, 1956.
Showtime at the Apollo, 1955.
Sunday Morning with Charles Kuralt, CBS-TV, 9-23-84.

Unpublished Interviews by Others

Embree, Jerry, Interview with Fats Domino, 1999.
Foose, Jonathan and Tad Jones, Interview with Dave Bartholomew, 9-23-81.
Jones, Tad, Interview with Lew Chudd, 9-3-73.
Jones, Tad, Interview with Rip Roberts, 5-14-79.
Katz, David, Interview with Byron Lee, 7-17-02.
Katz, David, Interview with Prince Buster, 7-26-02.
Katz, David, Interview with Jimmy Cliff, 7-31-02.
Russell, William and Ralph Collins, Interview with Harrison Verrett, 8-10-61, Hogan Jazz Archives, Tulane University, New Orleans.
Russell, William and Ralph Collins, Interview with Walter Nelson, Sr., 10-6-60, Hogan Jazz Archives, Tulane University, New Orleans.

Legal Documents, Public Records, and Other Sources

American Federation of Musicians, Local 496, Book of Membership Dues, 5-15-48.
American Federation of Musicians contract for Lloyd Price session 3-13-52.
Blackwell, Bumps, Letter to Art Rupe, 9-55, in Specialty Records Files.
City of New Orleans, *Lower Ninth Ward Profile*, Ernest N. Morial, 5-78.
Complaint for the Support of an Infant and to Determine Paternity, No. 0587063: Theron Domino, A Minor, Earnestine Price Robinson, His Guardia Ad Litem, and Earnestine Price Robinson vs. Antoine Domino, the Honorable Superior Court of the State of California, in and for the County of Los Angeles, 2-21-61.
Domino, Antoine "Fats," Jr., Supplement to Contract, 1-20-62.
Domino, Antoine, Jr., unexecuted and undated contract with Motown Record Corporation.
Domino, Anthony, Jr., Parish of Orleans and City of New Orleans, Birth Certificate, 3-14-28.
Domino, Anthony, vs. James Garrison, Petition for Change of Name, Civil District Court for the Parish of Orleans, State of Louisiana, Docket No. 5, No. 486-735, 12-17-68.
Fortner, Emmett, City of New Orleans, State of Louisiana, Certificate of Death No. 157720008491.
Fortner, Emmett W., Criminal District Court for the Parish of Orleans: State of Louisiana versus Emmett W. Fortner, 6-17-69.
Fortner, Emmett W., State of Louisiana, Parish of Orleans, Arrest No. 132745, 11-26-69.

Hagans, Buddy, City of New Orleans, State of Louisiana Certificate of Death No. 11915646, 6-12-80.

Imperial, Minit, and Aladdin Artists File, 8-13-63.

St. James Parish Conveyance Records, 1860

St. James Parish Census, 1880, 1890, 1900.

State of Louisiana, Parish of St. James Court Records, 1855, in St. James Parish Historical Society, Cultural and Heritage Center Museum

Verrett, Harrison, the Succession of, Civil District Court for the Parish of Orleans, State of Louisiana, Division A, Docket 1, No. 441-398, 10-26-65.

Warner Brothers Records letters and memos, 1968–1971.

Index

Page number in **bold** denote Notes.